RAP &
HIP HOP

A DAY BY DAY
HISTORY GUIDE

BY MASON BROWN

G.E.M.
EDITIONS

Library of Congress Cataloging-in-Publication Data
Brown, Mason
      Rap and Hip Hop: A Day by Day History Guide
      ISBN 978-0980056167
      1. Rap (Music). 2. Hip-hop. 3. Rap Musicians

We send our thanks to all the individuals who helped us compile this book. Please contact the author to report any errors or omissions.

The various music award ceremonies cited in the text are the intellectual property of the respective copyright holders: the Grammy Awards, the MTV Video Music Awards, the Rock and Roll Hall of Fame, the American Music Awards, the Source Awards, the Soul Train Awards, and the People's Choice Awards. Additionally, these entities did not participate in the writing, editing or publication of this work.

Organizations and other groups interested in purchasing large quantities of this book should contact the publisher.

Printed in the U.S.A.

▶ TABLE OF CONTENTS

▶ INTRODUCTION

On a hot Saturday night in August 1973, an unknown DJ named Kool Herc hosted a block party. The 18-year-old former graffiti artist performed for a crowd of 300 people in the packed first-floor recreation room of an apartment building on Sedgwick Avenue in the Bronx. The "Back to School Jam" began at 9 P.M. and was scheduled to end at 4 A.M. The admission charge was 50 cents for "fellas" and 25 cents for "ladies."

Operating two turntables, DJ Kool Herc used two copies of the same record to extend the instrumental "break" portion of a song. As he was extending a break, a member of his crew, Coke La Rock, spontaneously began to rap over the music. The energized crowd enjoyed every minute of this new musical form. Not surprisingly, a who's who of first generation rappers were in attendance at Herc's first show including KRS-One, Grandmaster Flash, Busy Bee, Afrika Bambaataa and Grandmaster Caz of the Cold Crush Brothers. It was on this day that rap music was born.

Overnight, DJ Kool Herc had established a reputation as a turntable artist who did far more than simply spin records. As his reputation grew, so did his legions of admirers and competitors.

But while rap enjoyed a wave of popularity in the Bronx, the music was slow to spread across the rest of the country. Then in 1979, "Rapper's Delight" by the Sugarhill Gang was a surprise hit that sounded like nothing else on the radio. Although the 12-inch single sold several-million copies, it just barely cracked the national top-40 charts.

By the early 1980s, rap pioneers such as Kurtis Blow, LL Cool J and Grandmaster Flash had brought the genre into the mainstream. Although initially viewed as a fad not to be taken seriously, hip hop continued to thrive.

Hip hop music soon progressed from street parties and neighborhood dance clubs to concert stages and the top-10 charts. In the process, the musical structure and lyrical themes of rap evolved, as did the dance styles and clothing. By the end of the decade, crossover rappers such as Run-D.M.C., the Beastie Boys and MC Hammer continued to advance the rise of hip hop.

By the 1990s, rap dominated both urban and pop radio, and had grown into a billion-dollar industry that created superstars from Snoop Dogg to the Notorious B.I.G. and from Tupac Shakur to Eminem. At the same time, rap music had diversified into various styles and sub-genres including Southern rap, crunk, trip-hop, Midwest rap, alternative rap, gangsta rap, grime, rap-rock, East Coast rap, West Coast rap and more.

As hip hop was embraced by popular culture, rappers appeared in television commercials as spokesmen for soft drinks and champagnes, as authors, as television personalities and as Hollywood stars on the big screen. Will Smith became a major box-office draw as he starred in the blockbuster films, *Independence Day* and *Men In Black*.

Soon, many rap stars expanded their empires to include business ventures, from their own record companies and clothing lines to restaurants and liquor companies. Consequently, Dr. Dre earned far more as a businessman than he ever did as a performer with a microphone in his hand.

But rap music would also provide a voice to a segment of society, which had previously lacked access to political power and the mainstream media. Rappers were no longer mere entertainers, but chroniclers of their culture and history.

*   *   *   *   *

This book provides a comprehensive overview of the history of hip hop, from its earliest days on the street corners and block parties in the Bronx to the modern era of blinged-out limousines and stadium tours.

More than 3,500 entries are listed in chronological order, from January to December, in a day-by-day record of events including industry awards, television and film appearances, noteworthy concerts and music festivals, personal disputes and controversies, arrests and court trials as well as birthdays and deaths. There is also a strong focus on the biggest as well as the most influential songs and albums, from the golden age of rap to the modern era. Lastly, there are plenty of historical tidbits and interesting nuggets of trivia that gave hip hop its unique character and prominent status on the global stage.

Unfortunately, a few important dates in hip hop history – notable events and record release dates – remain elusive or were not chronicled. We do not know the exact date that a teenage Grand Wizzard Theodore "scratched" a record for the first time. In the often repeated story, he was practicing his deejay skills when his mother burst through his bedroom door and demanded that he turn down the volume. In response, he angrily manipulated a record, back and forth, and scratched for the very first time. Fascinated by the sound he had just made, he employed the technique when he began performing publically in 1977.

In the immediate years before and after the first major record company decided to issue a rap single in 1979, the genre was dominated by smaller labels. These tiny independent companies were more interested in getting airplay and selling a few records than in keeping detailed information about recording and release dates. As a result, the exact release dates of a few dozen groundbreaking rap records from the 1970s and even the 1980s are unknown.

In addition to traditional rap and hip hop, this book also includes a number of songs from the pop and R&B fields, which featured elements of rap. This was done to be more inclusive and to provide a more complete picture of the history of hip hop.

Lastly, due to the nature of this work, there will likely be some errors and omissions in the text. We welcome all feedback. Any revisions and additions will be included in the second edition of this book. The author can be contacted by email at rap45rpm@gmail.com.

▶ JANUARY

JANUARY 1

1967: Grandmaster Flash (birth name Joseph Saddler) was born in Bridgetown, Barbados, but grew up in the Bronx, New York. A hip hop pioneer, he introduced a number of innovations to the art of deejaying including back-spinning and punch-phrasing, and also helped to popularize scratching. Forming Grandmaster Flash and the Furious Five in 1979, he scored a hit in 1982 with the groundbreaking socially-conscious single, "The Message."

1984: Journalist Steven Hager published the first book about rap music, *Hip Hop: The Illustrated History Of Break Dancing, Rap Music, And Graffiti*. The 112-page book examined the emerging hip hop revolution in New York City. Hager would also write a script for the first hip hop film, *Beat Street*.

1987: Before forming N.W.A., Ice Cube released the 12-inch single, "My Posse," with his first group, C.I.A. The single was produced by Dr. Dre.

1988: Former break dancers Rob Pilatus and Fabrice Morvan were hired by German producer Frank Farian. Best known for his work with the hit group Boney M, Farian wanted a pair of good-looking frontmen for his new music project, Milli Vanilli.

1995: Following months of public rumors about an alleged marriage between R. Kelly and Aaliyah, *Vibe* magazine published a copy of their marriage certificate. The document listed Kelly's age as 25, two years younger than his actual age. But while Aaliyah's age was listed as 18, she was actually 15-years-old at the time. The marriage was later annulled.

1996: Rap artist Mr. Cee (birth name Hubert Kyle Church III) of the hip hop group RBL Posse was shot and killed at the age of 22, just weeks after his group had signed with a subsidiary of Atlantic Records. He was shot nine times while walking on a sidewalk about a mile from his home in the Bayview-Hunters Point district of San Francisco. The murder went unsolved.

2000: The action-crime film, *Hot Boyz*, was released by No Limit Records. Written and directed by Master P, the film starred Snoop Dogg, Silkk the Shocker, C-Murder and Mystikal. The film caused some friction between No Limit Records and Cash Money Records because "Hot Boys" was the name of a rap group (featuring Juvenile, Lil Wayne, Turk and B.G.) on Cash Money Records.

2006: Young MC was a contestant on the third season of the VH-1 series, *Celebrity Fit Club*. He was declared the winner after losing 38 pounds over an eight-week period. (One of the losing contestants was rapper Bizarre of the group D12.)

2006: Flavor Flav began hosting the dating reality show, *Flavor Of Love*, which aired on VH-1. On the program, the rapper selected a date from a group of 20 women, while living in a mansion. The series was a spinoff of his previous program, *Strange Love*. A ratings hit, *Flavor Of Love* ran for three seasons.

2008: Jay-Z left his position as the president of Def Jam Recordings after the two sides could not agree on the financial terms of a new contract.

2010: Record producer Shawty Redd (birth name Demetrius A. Stewart) fatally shot an acquaintance at his home in Hampton, Georgia, and was charged with murder. He claimed the shooting was an act of self-defense. Following a trial in November 2011, Redd was found not guilty.

2016: Record producer and label owner Jermaine Dupri starred in the reality series, *The Rap Game*, which aired on the Lifetime network. Set in Atlanta, the program featured five young rappers, ages 12 to 16 years old. The budding performers were mentored by Da Brat, T.I., Usher, Ludacris and Silentó.

JANUARY 2

1993: Snow released the crossover hit single, "Informer." The reggae-rooted rapper was sitting in a Canadian jail cell when the single was issued. The song is considered a "no snitching" anthem.

1996: Philadelphia rapper Cool C and two accomplices robbed a PNC Bank branch. While leaving the bank, the rapper shot and killed a police officer. While Cool C was convicted of first-degree murder and sentenced to death, both of his accomplices were convicted of second-degree murder and sentenced to life in prison.

1996: The members of the alternative, hip hop group Arrested Development announced their break up. They had released just two albums and were best known for their crossover hits, "Tennessee" and "Mr. Wendal."

1996: Gina Longo signed a recording contract with Death Row Records, and was the first and only white artist at the label. According to *The Los Angeles Times*, Death Row chief Suge Knight said that Longo had "the voice of a black woman in a white woman's body." Coincidentally, Longo's father, Deputy District Attorney Lawrence W. Longo, had recommended a plea deal for Knight the previous year. As a result, the embattled label owner received probation instead of a nine-year prison term for a 1992 assault conviction. The District Attorney's Office later investigated a possible conflict of interest between the Longo family and Death Row. Longo was subsequently fired from his position and disciplined by the State Bar of California.

2012: Snoop Dogg was a contestant on the CBS game show, *The Price Is Right*. His appearance was part of the program's "Celebrity Charity Week." A big winner, he earned $72,585 for his charity, Snoop Youth Football League.

2014: Ke$ha admitted herself into a rehab facility near Chicago to treat what was described as an "eating disorder." She spent nearly two-months at the facility.

JANUARY 3

1967: Tim Dog (birth name Timothy Blair) was born in the Bronx, New York. He is best known for the 1991 diss track, "Fuck Compton."

1975: Shawnna (birth name Rashawnna Guy) was born in Chicago. A member of the 1990s duo Infamous Syndicate, she is best known as the featured artist on the Ludacris hits, "What's Your Fantasy" and "Stand Up." Her father is blues legend Buddy Guy.

1980: Kurtis Blow became the first rap act to appear on the influential British music program, *Tops Of The Pops*. Dressed in a three-piece suit, he performed "Christmas Rappin'."

1989: The syndicated late-night program, *The Arsenio Hall Show*, made its premiere. A number of hip hop artists would appear on the program including N.W.A., Tupac Shakur, Naughty By Nature, De La Soul, Snoop Dogg, the Wu-Tang Clan and frequent guest M.C. Hammer.

1990: The German electronic/dance group Snap! released their crossover hit single, "The Power." The song featured the vocals of Penny Ford and a rap by Turbo B. But in the song's music video, Ford's vocals were lip-synced by Jackie Harris. The track sampled "Let The Words Flow" by Chill Rob G, "Love's Gonna Get You" by Jocelyn Brown and "King Of The Beats" by Mantronix.

1997: Lil' Kim released the track, "Crush On You" (featuring the Notorious B.I.G. and Lil Cease). A remixed version of the song was released as a single. The track sampled "Rain Dance" by the Jeff Lorber Fusion.

2004: Jay-Z started his new role as president and CEO of Def Jam Recordings.

2004: Chingy released the single, "One Call Away" (featuring J-Weav). The track sampled dialogue from an episode of the sitcom, *The King Of Queens*.

2010: Sisqó competed in the British reality show, *Celebrity Big Brother 2010*. He lasted 20 days on the series and was the fifth contestant evicted from the Big Brother house. British rapper Lady Sovereign was also a contestant on the program.

JANUARY 4

2001: Vanilla Ice spent a night in jail after ripping out some of his wife's hair. The couple was driving through Davie, Florida, when the incident occurred. Vanilla Ice, who claimed he was trying to prevent his wife from jumping out of the vehicle, was released from prison after paying the $3,500 bail.

2005: AJ Abdallah, the owner of a recording studio where Eminem recorded *Slim Shady* in 1997, was found dead from a gunshot wound. Shortly before he was killed, he had announced his intention to sell the studio and leave Detroit.

2005: RZA of the Wu-Tang Clan published the book, *The Wu-Tang Manual*.

2006: Queen Latifah was awarded a star on the Hollywood Walk of Fame. She was the first hip hop artist to receive the honor.

2008: Beyoncé was victorious in a legal battle over her hit song, "Baby Boy." An appeals court in Houston reaffirmed an earlier decision against a songwriter from Minnesota who had claimed copyright infringement.

2016: Cleveland Cavaliers player LeBron James told the press that he had not listened to a track by Kanye West, "Facts," which criticized the NBA's star for his endorsement deal with Nike. West had his own endorsement deal with Nike until 2013, when he signed a contract with Adidas.

JANUARY 5

1994: Singer Dionne Warwick and the National Political Congress of Black Women publically objected to the NAACP Image Awards decision to nominate Tupac Shakur. The rapper was competing in the category of Outstanding Actor In A Motion Picture for his role in the film, *Poetic Justice*.

1999: Lauryn Hill received ten Grammy nominations, the most by a female artist in Grammy history.

2006: Master P appeared as a contestant on season two of the ABC dance competition, *Dancing With The Stars*. His dance partner was professional dancer Ashly DelGrosso. The couple was the fourth team to be eliminated.

2007: The reality program, *The (White) Rapper Show*, debuted on the VH-1 network. Created by *Ego Trip* magazine and hosted by MC Serch of 3rd Bass, the program pitted ten aspiring, white rappers against each other for the opportunity to win a $100,000 grand prize. The series ran for eight episodes with Atlanta-based rapper $hamrock selected as the winner.

2008: The single "Low" by Flo Rida featuring T-Pain began a remarkable ten-week run at number-one on the U.S. charts.

2011: At the 37th annual People's Choice Awards which were staged at the Nokia Theatre in Los Angeles, "Love The Way You Lie" by Eminem featuring Rihanna won the award for Favorite Music Video; Eminem won the award for Favorite Male Artist; and Eminem won the award for Favorite Hip-Hop Artist. The ceremony was hosted by Queen Latifah.

2012: Taboo of the Black Eyes Peas published his autobiography, *Fallin' Up: My Story*.

2012: DMX was attacked by a fan about ten-minutes into his performance at Café Sevilla in Long Beach, California. The stage crasher was quickly dragged away by members of security. DMX was unhurt and finished the concert.

2015: New York rapper Joey Bada$$ (real name Jo-Vaughn Virginie Scott) was charged by Australian authorities in the assault of a security guard before a concert in Byron Bay, New South Wales. He allegedly struck and broke the nose of the security guard when asked to show some identification.

2015: Eminem was sued by a member of the Chicago rap group Hotstylz over an uncleared sample. According to rapper Raymond Jones, the Eminem hit track "Rap God" used a lengthy sample of "Lookin Boy" by Hotstylz.

JANUARY 6

2006: British rapper Ms. Dynamite was arrested for disorderly conduct after was she kicked out the Paragon Lounge in London. While in custody, she punched a police officer and was also charged with assault. She later pleaded guilty to the charges and was sentenced to 60 days of community service.

2010: At the 36th annual People's Choice Awards which were staged at the Nokia Theatre in Los Angeles, Eminem won the award for Favorite Hip-Hop Artist; and "Run This Town" by Jay-Z featuring Rihanna and Kanye West won the award for Favorite Music Collaboration. The ceremony was hosted by Queen Latifah.

2014: MC Serch of the group 3rd Bass began hosting a syndicated radio talk show, *Serch*. Produced by CBS, the program focused on relationship issues.

2015: Southern rapper 2 Chainz announced that he was launching his own independent record label, the Real University. The artists on his label included Young Dolph, Fresh, Cap 1, Skooly and Bankroll Fresh.

2016: Kanye West made a surprise appearance as a contestant at the San Francisco stop of the *American Idol* auditions. He introduced himself to the judges by saying, "My name is Kanye, I'm from the south side of Chicago. I'm originally a producer. I always wanted to rap and no one really believed in me, so I wanted to try some things out, you know?" After performing "Gold Digger," he passed the audition and received a gold ticket.

JANUARY 7

1993: A New York state radio station, WSUC (90.5 FM) in Cortland, was fined $23,700 by the FCC for playing the uncensored version of the song "Yo Da-Lin In The Valley" by rap-rocker Kid Rock.

1997: Sean "Puff Daddy" Combs released his debut solo single, "Can't Nobody Hold Me Down" (featuring Ma$e). The track topped the pop charts for six weeks. (Combs was previously a featured artist on Lil' Kim's 1996 hit, "No Time.")

2001: The British electronic/house music group KLF released a reworked pop version of their track, "3 a.m. Eternal." The single featured a rap by Ricardo da Force. The original 1999 version of the song was not a hit.

2003: 50 Cent released the hit single, "In Da Club." The chart-topping track was nominated for two Grammys in the categories of Best Male Rap Solo Performance and Best Rap Song, and won two MTV Video Music Awards in the categories of Best Rap Video and Best New Artist In A Video. The song was originally offered to Eminem's side group D12, which turned it down.

2009: At the 35th annual People's Choice Awards which were staged at the Shrine Auditorium in Los Angeles, Chris Brown won the award for Favorite Male Singer; and "Low" by Flo Rida featuring T-Pain won the award for Favorite Hip-Hop Song. The ceremony was hosted by Queen Latifah.

2012: Jay-Z and Beyoncé welcomed the birth of their daughter, Blue Ivy Carter.

2013: Florida State University introduced a three-credit course, "The Sociology of Hip Hop."

2015: At the 41st annual People's Choice Awards which were staged at the Nokia Theatre in Los Angeles, Iggy Azalea won the award for Favorite Hip-Hop Artist.

2016: The reality show *Growing Up Hip Hop* premiered on the WE-tv network. The cast included Damon "Boogie" Dash (the son of former Roc-A-Fella Records executive Damon Dash), Angela Simmons (the daughter of Run-D.M.C. member Reverend Run), Kristinia DeBarge (the daughter of James DeBarge), TJ Mizell (the son of Jam Master Jay) and Maserati Rome (the son of Master P).

JANUARY 8

1967: R. Kelly (birth name Robert Sylvester Kelly) was born in Chicago. The singer and producer enjoyed a long career in the R&B and hip hop fields with hits such as "Bump N' Grind," "I'm A Flirt" and the Grammy-winning "I Believe I Can Fly."

1994: The Jamaican duo Chaka Demus and Pliers topped the British charts with a reggae-rap version of the pop-rock standard, "Twist And Shout."

2001: At the 28th annual American Music Awards, Dr. Dre won the award for Favorite Rap/Hip-Hop Artist. The ceremony was co-hosted by LL Cool J.

2004: Tony Yayo of the hip hop group G-Unit was paroled after he served a year in prison. Yayo had been sentenced for bail jumping after police discovered two handguns inside the trunk of his car during an arrest outside of the Copacabana nightclub in Manhattan on December 31, 2002. One day after his release from prison, he was re-arrested on a charge of possessing a forged passport.

2004: Hip hop entrepreneur Russell Simmons announced the sale of his Phat Farm and Baby Phat urban clothing lines to Kellwood Co. for $140 million.

2008: Jay-Z began his headlining set at the Glastonbury Festival with a purposely off-key verse of the song "Wonderwall" by Oasis. Jay-Z was responding to a comment made by Noel Gallagher of Oasis who said that it was "wrong" to include hip hop at the festival.

2008: At the 34th annual People's Choice Awards which were staged at the Shrine Auditorium in Los Angeles, "Give It To Me" by Timbaland with Justin Timberlake and Nelly Furtado won the award for Favorite Hip-Hop Song. The ceremony was hosted by Queen Latifah.

2014: At the 40th annual People's Choice Awards which were staged at the Nokia Theatre in Los Angeles, Ariana Grande won the award for Favorite Breakout Artist; "E.T." by Katy Perry featuring Kanye West won the award for Favorite Song of the Year; and Eminem won the award for Favorite Hip-Hop Artist.

2014: The members of Insane Clown Posse sued the FBI and the Justice Department over the U.S. government's classification of the group's fans – known as "Juggalos" – as gang members. In 2011, the Justice Department had declared that Juggalos were a "loosely organized hybrid gang."

2015: Cool C, a convicted murderer, was granted a stay of execution by Judge L. Felipe Restrepo. He had been scheduled to face death by lethal injection. Cool C had been convicted of killing a police officer in 1996 during a Philadelphia bank robbery.

JANUARY 9

1971: MF Doom (birth name Daniel Dumile) was born in London, England, but was raised in Long Island, New York. Known for his villainous stage attire, he was a member of the hip hop group KMD before he launched a solo career.

1999: Guru of the duo Gang Starr was robbed by three masked men outside of a recording studio in Queens, New York. The thieves made off with $10,000 in jewelry.

2002: At the 29th annual American Music Awards, Nelly won the award for Favorite Rap/Hip-Hop Artist. The ceremony was co-hosted by Sean "P. Diddy" Combs.

2003: MC Hammer was a member of the cast on the first season of the reality show, *The Surreal Life*. The series ran for nine episodes.

2005: At the 31st annual People's Choice Awards which were staged at the Pasadena Civic Auditorium, Alicia Keys won the award for Favorite Female Musical Performer; and Usher won the award for Favorite Male Musical Performer.

2005: MTV debuted the 11-episode reality series, *Strange Love*, which examined the relationship between rapper Flavor Flav and model Brigitte Nielsen. The two had met the previous year while filming another MTV reality series, *The Surreal Life*.

2005: Biz Markie was a contestant on the first season of the VH-1 series, *Celebrity Fit Club*. He was declared the winner after losing 40 pounds over an eight-week period.

2007: 50 Cent co-wrote a novel with writer K. Elliott, *The Ski Mask Way*. The fictional book chronicled the exploits of an ex-convict on the New York City streets.

2010: DJ Premier teamed with Nike to introduce the "Air Force 1" athletic shoes.

2010: Alicia Keys was the musical guest on *Saturday Night Live*. She performed "Try Sleeping With A Broken Heart" and "Empire State Of Mind (Part II) Broken Down."

2011: Fergie of the Black Eyed Peas starred in a television commercial for Dr Pepper Cherry. Her hit single, "Here I Come," was featured in the commercial.

2013: At the 38th annual People's Choice Awards which were staged at the Nokia Theatre in Los Angeles, Nicki Minaj won the award for Favorite Hip-Hop Artist.

JANUARY 10

1979: Daddy Mac (birth name Christopher Smith) was born in Atlanta. As a member of the teenage rap duo Kris Kross, he scored a smash hit in 1992 with "Jump." The members of the duo were known for wearing their clothes backwards.

1995: The hip hop duo Smif-N-Wessun released their debut album, *Dah Shinin'*. The duo was formed by Brooklyn natives Tek and Steele. The album spawned several hits including "Bucktown" and "Wrekonize."

2000: Shaggy 2 Dope of the rap group Insane Clown Posse collapsed while performing onstage at the House of Blues in Chicago. He was rushed to a hospital.

2004: The Black Eyes Peas were the musical guests on *Saturday Night Live*. They performed "Where Is The Love?" and "Hey Mama."

2009: Fergie of the Black Eyed Peas married actor Josh Duhamel in a ceremony at the Church Estates Vineyards in Malibu.

2011: Bun B (real name Bernard Freeman) of the rap duo UGZ was hired as a guest lecturer by Rice University to teach a course on the history of hip hop.

2012: Flavor Flav appeared on the television reality series, *Celebrity Wife Swap*. He swapped spouses for one week with heavy metal singer Dee Snider of the group Twisted Sister.

2015: Snoop Dogg welcomed the birth of his first grandchild, a boy named Zion.

JANUARY 11

1956: Big Bank Hank (birth name Henry Lee Jackson) of the pioneering rap group, the Sugarhill Gang, was born in Englewood, New Jersey. He died in 2014 at the age of 58.

1971: Mary J. Blige (full name Mary Jane Blige) was born in the Bronx, New York. She began her musical career in 1989 as a back-up singer at Uptown Records. She released her debut solo album in 1992, *What's The 411?*

1985: Ice-T appeared in the film, *Breakin' 2*, which was a sequel of the 1984 break dancing film, *Breakin'*. The film's soundtrack album spawned a pair of singles "Electric Boogaloo" by Ollie & Jerry and "Din Daa Daa" by George Kranz.

1992: Vanilla Ice claimed he was asleep when burglars robbed his home. The thieves ransacked his Miami Beach mansion and stole nearly $100,000 of items including a $20,000 Rolex watch.

1995: Rappers Ice Cube and Omar Epps starred in the drama film, *Higher Learning*. The movie was set at the fictional Columbus University. The film earned nearly $40 million in the U.S.

1999: At the 26th annual American Music Awards, Master P won the award for Favorite Rap/Hip-Hop Artist. The ceremony was co-hosted by Brandy.

2004: At the 30th annual People's Choice Awards which were staged at Pasadena Civic Auditorium, Beyoncé was the co-winner along with Faith Hill for Favorite Female Musical Performer.

2004: Vanilla Ice was a member of the cast on the second season of the reality show, *The Surreal Life*. In one episode, Vanilla Ice held the diminutive actor Gary Coleman over a deep fryer until he uttered his famous catchphrase, "What'chu talkin' 'bout, Willis?" The series ran for six episodes.

2005: T.I., released the single, "U Don't Know Me." The song was nominated for a Grammy in the category of Best Rap Solo Performance.

2010: *Fantasia For Real* debuted on VH-1. The reality series starred *American Idol* season 3 winner Fantasia Barrino. The program chronicled her personal and career struggles. The series ran for two seasons.

2011: The documentary, *Mr. Immortality: The Life And Times Of Twista*, chronicled the life of the Chicago rapper as he prepared to release his album, *The Perfect Storm*. The film featured appearances by Ne-Yo, The-Dream, Big Boi and NBA player Ron Artest.

2012: At the 38th annual People's Choice Awards which were staged at the Nokia Theatre in Los Angeles, "E.T." by Katy Perry featuring Kanye West won the award for Favorite Song of the Year; and Eminem won the award for Favorite Hip-Hop Artist.

2015: At least five people were shot during a Chris Brown concert at the Fiesta nightclub in San Jose, California. Brown had stopped the concert after he noticed a large fight had broken out in the audience. Seconds later, multiple gunshots were fired.

JANUARY 12

1970: Raekwon (birth name Corey Quontrell Woods) was born in born in Staten Island, New York. A member of the groundbreaking group the Wu-Tung Clan, he pursued a solo career in 1995 beginning with the album, *Only Built 4 Cuban Linx...*, which featured Ghostface Killah as the guest star.

1975: DJ Paul (birth named Paul Beauregard) was born in Memphis, Tennessee. He was a founding member of the hip hop group, Three 6 Mafia. DJ Paul is the half-brother of rapper Lord Infamous.

1981: Blondie released the very first number-one pop single to feature rapping, "Rapture." The song's music video included appearances by rapper Fab 5 Freddy and graffiti artists Lee Quiñones and Jean-Michel Basquiat.

1991: Vanilla Ice was the musical guest on *Saturday Night Live*. He performed "Ice Ice Baby" and "Play That Funky Music."

1993: Redman released the single, "Time 4 Sum Aksion." The track sampled "Tramp" by Lowell Fulson, "How I Could Just Kill A Man" by Cypress Hill and several other songs.

1994: The members of the musical duo Kid 'n Play reprised their roles as students in the hip hop film sequel, *House Party 3*. In the film, Christopher "Play" Martin managed a female rap act called Sex As A Weapon.

1996: The hip hop parody film, *Don't Be A Menace To South Central While Drinking Your Juice In The Hood*, was released. The film included many references to urban classics such as *Boyz N The Hood*, *South Central*, *Menace II Society* and *Juice*.

2003: At the 29th annual People's Choice Awards which were staged at the Shrine Auditorium in Los Angeles, Eminem won the award for Favorite Male Musical Performer.

2005: Missy Elliott hosted the competitive reality program, *The Road To Stardom With Missy Elliott*. In addition to Elliott, the program also starred singer Teena Marie, producer Dallas Austin and manager Mona Scott. The show was not renewed by UPN for a second season.

2006: Chamillionaire released his debut single, "Ridin'" (featuring Krayzie Bone). The chart-topping track was nominated for a Grammy in the category of Best Rap Song and won a Grammy for Best Rap Performance by a Duo or Group.

2007: Toni Braxton filed a federal lawsuit against her former personal manager, Barry Hankerson, for $10 million. According to court papers, she alleged that "Hankerson placed his own financial interests ahead of Braxton's and – through fraud, deception and double-dealing – induced her to leave a lucrative deal with Arista Records and enter into an exclusive recording agreement with Hankerson's wholly-owned record company."

2007: Chris Brown and Ne-Yo co-starred in the dance film, *Stomp The Yard*. The movie centered on a stepping competition at a fictional black college.

2016: Wale became the very first rapper to open a State of the Union Address. Performing a brief 15-minute set, he had been invited to the annual event by President Barack Obama.

JANUARY 13

1990: MC Hammer released his smash hit, "U Can't Touch This," which was the debut single from his chart-topping album, *Please Hammer, Don't Hurt 'Em*. The song was built upon a sample of the 1981 funk classic, "Super Freak" by Rick James. The song won two Grammys, including the award for Best Rap Solo Performance. The song's music video featured the rapper performing what was dubbed "the Hammer Dance."

1998: LL Cool J released the hit single, "Father." The song was an autobiographical narrative about the abuse experienced by the rapper during his childhood. The track was built upon a sample of the ballad "Father Figure" by George Michael.

1998: Master P released the single, "Make Em Say Uhh!" (featuring Fiend, Silkk The Shocker, Mia X & Mystikal). The song's music video was filmed on a basketball court and featured NBA star Shaquille O'Neal.

2001: Nelly Furtado was the musical guest on *Saturday Night Live*. She performed "I'm Like A Bird."

2003: At the 30th annual American Music Awards, the winners were: OutKast for Favorite Hip Hop/R&B Band, Duo, or Group; *The Eminem Show* by Eminem for Favorite Hip Hop/R&B Album; and Ashanti for Favorite Hip Hop/R&B New Artist.

2006: LL Cool J and Queen Latifah starred in the comedy drama film, *Last Holiday*. In the movie, LL Cool J portrayed the love interest of Queen Latifah.

2009: T.I. released the single, "Dead And Gone" (featuring Justin Timberlake). The duo had previously recorded a track on Timberlake's album *FutureSex/LoveSounds*, "My Love." The single "Dead And Gone" was nominated for two Grammys in the categories of Best Rap/Sung Collaboration and Best Rap Song. The song sold three-million copies in the U.S.

2012: Simone Green published the book, *Time Served: My Days And Nights On Death Row Records*. Green was the chief photographer for the legendary West Coast label.

2016: When DJ Khaled accidentally posted a photo of his credit card on the website Snapchat, nearly $80,000 of purchases were made by various internet users in less than 30-seconds.

JANUARY 14

1968: LL Cool J (birth name James Todd Smith) was born in Queens, New York. His stage name stands for "Ladies Love Cool James." He was the first rapper at Def Jam Recordings to achieve widespread success.

1992: The Pharcyde appeared in the Michael Jackson music video for his single, "Remember The Time." The members of the group portrayed dancing Egyptians.

2000: Chi Ali Griffith shot and killed his sister's boyfriend. Fleeing the scene, he was not captured until the following year. In a plea deal, he pleaded guilty to a charge of first-degree manslaughter. He was sentenced to 14 years in prison but released after serving 12 years.

2003: Benzino released his second album, *Redemption*. The album's most talked about song was the diss track "Pull Your Skirt Up," which attacked D12, G-Unit, Dr. Dre, Obie Trice, 50 Cent and especially Eminem. Later, Eminem responded with his own diss tracks, "The Sauce" and "Nail In The Coffin."

2006: Eminem remarried his ex-wife, Kim Mathers, in a ceremony at Meadow Brook Hall in Rochester, Michigan. Eminem would file for divorce just three-months later.

JANUARY 15

1965: Pioneering British rapper and deejay Derek B (birth name Derek Boland) was born in Hammersmith, West London, England. He was one of the first hip hop acts to appear on the leading U.K. music program, *Tops Of The Tops*, and on the cover of *Smash Hits* magazine. He passed away in 2009 at the age of 44.

1975: 9th Wonder (birth name Patrick Denard Douthit) was born in Winston-Salem, North Carolina. Best known as a hip hop producer, he was also a rapper, a record executive and a hip hop historian who has taught on the college level.

1979: Young Dro (birth name D'Juan Montrel Hart) was born in Atlanta, Georgia. After signing with rapper T.I.'s label, Grand Hustle Records, Young Dro released his major-label debut album, *Best Thang Smokin'*.

1981: Pitbull (birth name Armando Christian Pérez) was born in Miami, Florida, the son of Cuban immigrants. He released his breakthrough album in 2004, *M.I.A.M.I.* In 2009, he scored his first major hit with "I Know You Want Me (Calle Ocho)."

1994: Snoop Doggy Dogg released his second solo single, "Gin And Juice." The track sampled "Watching You" by Slave and "I Get Lifted" by George McCrae. The song was nominated for a Grammy in the category of Best Rap Solo Performance.

1999: Ol' Dirty Bastard was charged with attempted murder after he allegedly shot at a police officer in New York. After a grand jury chose not to indict the rapper, the charges were dropped.

2004: Mystikal was sentenced to six years in prison after he was convicted on a charge of sexual battery for a 2002 attack of his hairdresser.

2009: Death Row Records was auctioned off for $18 million. The winning bidder, WIDEawake Entertainment Group, assumed control of the label's catalogue, which included music by a number of leading hip hop artists including Tupac Shakur, Snoop Dogg and Dr. Dre. The court-ordered auction followed the personal bankruptcy of label owner Suge Knight.

2009: The documentary, *The Carter*, was released. The film chronicled the life of rapper Dwayne Michael Carter, Jr., who is better known as Lil Wayne.

JANUARY 16

1979: Aaliyah (full name Aaliyah Dana Haughton) was born in Brooklyn, New York. Signing a recording contract at age 12, she was mentored by R. Kelly. Nicknamed "The Princess of R&B," she became an overnight sensation following the release of her debut album, *Age Ain't Nothing But A Number*, which sold three-million copies in the U.S. In 2001, she perished in an airplane crash.

1987: The Beastie Boys appeared on *American Bandstand*. For much of their performance, the members of the group did not bother to lip-sync along to their hit, "(You Gotta) Fight For Your Right (To Party!)." The group's performance was censored by the ABC network after Ad-Rock grabbed his crotch.

2004: DJ Spigg Nice (real name Ronald Blackwell) of the hip hop group Lost Boyz was sentenced by a New Jersey court to 37-years in prison for his role in multiple bank robberies across the state. Along with three co-defendants, he was also ordered to pay nearly $1 million in restitution.

2004: Ice Cube starred in the action film, *Torque*. The rapper played the role of Trey Wallace, the leader of a black biker gang called the Reapers.

2007: DJ Drama and Don Cannon were arrested in Atlanta for manufacturing and selling mixtapes. The action occurred following complaints by the RIAA, which considered the unlicensed compilations no different than counterfeit CD or tapes. The authorities confiscated four vehicles, various pieces of professional recording equipment and more than 81,000 CDs. Both men were charged with felony violations of Georgia's RICO law. The arrests sent shockwaves throughout the hip hop community which viewed mixtapes as an essential part of music promotion.

2009: In a television commercial for State Farm Insurance, LeBron James held a Kid 'n Play CD and then attempted to perform the duo's signature dance.

2009: Brooklyn-based rapper Gravy (real name Jamal Woolard) played the lead role in the film biography of the Notorious B.I.G., *Notorious*. Biggie's wife Faith Evans was played by Antonique Smith and Tupac Shakur was portrayed by Anthony Mackie. Biggie's son Christopher Wallace, Jr., portrayed the rapper as a child. The film grossed nearly $45 million in the U.S.

2014: Pharrell Williams was nominated for an Oscar in the category of Best Original Song for the track, "Happy," from the film *Despicable Me 2*. He lost to "Let It Go" from the film, *Frozen*.

JANUARY 17

1966: Shabba Ranks (birth name Rexton Rawlston Fernando Gordon) was born in Sturgetown, Jamaica. A dancehall/reggae-based musician and deejay, he scored a series of international hits including "Mr. Loverman" and "The Jam."

1971: Lil Jon (birth name Jonathan Smith) was born in Atlanta. A former nightclub deejay, he formed the crunk-style hip hop group Lil Jon & The East Side Boyz in 1997. He later pursued a solo career and released his debut album in 2010, *Crunk Rock*.

1971: Rap-rock singer Kid Rock (birth name Robert James Ritchie) was born in Romeo, Michigan. His debut 1998 album, *Devil Without A Cause*, was a smash hit.

1992: A number of hip hop artists starred in the urban crime-drama film, *Juice,* including Tupac Shakur, Omar Epps and Queen Latifah. The film featured cameo appearances by Fab 5 Freddy, EPMD, Special Ed, Yo-Yo, Anthony "Treach" Criss and the co-hosts of *Yo! MTV Raps,* Ed Lover and Doctor Dré.

2000: At the 27th annual American Music Awards, DMX won the award for Favorite Rap/Hip-Hop Artist.

2004: G-Unit were the musical guests on *Saturday Night Live*. They performed "Stunt 101" and "Wanna Get To Know You."

2006: Dem Franchize Boyz released the single, "Lean Wit It, Rock Wit It" (featuring Peanut and Charlay). The song sold more than one-million copies in the U.S.

2011: Florida A&M University established the Institute for Hip Hop and Music Industry Studies. It was later renamed the Institute for Research in Music and Entertainment.

2016: Soul singer Clarence Reid passed away at the age of 76. Beginning in 1971, he recorded a series of risque, proto-rap albums under the name, Blowfly.

JANUARY 18

1980: Soul/hip hop singer Estelle (full name Estelle Fanta Swaray) was born in West London, England.

1997: Snoop Doggy Dogg was the musical guest on *Saturday Night Live*. He performed "Snoop's Upside Ya Head" and "Vapors."

2002: Sisqó co-starred in the hit comedy film, *Snow Dogs*. He played the role of a dentist named Dr. Rupert Brooks.

2002: C-Murder (real name Cory Miller) was charged with the murder of 16-year-old Steve Thomas outside of the Platinum Club in Harvey, Louisiana. The victim was shot in the chest following an argument. Despite a series of legal maneuvers and multiple trials, C-Murder was convicted of the crime and sentenced to life in prison. While behind bars, he allegedly continued to record music.

2002: The crime film, *State Property*, was released. Set in Philadelphia, the film starred hip hop artists Beanie Sigel, Omillio Sparks, Memphis Bleek, Jay-Z and Damon Dash. A sequel, *State Property 2*, was released in 2005.

2003: DJ Quik (birth name David Marvin Blake) was born in Compton, California. The rapper is best known for his 1991 debut album, *Quik Is The Name*.

2011: Rapper and producer David Banner was inducted into the Mississippi Musicians Hall of Fame.

2011: Kanye West released the single, "All Of The Lights" (featuring Rihanna). Also appearing on the track were guest vocalists John Legend, Elly Jackson, Alicia Keys, Fergie, Kid Cudi, Elton John, Drake and The-Dream. The song was nominated for three Grammys and won two awards in the categories of Best Rap Song and Best Rap/Sung Collaboration.

2014: Ice Cube co-produced and starred in the action-comedy film, *Ride Along*. He played the role of an undercover detective named James Payton. The film was a box office hit and earned nearly $155 million. (Ice Cube also appeared in the 2016 sequel, *Ride Along 2*.)

2014: Drake was both the guest host and featured musical performer on *Saturday Night Live*. He performed a medley of "Started From The Bottom" and "Trophies" and a medley of "Hold On, We're Going Home" and "From Time."

2015: A$AP Yams (real name Steven Rodriguez), a co-founder of the hip hop collective A$AP Mob, died at the age of 26. He was found dead in his Brooklyn apartment. The cause of death was attributed to accidental, acute drug intoxication.

JANUARY 19

1977: Z-Ro (birth name Joseph Wayne McVey) was born in Houston, Texas. Also known as the Mo City Don, he released his debut studio album in 1998, *Look What You Did To Me*.

1979: British rapper Wiley (birth name Richard Kylea Cowie) was born in East London, England. Originally a member of the group Pay As U Go, he later pursued a solo career. Nicknamed "The Father of Grime," he scored a series of hits including "Wearing My Rolex," "Never Be Your Woman" and "Heatwave."

1992: Mac Miller (birth name Malcolm James McCormick) was born in Pittsburgh, Pennsylvania. A rapper, he topped the pop charts in 2010 with his independently released album, *Blue Slide Park*. As a producer, he worked under the name Larry Fisherman.

1993: Snow released his debut album, *12 Inches Of Snow*. The project fused reggae with hip hop on the singles "Informer" and "Girl I've Been Hurt." Snow had finished recording the album shortly before he began an eight-month prison term.

1999: Silkk The Shocker released his third studio album, *Made Man*. The chart-topping album spawned the hit singles, "Somebody Like Me," "It Ain't My Fault Pt. 2" and "Ghetto Rain." The album featured guest appearances by Jay-Z, Snoop Dogg and Mýa.

2002: *The Nick Cannon Show* premiered on the Nickelodeon network. Running for two seasons, the comedy program featured appearances by a number of hip hop artists including Usher, Kel Mitchell, Mary J. Blige and Lil' Romeo. The program was a spinoff of another Nickelodeon series, *All That*.

2005: Ja Rule co-starred in the action-thriller film, *Assault On Precinct 13*. He played the role of a counterfeiter named Smiley.

2009: During a prison interview, rapper DMX admitted his desire to become a Christian pastor.

2010: Waka Flocka Flame was shot in the arm and robbed at a car wash in Atlanta.

JANUARY 20

1971: Questlove (birth name Ahmir Khalib Thompson) was born in Philadelphia. Trained as a drummer, he co-founded the hip hop group the Roots. In 1993, the group recorded its debut album, *Organix*. In 2014, the Roots were selected as the house band for *The Tonight Show*. Questlove's father led the popular 1950s doo-wop group, Lee Andrews & The Hearts.

1990: Digital Underground released the crossover hit single, "The Humpty Dance." The group's lead singer Shock G adopted an alternate persona, Humpty Hump, when performing the song on stage. Tupac Shakur made an appearance in the song's music video.

1990: 2 Live Crew released their controversial, crossover hit single, "Me So Horny." The song sampled "Firecracker" by Mass Production as well as dialogue from two films, *Full Metal Jacket* and Richard Pryor's *Which Way Is Up?*

2013: Lupe Fiasco was escorted from the stage by security guards after making anti-Barack Obama comments at a performance in Washington, D.C. Ironically, the private concert was staged in celebration of Obama's second presidential inauguration.

2016: West Coast rapper E-40 introduced a malt liquor beverage called "E40."

JANUARY 21

1998: Record industry executive Dick Griffey filed a $6 million lawsuit against Dr. Dre for breach of contract. Griffey alleged that a 1991 agreement entitled him to 25-percent of Dre's earnings.

2000: A concert headlined by Eve, Juvenile and B.G. at the Oakland Coliseum was cancelled when a large group of people without tickets broke down the facility's doors and fought with those inside the auditorium. More than 25 people were injured.

2001: Shyne (real name Jamal Barrow) was arrested for an auto accident in New York City that left two pedestrians seriously injured. At the time, Shyne was a co-defendant in the gun possession trial of Sean "Puffy" Combs.

2003: Snoop Dogg released the single, "Beautiful" (featuring Pharrell Williams and "Uncle" Charlie Wilson). The song's music video was shot in Rio de Janeiro, Brazil.

2005: Ice Cube starred in the comedy film, *Are We There Yet?* He played the role of Nick Persons, a child-hating bachelor. A surprise hit, the film earned nearly $98 million at the box office.

2006: Chingy released the single, "Pullin' Me Back" (featuring Tyrese). The track sampled "Rain" by SWV.

2008: After he was caught going more than 100 MPH on a Phoenix highway, DMX was charged with reckless driving, two counts of endangerment, three counts of speeding and driving on a suspended license.

2009: Jay-Z performed at the Staff Ball, the final event of Barack Obama's first presidential inauguration. Opening up for Jay-Z was the rock band, Arcade Fire. Staged at the D.C. Armory, the event drew nearly 10,000 attendees but was closed to the media.

JANUARY 22

1965: DJ Jazzy Jeff (birth name Jeffrey Allan Townes) was born in Philadelphia. Along with the Fresh Prince, he won the first ever Grammy Award in the newly launched rap category in 1989.

1983: Street Dance released the pioneering hip hop song, "Break Machine." Produced by Jacques Morali and Henri Belolo – best known for their work with the Village People – the song was a major European hit and reached the top-10 in the U.K.

1990: At the 17th annual American Music Awards, the winners were: M.C. Hammer for Favorite Rap/Hip-Hop Artist; *Let's Get It Started* by M.C. Hammer for Favorite Rap/Hip-Hop Album; and Young M.C. for Favorite Rap/Hip-Hop New Artist.

1998: Silentó (birth name Richard Lamar Hawk) was born in Atlanta. Signing with Capitol Records, he scored a top-10 hit with his debut single in 2015, "Watch Me (Whip/Nae Nae)."

2003: Dave Chappelle launched the Comedy Central series, *Chappelle's Show*. The program featured Questlove as the house deejay. Guest artists included Big Boi, Common, Snoop Dogg, Kanye West, Talib Kweli and Mos Def. The program's most popular skit featured Chappelle as rapper Lil Jon. The series ran for three seasons.

2005: Ludacris featuring Sum 41 were the musical guests on *Saturday Night Live*. Ludacris performed "Number One Spot" and was joined by Sum 41 on "Get Back."

2010: Apache (real name Anthony Peaks) died of heart failure at the age of 45. The New Jersey-based rapper began his career in the hip hop group, the Flavor Unit. Signing with Tommy Boy Records as a solo artist, he released his debut album in 1992, *Apache Ain't Shit*, which featured the hit, "Gangsta Bitch." He also worked with Tupac Shakur, Fat Joe and Naughty By Nature.

2010: Jay-Z, Bono, The Edge and Rihanna performed the charity single, "Stranded (Haiti Mon Amour)," as part of the telethon, Hope for Haiti Now: A Global Benefit for Earthquake Relief. The track was released the next day and became a hit in a number of countries. The song was written by Jay-Z, The Edge and Bono and produced by Swizz Beatz.

2016: Big Daddy Kane co-starred in the thriller film, *Exposed*.

JANUARY 23

1989: Tone Loc released his debut album, *Loc-ed After Dark*. The album was highlighted by two crossover top-10 singles, "Wild Thing" and "Funky Cold Medina," and sold two-million copies in the U.S. It was the second rap album to reach the number-one position on the U.S. charts.

1996: Singer Brandy began her run as the star of the sitcom, *Moesha*, which aired on the UPN network. The series featured Brandy as a high school student named Moesha Mitchell who lived with her family in the South Central section of Los Angeles. Brandy's real-life brother William "Ray J" Norwood portrayed Moesha's cousin, Dorian "D-Money" Long, for the last two seasons of the program. Additionally, rapper Fredro Starr portrayed Moesha's boyfriend/fiancee. The program was a ratings success and ran for six seasons.

2000: Russell Simmons was the subject of an episode of the VH-1 program, *Behind The Music*.

2007: Fergie released the solo single, "Glamorous." The chart-topping track featured rapper Ludacris.

2007: Mims released the single, "This Is Why I'm Hot" which appeared on his debut album, *Music Is My Savior*. The track sampled "Jesus Walks" by Kanye West, "Tell Me When To Go" by E-40, "Nuthin' But A 'G' Thang" by Dr. Dre and "Shook Ones Part II" by Mobb Deep.

2015: Luxury car maker Rolls-Royce filed a lawsuit against Rolls Royce Rizzy in a New Jersey federal court in an effort to stop the rapper from using the company's name and logo. Rizzy had previously ignored multiple "cease and desist" letters from Rolls-Royce.

JANUARY 24

1983: Afrika Bambaataa & Soulsonic Force released the 12-inch single "Looking For The Perfect Beat." It was the first hip hop song to use digital sampling.

1987: The Beastie Boys performed on the long-running television program, *American Bandstand*. This was their first of two appearances on the show.

2011: Flavor Flav teamed with business partner Nick Cimino to open Flav's Fried Chicken Flavor in Clinton, Iowa. The restaurant closed on April 24 after just 13 weeks in operation. Flavor Flav later opened another restaurant in Las Vegas.

2015: Paul McCartney teamed with Rihanna and Kanye West on the single, "FourFiveSeconds." The trio performed the song at the 57th Annual Grammy Awards on February 8. This was McCartney's first top-10 U.S. hit in 30 years. The track sold two-million copies in the U.S.

JANUARY 25

1993: At the 20th annual American Music Awards, the winners were: Sir Mix-A-Lot for Favorite Rap/Hip-Hop Artist; and Kris Kross for Favorite Rap/Hip-Hop New Artist. The ceremony was co-hosted by Bobby Brown.

1998: Queen Latifah became the first hip act to perform during the halftime show at the Super Bowl. Staged at Qualcomm Stadium in San Diego, the Motown-themed program also featured Boyz II Men, Smokey Robinson, Martha Reeves, the Temptations and the Grambling State University Band.

1999: Eminem released his breakthrough single, "My Name Is," from his major label debut album, *The Slim Shady LP*. The track sampled "I Got The..." by Labi Siffre. The single won a Grammy in the category of Best Rap Solo Performance.

2000: NBA player and aspiring rapper Kobe Bryant released the single, "K.O.B.E." The track featured model Tyra Banks. (The B-side "Thug Poet" featured Nas, 50 Cent and Broady Boy.) Sony Records later decided not to release Bryant's album.

2008: Sisqó surprised his fans by appearing as a contestant on the six-episode CMT reality show, *Gone Country*. The rapper competed against six other singers in the county music competition. The winner earned a recording session produced by John Rich of the hit duo, Big & Rich. R&B singer Bobby Brown was also a contestant on the series. Neither Sisqó nor Brown won the competition.

2009: The contents of the Death Row Records offices in Los Angeles were sold at an auction on the orders of a bankruptcy court. The inventory included an electric chair, a large portrait of Suge Knight, more than 17,000 copies of the Snoop Dogg CD *Tha Doggfather* as well as various music awards.

2011: The duo LMFAO released the smash hit single, "Party Rock Anthem." The track featured guest vocals by producer GoonRock and British singer Lauren Bennett. The song sold ten-million digital copies and the video was viewed over one-billion times on YouTube. The song's music video revived a popular hip hop dance, "The Running Man." The track was also featured in a number of televison commercials including a popular spot for Kia Soul.

2011: Black Eyed Peas member will.i.am was hired as the Director of Creative Innovation by Intel, the computer electronics company. The computer savvy rapper explained at a news conference: "Nearly everything I do involves processors and computers, and when I see an Intel chip I think of all the creative minds involved that help to amplify my own creativity."

2012: According to published reports, Nas reportedly owed nearly $6.5 million in back taxes to the IRS. The federal agency filed liens with the rapper's publishing company in order to collect the unpaid taxes.

JANUARY 26

1971: Soul/hip hop performer Erykah Badu (birth name Erica Abi Wright) was born in Dallas. Her professional career began in 1994 when she was hired as the opening act for D'Angelo.

1998: At the 25th annual American Music Awards, Bone Thugs-N-Harmony won the award for Favorite Rap/Hip-Hop Artist.

2006: The documentary *Hip-Hop: Beyond Beats And Rhymes* premiered at the Sundance Film Festival. Written, produced, and directed by Byron Hurt, the documentary explored various social issues within hip hop culture. The film featured interviews with rap performers and fans as well as various researchers and writers. The documentary aired on PBS the following year.

2013: Kendrick Lamar was the musical guest on *Saturday Night Live*. He performed "Swimming Pools (Drank)" and "Poetic Justice."

2014: At the 56th Annual Grammy Awards, the winners were: "Thrift Shop" by Macklemore & Ryan Lewis featuring Wanz in the category of Best Rap Performance; "Holy Grail" by Jay-Z and Justin Timberlake in the category of Best Rap/Sung Collaboration; "Thrift Shop" by Macklemore & Ryan Lewis in the category of Best Rap Song; *The Heist* by Macklemore & Ryan Lewis in the category of Best Rap Album; and Macklemore & Ryan Lewis in the category of Best New Artist. The ceremony was hosted for the third year in a row by LL Cool J.

2014: Macklemore of the duo Macklemore & Ryan Lewis apologized to Kendrick Lamar following the Grammy Awards ceremony. In a text, he wrote "You got robbed. I wanted you to win. You should have. It's weird and sucks that I robbed you." While Macklemore & Ryan Lewis won four Grammys – including three rap awards – Lamar was shut out of the winner's circle despite his seven nominations.

JANUARY 27

1988: From his third album, LL Cool J released the first single, "Going Back To Cali." The track originally appeared on the soundtrack of the 1987 hit film, *Less Than Zero*. The million-selling single was produced and co-written by Rick Rubin.

1991: Denise "Dee" Barnes, the host of the Fox network hip hop program *Pump It Up!*, was allegedly assaulted by Dr. Dre of N.W.A., in the wake of the negative portrayal of the group on her television show. Dr. Dre was later charged with assault. After pleading no contest, he was sentenced to 240 hours of community service and two years of probation and was also fined $2,513. Barnes filed a civil suit against the rapper, which was later settled out of court.

1997: At the 24th annual American Music Awards, Tupac Shakur won the award for Favorite Rap/Hip-Hop Artist. The ceremony was hosted by Sinbad.

1998: The hip hop duo Lord Tariq and Peter Gunz released the single, "Deja Vu (Uptown Baby)." The track sampled "Black Cow" by Steely Dan and "Amores Como El Nuestro" by Jerry Rivera.

1998: Sylk-E. Fyne released the single, "Romeo And Juliet" (featuring Chill), which was her only top-40 pop hit. The track appeared on her debut album, *Raw Sylk*. The track included an interpolation of "You Don't Have To Cry" by Rene & Angela.

2003: Eminem released the single, "Superman." The diss song sparked a feud with Mariah Carey. In 2009, Eminem dissed both Carey and her husband at the time, Nick Cannon, on the track, "Bagpipes From Baghdad."

2004: Chicago-based rapper Twista released his breakthrough album, *Kamikaze*. The chart-topping album featured guest artists Kanye West, Jamie Foxx and R. Kelly. The album spawned five singles: "Slow Jamz," "Overnight Celebrity," "So Sexy" and "Sunshine." The bonus single "So Sexy: Chapter II (Like This)" was included on the re-released version of the album.

2009: Flo Rida released the single, "Right Round" (featuring Ke$ha). The song was built upon a sample of "You Spin Me Round (Like A Record)" by Dead Or Alive.

JANUARY 28

1984: Def Jam Recordings released their very first record, "It's Yours" by T La Rock & Jazzy Jay. The session was recorded at Power Play Studios in Queens, New York. At the time, the label operated out of Rick Rubin's dorm room at New York University.

1985: J. Cole (birth name Jermaine Lamarr Cole) was born in Frankfurt, Germany, but raised in Fayetteville, North Carolina. He released his breakthrough album in 2011, *Cole World: The Sideline Story*.

1991: At the 18th annual American Music Awards, the winners were: M.C. Hammer for Favorite Rap/Hip-Hop Artist; *Please Hammer, Don't Hurt 'Em* by M.C. Hammer for Favorite Rap/Hip-Hop Album; and Vanilla Ice for Favorite Rap/Hip-Hop New Artist.

1995: TLC began a four-week run at number-one on the U.S. singles chart with "Creep."

2001: Hip hop artists Mary J. Blige and Nelly performed during the halftime show at Super Bowl XXXV, which was staged at Raymond James Stadium in Tampa, Florida. The theme of the program was "The Kings of Rock and Pop." Blige and Nelly performed "Walk This Way" with Aerosmith, 'N Sync and Britney Spears.

2003: "The Message," a 1982 hit by Grandmaster Flash and the Furious Five, was the first rap song added to the prestigious U.S. National Recording Registry of Historic Songs.

2004: Turk (real name Tab Virgil) of the New Orleans hip hop group the Hot Boys was charged with first-degree attempted murder, after shooting two police officers who had entered his apartment in Memphis. After agreeing to a plea deal, the rapper pleaded guilty to charges of attempted second-degree murder. He served nine-years of a twelve-year prison term.

2005: The Game released the single, "Hate It Or Love It" (featuring 50 Cent). The track sampled "Rubber Band" by the Trammps. The song was nominated for two Grammys in the categories of Best Rap Song and Best Rap Performance by a Duo or Group.

2006: T.I. released the single, "What You Know." The track was used as the theme of his first feature film, *ATL*. The single sold two-million copies in the U.S., was nominated for a Grammy in the category of Best Rap Song and won a Grammy for Best Rap Solo Performance.

2013: While driving his Rolls-Royce in Fort Lauderdale, Rick Ross was forced to swerve his vehicle in order to avoid a hail of gunfire. In the process, he struck the side of a house. Neither Ross nor his female passenger was injured.

2015: Lil Wayne sued his record label, Cash Money, over contractual violations and the nonpayment of royalties. He asked for $51 million in damages.

JANUARY 29

1982: Riff Raff (birth name Horst Christian Simco) was born in Houston. Before pursuing a solo career, he was a member of the group, Three Loco.

1996: At the 23rd annual American Music Awards, Coolio won the award for Favorite Rap/Hip-Hop Artist. The program was hosted by Sinbad.

2011: Nicki Minaj was the musical guest on *Saturday Night Live*. She performed "Right Thru Me" and "Moment 4 Life." She also appeared in a skit, "Bride of Blackenstein."

2016: A Beastie Boys exhibit was unveiled at the Rock and Roll Hall of Fame in Cleveland. Among the artifacts were Mike D's Volkswagen medallion, the original handwritten lyrics of the track "Brass Monkey" and the group's outfits from the "Intergalactic" music video.

2016: Kevin Gates released his breakthrough album, *Islah*. Several singles were issued from the album including "Really Really" and "2 Phones."

JANUARY 30

1984: Kid Cudi (birth name Scott Ramon Seguro Mescudi) was born in Cleveland, Ohio. Discovered by Kanye West, Cudi was signed in 2008 to West's label G.O.O.D. Music. Cudi's debut album, *Man On The Moon: The End Of Day*, spawned the breakthrough single, "Day 'n' Nite."

1989: At the 16th annual American Music Awards, the winners were: DJ Jazzy Jeff & The Fresh Prince for Favorite Rap/Hip-Hop Artist; and *He's The DJ, I'm The Rapper* by DJ Jazzy Jeff & The Fresh Prince for Favorite Rap/Hip-Hop Album. This was the first year for the two rap/hip hop categories.

1991: *DJ Magazine* was founded in Britain. The monthly periodical chronicled the popularity of deejay culture.

1995: At the 22nd annual American Music Awards, Snoop Doggy Dogg won the award for Favorite Rap/Hip-Hop Artist.

1996: Rapper and activist Sister Souljah published her autobiography, *No Disrespect*.

2004: The musical drama film, *You Got Served*, was released. The film followed the exploits of a group of Los Angeles teens who battled each other in street dance competitions. The film starred the R&B boy band B2K and featured an appearance by Lil' Kim.

2007: Brandy rear-ended another car while driving on the 405 Freeway in Los Angeles. The impact started a multiple-vehicle crash that resulted in the death of a 38-year-old woman. Although she was not criminally charged for the accident, Brandy was later sued by the family of the deceased victim and the drivers of the other damaged vehicles. All of the lawsuits were settled out of court.

2010: Shyne was not permitted to enter the United Kingdom due to his past criminal convictions. He was hoping to start recording a new album at a studio in London. The rapper was sent back to his native country, Belize.

2015: Marion "Suge" Knight was arrested on charges of suspicion of murder following a fatal hit and run incident. The incident occurred in the parking lot of a restaurant in Compton following a heated argument.

2016: Drake released the single, "Summer Sixteen," which was the lead track from his sixth album, *Views From The 6*. The track sampled "The Question Is" by the Winans and "Glass Tubes" by Brian Bennett.

JANUARY 31

1994: The Wu-Tang Clan released the hit single, "C.R.E.A.M." ("Cash Rules Everything Around Me"). This was the group's best known hit.

2000: Jay-Z was indicted in the stabbing of record executive Lance "Un" Rivera at the Kit Kat Club in Manhattan. In October 2000, he pleaded guilty to the charge and received a sentence of probation.

2010: At the 52nd Annual Grammy Awards, the winners were: "D.O.A. (Death Of Auto-Tune)" by Jay-Z in the category of Best Rap Solo Performance; "Crack A Bottle" by Eminem, Dr. Dre & 50 Cent in the category of Best Rap Performance by a Duo or Group; "Run This Town" by Jay-Z, Rihanna & Kanye West in the category of Best Rap/Sung Collaboration; "Run This Town" by Jay-Z, Rihanna & Kanye West in the category of Best Rap Song; and *Relapse* by Eminem in the category of Best Rap Album.

2010: Paul Lawrence Fuemana, the lead singer of the New Zealand-based duo OMC, passed away after battling a neurological disease. OMC is best known for their 1995 hit, "How Bizarre." Fuemana was 40-years-old.

2013: Donald Trump threatened legal action against rapper Mac Miller for recording the track "Donald Trump" without first securing permission from the business tycoon.

▶ FEBRUARY

FEBRUARY 1

1975: Big Boi (birth name Antwan André Patton) was born in Savannah, Georgia. Best known as a member of the popular hip hop duo OutKast, he also pursued a solo career.

1992: Marvel Comics published the first *Kid 'n Play* comic book. In all, nine issues were produced.

1994: Ice T published the book, *The Ice Opinion*.

1994: The Fugees released their debut album, *Blunted On Reality*. Only a moderate hit, the album had been recorded two years earlier but was delayed due to problems with the group's record label.

1997: The documentary, *Battle Sounds*, examined the competitive world of hip hop deejays. The project was filmed over a three-year period.

1998: Pastor Mason Betha (also known as Ma$e) published his autobiography, *Revelations: There's A Light After The Lime*. The book examined the former rapper's religious transformation and his establishment of the non-denominational movement, S.A.N.E. (Saving a Nation Endangered) Ministries.

1999: In *Blaze* magazine's ranking of the Top 50 MCs of all Time, the number-one MC was Rakim. At number-two was KRS-One.

2004: The halftime performers at Super Bowl XXXVIII included P. Diddy, Nelly, Janet Jackson, Justin Timberlake and rap-rock singer Kid Rock. This was the first time in history that more than half of the performers at the halftime show were hip hop acts. At the end of the performance, Janet Jackson experienced her infamous "wardrobe malfunction." Staged at Reliant Stadium in Houston, the concert featured a "Rock the Vote" theme.

2009: Erykah Badu and Jay Electronica welcomed the birth of their daughter, Mars.

2010: Controversial rapper Luther Campbell of the group 2 Live Crew was hired as a columnist for the entertainment magazine, *The Miami New Times*.

2011: Dr. Dre released the single, "I Need A Doctor" (featuring Eminem and Skylar Grey). The track was intended for Dre's third solo album, *Detox*, which was not released. The track was nominated for two Grammys in the categories of Best Rap/Sung Collaboration and Best Rap Song. The song's music video featured a cameo appearance by actress Sandra Bullock.

2011: Chris Brown released the single, "Look At Me Now" (featuring Lil Wayne and Busta Rhymes). The song's music video featured a Step Up-style dance competition. The song was nominated for two Grammys in the categories of Best Rap Performance and Best Rap Song.

2015: J. Ivy published the book, *Dear Father: Turning My Pain Into Power*.

2015: Missy Elliott, Katy Perry, Lenny Kravitz and the Arizona State University Sun Devil Marching Band were the musical performers at the Super Bowl XLIX halftime show, staged at the University of Phoenix Stadium in Glendale, Arizona.

FEBRUARY 2

1993: Fat Boys member Prince Markie Dee teamed with the Soul Convention on the single, "Typical Reasons (Swing My Way)." The track sampled "Outstanding" by the Gap Band.

1994: Ice Cube released the single, "You Know How We Do It," which has become a West Coast classic. The track sampled "The Show Is Over" by Evelyn "Champagne" King.

2002: LL Cool J starred in a remake of the 1975 science-fiction film, *Rollerball*. He portrayed Marcus Ridley, an athlete who competed in the violent sport of rollerball.

2009: Eminem released the hit single, "Crack A Bottle," which featured Dr. Dre and 50 Cent. It was the debut release from his sixth studio album, *Relapse*.

2010: B.o.B released the single, "Nothin' On You" (featuring Bruno Mars). The remixed version of the track also featured Big Boi. The song was nominated for three Grammys.

2012: R&B singer Ericka Lee filed a lawsuit in a California federal court against Drake, claiming she had not received royalties for the use of her voice on the rapper's hit single "Marvin's Room."

2013: Macklemore and Ryan Lewis began a four-week run at number-one on the U.S. singles chart with "Thrift Shop."

2013: Mary J. Blige portrayed Betty Shabazz, the widow of Malcolm X, in the Lifetime network film, *Betty & Coretta*.

2015: West Coast rapper "The Jacka" (real name Dominic Newton) was murdered in his hometown of Oakland at the age of 37. He was standing on a sidewalk next to a van when he was shot by an unknown assailant.

2016: L.A. Reid published his autobiography, *Sing To Me: My Story Of Making Music, Finding Magic, And Searching For Who's Next*.

2016: DJ Big Kap (real name Keith Carter) passed away at the age of 45. He was a member of the East Coast hip hop collective, the Flip, and worked with the Notorious B.I.G.

FEBRUARY 3

1990: Sean Kingston (birth name Kisean Anderson) was born in Miami but raised in Jamaica. After he was discovered on MySpace, Kingston signed a recording contract in 2007. He scored a sizable hit with his debut single, "Beautiful Girls."

1995: J-Dee (real name Dasean Cooper), a member of the Los Angeles gangsta rap trio Da Lench Mob, was sentenced to 29-years to life in prison for the murder of his girlfriend's roommate.

1996: Tone Loc provided the voice of a cartoon teddy bear named C-Bear in the Fox Kids animated television series, *C-Bear And Jamal*. The program ran for 13 episodes.

1997: Scarface released the single, "Smile" (featuring 2Pac and Johnny P.). The track featured an interpolation of "Tell Me If You Still Care" by the S.O.S. Band. The song's controversial music video featured a 2Pac look-alike who was symbolically crucified on a cross.

1998: Fat Pat (real name Patrick Lamark Hawkins) was killed in Houston. He was shot dead after leaving a concert promoter's apartment. Fat Pat was a member of the Houston rap collective, the Screwed Up Click, and was best known for the 1998 solo single, "Tops Drop." He was 27-years-old.

2004: Antonio "L.A." Reid was named the Chairman and CEO of the Island Def Jam Music Group. He remained at the post for seven-years.

2013: Beyoncé and Destiny's Child were the performers at the Super Bowl XLVII halftime show, which was staged at the Mercedes-Benz Superdome in New Orleans.

FEBRUARY 4

1976: Cam'ron (birth name Cameron Ezike Giles) was born in Harlem, New York. A successful solo artist, he was also a member of the groups, the Diplomats, Children Of The Corn and the U.N. He released his debut solo album in 1998, *Confessions Of Fire*.

1991: Vanilla Ice published his autobiography, *Ice By Ice: The Vanilla Ice Story In His Own Words*.

1994: Tone Loc co-starred in the Jim Carrey comedy film, *Ace Ventura: Pet Detective*. Loc portrayed a police officer named Emilio.

2003: 50 Cent released his debut album, *Get Rich Or Die Tryin'*. The album spawned four singles, "In Da Club," "21 Questions," "P.I.M.P." and "If I Can't." A smash hit, the album sold more than eight-million copies in the U.S. and was nominated for a Grammy in the category of Best Rap Album.

2003: Jay-Z released the single, "Excuse Me Miss." Pharrell provided the falsetto vocals on the song's chorus. The track sampled "Take You Out" by Luther Vandross and "Big Poppa" by the Notorious B.I.G. Jay-Z later recorded a sequel to "Excuse Me Miss," which was titled "La-La-La (Excuse Me Miss Again)."

2006: The single "Check On It" by Beyoncé featuring Slim Thug began a five-week run at number-one on the U.S. charts.

2007: Timbaland released his second solo album, *Shock Value*. The album – which was the first release on his own label, Mosley Music Group – featured a number of notable guest artists including Justin Timberlake, the Hives, Nelly Furtado, Missy Elliott, 50 Cent, Dr. Dre, Elton John, Fall Out Boy and Magoo. The album spawned five singles: "Give It To Me," "The Way I Are," "Apologize," "Scream" and "Throw It On Me."

2011: Salt-n-Pepa began a headlining U.S. tour, which was billed as "Salt N Pepa's Legends of Hip Hop Tour." The supporting acts included Rob Base, Whodini, Naughty By Nature, Kurtis Blow, Doug E. Fresh, Biz Markie, MC Lyte, Big Daddy Kane, Kool Moe Dee, Slick Rick and Chubb Rock.

2012: Cymphonique Miller, the 15-year-old daughter of rapper Master P, starred on the Nickelodeon television program, *How To Rock*. Her brother, rapper Lil' Romeo, starred in his own series on the same network from 2003 to 2006.

2012: Madonna, LMFAO, Nicki Minaj, M.I.A. and Cee Lo Green were the musical performers at the Super Bowl XLVI halftime show, which was staged at Lucas Oil Stadium in Indianapolis, Indiana.

FEBRUARY 5

1986: Kevin Gates (birth name Kevin Jerome Gilyard) was born in Baton Rouge, Louisiana. He was a regional star who released a number of popular rap mixtapes before attracting the attention of Atlantic Records in 2013. His breakthrough album, *Islah*, was released in 2016.

1987: Fazer (birth name Richard Rawson) of the British hip hop trio, N-Dubz, was born in Camden, London, England.

1991: A hip hop group formed by inmates at East Jersey State Prison in New Jersey released an EP on a major label, Hollywood Records. MTV refused to air the group's music video for the track, "Belly Of The Beast."

1994: Salt-n-Pepa were the musical guests on *Saturday Night Live*. They performed "Shoop" and "Whatta Man."

2002: Fat Joe released the single, "What's Luv?," which featured Ashanti. (Ja Rule was the featured artist on the remixed version of the song.) The track sampled "Niggaz Nature" by 2Pac. This was the biggest solo hit of Fat Joe's career.

2006: LL Cool J released the hit single, "Control Myself," which featured Jennifer Lopez. The track sampled two songs by Afrika Bambaataa & Soulsonic Force, "Looking For The Perfect Beat" and "Planet Rock."

2008: Kid Cudi released the hit single, "Day 'n' Nite." The track appeared on his mixtape, *A Kid Named Cudi*, as well as on his debut studio album, *Man On The Moon: The End Of Day*. Three different music videos were filmed for the track.

2011: The Grammy Museum in Los Angeles unveiled its first hip hop exhibition, "Hip-Hop: A Cultural Odyssey." Among the exhibits were handwritten song lyrics by Tupac Shakur, Grandmaster Flash's turntables and LL Cool J's Troop suit and Kangol hat.

2011: The rap-metal group Linkin Park were the musical guests on *Saturday Night Live*. They performed "Waiting For The End" and "When They Come For Me."

2012: Flavor Flav, Elton John and Melanie Amaro appeared in a television commercial for Pepsi, which made its debut during Super Bowl XLVI.

FEBRUARY 6

1989: Jamaican sound engineer King Tubby (real name Osbourne Ruddock) was shot and killed outside of his home in the Duhaney Park section of Kingston, shortly after a recording session. He was influential in the rise of dub and electronic music.

1992: The hip hop duo Kris Kross released their debut single, the smash hit "Jump." The track sampled several songs including "I Want You Back" by the Jackson 5 and "Funky Worm" by the Ohio Players. The single sold more than two-million copies in the U.S.

1993: An episode of the television series, *MTV Unplugged*, featured a number of hip hop artists. Titled *Uptown Unplugged*, the program was filmed at Universal Studios in Los Angeles and featured Mary J. Blige, Jodeci, Father MC, Christopher Williams and Heavy D.

2007: Timbaland released his debut solo single, "Give It To Me" (featuring Nelly Furtado and Justin Timberlake). The chart-topping song was nominated for a Grammy in the category of Best Pop Collaboration with Vocals.

2011: The Black Eyed Peas, Usher and Slash (of Guns N' Roses) were the performers at the Super Bowl XLV halftime show, which was staged at Cowboys Stadium in Arlington, Texas.

2013: Drake released the track, "Started From The Bottom," which was the debut single from his third album, *Nothing Was The Same*. Drake's mother, Sandi, appeared in the song's music video. The track was nominated for a Grammy in two categories.

FEBRUARY 7

1980: The Sugarhill Gang released their debut album, *Sugarhill Gang*. The album was highlighted by the tracks, "Rapper's Reprise" and the groundbreaking rap classic "Rapper's Delight."

1993: Before she became an actress, Carmen Electra released a hip hop album, *Carmen Electra*. The album was produced by Prince, whom was she was dating at the time.

1994: At the 21st annual American Music Awards, Dr. Dre won both of the rap/hip hop awards: Favorite Rap/Hip-Hop Artist and Favorite Rap/Hip-Hop New Artist.

1995: Tupac Shakur was sentenced to 18 to 54 months in prison for a December 1994 conviction on a charge of sexual abuse. He was sent to the Clinton Correctional Facility in Dannemora, New York.

1995: Mobb Deep released the single, "Shook Ones (Part II)." The track sampled "Jessica" by Herbie Hancock, "Kitty With The Bent Frame" by Quincy Jones and "Dirty Feet" by Daly-Wilson Big Band featuring Kerrie Biddell. The song was considered a follow-up to the 1984 track, "Shook Ones."

2003: LL Cool J starred in the romantic-comedy film, *Deliver Us From Eva*. The rapper portrayed Ray Adams, a casanova who fell in love with a woman he was paid to date. This was the first film in which the rapper was billed as James Todd Smith instead of LL Cool J.

2008: KRS-One began recording a new version of the anti-violence rap classic, "Self-Destruction," which he titled "Self-Construction." The track was recorded over a three-day period and featured 55 musical artists including Nelly, Method Man, the Game, David Banner, Redman, Rah Digga, Awol One, Lil' AJ, Ne-Yo, Talib Kweli, Styles P, Busta Rhymes, Fat Joe, Cassidy, MC Lyte, 50 Cent and others. The track was recorded at the Los Angeles Recording School.

2010: Nicki Minaj offered a $50,000 reward for the return of her lost stuffed animal, Oscar, which had accompanied her on a trip from Miami to New York for an appearance on *The Late Show With David Letterman*.

2016: Beyoncé joined Coldplay and Bruno Mars at the Super Bowl halftime show at Levi's Stadium in suburban San Francisco. Beyoncé's performance sparked a controversy for her Black Panthers-inspired uniform, Black Power salute and Malcolm X references.

FEBRUARY 8

1969: Paul Lawrence Fuemana, the lead singer of the New Zealand-based duo OMC, was born in Auckland, New Zealand. OMC is best known for the 1995 hit, "How Bizarre."

1976: Capone (birth name Kiam Akasi Holley) was born in Queens, New York. In 1995, he teamed with Noreaga to form the hip hop duo, Capone-N-Noreaga. Both members of the duo later pursued solo careers.

1987: Run-D.M.C. released the single, "It's Tricky." The Knack later sued over the claim that the song included an unauthorized sample from their number-one hit, "My Sharona." The song's music video was shot in Los Angeles and featured magicians Penn and Teller.

1992: C&C Music Factory were the musical guests on *Saturday Night Live*. They performed "Here We Go (Let's Rock & Roll)," "Gonna Make You Sweat (Everybody Dance Now)" and "A Deeper Love."

1995: The Oakland-based hip hop duo Luniz released the single, "I Got 5 On It" (featuring Michael Marshall). The track sampled "Why You Treat Me So Bad" by Club Nouveau, "Jungle Boogie" by Kool & The Gang and "Top Billin'" by Audio Two.

2001: Eve released the debut single, "Who's That Girl?," from her second album, *Scorpion*.

2002: Sean "Puffy" Combs and Mos Def co-starred in the romantic-drama film, *Monster's Ball*.

2003: The single "All I Have" by Jennifer Lopez featuring LL Cool J began a four-week run at number-one on the U.S. charts.

2004: At the 46th Annual Grammy Awards, the winners were: "Work It" by Missy Elliott in the category of Best Female Rap Solo Performance; "Lose Yourself" by Eminem in the category of Best Male Rap Solo Performance; "Shake Ya Tailfeather" by Nelly, P. Diddy & Murphy Lee in the category of Best Rap Performance by a Duo or Group; "Crazy in Love" by Beyoncé & Jay-Z in the category of Best Rap/Sung Collaboration; *Speakerboxxx/The Love Below* by OutKast

2005: 50 Cent released the hit single, "Candy Shop" (featuring Olivia). Due to the song's risque lyrics, most radio stations played a heavily edited version of the track. The song was nominated for a Grammy in the category of Best Rap Song.

2006: At the 48th Annual Grammy Awards, the winners were: "Gold Digger" by Kanye West in the category of Best Rap Solo Performance; "Don't Phunk With My Heart" by the Black Eyed Peas in the category of Best Rap Performance by a Duo or Group; "Numb/Encore" by Jay-Z & Linkin Park in the category of Best Rap/Sung Collaboration; "Diamonds From Sierra Leone" by Kanye West in the category of Best Rap Song; and *Late Registration* by Kanye West in the category of Best Rap Album.

2006: The Game announced a partnership with automotive specialists, 310 Motoring, in the launch of a signature sneaker line, "Hurricane by 310."

2008: The Smithsonian Institution in Washington, D.C., debuted a photographic exhibition of hip hop artists, *RECOGNIZE! Hip Hop and Contemporary Portraiture*. The event was staged at the museum's National Portrait Gallery.

2009: At the 51st Annual Grammy Awards, the winners were: "A Milli" by Lil Wayne in the category of Best Rap Solo Performance; "Swagga Like Us" by Jay-Z & T.I. featuring Kanye West, & Lil Wayne in the category of Best Rap Performance by a Duo or Group; "American Boy" by Estelle & Kanye West in the category of Best Rap/Sung Collaboration; "Lollipop" Lil Wayne & Static Major in the category of Best Rap Song; and *Tha Carter III* by Lil Wayne in the category of Best Rap Album.

2009: Chris Brown allegedly struck his then-girlfriend Rihanna during an argument inside his rented Lamborghini, after the couple had left a pre-Grammy party hosted by record executive Clive Davis. Rihanna was treated at Cedars-Sinai Medical Center for her injuries. Brown was arrested and released after paying a $50,000 bail. Both Brown and Rihanna cancelled their scheduled performances at the Grammy Awards.

2013: Rapper T.I. appeared in the crime film, *Identity Thief*, which starred Jason Bateman and Melissa McCarthy. In the film, T.I. was billed as Tip "T.I." Harris.

2014: The single "Dark Horse" by Katy Perry featuring Juicy J began a four-week run at number-one on the U.S. charts.

2015: At the 57th Annual Grammy Awards, the winners were: "i" by Kendrick Lamar in the category of Best Rap Performance; "The Monster" by Eminem featuring Rihanna in the category of Best Rap/Sung Collaboration; "i" by Kendrick Lamar in the category of Best Rap Song; and *The Marshall Mathers LP 2 by* Eminem in the category of Best Rap Album. The ceremony was hosted for the fourth year in a row by LL Cool J.

2015: Pharrell Williams portrayed a cartoon version of himself on *The Simpsons*. In an episode titled "Walking Big & Tall," Williams recited some of the lyrics from his hit song, "Happy."

FEBRUARY 9

1999: JT Money, a former member of the hip hop group Poison Clan, released the crossover hit single, "Who Dat" (featuring Solé). Later in year, JT Money returned the favor and was a featured artist on Solé's hit single, "4,5,6."

2006: Kanye West was criticized for his photo on the cover of *Rolling Stone* magazine. Portrayed as Christ, the rapper wore a tunic and a crown of thorns.

2007: Nick Cannon portrayed a fictional soccer player named TJ Harper in the British film, *Goal II: Living The Dream*.

2012: Converse introduced four new styles of footwear in collaboration with the British rap-rock group, Gorillaz.

2013: Chris Brown crashed his Porsche into a cement wall in Beverly Hills, allegedly while trying to elude paparazzi. He escaped serious injury and was able to walk away from his totaled vehicle. The accident occurred one day before he was scheduled to perform at the Grammy Awards.

FEBRUARY 10

1987: Public Enemy released their debut album, the critically-acclaimed *Yo! Bum Rush The Show*. The album spawned two singles, "Public Enemy No. 1" and "You're Gonna Get Yours."

1990: Tevin Campbell, Kool Moe Dee and Big Daddy Kane were the musical guests on *Saturday Night Live*. They performed "Back On The Block" and "Wee B. Dooinit."

1996: Coolio was the musical guest on *Saturday Night Live*. He performed "1, 2, 3, 4 (Sumpin' New)" and "Gangsta's Paradise."

2004: J-Kwon released the single, "Tipsy." The track sampled "We Will Rock You" by Queen and "It's Funky Enough" by the D.O.C. The song's music video featured Da Brat, Daz Dillinger, Jermaine Dupri, Murphy Lee and comedian Lavell Crawford.

2004: Kanye West released his debut album, *The College Dropout*, which was recorded over a period of four-years. The critically-acclaimed album spawned five singles: "Through The Wire," "Slow Jamz," "All Falls Down," "Jesus Walks" and "The New Workout Plan." The album won a Grammy in the category of Best Rap Album and sold more than three-million copies in the U.S.

2006: J Dilla (real name James Dewitt Yancey) passed away at the age of 32 from complications of Lupus. He worked with a number of hip hop artists including Common, A Tribe Called Quest, De La Soul, Busta Rhymes, Erykah Badu and the Pharcyde.

2007: The BET network premiered the documentary, *Wu: The Story Of The Wu-Tang Clan*.

2008: At the 50th Annual Grammy Awards, the winners were: "Stronger" by Kanye West in the category of Best Rap Solo Performance; "Southside" by Common & Kanye West in the category of Best Rap Performance by a Duo or Group; "Umbrella" by Rihanna & Jay-Z in the category of Best Rap/Sung Collaboration; "Good Life" by Kanye West & T-Pain in the category of Best Rap Song; and *Graduation* by Kanye West in the category of Best Rap Album.

2009: T.I. starred in the MTV reality program, *T.I.'s Road To Redemption*. The program chronicled the rapper's life shortly before he entered prison for a weapons conviction. The series ran for nine episodes.

2013: At the 55th Annual Grammy Awards, the winners were: "Niggas In Paris" by Jay-Z and Kanye West in the category of Best Rap Performance; "No Church In The Wild" by Jay-Z and Kanye West featuring Frank Ocean & The-Dream in the category of Best Rap/Sung Collaboration; "Niggas In Paris" by Jay-Z and Kanye West in the category of Best Rap Song; and *Take Care* by Drake in the category of Best Rap Album. The ceremony was hosted for the second year by LL Cool J.

FEBRUARY 11

1971: Nikki D (birth name Nichelle Strong) was born in Canada. The first female performer signed to Def Jam Recordings, her biggest hit came in 1991 with "Daddy's Little Girl."

1979: Singer/actress Brandy (birth name Brandy Rayana Norwood) was born in McCabe, Mississippi. In 2009, she adopted the name Bran'Nu when she rapped on Timbaland's album, *Timbaland Presents Shock Value 2*.

1994: Tone Loc co-starred in the comedy film, *Blank Check*. Loc portrayed a criminal named Juice.

1997: Soul/hip hop singer Erykah Badu released her debut album, *Baduizm*. The project spawned three singles, "On & On," "Next Lifetime" and "Otherside Of The Game." The album sold three-million copies in the U.S.

2005: Will Smith starred in the romantic-comedy film, *Hitch*. He portrayed a dating trainer named Alex "Hitch" Hitchens. The film grossed nearly $370 million.

2007: At the 49th Annual Grammy Awards, the winners were: "What You Know" by T.I. in the category of Best Rap Solo Performance; "Ridin'" by Chamillionaire & Krayzie Bone in the category of Best Rap Performance by a Duo or Group; "My Love" by Justin Timberlake & T.I. in the category of Best Rap/Sung Collaboration; "Money Maker" by Ludacris & Pharrell in the category of Best Rap Song; and *Release Therapy* by Ludacris in the category of Best Rap Album.

2008: Maya released her hit single, "Paper Planes." The ballad was written by M.I.A. and Diplo, and was built upon a sample of "Straight To Hell" by the Clash. "Paper Planes" was nominated for a Grammy in the prestigious category of Record of the Year and was named the #5 song of the decade, 2000 to 2010, by *Rolling Stone* magazine.

2016: Martin Shkreli offered $10 million to Kanye West and his record company for the rapper's next album, *The Life Of Pablo*. The previous year, Shkreli spent $2 million to purchase the only copy of Wu-Tang Clan's comeback album, *Once Upon A Time In Shaolin*.

FEBRUARY 12

1980: Gucci Mane (birth name Radric Davis) was born in Bessemer, Alabama, but raised in Atlanta. After signing with Warner Brothers in 2009, he released his breakthrough album, *The State vs. Radric Davis*. Mane later founded the label, 1017 Brick Squad Records.

1990: MC Hammer released his third album, the chart-topping smash, *Please Hammer, Don't Hurt 'Em*. The album was propelled by the crossover hit, "Can't Touch This." The album's other hits included "Here Comes The Hammer" and a remake of the Chi-Lites' 1971 soul classic "Have You Seen Her." With 10-million copies sold in the U.S., *Please Hammer, Don't Hurt 'Em* was the second best-selling rap album of the 20th century, behind by TLC's *CrazySexyCool* which sold 11-million copies.

1991: Master P released his debut studio album, *Get Away Clean*.

1997: Ice Cube starred in the action-thriller film, *Dangerous Ground*. He played the role of a protestor named Vusi Madlazi who was forced to leave his South African village.

2000: DMX was the musical guest on *Saturday Night Live*. He performed "Party Up" and "What's My Name."

2007: Ludacris released the socially-conscious single, "Runaway Love" (featuring Mary J. Blige).

2010: A motorcycle owned by Ludacris was featured in an exhibit at the Harley-Davidson Museum in Milwaukee. Also on display were motorcycles owned by Clark Gable and Steve McQueen.

2011: Chris Brown was the musical guest on *Saturday Night Live*. He performed "Yeah 3x" and "No BS."

2012: At the 54th Annual Grammy Awards, the winners were: "Otis" by Jay-Z & Kanye West featuring Otis Redding in the category of Best Rap Performance; "All Of The Lights" by Kanye West, Rihanna, Fergie & Kid Cudi in the category of Best Rap/Sung Collaboration; "All Of The Lights" by Kanye West, Rihanna, Fergie & Kid Cudi in the category of Best Rap Song; and *My Beautiful Dark Twisted Fantasy* by Kanye West in the category of Best Rap Album. The ceremony was hosted by LL Cool J.

2014: Los Angeles hip hop group Odd Future was banned from entering New Zealand. The group was scheduled to perform on a bill with Eminem. According to the country's immigration officials, the decision was made due to "incidents at past performances in which they have incited violence."

2016: Rihanna staged a fashion show in New York City to introduce her clothing collection, Fenty Puma by Rihanna. Among the celebrities in attendance were Naomi Campbell, Chris Rock, Ne-Yo and Pete Wentz.

2016: Drake was given an honorary "key to the city" by the mayor of his hometown, Toronto, Canada.

FEBRUARY 13

1966: Freedom Williams (birth name Frederick Brandon Williams) was born in Brooklyn, New York. As the rapper and co-leader of the dance group C+C Music Factory, he appeared on their radio and club hits, "Gonna Make You Sweat (Everybody Dance Now)," "Things That Make You Go Hmmm..." and "Here We Go (Let's Rock & Roll)."

1996: Tupac Shakur released his fourth album, the chart-topping *All Eyez On Me*. One of the most celebrated albums of the classic rap era, it would propel the gangsta rapper to superstar status. The politically-charged album was highlighted by the chart-topping singles, "How Do U Want It" and "California Love," as well as the tracks, "2 Of Amerikaz Most Wanted," "All Bout U" and "I Ain't Mad At Cha."

1996: The Fugees released their breakthrough album, *The Score*. The chart-topping album spawned the hit singles "Fu-Gee-La," "Ready Or Not," a remake of the Bob Marley reggae standard "No Woman, No Cry" and a remake of the Roberta Flack soul classic, "Killing Me Softly." The album sold more than six-million copies in the U.S.

1998: Ellen Albertini Dow, nicknamed the hip hop granny, performed the rap classic "Rapper's Delight" in the comedy film, *The Wedding Singer*. The 85-year-old actress refused to lip-sync the song, which was also included on the film's soundtrack album. (She passed away in 2015 at the age of 101.)

1999: Busta Rhymes and the Roots were the musical guests on *Saturday Night Live*. They performed "Gimme Some More" and "Tear da Roof Off."

2003: After Russell Simmons of Def Jam Recordings threatened to call for a boycott of Pepsi products – in the wake of the soda maker's firing of Ludacris as their spokesman – Pepsi agreed to donate a sum of $3 million to urban charity groups.

2005: 50 Cent portrayed a cartoon version of himself on *The Simpsons*. In an episode titled "Pranksta Rap," 50 Cent traded rap verses with Bart Simpson.

2005: At the 47th Annual Grammy Awards, the winners were: "99 Problems" by Jay-Z in the category of Best Rap Solo Performance; "Let's Get It Started" by the Black Eyed Peas in the category of Best Rap Performance by a Duo or Group; "Yeah!" by Usher featuring Lil Jon & Ludacris in the category of Best Rap/Sung Collaboration; "Jesus Walks" by Kanye West in the category of Best Rap Song; and *The College Dropout* by Kanye West in the category of Best Rap Album.

2007: Cupid (real name Bryson Bernard) released the single, "Cupid Shuffle," which launched a popular dance craze of the same name. The song was performed in a closing scene of the film, *Jumping The Broom*.

2011: At the 53rd Annual Grammy Awards, the winners were: "Not Afraid" by Eminem in the category of Best Rap Solo Performance; "On To The Next One" by Jay Z & Swiss Beatz in the category of Best Rap Performance by a Duo or Group; "Empire State Of Mind" by Jay-Z & Alicia Keys in the category of Best Rap/Sung Collaboration; "Empire State Of Mind" by Jay-Z & Alicia Keys in the category of Best Rap Song; and *Recovery* by Eminem in the category of Best Rap Album.

2012: Sean "Diddy" Combs was hospitalized after suffering severe headaches, one day after he hosted a post-Grammy party at the Playboy Mansion.

2014: Will Smith portrayed the role of Satan in the romantic-drama film, *Winter's Tale*.

2015: Drake released his fourth studio album, *If You're Reading This It's Too Late*. Two singles were released from the project, "Preach" and "Energy." The album sold two-million copies in the U.S.

2016: Kanye West was the guest musical artist on *Saturday Night Live*. According to news reports, he almost cancelled his performance at the last minute.

2016: Kanye West admitted that he was $53 million in debt. He made the announcement on Twitter. A year earlier, he claimed to be $16 million in debt.

2016: Kendrick Lamar was given an honorary "key to the city" by the mayor of his hometown, Compton, California.

FEBRUARY 14

1981: The Funky Four Plus One were the first hip act to perform on *Saturday Night Live*. They were invited by Debbie Harry (of Blondie), who as the guest host was told she could select any musical artist to appear on the show. The group performed "That's The Joint."

1989: Rap trio De La Soul released their debut album, *3 Feet High And Rising*. The album was highlighted by the singles, "The Magic Number," "Buddy," "Eye Know" and the crossover hit "Me Myself And I."

1995: Eazy-E made his final appearance in a music video when he guest starred in the clip, "Foe Tha Love Of $" by Bone Thugs-N-Harmony.

1998: Missy Elliott was the musical guest on *Saturday Night Live*. She performed "Sock It 2 Me" and "Beep Me 911."

2000: On Valentine's Day, Sean "Puff Daddy" Combs and Jennifer Lopez publically confirmed their break up, which had been rumored for two months. The couple had dated for 17 months.

2002: Treach of Naughty By Nature starred in the romantic-comedy film, *Book Of Love: The Definitive Reason Why Men Are Dogs*. He portrayed a frustrated bachelor named Jay Black. Sandra "Pepa" Denton and the group Jagged Edge made cameo appearances in the film.

2010: Kid Cudi co-starred in the HBO comedy-drama series, *How To Make It In America*. He portrayed a character named Domingo Brown.

2010: British soul/hip hop singer Estelle performed at the Winter Olympics in Vancouver, Canada.

2012: Ciara starred in the film, *Mama, I Want To Sing!* The film was based on the life of 1960s soul singer Doris Troy, who was discovered by James Brown.

2013: Tim Dog (real name Timothy Blair) died from complications of diabetes. The Bronx-born rapper was best known for the 1991 diss track, "Fuck Compton." Over the next 19-months, rumors persisted that he had faked his own death. But in September 2014, investigators from the television program *Dateline NBC* located his death certificate in Dekalb County, Georgia.

FEBRUARY 15

1969: Birdman (birth name Bryan Williams) was born in New Orleans. A producer and rapper, he co-founded the duo Big Tymers. Also a successful entrepreneur, he co-founded Cash Money Records.

1981: Soul/hip hop singer Olivia (birth name Theresa Longott) was born in Brooklyn, New York. A solo artist, she is best known for providing the female vocals on 50 Cent's smash single, "Candy Shop." She also starred on the VH-1 reality series, *Love & Hip Hop*.

1999: Rapper Big L was murdered in a drive-by shooting in his hometown of Harlem, New York, at the age of 24. While standing on the sidewalk on West 139th Street, he was shot a total of nine times in the face and chest. Although one of Big L's childhood friends was initially arrested for the crime, he was subsequently released and not charged. The shooter has never been identified and the murder remains unsolved.

2002: The documentary, *Scratch*, was released. The film examined the art of the hip hop deejay and featured a number of pioneering turntable artists including Grand Wizard Theodore, Afrika Bambaataa and DJ Jazzy Jay.

2014: Adidas introduced a line of athletic shoes to commemorate the first headlining tour by rapper 2 Chainz. The "2 Good to be T.R.U." shoes were priced at $130 per pair.

2016: At the 58th Annual Grammy Awards, the winners were: "Alright" by Kendrick Lamar in the category of Best Rap Performance; "These Walls" by Kendrick Lamar featuring Bilal, Anna Wise and Thundercat in the category of Best Rap/Sung Collaboration; "Alright" by Kendrick Lamar in the category of Best Rap Song; and *To Pimp A Butterfly* by Kendrick Lamar in the category of Best Rap Album. Also, Run-D.M.C. was honored with a prestigious Lifetime Achievement Award. The pioneering hip hop group had never won a Grammy. The ceremony was hosted for the fifth year in a row by LL Cool J.

2016: West Coast rapper Jay Rock was seriously injured in a motorcycle accident. He fractured multiple bones and was hospitalized for a week.

FEBRUARY 16

1982: Lupe Fiasco (birth name Wasalu Muhammad Jaco) was born in Chicago. The rapper released his breakthrough solo album in 2006, *Lupe Fiasco's Food & Liquor*. Also a successful entrepreneur, he launched two clothing lines and was the CEO of 1st & 15th Entertainment.

1988: Eric B. & Rakim released the single, "Paid In Full." The track sampled "Don't Look Any Further" by Dennis Edwards featuring Siedah Garrett, "Ashley's Roachclip" by the Soul Searchers and "Change The Beat (Female Version)" by Beside. A remixed version of "Paid In Full" by the U.K. production duo Coldcut – which was titled "Paid In Full (Seven Minutes Of Madness)" – was a popular club hit in the U.S. and a radio hit in several European countries

1993: Tupac Shakur released his second album, *Strictly 4 My N.I.G.G.A.Z.* The politically-charged album spawned the hits "Keep Ya Head Up" and "I Get Around." The project featured a number of guest vocalists including Ice-T, Ice Cube, Dave Hollister, Treach, Apache, Poppi, Deadly Threat, Digital Underground and Shakur's stepbrother, Mopreme. The album sold nearly two-million copies in the U.S.

1995: Kid Rock was arrested after he allegedly punched a deejay at Christie's Cabaret in Nashville after the pair argued over the choice of music in the club. The rap-rock singer was released from jail after paying a $3,000 bond.

1999: Ol' Dirty Bastard of the Wu-Tang Clan was arrested in Hollywood for wearing a bulletproof vest. In California, convicted felons are barred from wearing body armor. He was released after paying an $18,000 bond.

2007: Eminem's ex-wife Kim Mathers criticized the rapper during an interview on a Detroit radio station, WKQI-FM. She said: "I vomit in my mouth whenever I'm around him."

2009: Marion "Suge" Knight was assaulted by a member of Akon's entourage at a hotel in Scottsdale, Arizona. The suspect was arrested at the scene and charged with felony aggravated assault. Knight suffered a number of broken bones in his face.

2010: Sandy Denton of Salt-n-Pepa published her autobiography, *Let's Talk About Pep*.

2013: Adidas released a pair of sports shoes designed by singer/actress Teyana Taylor. The shoes were called Originals Harlem GLC and were priced at $140 per pair.

2013: A biography of Beyoncé, *Life Is But A Dream*, aired on HBO. The singer directed the made for television film.

FEBRUARY 17

1981: The Tom Tom Club released the single, "Wordy Rappinghood." It was one of the first chart hits in the U.K. to feature rapping, which was provided by the group's female member, Tina Weymouth.

1988: DJ Jazzy Jeff & The Fresh Prince released the crossover hit single, "Parents Just Don't Understand." The song won a Grammy in a newly introduced category, Best Rap Performance.

1996: Tupac Shakur was the musical guest on *Saturday Night Live*. Joined by Danny Boy and Roger Troutman, Shakur performed "Shed So Many Tears," "I Ain't Mad At Cha" and "California Love."

2001: Shaggy was the musical guest on *Saturday Night Live*. He performed "It Wasn't Me" and "Angel."

2002: Busta Rhymes was the subject of an episode of the VH-1 program, *Behind The Music*.

2009: Snoop Dogg hosted a variety program on MTV, *Dogg After Dark*. The series was filmed at Kress, a nightclub in Los Angeles. Featuring interviews and skits, the program also included performances by Snoop Dogg and his band, the Snoopadelics. The series ran for just seven episodes.

2014: Iggy Azalea released her smash hit, "Fancy" (featuring Charli XCX). The track was the fourth single from her debut album, *The New Classic*. The song's music video was inspired by the comedy film, *Clueless*. The track sold more than four-million copies in the U.S.

2014: The Roots began their run as the house band on the NBC talk show, *The Tonight Show Starring Jimmy Fallon*. The group had followed Fallon from his previous program, *Late Night With Jimmy Fallon*.

2015: Afroman was arrested after punching a woman in the face during a concert in Biloxi, Mississippi. The woman had been dancing next to the rapper when she was struck. In the aftermath of the assault, many of his concerts were cancelled by promoters. Afroman was later sentenced to probation and ordered to attend anger management classes.

2016: Kanye West admitted on Twitter: "My number one enemy has been my ego.... A wise man should be humble enough to admit when he's wrong and change his mind based on new information."

FEBRUARY 18

1965: Dr. Dre (birth name Andre Romelle Young) was born in Compton, California. A member of the World Class Wreckin' Cru and the groundbreaking gangsta rap group N.W.A., he later enjoyed a successful solo career. Also a talented producer, he worked with hit acts such Eminem, the D.O.C., Snoop Dogg, Xzibit, the Game, Kendrick Lamar and 50 Cent. Also an entrepreneur, he started his own label, Aftermath Entertainment, and introduced a popular headphone line in 2008, Beats By Dre.

1982: Juelz Santana (birth name LaRon Louis James) was born in Harlem, New York. A member of the hip hop group the Diplomats, he also appeared as a guest vocalist on hits by Cam'ron, Chris Brown and others. Also a solo artist, he released his debut album in 2003, *From Me To U.*

1994: T-Bone (real name Terry E. Gray), a member of the Los Angeles gangsta rap trio Da Lench Mob, was arrested on charges of murder after two men were fatally shot at a southern California bowling alley. T-Bone, who claimed it was a case of mistaken identity, was later acquitted of the charges. (Another member of Da Lench Mob, J-Dee, was accused of murder the previous year.)

1997: New Orleans hip hop trio TRU released their album, *Tru 2 da Game.* The group consisted of brothers Master P, C-Murder and Silkk the Shocker. The album sold two-million copies and was highlighted by the hit singles "I Always Feel Like" and "FEDz."

FEBRUARY 19

1960: Prince Markie Dee (birth name Mark Anthony Morales) was born in Brooklyn, New York. In 1982, he co-founded the pioneering rap group, the Fat Boys. He later pursued a solo career.

1998: New Ark, a group of studio musicians, filed a lawsuit against Lauryn Hill over the songwriting and production credits on her smash album, *The Miseducation Of Lauryn Hill*. The suit was settled out of court in February 2001.

2003: Lil Jon & The East Side Boyz released the single, "Get Low" (featuring the Ying Yang Twins). This was one of the first crunk-style, crossover pop hits.

2005: 50 Cent was the musical guest on *Saturday Night Live*. He performed "Disco Inferno" and was joined by Olivia on "Candy Shop."

2008: André 3000 of OutKast starred along with Will Ferrell and Woody Harrelson in the sports-comedy film, *Semi-Pro*. He portrayed a basketball player named Clarence Withers who dreamed about playing in the NBA.

2012: Rick Ross was selected as the winner of MTV's annual "Hottest MCs in the Game."

2016: Chino (real name Pachino Braxton) was shot in the head during a drive-by shooting in Baltimore. He recovered from his injuries. The rapper was a member of Dreamchasers.

FEBRUARY 20

1991: At the 33rd Annual Grammy Awards, the winners were: "U Can't Touch This" by M.C. Hammer in the category of Best Rap Solo Performance; and "Back On The Block" by Big Daddy Kane, Ice-T, Kool Moe Dee, Melle Mel, Quincy D. III and Quincy Jones in the category of Best Rap Performance by a Duo or Group.

1995: The Notorious B.I.G. released the single, "Big Poppa." The track sampled "Between The Sheets" by the Isley Brothers. "Big Poppa" was nominated for a Grammy in the category of Best Rap Solo Performance.

1996: Snoop Doggy Dogg and his bodyguard were both acquitted of assault and murder charges by a Los Angeles jury. The two men had been charged in the 1993 shooting death of Philip Woldemariam.

1996: Jay-Z released the influential single, "Dead Presidents." The single version of the track was much different than the album version, which appeared on his debut release, *Reasonable Doubt*. Although the single failed to chart, it managed to sell more than half a million copies and was certified Gold by the RIAA.

2000: Run-D.M.C. was the subject of an episode of the VH-1 program, *Behind The Music*.

2001: Rap-rock group Crazy Town released the hit single, "Butterfly." The track sampled "Pretty Little Ditty" by Red Hot Chili Peppers.

2007: T-Pain released the single, "Buy U A Drank (Shawty Snappin')," which featured Yung Joc. This was T-Pain's biggest crossover pop hit. The song's music video featured cameo appearances by Tay Dizm, E-40, Gorilla Zoe, Huey, Shawnna, Jay Lyriq, Brandon T. Jackson and others.

2008: A free concert by Akon at the Field's shopping center near Copenhagen, Denmark, turned violent when someone set off a false fire alarm. As police began evacuating the mall, many of the attendees turned violent and began throwing rocks and bottles. At least eight people were injured.

2011: A Guinness world record was set when 2,387 people at the Anaheim Convention Center performed the "Ch-Cha Slide," a line dance created by DJ Casper.

2014: Chris Brown and his bodyguard were sued for $3 million by a 25-year-old man, following a fight outside of the W Hotel in Washington, D.C., in October 2013. Brown later settled the lawsuit for $100,000.

2016: Ne-Yo married his fiancee Crystal Renay in a ceremony at the Terranea Resort in Rancho Palos Verdes, California.

FEBRUARY 21

1990: At the 32nd Annual Grammy Awards, Young MC won a Grammy in the category of Best Rap Performance for "Bust A Move."

1995: 2Pac released "Dear Mama," the debut single from his third album, *Me Against The World*. The song was a musical tribute to his mother, Afeni Shakur.

1996: MCA Records announced a $200 million deal to acquire 50-percent of Interscope Records. Interscope had been the distributor for Death Row Records since 1992.

2001: Eminem and Elton John teamed up for a performance of "Stan" at the 43rd annual Grammy Awards. At the event, Eminem won three Grammys in the categories of Best Rap Solo Performance, Best Rap Album, and with Dr. Dre for Best Rap Performance by a Duo or Group.

2003: An SUV owned by Busta Rhymes was struck by six bullets just a few minutes after he had parked the vehicle on a New York City street. The shooting occurred near the offices of his label, Violator Records.

2003: The opening theme song of the HBO series, *Real Time With Bill Maher*, was written by Christopher Reid of the hip hop duo, Kid 'n Play.

2012: Drake released the hit single, "Take Care," which featured Rihanna. The song sampled the remixed version of "I'll Take Care Of You" by Gil Scott-Heron.

2012: Sean "Diddy" Combs announced the launch of his new cable network, REVOLT. The network began broadcasting on October 21, 2013.

2012: An appeals court in North Carolina upheld a 2010 judgement against the Game. The rapper had been ordered to pay $5 million in compensatory damages to five Greensboro police officers who were allegedly slandered on the DVD, *Stop Snitchin', Stop Lyin'*.

2012: Tyga released his breakthrough album, *Careless World: Rise Of The Last King*. The album spawned five singles including "Far Away" and "Rack City." The album's title track contained a portion of a speech by Martin Luther King, Jr.

2013: Actress Lindsay Lohan lost her lawsuit against Pitbull. She had claimed defamation after the rapper mentioned her by name on the 2011 track, "Give Me Everything." A judge ruled that Pitbull's song was protected by the First Amendment.

FEBRUARY 22

1989: At the 31st Annual Grammy Awards, DJ Jazzy Jeff & The Fresh Prince won a Grammy in the category of Best Rap Performance for "Parents Just Don't Understand."

1990: Above The Law introduced the "G-funk" sound to hip hop with their debut album, *Livin' Like Hustlers*. Dr. Dre popularized the G-funk style with his 1992 hit album, *The Chronic*.

1990: Governor Bob Martinez of Florida called for an obscenity investigation of 2 Live Crew following the release of their album, *As Nasty As They Wanna Be*. State prosecutor Peter Antonacci refused the order and suggested that any investigations should occur on a county, not statewide, level.

2008: Jennifer Lopez and Marc Anthony welcomed the birth of fraternal twins, Emme Maribel Muñiz and Maximilian David Muñiz.

2011: Chicago rapper Rhymefest nearly won the race for alderman of the city's 20th ward. He lost by a margin of 54 to 46 percent. He is best known for co-writing the Kanye West hit, "Jesus Walks."

2011: Layzie Bone released two albums on the same day, *The Definition* and *The Meaning*.

2015: The song "Glory" by Common and John Legend won an Oscar for Best Original Song at the 87th annual Academy Awards.

FEBRUARY 23

1979: D-Roc (birth name Deongelo Holmes) of the Ying Yang Twins was born in Atlanta. The duo first hit the charts in 2000 with the single, "Whistle While You Twurk."

1993: Ice Cube released the single, "It Was A Good Day," which became the gangsta rapper's best known song. The track sampled "Footsteps In The Dark" by the Isley Brothers and "Sexy Mama" by the Moments.

1999: Eminem released his breakthrough album, *The Slim Shady LP*. Aided by his mentor Dr. Dre of Interscope Records, Eminem channeled his alter ego "Slim Shady" on the album. After releasing the debut single, "Just Don't Give A Fuck," Eminem scored his first hit with the follow-up single, "My Name Is." Two more singles were issued from the album, "Role Model" and "Guilty Conscience."

2000: At the 42nd Annual Grammy Awards, the winners were: "My Name Is" by Eminem in the category of Best Rap Solo Performance; "You Got Me" by Erykah Badu & The Roots in the category of Best Rap Performance by a Duo or Group; and *The Slim Shady LP* by Eminem in the category of Best Rap Album.

2001: DJ Q-Bert premiered his animated film, *Wave Twisters*, which was based on his album of the same name. The album mixed computer graphics, live-action footage and traditional cel animation. In the film, DJ Q-Bert portrayed the role of Darth Fader.

2003: Dutch beermaker Heineken debuted a commercial featuring Jay-Z which was titled, "The Takeover." The ad aired during the Grammys.

2003: At the 45th Annual Grammy Awards, the winners were: "Scream a.k.a. Itchin" by Missy Elliott in the new category of Best Female Rap Solo Performance; "Hot In Herre" by Nelly in the new category of Best Male Rap Solo Performance; "The Whole World" by OutKast & Killer Mike in the category of Best Rap Performance by a Duo or Group; "Dilemma" by Nelly & Kelly Rowland in the category of Best Rap/Sung Collaboration; and *The Eminem Show* by Eminem in the category of Best Rap Album.

2010: Bassist and rapper Chilly B (real name Robert Crafton III) of the group Newcleus died at the age of 43. Newcleus was an electronic/rap group best known for the 1980s club hits, "Jam-On's Revenge" and "Jam On It." After battling chronic diabetes and kidney disease, he suffered a fatal stroke.

2011: Rapper Tru Life (real name Roberto Guzman Rosado, Jr.) and his brother were sentenced in the attacks of two men in a Manhattan apartment building, which left one of the men dead. Tru Life pleaded guilty to charges of second-degree gang assault and his brother pleaded guilty to first-degree manslaughter. While Tru Life was sentenced to eight-years in prison, his brother was sentenced to ten-years.

FEBRUARY 24

1993: Arrested Development were the first hip hop act to win a Grammy in the category of Best New Artist. The teen duo Kris Kross was also nominated for the award. The other winners were: "Baby Got Back" by Sir Mix-A-Lot in the category of Best Rap Solo Performance; and "Tennessee" by Arrested Development in the category of Best Rap Performance by a Duo or Group.

1999: Juvenile released the single, "Back That Thang Up" (featuring Mannie Fresh and Lil Wayne). The explicit version of the track was titled "Back That Azz Up." Juvenile was later accused of copyright infringement by DJ Jubilee who recorded a song with a similar title. The court case was settled in 2004 in Juvenile's favor.

1999: At the 41st Annual Grammy Awards, the winners were: "Gettin' Jiggy Wit It" by Will Smith in the category of Best Rap Solo Performance; "Intergalactic" by the Beastie Boys in the category of Best Rap Performance by a Duo or Group; and *Vol. 2... Hard Knock Life* by Jay-Z in the category of Best Rap Album. Also, Lauryn Hill won a total of five Grammys, including in the categories of Best New Artist and Album Of The Year for *The Miseducation of Lauryn Hill.*

2001: The single "Stutter" by Joe featuring Mystikal began a four-week run at number-one on the U.S. charts.

2004: Kanye West released the single, "All Falls Down." After West was unable to secure permission to sample "Mystery Of Iniquity" by Lauryn Hill, he instead used a newly-recorded interpolation of the song. The track was nominated for a Grammy in the category of Best Rap/Sung Collaboration. In the song's music video, actress Stacey Dash portrayed West's girlfriend.

2009: Pitbull released his first major hit, "I Know You Want Me (Calle Ocho)." The track sampled "The Bomb! (These Sounds Fall Into My Mind)" by the Bucketheads and "75, Brazil Street" by Nicola Fasano versus Pat Rich. "Calle Ocho" referred to a street in the Little Havana district of Miami.

2010: 50 Cent was sued by a Florida woman over the unauthorized release of a sex tape. He allegedly posted the 13-minute video on the internet.

FEBRUARY 25

1992: A launch party for the newly formed Death Row Records was staged at a swanky West Hollywood restaurant, Chasen's.

1992: At the 34th Annual Grammy Awards, the winners were: "Mama Said Knock You Out" by LL Cool J in the category of Best Rap Solo Performance; and "Summertime" by D.J. Jazzy Jeff & The Fresh Prince in the category of Best Rap Performance by a Duo or Group.

1992: The fifth and final album by Boogie Down Productions, *Sex And Violence*, was released. One of the group's members, KRS-One, would begin a successful solo career the following year.

1998: At the 40th Annual Grammy Awards, the winners were: "Men In Black" by Will Smith in the category of Best Rap Solo Performance; "I'll Be Missing You" by Puff Daddy, Faith Evans & 112 in the category of Best Rap Performance by a Duo or Group; and *No Way Out* by Puff Daddy & The Family in the category of Best Rap Album. At the awards ceremony, Ol' Dirty Bastard rushed the stage during the presentation of the Song of the Year award to Shawn Colvin. Upset that the Wu-Tang Clan did not win the Best Rap Album award, he told the audience, "I went and bought me an outfit today that cost me a lot of money, because I figured that Wu-Tang was gonna win."

2001: The entourages of rappers Lil' Kim and Foxy Brown were involved in a violent scuffle outside the studios of radio station Hot 97 in New York City. One person was shot during the melee. In 2005, Lil' Kim was convicted of perjury for attempting to shield her colleagues from prosecution.

2004: During the second season of *Chappelle's Show*, comedian Dave Chappelle introduced a popular, recurring skit in which he portrayed rapper Lil Jon.

2008: Sean "P. Diddy" Combs co-produced and starred in the television adaptation of the classic play, *A Raisin In The Sun*. Combs played the role of Walter Lee Younger. The film was nominated for an Emmy Award in the category of Outstanding Made For Television Movie.

2008: Songwriter and rapper Static Major (real name Stephen Ellis Garrett) died at age 33 after undergoing a procedure to treat an auto-immune disease, myasthenia gravis. He was best known for his work with Aaliyah and as a featured artist on Lil Wayne's smash hit, "Lollipop."

2015: When Kanye West performed his new single, "All Day," at the annual BRIT Awards ceremony, much of the song was censored due to its explicit lyrics.

2015: Chris Brown was denied entry into Canada due to his past criminal convictions. As a result, he was forced to cancel a number of concerts.

2016: A$AP Rocky was attacked by three men as he entered an elevator at the Pullman Hotel in Auckland, New Zealand. He had performed at the 12,000 seat Vector Arena a few hours earlier.

FEBRUARY 26

1991: LL Cool J released the crossover hit single, "Mama Said Knock You Out." In 2014, rap-metal band Five Finger Death Punch scored a hit with a remake of the song.

1995: Tupac Shakur began a prison sentence at the Clinton Correctional Facility in New York after he was convicted on a charge of sexual abuse. Although he was sentenced to remain behind bars for a term of 18 to 54 months, he was released after serving 10 months.

1997: At the 39th Annual Grammy Awards, the winners were: "Hey Lover" by LL Cool J in the category of Best Rap Solo Performance; "Tha Crossroads" by Bone Thugs-N-Harmony in the category of Best Rap Performance by a Duo or Group; and *The Score* by the Fugees in the category of Best Rap Album. Babyface also won Grammys in the categories of Producer Of The Year and for his work as a producer on the Eric Clapton song "Change The World" in the category of Record Of The Year.

1999: Xzibit made his acting debut in the comedy film, *The Breaks*.

2001: The Black Eyed Peas released their hit single, "Request + Line." The track featured soul singer Macy Gray on lead vocals.

2012: Nicki Minaj performed before the start of the NBA All-Star Game at the Amway Center in Orlando, Florida.

FEBRUARY 27

1992: The Bronx-based hip hop group Nice & Smooth released their hit, "Sometimes I Rhyme Slow." The track was constructed over a looped sample of the guitar intro from "Fast Car" by Tracy Chapman.

1996: The Florida hip hop group Quad City DJ's released the club hit, "C'Mon N' Ride It (The Train)." The track sampled the theme from the film *Together Brothers* by Barry White.

1998: At the 12th annual Soul Train Music Awards which were staged in Los Angeles, Puff Daddy won the Sammy Davis Jr. Award for Entertainer of the Year.

2001: The rap trio City High released the single, "What Would You Do." The track was featured on both their debut album, *City High*, as well as on the soundtrack of the Eddie Murphy and Martin Lawrence film, *Life*.

2002: At the 44th Annual Grammy Awards, the winners were: "Get Ur Freak On" by Missy Elliott in the category of Best Rap Solo Performance; "Ms. Jackson" by OutKast in the category of Best Rap Performance by a Duo or Group; David Sheats (producer) & OutKast for Stankonia in the category of Best Rap Album; and "Let Me Blow Ya Mind" by Eve & Gwen Stefani in the new category of Best Rap/Sung Collaboration. Also, Alicia Keys won two notable Grammys, Best New Artist and Song Of The Year for her track "Fallin'."

2006: The Smithsonian Institution in Washington, D.C., announced a multi-year initiative to gather various artifacts of hip hop music and culture for a forthcoming exhibit: "Hip-Hop Won't Stop: The Beat, The Rhymes, The Life." The announcement was marked by a ceremony in New York City that featured a number of hip hop pioneers including Russell Simmons, Afrika Bambaataa, Grandmaster Flash, DJ Kool Herc, Fab 5 Freddy and Ice-T.

2009: Taboo of the Black Eyed Peas co-starred in the action film, *Street Fighter: The Legend Of Chun-Li*. He portrayed a street fighter named Vega.

2010: Jennifer Lopez was both the guest host and featured musical performer on *Saturday Night Live*.

2015: Will Smith starred opposite Margot Robbie in the romantic-comedy film, *Focus*. Smith played the role of an experienced con-man named Nicky Spurgeon. The film grossed nearly $160 million worldwide.

FEBRUARY 28

1996: At the 38th Annual Grammy Awards, the winners were: "Gangsta's Paradise" by Coolio in the category of Best Rap Solo Performance; "I'll Be There For You"/ "You're All I Need To Get By" by Mary J. Blige & Method Man in the category of Best Rap Performance by a Duo or Group; and *Poverty's Paradise* by Naughty By Nature in the new category of Best Rap Album.

2004: The single "Yeah!" by Usher featuring Lil John and Ludacris began a remarkable twelve-week run at number-one on the U.S. charts.

2006: The single "Hips Don't Lie" by Columbian-born singer Shakira was released. An international smash hit, the song heavily sampled "Dance Like This" by Jean Wyclef. In June of the same year, Shakira and Jean performed "Hips Don't Lie" during the opening ceremony of the FIFA World Cup in Munich.

2009: Flo Rida began a six-week run at number-one on the U.S. singles chart with "Right Round."

2010: Canadian alternative rapper k-os (real name Kevin Brereton) performed at the closing ceremonies of 2010 Winter Olympics in Vancouver, Canada.

2013: Following a concert by rapper French Montana at the Theatre of Living Arts in Philadelphia, an assailant with a machine gun opened fire on Montana and a large group of autograph seekers. While the rapper escaped injury, two fans were struck – one fatally.

2015: Two people were shot at a hip hop concert in Charlotte, North Carolina, that featured T.I., Jeezy, Yo Gotti and P. Diddy.

FEBRUARY 29

1976: Ja Rule (birth name Jeffrey Atkins) was born in Queens, New York. The popular rapper released his debut album in 1999, *Venni Vetti Vecci*.

2000: Sean "Puff Daddy" Combs pleaded not guilty to a charge of attempting to bribe a chauffeur to take responsibility for a shooting that occurred the previous year.

2000: Nelly released his debut solo single, "Country Grammar (Hot Shit)." The smash hit propelled the Texas-born rapper to stardom. The song's melody and chorus were based on the children's song, "Down Down Baby."

2004: The Detroit studio where Eminem recorded his rap classic, "My Name Is," was listed for sale on Ebay.

2012: A scheduled concert by Erykah Badu in Malaysia was cancelled after numerous complaints in the predominantly Muslim nation. The country's information minister ordered the cancellation as the result of a promotional photo of the singer which featured the word "Allah" on her shoulders.

▶ MARCH

MARCH 1

1986: LL Cool J appeared on the long-running television program, *American Bandstand*. After performing "Can't Live Without My Radio," he was asked by host Dick Clark how success has changed him. The rapper responded, "My pant sizes are bigger and my pockets are fatter." LL Cool J was the only hip hop act to appear on *American Bandstand* three times.

1987: The Beastie Boys released the single, "No Sleep Till Brooklyn." The track featured the guitarwork of Kerry King of the group Slayer. (During this period, producer Rick Rubin was working with both the Beastie Boys and Slayer.) The song's music video parodied 1980s heavy metal.

1987: The Beastie Boys were the first rap act featured on the cover of *Spin* magazine.

1990: Rob Pilatus of the disgraced duo Milli Vanilli proclaimed in a *Time* magazine interview: "Musically, we're more talented than any Bob Dylan or Paul McCartney. Mick Jagger can't produce a sound. I'm the new Elvis."

1994: At the 36th Annual Grammy Awards, the winners were: "Let Me Ride" by Dr. Dre in the category of Best Rap Solo Performance; and "Rebirth Of Slick (Cool Like Dat)" by Digable Planets in the category of Best Rap Performance by a Duo or Group.

1995: At the 37th Annual Grammy Awards, the winners were: "U.N.I.T.Y." by Queen Latifah in the category of Best Rap Solo Performance; and "None of Your Business" by Salt-n-Pepa in the category of Best Rap Performance by a Duo or Group.

2002: Do'reen (real name Doreen Waddell) of the group Soul II Soul was killed while crossing the busy A27 highway in Shoreham, West Sussex, England. She ran across the motorway after she was accused of shoplifting at a Tesco grocery store. Waddell was 36-years-old.

2004: Juvenile released the single, "Slow Motion" (featuring Soulja Slim). This was the first number-one pop single by an artist on Cash Money Records. The song's music video was a tribute to Soulja Slim who had passed away the previous year.

2005: Usher became a minority owner of the Cleveland Cavaliers NBA team. He was part of a group headed by Dan Gilbert, which paid $375 million for the basketball franchise.

2011: Big Sean released the single, "My Last" (featuring Chris Brown). The track sampled "Can You Stand The Rain" by New Edition. The song's music video featured appearances by Kid Cudi and Teyana Taylor.

2012: British rapper Mike Skinner published his autobiography, *The Story Of The Streets*.

2012: T.I. announced that he had signed three recording artists – Iggy Azalea, Chipmunk (later known as Chip) and Trae Tha Truth – to his record label, Grand Hustle.

2013: New Orleans rapper Magic (real name Awood Johnson) and his wife died in an auto accident in Hattiesburg, Mississippi. Their 12-year-old daughter survived the crash. Magic was 37-years-old.

MARCH 2

1971: Method Man (birth name Clifford Smith) was born in Staten Island, New York. Emerging from the East Coast hip hop collective Wu-Tang Clan, he enjoyed a successful career as a solo artist and producer.

1992: Luther Campbell published his autobiography, *As Nasty As They Wanna Be: The Uncensored Story Of Luther Campbell Of The 2 Live Crew.*

1997: D12, a Detroit hip hop group featuring Eminem, released their debut effort, *The Underground EP.*

1999: Ja Rule released his debut single, "Holla Holla," from his first album, *Venni Vetti Vecci.*

1999: The "Hard Knock Life" tour began with a stop at the MCI Center in Washington, D.C. The 47-date tour featured rap and rock acts Jay-Z, DMX, Method Man, Redman, Korn and Rob Zombie. The tour grossed $18 million.

2002: Tommy Boy Records – a pioneering hip hop label with a roster that included Coolio, De La Soul and Naughty By Nature – announced it was moving away from rap in favor of dance music. The label explained that it had become too expensive to produce rap music.

2002: OutKast were the musical guests on *Saturday Night Live*. They performed "The Whole World" and "Ms. Jackson."

2004: Jay-Z released the single, "Dirt Off Your Shoulder." The song's title became a popular catchphrase. The track was later mashed-up with "Lying From You" by Linkin Park and was included on the album, *Collision Course.*

2004: Heavy D co-starred in the comedy film, *Larceny*. He played the role of an independently wealthy playboy named Charlie.

2006: Rap-rock singer Kid Rock was the subject of an episode of the VH-1 program, *Behind The Music.*

2007: The faux documentary, *Gangsta Rap: The Glockumentary*, was released. The comedy film starred Too $hort and followed a fictional, middle-aged "gangsta rap" group that was trying to make a comeback.

2007: R. Kelly released the remixed version of "I'm A Flirt" (featuring T.I. and T-Pain). The original version of the song was recorded by Bow Wow and featured R. Kelly. While both versions received strong airplay, R. Kelly's remix was the bigger hit.

2009: The Roots began their run as the house band on the NBC talk show, *Late Night With Jimmy Fallon*. The group would later follow Fallon to his new program in 2014, *The Tonight Show Starring Jimmy Fallon.*

2012: At least 14 people were injured before a Nipsey Hussle concert in Tempe, Arizona. Several fights broke out among groups of concertgoers who were waiting in line to enter the Clubhouse Music Venue. Multiple shots were fired during the scuffles.

2013: Macklemore and Ryan Lewis were the musical guests on *Saturday Night Live*. They performed "Thrift Shop" and "Can't Hold Us."

2013: Baauer began a five-week run at number-one on the U.S. singles chart with "Harlem Shake."

2015: Kanye West released the track "All Day," which featured Theophilus London, Allan Kingdom and Paul McCartney. The track employed an interpolation of "Dance With Me" by Noel Ellis and featured a sample of an unreleased Paul McCartney song from 1969. "All Day" was nominated for two Grammys in the categories of Best Rap Song and Best Rap Performance. This was the third collaboration between West and McCartney.

MARCH 3

1966: Tone Loc (birth name Anthony Terrell Smith) was born in Los Angeles. The gravelly voiced singer is best known for his two top-10 crossover hits, "Wild Thing" and "Funky Cold Medina."

1981: Lil' Flip (birth name Wesley Eric Weston, Jr.) was born in Houston, Texas. The rapper began his recording career in 2000 and is best known for the hits, "The Way We Ball," "Sunshine" and "Game Over."

1986: Music manager Jerry Heller met rapper Eazy-E at a record pressing plant in Hollywood, California. After Heller listened to Eazy-E's music, the two men decided to form a label, Ruthless Records. In addition to Eazy-E and his group N.W.A., the label signed dozens of hip hop acts including MC Ren, the D.O.C., J.J. Fad, Michel'le, Bone Thugs-N-Harmony and Kid Frost.

1987: Boogie Down Productions released their influential debut album, *Criminal Minded*. The group consisted of KRS-One, D-Nice and Scott La Rock. A pioneering "gangsta rap" album, it was highlighted by the tracks, "South Bronx," "The Bridge Is Over" and "9mm Goes Bang." Scott La Rock was murdered one month after the album was released.

2005: 50 Cent released his second album, *The Massacre*. The project spawned four singles, "Disco Inferno," "Candy Shop," "Just A Lil Bit" and "Outta Control." The album sold more than five-million copies in the U.S. and was nominated for a Grammy in the category of Best Rap Album.

2006: The film, *Dave Chappelle's Block Party*, was released. In the film, the comedian filled a bus with residents from his hometown in Ohio and sent them to Brooklyn, New York, to experience the world of hip hop. Taken to an outdoor block party, the Ohio natives were exposed to performances by Kanye West, Big Daddy Kane, Common, Mos Def, Talib Kweli, the reunited Fugees and others.

2009: Ciara released the single, "Love Sex Magic" (featuring Justin Timberlake). Veering from her traditional Crunk&B sound, the track was more pop and funk oriented. The song was nominated for a Grammy in the category of Best Pop Collaboration with Vocals.

2013: Several musical performers were contestants on the reality show, *Celebrity Apprentice 4*, which was hosted by Donald Trump. Country singer John Rich was selected as the winner of the competition after he defeated Lil Jon, La Toya Jackson, Trace Adkins, Dee Snider and others.

MARCH 4

1966: Grand Puba (birth name Maxwell Dixon) was born in New Rochelle, New York. He was a member of the groups, Brand Nubian and Masters of Ceremony. As a solo artist, he released his first album in 1991, *Reel To Reel*.

1990: Heavy D was the featured vocalist of the remixed version of "Alright" by Janet Jackson, which was recorded for the song's music video.

1997: Foxy Brown released the single, "I'll Be" (featuring Jay-Z). The track sampled "I'll Be Good" by René & Angela.

2004: The reality series *Pimp My Ride* debuted on the MTV network. The program was hosted by rapper Xzibit. The series ran for six seasons and spawned a pair of spinoff shows, *Pimp My Ride UK* and *Pimp My Ride International*.

2012: Young Buck was the victim of a drive-by shooting in Memphis. In spite the fact that his vehicle was struck 11 times, the rapper was not injured.

MARCH 5

1963: Grand Wizzard Theodore (birth name Theodore Livingston) was born in the Bronx, New York. A rap pioneer, he introduced "scratching" to the genre in 1977. In his youth, he trained under Grandmaster Flash and later formed the group, Grand Wizard Theodore & The Fantastic Five MCs.

1992: Das EFX released their debut single, "They Want EFX." The track sampled "Buffalo Gals" by Malcolm McLaren and "Blind Man Can See It" by James Brown.

1997: The documentary, *Rhyme & Reason*, was released. The film examined the history of hip hop and featured an all-star cast which included KRS-One, Kurtis Blow, Master P, Method Man, Nas, Treach, Whodini, the Wu-Tang Clan, Wyclef Jean, Xzibit and many others.

2003: Luther Campbell of 2 Live Crew was charged with a felony after he gave a "sexually charged" performance at the End Zone nightclub in North Charleston, South Carolina. According to authorities, a woman went on stage and took off her clothes during the concert. At a trial in November, Campbell pleaded guilty and was given a suspended six-month jail sentence. He was also barred from staging concerts in South Carolina for five years.

2004: Snoop Dogg portrayed underworld boss Huggy Bear Brown in the film adaptation of the 1970s television series, *Starsky & Hutch*. The film grossed nearly $90 million in the U.S.

2005: The single "Candy Shop" by 50 Cent featuring Olivia began a nine-week run at number-one on the U.S. charts.

2006: The track, "It's Hard Out Here For A Pimp" from the film *Hustle & Flow*, won an Oscar at the Academy Awards in the category of Best Original Song. The song was co-written by DJ Paul, Juicy J, Crunchy Black and Frayser Boy.

2008: Soulja Boy launched his own fashion line, S.O.D clothing. Later that year, he also introduced a line of athletic shoes, Yums.

2013: Coolio appeared on the television reality series, *Celebrity Wife Swap*. He swapped partners for one week with rock singer Mark McGrath. Coolio later claimed he wasn't dating the woman who portrayed his girlfriend on the program.

2014: Lil Boosie was released from the Louisiana State Penitentiary after serving five-years of an eight-year sentence. In 2009, he had pleaded guilty to drug charges.

MARCH 6

1936: Sylvia Robinson (birth name Sylvia Vanderpool) was born in New York City. A former R&B singer, she co-founded the pioneering hip hop label Sugarhill Records and was instrumental in crafting two landmark singles, "Rapper's Delight" by the Sugarhill Gang and "The Message" by Grandmaster Flash & The Furious Five.

1974: Beanie Sigel (birth name Dwight E. Grant) was born in Philadelphia. The rapper recorded for Roc-A-Fella Records and Damon Dash's Dame Dash Music Group.

1977: Bubba Sparxxx (birth name Warren Anderson Mathis) was born in LaGrange, Georgia. The Southern rapper is best known for his hit "Ms. New Booty."

1998: Chuck D filed a lawsuit in the United States District Court of New York against the estate of the Notorious B.I.G. over the unauthorized use of Chuck D's voice on the deceased rapper's 1997 track, "Ten Crack Commandments." The vocal was taken from Public Enemy's 1991 hit, "Shut 'Em Down."

2000: Foxy Brown was injured after she drove her car into a fence in Brooklyn, New York. After police arrived, they discovered that the 20-year-old rapper was driving with a suspended driver's license.

2001: Missy "Misdemeanor" Elliott released the single, "Get Ur Freak On." The track featured a man speaking in Japanese and an Indian instrument called a tumbi, and sampled "Ugly" by Bubba Sparxxx. The single won a Grammy in the category of Best Rap Solo Performance. The song's music video featured appearances by LL Cool J, Timbaland, Ja Rule, Ludacris, Busta Rhymes, Nate Dogg Master P, Lil' Romeo and Eve.

2001: Shaggy released the single, "Angel" (featuring Rayvon). The track sampled "The Joker" by the Steve Miller Band and employed the melody of the 1960s pop standard, "Angel Of The Morning."

2001: Fabolous made his recording debut on a hit single by Lil' Mo, "Superwoman Pt. II."

2007: Jay-Z announced that he had sold his urban clothing line, Rocawear, to the Iconix Brand Group for $204 million. As part of the agreement, the rapper retained control of Rocawear's men's line. He also remained with the parent company in charge of marketing, licensing and product development. Jay-Z and Damon Dash had co-founded the company in 1999. In 2005, Jay-Z bought out Dash's share of the business.

2014: In celebration of the 25th anniversary of *Billboard's* rap singles chart, the magazine ranked the top-100 hip hop songs of the era. Topping the list was "Thrift Shop" by Macklemore & Ryan Lewis featuring Wanz. In second place was "Tootsee Roll" by 69 Boyz.

2014: Rising unsigned rapper Speaker Knockerz (real name Derek McAllister, Jr.) was found dead in the garage of his home in Columbia, South Carolina. An internet sensation, he was best known for the track, "Lonely." He was 19-years-old.

2015: At least six people were stabbed during a concert by Migos at the Washington Avenue Armory in Albany, New York.

MARCH 7

1987: *Licensed To Ill* by the Beastie Boys was the first rap album to top the *Billboard* magazine sales chart.

1989: The disgraced lip-syncing duo Milli Vanilli released the album, *Girl You Know It's True*. It was a worldwide hit and sold six-million copies in the U.S. But following the admission that Fab Morvan and Rob Pilatus did not actually perform on any of the tracks, Arista Records dropped the duo and pulled the album.

1992: Ice Cube released the album, *The Predator*. Issued a few months after the 1992 Los Angeles riots, the project explored a number of racial issues. The album spawned the singles, "Wicked," "It Was A Good Day" and "Check Yo Self." The album sold more than two-million copies in the U.S.

1994: The U.S. Supreme Court ruled that 2 Live Crew's version of the song, "Oh, Pretty Woman" (originally recorded by Roy Orbison), was a commercial parody that qualified under the "fair use" rule and did not violate the copyright held by the publishing company, Acuff-Rose Music.

1997: At the 11th annual Soul Train Music Awards which were staged in Los Angeles, Babyface won the Sammy Davis Jr. Award for Entertainer of the Year. The "Best Rap Album" category was dropped from the annual ceremony.

2000: Big Punisher (real name Christopher Lee Rios) suffered a fatal heart attack at the Crowne Plaza Hotel in White Plains, New York. Morbidly obese for most of his life, he weighed 698 pounds at the time of his death. He was 28-years-old.

2010: A number of hip hop artists starred in the animated film, *Freaknik: The Musical*. The made for television project starred T-Pain (as the Ghost of Freaknik) and featured the voices of Snoop Dogg, Lil Wayne, Young Cash, Sophia Fresh, DJ Pooh, Mack Maine, Cee Lo Green, Rick Ross and Kid 'n Play.

2011: Nelly was the subject of an episode of the VH-1 program, *Behind The Music*.

MARCH 8

1991: The crime-action film, *New Jack City*, was released. The film starred Ice-T, Wesley Snipes, Allen Payne, Chris Rock and Judd Nelson. Ice-T portrayed a detective named Scotty Appleton who went undercover as a member of a gang headed by Wesley Snipes' character, Nino Brown. R&B singers Nick Ashford and Keith Sweat also appeared in the film. *New Jack City* was the highest-grossing independent film of the year.

1993: P.M. Dawn released the hit single, "Looking Through Patient Eyes." The song featured the backing vocals of Cathy Dennis and sampled "Father Figure" by George Michael. The song's music video was shot inside of a church.

1994: Coolio released the single, "Fantastic Voyage" (featuring G.A.T.). The track sampled "Fantastic Voyage" by Lakeside.

2003: Ms. Dynamite was the musical guest on *Saturday Night Live*. She performed "Dy-Na-Mi-Tee." Queen Latifah was the show's guest host.

2003: 50 Cent began a nine-week run at number-one on the U.S. singles chart with "In Da Club."

2010: Drake released the track, "Over," which was the debut single from his first full-length studio album, *Thank Me Later*. Singer Rita Ora portrayed Drake's love interest in the song's music video. The track was nominated for a Grammy in the category of Best Rap Solo Performance.

2013: Kendrick Lamar was selected as the winner of MTV's annual "Hottest MCs in the Game."

MARCH 9

1971: C-Murder (birth name Corey Miller) was born in New Orleans. He is the brother of rappers Master P and Silkk the Shocker, and the uncle of Romeo Miller (a.k.a. Lil Romeo) and Cymphonique Miller. After he was convicted of murder in 2009, C-Murder was sentenced to life in prison.

1972: AZ (birth name Anthony Cruz) was born in Brooklyn, New York. He was a member of the hip hop group the Firm (which also included Nas, Foxy Brown, Cormega and Nature). Pursuing a solo career beginning with his 1995 debut album *Doe Or Die*, he later earned a Grammy nomination for the track, "The Essence."

1980: Chingy (birth name Howard Bailey, Jr.) was born in St. Louis. His stage name was taken from a slang term for "money." He scored his breakthrough hit in 2003 with the single, "Right Thurr."

1985: Wretch 32 (birth name Jermaine Scott Sinclair) was born in the Tottenham section of London, England. A grime-style rapper, he was a member of Combination Chain Gang. He later co-founded the hip hop group, the Movement. As a solo artist, he released his first single in 2011, "Traktor."

1987: Bow Wow (birth name Shad Gregory Moss) was born in Columbus, Ohio. Originally known as Lil' Bow Wow, he was discovered at age 11 by music producer Jermaine Dupri, and released his debut album two years later.

1990: YG (birth name Keenon Daequan Ray Jackson) was born in Compton, California. The rapper scored his first hit in 2009 with the single, "Toot It And Boot It" (featuring Ty Dolla $ign).

1990: The comedy film, *House Party*, starred the members of the hip hop duo, Kid 'n Play. The popular film spawned two sequels, *House Party 2* and *House Party 3*.

1990: Mellow Man Ace released the single, "Mentirosa," from his debut album, *Escape From Havana*. The track sampled two songs by Santana, "No One To Depend On" and "Evil Ways."

1991: A concert by KRS-One in suburban Paris was stopped after hundreds of spectators began fighting and trying to jump on stage. A total of six people were hospitalized.

1993: At the 7th annual Soul Train Music Awards which were staged in Los Angeles, *3 Years, 5 Months & 2 Days In The Life Of...* by Arrested Development won the award for Best Rap Album.

1994: T-Bone (real name Terry E. Gray), a member of the Los Angeles gangsta rap trio Da Lench Mob, was cleared of murder charges by a jury in Torrance, California. He had been accused of shooting two men at a bowling alley, one of whom died. T-Bone repeatedly claimed he was a victim of mistaken identity.

1997: The Notorious B.I.G. was gunned down after leaving a party at the Peterson Automotive Museum in Los Angeles that was co-sponsored by *Vibe* magazine. Although the drive-by shooting remains unsolved, witnesses described the gunman as an African-American man in a suit and bow tie. Biggie had planned on spending the day in London but had changed his mind at the last minute. Just 16 days later, his second album, *Life After Death*, was released.

1999: C-Murder released his second album, *Bossalinie*. The album featured guest vocals from a number of his labelmates at No Limit Records including Snoop Dogg, Daz Dillinger and Kurupt. The album spawned the singles, "Like A Jungle" and "Gangsta Walk."

2001: Rappers Sisqó and Carmen Electra appeared in the comedy film, *Get Over It*.

2002: The single "Ain't It Funny" by Jennifer Lopez featuring Ja Rule began a six-week run at number-one on the U.S. charts.

2004: Twista released the single, "Overnight Celebrity" (featuring Kanye West). The track sampled "Cause I Love You" by Lenny Williams.

2006: Lil' Kim starred in the reality program, *Lil' Kim: Countdown To Lockdown*. Airing on the BET network, the six-episode series followed the rapper as she prepared to begin a prison term at the Federal Detention Center in Philadelphia.

2009: Lil' Kim appeared as a contestant on season two of the ABC dance competition, *Dancing With The Stars*. Her partner was professional dancer Derek Hough. The couple was the ninth team to be eliminated.

2010: Lil Wayne began a prison sentence after he pleaded guilty to a felony gun possession. He served eight-months of a one-year sentence at Rikers Island.

2015: Waka Flocka Flame cancelled a scheduled concert on the campus of the University of Oklahoma in response to a controversial online video that was produced by one of the school's fraternities.

MARCH 10

1963: Rick Rubin (birth name Frederick Jay Rubin) was born in Long Beach, New York. As a co-founder of Def Jam Recordings, he was instrumental in the development of rap music during the 1980s. At Def Jam, he teamed with Russell Simmons to cultivate a number of pioneering hip hop acts such as LL Cool J, the Beastie Boys, Public Enemy and Run–D.M.C. Rubin later headed Columbia Records before forming another label, American Recordings.

1964: Neneh Cherry (birth name Neneh Mariann Karlsson) was born in Stockholm, Sweden. She is best known for her 1988 hit single, "Buffalo Stance." Her stepfather is jazz musician Don Cherry.

1964: Biz Markie (birth name Marcel Theo Hall) was born in Egg Harbor Township, New Jersey. He is best known for his 1989 crossover hit, "Just A Friend."

1972: Timbaland (birth name Timothy Zachery Mosley) was born in Norfolk, Virginia. After a stint in the rap duo Timbaland & Magoo, Timbaland became a successful R&B and hip hop producer. He also enjoyed a successful solo career.

1977: Robin Thicke (full name Robin Charles Thicke) was born in Los Angeles. The son of actors Alan Thicke and Gloria Loring, he is best known for his 2013 smash hit "Blurred Lines," which featured T.I., and Pharrell Williams. Thicke has worked with a number of R&B and hip hop performers including Flo Rida, Kid Cudi, Mary J. Blige, Usher, Jennifer Hudson, Christina Aguilera and Nicki Minaj.

1984: In a dorm room at New York University, student Rick Rubin teamed with local concert promoter Russell Simmons to form the pioneering rap label, Def Jam Recordings. The company initially operated out of Rubin's dorm in Weinstein Hall. Before Simmons had joined the label, Rubin had released a record by his own rock group, Hose. After the arrival of Russell, Def Jam issued 12-inch singles by T La Rock & Jazzy Jay, LL Cool J and the Beastie Boys. As the result of their early success, the label was able to secure a lucrative distribution deal with CBS Records.

1992: At the 6th annual Soul Train Music Awards which were staged in Los Angeles, *Apocalypse '91 by* Public Enemy won for Best Rap Album.

1999: Master P (real name Percy Miller) signed a deal with Converse to launch a line of "All Star MP" athletic shoes.

2006: C-Murder was granted an appeal of his murder conviction. He was permitted to serve under house arrest until the completion of his second trial. When he was retried in 2009, the rapper was found guilty for the second time. He was sentenced to life in prison.

2015: A federal jury in Los Angeles ruled that the writers of the hit song "Blurred Lines" – Robin Thicke, T.I. and Pharrell Williams – copied Marvin Gaye's 1977 hit "Got To Give It Up." The jury awarded nearly $7.4 million to Gaye's estate.

MARCH 11

1981: Paul Wall (birth name Paul Michael Slayton) was born in Houston, Texas. Topping the pop charts in 2005 with the solo album *The Peoples Champ*, he also recorded a number of albums with Chamillionaire.

1989: *Billboard* magazine introduced its weekly Hot Rap Singles chart. The first number-one song was "Self-Destruction" by Stop The Violence Movement, a project that was launched by KRS-One.

1991: At the 17th annual People's Choice Awards which were staged at Universal Studios in Hollywood, M.C. Hammer won the award for Favorite Musical Performer; and "Ice Ice Baby" by Vanilla Ice won the award for Favorite New Song.

2005: Bow Wow released the single, "Let Me Hold You" (featuring Omarion). The track sampled "If Only For One Night" by Brenda Russell. The song sold one-million copies in the U.S.

2015: Madonna admitted on *The Howard Stern Show* that she had dated Tupac Shakur in 1994, two years before his death.

MARCH 12

1983: Run-D.M.C. released their groundbreaking single, "It's Like That" / "Sucker MCs." The single marked a change in the direction of hip hop from its R&B-based melodic structure to a more sparse and beat-heavy style. The trio developed their new sound by using a programmable drum machine, the Roland TR-808.

1991: At the 5th annual Soul Train Music Awards which were staged in Los Angeles, *Please Hammer Don't Hurt 'Em* by M.C. Hammer won the award for Best Rap Album. M.C. Hammer also won the Sammy Davis Jr. Award for Entertainer of the Year.

1992: During an interview with radio.com, Gene Simmons of the rock group Kiss said that hip hop has no place in the Rock and Roll Hall of Fame. He argued, "If you don't play guitar and you don't write your own songs, you don't belong there."

1993: Chris Rock and Deezer D starred in the comedy film, *CB4*, which chronicled a fictional rap group that was formed in prison. The film featured appearances by a number of rappers including Eazy-E, Flavor Flav, Ice-T and Ice Cube. The film grossed $18 million in the U.S.

1996: "Weird Al" Yankovic released a parody of Coolio's "Gangsta's Paradise" which he reworked as "Amish Paradise." Coolio was reportedly unhappy with the song.

2004: Beyoncé, Alicia Keys and Missy Elliott were the co-headliners of the 30-date "Verizon Ladies First Tour." Nicknamed the "urban Lilith Fair," the tour began in Sunrise, Florida, and ended in Anaheim, California.

2007: Grandmaster Flash and the Furious Five were inducted into the Rock and Roll Hall of Fame at a ceremony which was staged at the Waldorf Astoria Hotel in New York City. They were the first hip hop act to be inducted by the Rock Hall. The group consisted of Grandmaster Flash (real name Joseph Saddler), Keef Cowboy (real name Keith Wiggins), the Kidd Creole (real name Nathaniel Glover, Jr.), Melle Mel (Melvin Glover), Rahiem (real name Guy Todd Williams) and Scorpio (real name Eddie Morris).

2012: Donda West, the mother of Kanye West, published her autobiography, *Raising Kanye: Life Lessons From The Mother Of A Hip-Hop Superstar*.

2014: Kid Cudi co-starred in the action film, *Need For Speed*. He portrayed Sergeant Benny "Maverick" Jackson, a pilot and member of a street racing crew. The film earned more than $200 million.

MARCH 13

1990: Kid 'n Play released the best-selling album of their career, *Funhouse*. Their second album, it was highlighted by the hit tracks, "Funhouse" and "Back To Basics."

1992: A Tribe Called Quest released the single, "Scenario" (featuring Leaders of the New School). The track sampled "Oblighetto" by Jack McDuff, "Little Miss Lover" by Jimi Hendrix and "So What?" by Miles Davis. The song's music video featured appearances by Redman, Spike Lee, De La Soul, Brand Nubian and Fab 5 Freddy.

1993: Snow began a seven-week run at number-one on the U.S. singles chart with "Informer."

1993: Mary J. Blige was the musical guest on *Saturday Night Live*. She performed "Reminisce" and "Sweet Thing."

1995: At the 9th annual Soul Train Music Awards which were staged in Los Angeles, *Gangsta's Paradise* by Coolio won the award for Best Rap Album.

2004: TLC was the subject of an episode of the VH-1 program, *Behind The Music*. The episode, which was titled "The Final Chapter," focused on the group's demise.

2004: N*E*R*D were the musical guests on *Saturday Night Live*. They performed "She Wants To Move" and "Maybe."

2008: Lil Wayne released the single, "Lollipop," which featured Static Major. (R&B singer Static Major passed away two-weeks before the single was released.) A major hit, it sold four-million copies in the U.S. The rock band Framing Hanley scored a hit with a remake of the song.

MARCH 14

1965: Slick Rick (birth name Richard Martin Lloyd Walters) was born in London, England, but was raised in the Bronx, New York. A pioneering rapper, he often worked with Doug E. Fresh in the 1980s.

1990: At the 4th annual Soul Train Music Awards which were staged in Los Angeles, *Big Time* by Heavy D & The Boyz won the award for Best Rap Album.

1995: Tupac Shakur released his third studio album, *Me Against The World*. The album was released while Shakur was in prison, making him the first musical act to top the album charts while behind bars. As his most critically-acclaimed album, it was highlighted by the singles, "Dear Mama," "So Many Tears" and "Temptations." The album sold more than three-million copies in the U.S.

2004: D12 released the hit single, "My Band." The song's lyrics parodied the widely-held notion that Eminem was the lead singer of D12.

2009: Lil' Kim owed $979,090 in unpaid back taxes to the I.R.S., according to *The Detroit News*.

2011: The reality series *Love & Hip Hop* (sometimes called *Love & Hip Hop: New York*) premiered on VH-1. The program examined the lives of various women in the hip hop field. The first season's cast included Chrissy Lampkin, Emily Bustamante, Somaya "Boss" Reece and Olivia Longott. The program spawned six spin-off series: *Love & Hip Hop: Atlanta, Love & Hip Hop: Hollywood, Chrissy & Mr. Jones, The Gossip Game, This Is Hot 97* and *K. Michelle: My Life*.

2014: Atlanta rapper DG Yola (real name Mario Talley) was arrested on charges of murder and robbery. The 28-year-old rapper was accused of killing one man and robbing another.

MARCH 15

1975: Black Eyed Peas co-founder will.i.am (birth name William James Adams, Jr.) was born in Los Angeles. He also released a number of solo albums beginning with 2001's *Lost Change*. As a producer, he worked with dozens of acts including Lady Gaga, Michael Jackson, Justin Bieber, Eazy-E, Britney Spears, U2, Miley Cyrus, David Guetta, Rihanna, Lady Gaga, Usher, Justin Timberlake, Nicki Minaj, the Game, Nas and Bone Thugs-N-Harmony.

1981: Young Buck (birth name David Darnell Brown) was born in Nashville. Formerly a member of the hip hop group UTP Playas, he later joined G-Unit. Also a producer and entrepreneur, he launched his own label, Ca$hville Records.

1994: At the 8th annual Soul Train Music Awards which were staged in Los Angeles, *Bacdafucup* by Onyx won the award for Best Rap Album.

2011: Sean "Diddy" Combs was given the Man of the Year Award at the annual Jackie Robinson Foundation gala, which was staged at the Waldorf Astoria in New York City. The award was presented to Combs by hip hop entrepreneur Russell Simmons. The event raised $1.4 million for minority scholarships and mentoring programs.

2011: The documentary, *Rhyme And Punishment*, examined the phenomenon of rappers in prison. The film included interviews with Slick Rick, Beanie Sigel, Cassidy, Prodigy, Project Pat, Immortal Technique and others.

2012: Pitbull was the subject of an episode of the VH-1 program, *Behind The Music*.

2012: Pioneering West Coast rapper Nate Dogg (real name Nathaniel Dwayne Hale) passed away in Long Beach, California, after suffering a series of strokes.

2014: The NFL demanded $16.6 million from M.I.A. after the two sides failed to reach a financial settlement. The football league had fined the rapper after she raised her middle finger during her performance at the Super Bowl halftime show in 2012, which resulted in a breach of contract. M.I.A. settled her dispute with the NFL later in the year.

MARCH 16

1959: Flavor Flav (birth name William Jonathan Drayton, Jr.) of Public Enemy was born in Hempstead, New York. An actor and rapper, he was a member of the groundbreaking group Public Enemy.

1981: Danny Brown (birth name Daniel Dewan Sewell) was born in Detroit. The rapper released his breakthrough album in 2013, *Old*.

1993: Boss released her debut single, "Deeper." The track sampled several songs including "90% Of Me Is You" by Gwen McCrae and "Under The Bridge" by Red Hot Chili Peppers.

2001: Sean "Puff Daddy" Combs was found not guilty on four counts of illegal possession of a firearm and one count of bribery in a Manhattan courtroom. Combs' bodyguard, Anthony "Wolf" Jones, was also found not guilty of similar charges. However, Combs' protege Shyne (real name Jamal Barrow) was convicted on five of eight charges and sentenced to nine-years in prison. The men had been charged after a shooting in a Manhattan nightclub that injured three clubgoers. The trial lasted seven weeks and included testimony from 60 witnesses.

2012: Flavor Flav opened a restaurant in Las Vegas, Flavor Flav's House of Flavor. The business closed its doors after six months.

2015: Redfoo of the hip hop/electro-pop group LMFAO appeared as a contestant on season twenty of the ABC dance competition, *Dancing With The Stars*. His partner was professional dancer Emma Slater. The couple was the first team to be eliminated.

MARCH 17

1972: Domino (birth name Shawn Antoine Ivy) was born in St. Louis but raised in Long Beach, California. He is best known for the solo album, *Domino*, which featured the hits, "Getto Jam" and "Sweet Potato Pie." He was also a member of the hip hop group, Bloods & Crips.

1988: C-Murder released his debut album, *Life Or Death*. A top-10 hit, it spawned the singles, "A 2nd Chance" and "Making Moves." This was the best-selling album of C-Murder's career.

1992: The hip hop duo Kris Kross released their debut album, *Totally Krossed Out*. Most of the tracks were written by the duo's producer, Jermaine Dupri. The chart-topping album spawned the hits, "Warm It Up," "I Missed The Bus," "It's A Shame" and the smash, "Jump."

1992: Sister Souljah released her only album, *360 Degrees Of Power*.

1998: Puff Daddy released the single, "Victory" (featuring the Notorious B.I.G. and Busta Rhymes), from his debut album, *No Way Out*. The track featured the final recorded vocals by the Notorious B.I.G. before his death. The track sampled "Going The Distance" by Bill Conti. Puff Daddy spent an astounding $2.7 million on the song's music video.

1998: The LOX – a group consisting of Sheek Louch, Styles P and Jadakiss – released the single, "Money, Power & Respect" (featuring DMX and Lil' Kim). The track sampled "New Beginning" by Dexter Wansel and dialogue from the 1983 film *Scarface*.

2006: Professor X (real name Lumumba Carson) of the hip hop group, X Clan, passed away at the age of 49 after battling spinal meningitis. He was also known as PXO, Baba and Professor X The Overseer. His father is Black Nationalist leader Sonny Carson.

2010: Erykah Badu filmed a controversial music video for her track, "Window Seat." The video featured the singer taking off her clothes while walking down a sidewalk in Dallas, near the spot where President Kennedy was assassinated in 1963. Badu was later charged with disorderly conduct. She was sentenced to six-months of probation and ordered to pay a $500 fine.

2015: Wiz Khalifa released the track, "See You Again" (featuring Charlie Puth). The rap ballad appeared on the soundtrack of the film, *Furious 7*. A huge hit, the song was nominated for three Grammys and sold four-million copies in the U.S.

MARCH 18

1967: Dres (birth name Andres Titus) was born in Queens, New York. In 1989, he teamed with William "Mista Lawnge" McLean to form the alternative hip hop duo, Black Sheep. The duo garnered success with their debut album, *A Wolf In Sheep's Clothing*. Dres' son is the lead singer of the punk rock band Cerebral Ballzy.

1970: Singer and actress Queen Latifah (birth name Dana Owens) was born in East Orange, New Jersey. She released her debut album in 1989, *All Hail The Queen*. She had far greater success as a television and film actress.

1991: After donating $2,500 to the Republican Party, N.W.A. member Eazy-E was invited by Senator Bob Dole to a Washington luncheon with President George H.W. Bush in attendance. Eazy-E later told *Rolling Stone* magazine, "I ain't shit – ain't a Republican or Democrat. I didn't even vote. My vote ain't going to help."

1993: The Pharcyde scored their first hit with the single, "Passin' Me By." The track sampled "Summer In The City" by Quincy Jones, "125th Street Congress" by Weather Report and "Are You Experienced?" by the Jimi Hendrix Experience. "Passin' Me By" was later featured in the Adam Sandler film, *Big Daddy*.

2011: Chris Brown released his fourth album, *F.A.M.E.*, which featured a number of guest vocalists including Busta Rhymes, Tyga, Lil Wayne, Ludacris, Justin Bieber, Wiz Khalifa, the Game, Big Sean and Timbaland. The album spawned the hits, "Yeah 3x," "Look At Me Now" and "Beautiful People." The chart-topping album won a Grammy in the category of Best R&B Album.

MARCH 19

1973: Bun B (birth name Bernard Freeman) was born in Port Arthur, Texas. A former member of the hip hop duo UGK, he later pursued a solo career. After issuing a mixtape, he released his first solo album in 2005, *Trill*.

1987: DJ Jazzy Jeff & The Fresh Prince released their debut album, *Rock The House*. The album spawned three singles: "The Magnificent Jazzy Jeff," "A Touch Of Jazz" and "Girls Ain't Nothing But Trouble."

1990: Tone Loc was featured on the cover of *Newsweek* magazine. The headline read: "Rap Rage: Yo! Street rhyme has gone big time; But are those sounds out of bounds?"

1991: The hit single "You Can't Play With My Yo-Yo" by Yo-Yo (featuring Ice Cube) was released. The track sampled "Devotion" by Earth, Wind & Fire, "Wrath Of My Madness" by Queen Latifah, "You Can Make It If You Try" by Sly & The Family Stone and "Save The World" by Southside Movement.

1994: Snoop Doggy Dogg was the musical guest on *Saturday Night Live*. He performed "Gin And Juice" and "Lodi Dodi."

2004: LL Cool J starred in the crime-thriller film, *Mindhunters*. The rapper portrayed a killer named Gabe Jensen.

2011: While visiting Port-au-Prince, Haiti, Wyclef Jean was shot in the right hand. The local authorities disputed his account and claimed that the rapper was actually cut by a piece of broken glass.

2012: Multiple gunshots were fired at Tyga's tour bus following a concert in Omaha, Nebraska. Two passengers on the bus, including rapper Honey Cocaine, were injured.

2015: Sir Mix-A-Lot was sued in a federal court by his former songwriting partner David Ford (a.k.a. DJ Punish) over the copyrights of several songs including "Baby Got Back" and "Anaconda." The lawsuit was settled later in the year with Sir Mix-A-Lot prevailing.

MARCH 20

1969: Mannie Fresh (birth name Byron O. Thomas) was born in New Orleans. A successful producer at Cash Money Records, he was also a member of the successful hip hop duo, Big Tymers. He later pursued a solo career and formed his own label, Chubby Boy Records.

2012: Kanye West and Jay-Z released the single, "No Church In The Wild" (featuring Frank Ocean). It was the first single from the duo's collaborative album, *Watch The Throne*. The single won a Grammy in the category of Best Rap/Sung Collaboration. The song's music video did not feature any of the artists who performed on the track.

2015: Marion "Suge" Knight collapsed in court after a judge set the rapper's bail at $25 million in his murder trial. Even though the court later reduced the bail to $10 million, Knight remained behind bars.

MARCH 21

1966: DJ Premiere (birth name Christopher Edward Martin) was born in Houston but later settled in Brooklyn, New York. A talented producer, he joined the hip hop act Gang Starr in 1989.

1989: Tone Loc released the top-10 crossover hit, "Funky Cold Medina." The song was co-written by rapper Young MC. The track sampled several songs including "Get Off Your Ass And Jam" by Funkadelic, "Honky Tonk Women" by the Rolling Stones, "Hot Blooded" by Foreigner, "Christine Sixteen" by Kiss, "All Right Now" by Free and "You Ain't Seen Nothing Yet" by Bachman-Turner Overdrive.

1990: Rapper Tairrie B claimed that Dr. Dre assaulted her at a Grammy Awards after-party. She alleged that he punched her in the eye and mouth.

1996: Dr. Dre left Death Row Records following a contractual dispute with Suge Knight. Dr. Dre was also unhappy with Knight's aggressive business practices. After leaving the label, Dr. Dre was criticized in the press by Knight and former labelmate Tupac Shakur. By the end of the year, Dr. Dre had launched his own label, Aftermath Entertainment.

2000: Snoop Dogg and Ice-T starred in the urban-action film, *The Wrecking Crew*.

2008: The documentary, *Planet B-Boy*, was released. Directed by Benson Lee, the film chronicled the history of hip hop dancing around the world.

2011: Romeo Miller (a.k.a. Lil' Romeo) appeared as a contestant on season twelve of the ABC dance competition, *Dancing With The Stars*. His partner was professional dancer Chelsie Hightower. The couple was the seventh team to be eliminated.

2012: Ne-Yo staged a launch party at Liberty Theater in New York City to introduce his new drink, a tequila-flavored rum called Malibu Red.

MARCH 22

1981: Mims (birth name Shawn Mims) was born in Manhattan, New York. The rapper is best known for his 2007 single, "This Is Why I'm Hot."

1983: The soundtrack of the hip hop film, *Wild Style*, was released. Although the film was overlooked at the time, the accompanying album was instrumental in the rise of rap music. Although the album produced no hit singles, it was highlighted by the tracks "Cold Crush Brothers At The Dixie" by the Cold Crush Brothers and "MC Battle" by Busy Bee Starski vs. Rodney Cee.

1990: The uncensored versions of albums by 2 Live Crew were removed by Musicland and Sam Goody record stores at all 750 of their locations in the U.S.

1991: Vanilla Ice appeared in the children's action film, *Teenage Mutant Ninja Turtles II: The Secret Of The Ooze*. In the film, he performed the song, "Ninja Rap." Although the movie was a box office success, the rapper's image took a hit.

1994: The soundtrack of the film *Above The Rim* was released by Death Row Records. The 18-song album featured tracks by Warren G, Nate Dogg, Snoop Dogg as well as one the film's stars, Tupac Shakur. The soundtrack was released one day before the film's premiere.

1997: The single "Can't Nobody Hold Me Down" by Puff Daddy featuring Ma$e began a six-week run at number-one on the U.S. charts.

2005: C-Murder released his fifth album, *The Truest Shit I Ever Said*. The album was allegedly recorded while the rapper was in jail, using a portable tape recorder provided by his attorney during visiting hours. The album also contained interviews with C-Murder's friends and family members.

2010: Hundreds of people protesting a planned concert by Akon stormed the offices of a Sri Lankan broadcasting company that was sponsoring the event. The protestors were unhappy with music video, "Sexy Chick" by David Guetta and featuring Akon, which showed women in bikinis dancing in front of a statue of Buddha. As a result of the protests, the concert was cancelled and Akon was banned from entering the country.

2011: Black Eyed Peas member will.i.am provided the voice of a rapping, red-crested cardinal named Pedro in the animated hit film, *Rio*. The film earned more than $140 million in the U.S. He reprised his role in the sequel film, *Rio 2*.

2012: The Game was the subject of an episode of the VH-1 program, *Behind The Music*.

MARCH 23

1987: At the first annual Soul Train Music Awards, Run-D.M.C. became the first hip hop act to win an award. The trio won in two categories: *Raising Hell* for Best Rap Album and "Walk This Way" for Best Rap Single.

1996: The Notorious B.I.G. was arrested near the Palladium nightclub in Manhattan after he chased and threatened a pair of autograph seekers. After the two fans had left in a taxi, he followed them and broke the windows of the vehicle with a baseball bat. He was later convicted of harassment.

1998: At 19-years-old, Aaliyah was the youngest person to perform a song at the Academy Awards ceremony. She sang "Journey To The Past" from the movie *Anastasia*.

2003: The track, "Lose Yourself" from the film *8 Mile*, won an Oscar at the Academy Awards for Best Original Song. The song was co-written by Eminem, Jeff Bass and Luis Resto. This was the first time a rap song had been nominated for an Oscar.

MARCH 24

1970: Maseo (birth named Vincent Lamont Mason, Jr.) of the rap trio De La Soul was born in Brooklyn, New York. He also used the stage names, P.A. Pasemaster Mase and Plug Three.

1992: A judge in Chicago approved a settlement which gave cash rebates of up to $3 to buyers of Milli Vanilli recordings. The class-action lawsuit had been filed in November 1990.

1992: Melle Mel of Grandmaster Flash and the Furious Five entered a boxing ring to fight Willie D of the Geto Boys. The event aired on *MTV Raps* and was billed as the Celebrity Rappers Boxing Match. Willie D won the fight with a knock-out punch.

1992: Arrested Development released their debut album, *3 Years, 5 Months & 2 Days In The Life Of...* The title referred to amount of time it took for the group to secure a recording contract. The album was highlighted by the tracks, "People Everyday," "Tennessee" and "Mr. Wendal." The progressive hip hop group won two Grammys in the categories of Best Rap Single and Best New Artist.

2000: P. Diddy was the judge on the ABC/MTV reality competition, *Making The Band*, which pitted unknown musical acts against each other. The series was responsible for the discovery and success of a number of acts including hip hop group Da Band as well as Donnie King, O-Town, Day 26 and Danity Kane. The popular program aired for multiple seasons and was cancelled in 2009.

2006: Sean "Diddy" Combs and his label Bad Boy Records lost a copyright infringement lawsuit to Bridgeport Music and Westbound Records, which had claimed that the debut album by the Notorious B.I.G. had used unlicensed samples. A jury awarded the plaintiffs nearly $3.7 million in damages. Upon appeal, the award was reduced by $2.8 million.

2007: Tony Yayo of G-Unit was arrested for allegedly assaulting the teenage son of the Game's manager, Jimmy "The Henchmen" Rosemond, on March 20. Rosemond's 14-year-old son claimed he was slapped several times because Yayo objected to the teen's t-shirt which featured a logo of Czar Entertainment. The charges were later reduced with Yayo reaching a plea deal. He was sentenced to ten days of community service.

2011: Pitbull announced a partnership with Voli to produce a low-calorie vodka. In addition to becoming the company's spokesman, he also became a part-owner of the brand.

2012: Black Eyed Peas member will.i.am began his first of several seasons as a coach on the British music talent show, *The Voice UK*.

2014: Nick Cannon posted photos of himself on Instagram wearing whiteface makeup, a red wig and ski cap to promote his new album, *White People Party Music*. Calling himself Connor Smallnut and declaring, "It's official... I'm White!!!," Cannon sparked a public controversy. Cannon later defended his actions during an interview on *Good Morning America*.

2015: Former rap promoter Jimmy "The Henchman" Rosemond was sentenced to life in prison plus 20 years after he was convicted of a murder-for-hire plot that resulted in the death of an associate of the rap group, G-Unit.

2015: Kendrick Lamar surprised his fans by staging a free outdoor concert in West Hollywood. Performing on the back of a flatbed truck, he was celebrating the release of his second album, *To Pimp A Butterfly*. He had announced the show earlier in the day on his Twitter account.

MARCH 25

1975: Juvenile (birth name Terius Gray) was born in New Orleans. Breaking into music as a member of the hip hop group the Hot Boys, he later pursued a solo career. He scored his first major hit in 1999 with the single, "Back That Thang Up."

1979: The Fatback Band released the pioneering hip hop single, "King Tim III (Personality Jock)." The B-side hit featured an MC from the Bronx, Timothy Washington. The song represented the transition between disco, which was fading at the time, and rap. The single was issued nearly six-months before the Sugarhill Gang released "Rapper's Delight."

1988: Ryan Lewis was born in Spokane, Washington. The DJ, photographer and producer teamed with rapper Macklemore in 2009 to form a hip hop duo. In 2012, Macklemore & Ryan Lewis issued their self-financed independent album, *The Heist*. A surprise hit, the project spawned five singles, most notably "Thrift Shop." As a result of the album's success, the duo won four Grammys.

1988: Big Sean (birth name Sean Michael Leonard Anderson) was born in Santa Monica, California, but raised in Detroit. The rapper released his debut album in 2011, *Finally Famous*.

1997: *Life After Death*, the second studio album by the Notorious B.I.G., was released just 16 days after he was murdered in Los Angeles. The album featured collaborations with Jay-Z, Lil' Kim, 112, Ma$e, Bone Thugs-N-Harmony, Too $hort, Angela Winbush, Puff Daddy, R. Kelly and others. The album spawned the singles, "Hypnotize," "Mo Money Mo Problems" and "Sky's The Limit." The album was nominated for three Grammys in the categories of Best Rap Album, Best Rap Solo Performance for the track "Hypnotize" and Best Rap Performance by a Duo or Group for the track "Mo Money Mo Problems." The album sold more than ten-million copies in the U.S.

2000: "Wild Wild West" by Will Smith was selected as the Worst Original Song at the 20th annual Golden Raspberry Awards.

2011: Rick Ross was arrested in Shreveport, Louisiana, for the possession of marijuana. Ross was in the city for a concert at the Kokopellis nightclub.

2013: Usher began his first of two seasons as a judge on the television singing competition, *The Voice*.

MARCH 26

1987: The Fat Boy released their best-selling album, *Crushin'*. The million-selling album was highlighted by the singles "Falling In Love" and a remake of the rock standard "Wipe Out."

1988: Joseph D. Baugh, the Attorney General for the 21st District of Tennessee, ruled that N.W.A.'s album *Straight Outta Compton* and 2 Live Crew's album *As Nasty As They Wanna Be* both violated the state's obscenity laws.

1991: Yo-Yo released her debut solo single, "You Can't Play With My Yo-Yo," which featured Ice Cube. The track sampled "Devotion" by Earth, Wind & Fire, "Wrath Of My Madness" by Queen Latifah, "You Can Make It If You Try" by Sly & The Family Stone and "Save The World" by Southside Movement.

1995: Eazy-E (real name Eric Lynn Wright) of the gangsta rap group N.W.A. died from complications of AIDS. He had checked into Cedars-Sinai Hospital in Los Angeles a month earlier believing he was suffering an asthma attack. He was 30-years-old.

1996: Jay-Z released the single, "Ain't No Nigga" (featuring Foxy Brown). It was his first chart hit and was included on both his debut album, *Reasonable Doubt*, and on the soundtrack of the Eddie Murphy film, *The Nutty Professor*. The track sampled "Seven Minutes Of Fun" by the Whole Darn Family and interpolated "Ain't No Woman (Like The One I've Got)" by the Four Tops.

2006: Rappers Xzibit and Busta Rhymes starred in the action-thriller film, *Full Clip*.

2007: NBA star Tony Parker released the rap album, *TP*. All of the tracks were sung in French. The project featured guest appearances by Jamie Foxx and French rapper Booba. (In 2013, Parker announced he was retiring from his "rap career.")

2012: A documentary chronicling the career of the late rapper Heavy D, *Be Inspired: The Life Of Heavy D*, aired on the Centric TV network.

2013: Jodeci were booed off the stage during their performance at Wembley Arena in London. Three of the four original members – K-Ci, JoJo and Mr. Dalvin – had reunited for the concert. At one point, Mr. Dalvin awkwardly jumped off the stage and into the audience, but was unable to climb back onto the stage without the help of a security guard. Also on the bill were SWV, BLACKstreet, Dru Hill, Damage and Changing Faces.

2013: Rihanna was loudly booed by an Australian audience after she was 80–minutes late for her headlining performance at a concert in the city of Adelaide.

2013: Robin Thicke released the single, "Blurred Lines," which featured the song's two co-writers, T.I. and Pharrell Williams. Thicke released two music videos for the track – one of which featured nudity and was banned by YouTube. A smash hit, the track sold more than seven-million copies in the U.S. The song was nominated for two Grammys in the categories of Record of the Year and Best Pop Duo/Group Performance. The estate of Marvin Gaye later sued over the song's similarity to Gaye's 1977 hit, "Got To Give It Up."

MARCH 27

1975: Fergie (birth name Stacy Ann Ferguson) was born in Hacienda Heights, California. Afer a stint in the girl group Wild Orchid, she joined the Black Eyed Peas in 2002. As a solo artist, she released her smash debut album in 2006, *The Dutchess*.

1975: Skee-Lo (birth name Antoine Roundtree) was born in Chicago. The rapper is best known for his 1995 Grammy-nominated hit, "I Wish."

1984: Run–D.M.C. released their groundbreaking debut album, *Run–D.M.C.* The project took rap in a new direction with its stripped-down, beat-heavy sound. The album was highlighted by the tracks, "Rock Box," "Jam-Master Jay," "Scratchin'," "Hollis Crew" and the single, "It's Like That" / "Sucker MCs."

1989: De La Soul released the smash, crossover hit, "Me Myself And I." The song's lyrics combined humor with political commentary.

1990: *Star Wars* filmmaker George Lucas sued Luther Campbell of 2 Live Crew over the rapper's stage name, Luke Skyywalker. Lucas accused the rapper of trademark infringement and asked for $300 million in damages. The case was dismissed later in the year with Campbell paying $300,000 to Lucas in an out of court settlement.

1996: Busta Rhymes released his debut solo album, *The Coming*. The album spawned the singles, "Woo-Hah!! Got You All I Check" and "It's A Party." The album was nominated for a Grammy in the category of Best Rap Solo Performance.

1998: Big Pun released the single, "Still Not A Player." This was his first crossover hit. The song was a remixed version of his earlier hit, "Not A Player," and sampled "Don't Wanna Be A Player" by Joe and "A Little Bit Of Love" by Brenda Russell. Rapper Cormega made an appearance in the song's music video.

2001: A remake of the classic R&B song, "Lady Marmalade," was recorded by a quartet of female vocalists, Lil' Kim, Christina Aguilera, Mýa and Pink. The chart-topping single was featured on the soundtrack of the hit film, *Moulin Rouge!*

2008: Remy Ma (real name Reminisce Smith) was found guilty of assault. She had been on trial for shooting a female friend while the two fought inside a car. Remy Ma served six-years of an eight-year prison sentence and was released in August 2014.

2011: Ice Cube became a spokesman for Coors Light beer and appeared in a number of television commercials.

2014: The Wu-Tang Clan announced on their website they would be selling only one copy of their next album, *Once Upon A Time In Shaolin*. The hip hop group had been working on the long-awaited project since 2007. It was purchased in an auction for a reported $2 million by a 32-year-old pharmaceutical executive.

2015: T.I. (real name Clifford Harris) staged a ribbon cutting ceremony in honor of the opening of his new restaurant in Atlanta, Scales 925.

MARCH 28

1966: Cheryl "Salt" James of the 1980s female rap trio Salt-n-Pepa was born in Brooklyn, New York. She co-founded the group in 1984.

1971: Mr. Cheeks (birth name Terrance Kelly) was born in Queens, New York. In addition to his membership in the hip hop group Lost Boyz, he also enjoyed a successful solo career.

1986: J-Kwon (birth name Jerrell C. Jones) was born in St. Louis, Missouri. He is best known for the 2004 hit, "Tipsy."

1998: Ol' Dirty Bastard of the Wu-Tang Clan released his debut solo album, *Return To The 36 Chambers: The Dirty Version*. The platinum-selling album spawned the singles, "Brooklyn Zoo" and "Shimmy Shimmy Ya."

1999: Vanilla Ice was the subject of an episode of the VH-1 series, *Behind The Music*.

1999: Freaky Tah (real name Raymond Rogers) was shot and killed in a hotel parking lot in Queens, New York, at the age of 27. He was a member of the hip hop group, the Lost Boyz. The shooter later pleaded guilty to a charge of murder and was sentenced to 15-years to life in prison.

2000: 504 Boyz released their debut single, "Wobble Wobble." The all-star group was led by Master P and included C-Murder, Silkk The Shocker, Mac, Magic, Krazy and Mystikal. The track appeared on the group's hit album, *Goodfellas*.

2001: Puff Daddy told an MTV interviewer that he had changed his name to "P. Diddy."

2006: T.I. released his fourth album, *King*. The album spawned the singles, "What You Know," "Why You Wanna," "Live In The Sky" and "Top Back (Remix)." The project also served as the soundtrack of a film that featured T.I. in the starring role, *ATL*. The album sold two-million copies in the U.S. and was nominated for Grammys in the categories of Best Rap Album and Best Rap Song, and won the award for Best Rap Solo Performance for the track, "What You Know."

2009: André 3000 of OutKast was arrested in Henry County, just south of Atlanta, for driving 109 mph in a 65 mph zone. He was behind the wheel of a 2007 Porsche Carrera.

2010: Flesh-n-Bone was arrested while performing at a concert in Cleveland with his band, Bone Thugs-N-Harmony. He was picked up on a 10-year-old felony warrant. The charges were later dropped.

2012: A Gainesville, Florida, judge overturned a jury's guilty verdict against Plies (real name Algernod Washington) after the rapper was found liable for multiple shootings at a 2006 concert that left five people injured. The judge explained that the rapper did not participate in the shootings and was not responsible for the victims' injuries.

MARCH 29

1988: DJ Jazzy Jeff & The Fresh Prince released their breakthrough album, *He's The DJ, I'm The Rapper*. This was the very first rap double-album. The album spawned the hits, "Brand New Funk," "Parents Just Don't Understand" and "A Nightmare On My Street." The album sold more than three-million copies in the U.S.

1991: KDAY in Los Angeles, the first "all hip hop" radio station in the U.S., was sold. The new owners dropped the format after a seven-year run.

1992: Tone Loc began his recurring role on the Fox television sitcom, *Roc*. He portrayed an anti-crime vigilante named Ronnie Paxton.

1992: "Addams Groove" by MC Hammer was selected as the Worst Original Song at the 12th annual Golden Raspberry Awards.

1995: After Ol' Dirty Bastard used his food stamp ID for the cover art of his debut solo album, he invited an MTV news crew for a ride in a limousine as he collected his monthly food stamps. But when an employee at the welfare office saw the MTV report, the rapper lost his benefits.

1996: After leaving *The Soul Train Awards* ceremony in Los Angeles, various members of Bad Boy Records and Death Row Records confronted each other. At one point, someone pulled out a gun. The simmering feud between the two camps would continue for years.

2011: Snoop Dogg sang a duet with country music legend Willie Nelson on *The Late Show With David Letterman*. The track, "Superman," was included on the rapper's album, *Doggumentary*.

2012: T-Pain was the subject of an episode of the VH-1 program, *Behind The Music*.

MARCH 30

1962: MC Hammer (birth name Stanley Kirk Burrell) was born in Oakland. He is best known for the 1990 smash hit "U Can't Touch This" from the album *Please Hammer, Don't Hurt 'Em*, which was the second best-selling rap album of the 20th century. After becoming an ordained minister in 1997, he began combining gospel with rap music.

1988: At the 2nd annual Soul Train Music Awards which were staged in Los Angeles, LL Cool J won both rap awards: *Bigger And Deffer* for Best Rap Album and "I Need Love" for Best Rap Album.

1992: The German electronic/dance group Snap! released the crossover hit single, "Rhythm Is A Dancer." The song featured the lead vocals of Thea Austin and rapping by Turbo B.

1993: Onyx released their debut album, *Bacdafucup*. The album was highlighted by the hit singles "Throw Your Gunz," "Slam" and "Shifftee."

2003: The single "21 Questions" by 50 Cent featuring Nate Dogg began a four-week run at number-one on the U.S. charts.

2006: Black Rob (born Robert Ross) had his prison sentence increased to seven years, up from the original two-to-six-years, after he failed to turn himself in on January 24. The rapper had been convicted on a charge of grand larceny after he stole $6,000 in jewelry from a hotel. He was released from prison in May 2010.

2010: The Black Eyed Peas became the first musical act to broadcast a concert in 3D. Performing at the Staples Center in Los Angeles, the group was seen in 500 theaters across the country in normal 2D and at one theater in 3D.

2015: De La Soul announced an online crowdsourcing campaign to raise $100,000 for the purpose of recording a new album. The group reached its goal in just nine-hours, and would ultimately raise $600,000. The resulting album, *And the Anonymous Nobody*, was released in 2016.

MARCH 31

1968: Mad Cobra (birth name Ewart Everton Brown) was born in Jamaica. He is best known for the 1992 crossover hit, "Flex."

1978: Tony Yayo (birth name Marvin Bernard) was born in Queens, New York. The rapper is best known as a member of the hip hop group, G-Unit. He released his breakthrough solo album in 2005, *Thoughts Of A Predicate Felon*.

1985: Jay Rock (birth name Johnny Reed McKinzie, Jr.) was born in the Watts section of Los Angeles. The rapper is best known for the 2008 single, "All My Life (In The Ghetto)."

1992: The musical film *Sisters In The Name Of Rap* premiered at the Hiphop Archive & Research Institute in Cambridge, Massachusetts. The project was filmed at the Ritz in New York City. It was hosted by Dee Barnes and featured Salt-n-Pepa, Queen Latifah, MC Lyte and other female rappers. It aired on the USA Network later in the year.

1992: Ice-T and his group Body Count released their debut album, *Body Count*. The heavy metal album contained the controversial track, "Cop Killer," which was criticized by police groups across the country. The band's label, Sire Records, later removed the track from the album.

1992: Arrested Development released their debut single, "Tennessee," which featured guest vocalist Dionne Farris. The crossover hit was written by the group's lead singer, Speech, about the deaths of his brother and grandmother. The song sampled "Alphabet St." by Prince.

1999: Civil rights pioneer Rosa Parks filed a lawsuit against OutKast and their label, LaFace Records, charging trademark infringement over the duo's 1998 hit track, "Rosa Parks." Although the initial lawsuit was dismissed, the case eventually wound its way to the Supreme Court which allowed the suit to proceed. The case was settled in 2005 with OutKast and others paying Parks an undisclosed settlement.

2006: T.I. starred in the film, *ATL*. He portrayed a fictional, up-and-coming Atlanta rapper named Rashad. The film also featured Big Boi of OutKast, who portrayed a drug dealer. T.I.'s album *King* served as the film's official soundtrack.

2009: The Black Eyed Peas released "Boom Boom Pow," the debut single from their album, *The E.N.D.* The song was the best-selling digital single of 2009 and won a Grammy in the category of Best Short Form Music Video.

2015: Tyga introduced a line of L.A. Gear athletic shoes, the Liquid Gold L.A. Lights collection. The rapper celebrated the unveiling of the shoe line with an appearance at Shiekh Shoes in Los Angeles.

▶ APRIL

APRIL 1

1949: Gil Scott-Heron, nicknamed the Godfather of Rap, was born in Chicago. Rooted in jazz and R&B, Scott-Heron was a "spoken word" performer whose vocal style greatly influenced early rap music. He died in 2011.

1971: Method Man (birth name Clifford Smith) was born in Hempstead, New York. He took his stage name from the 1979 martial arts film, *Method Man*. An original member of the East Coast hip hop collective, the Wu-Tang Clan, he released his debut solo album in 1994, *Tical*.

1996: DJ Kool released the single, "Let Me Clear My Throat," which featured Biz Markie and Doug E. Fresh. The live version of the track – which was taken from a performance at the Bahama Bay club in Philadelphia – was one of only a handful of live hip hop songs to receive strong radio airplay. (In 2015, the Buffalo Sabres of the NHL began using the track as their official goal song.)

1996: MC Hammer and his wife filed for bankruptcy in an Oakland court. The couple claimed more than $10 million in debts and only $1 million in assets.

1997: The single, "Hypnotize" by the Notorious B.I.G., was released. This was the fifth single in chart history to top the U.S. pop charts after an artist's death. The track sampled "Rise" by Herb Alpert and interpreted "La Di Da Di" by Slick Rick. The song's music video featured the final film appearance by the Notorious B.I.G. The track was nominated for a Grammy in the category of Best Rap Solo Performance.

2004: Chuck D of Public Enemy began co-hosting a politically-oriented talk show on the Air America network. His co-hosts on *Unfiltered* were Rachel Maddow and Lizz Winstead.

2010: The British hip hop trio N-Dubz published the autobiography, *Against All Odds: From Street Life To Chart Life*.

2011: The FBI released a 359-page document from their investigation of the murder of the Notorious B.I.G.

2012: A 30-year-old man was arrested after he broke into the home of Sean "Diddy" Combs in East Hampton, New York. After making his way inside, the burglar consumed the rapper's liquor, dressed in his clothing, smoked his cigars and slept in his bed.

2012: RZA of the Wu-Tang Clan made his first appearance on the television series, *Californication*. Portraying a wealthy hip hop mogul named Samurai Apocalypse, he would appear in nine episodes.

2014: Nick Cannon released his first album in over a decade, *White People Party Music*. To promote the album he posted photos of himself on Instagram in whiteface makeup, a red wig and ski cap, and adopted a white alter-ego, Conner Smallnut.

2015: The exhibition "Hip-Hop Revolution" opened at the Museum of the City of New York. The city's hip hop scene from 1977 to 1990 was documented through the photographs of Janette Beckman, Joe Conzo and Martha Cooper. The display featured pioneers such as the Beastie Boys, Run-D.M.C., Afrika Bambaataa, DJ Kool Herc, the Cold Crush Brothers and Rock Steady Crew.

2015: A full-sized wax figure of Pharrell Williams was unveiled at Madame Tussauds in New York City.

2016: The 1988 album *It Takes A Nation Of Millions To Hold Us Back* by Public Enemy was named the number-one album on *Q* magazine's list of "The Top 20 Albums of the Golden Age" of hip hop.

APRIL 2

1983: Yung Joc (birth name Jasiel Robinson) was born in Memphis. The Southern-styled rapper released his debut album in 2006, *New Joc City*.

1991: LL Cool J delivered a pair of athletic sports shoes to every student and teacher at the Thompson Middle School in Dorchester, Massachusetts, after the school won the Foot Locker Cool School Video contest.

1992: Pete Rock & CL Smooth released the single, "They Reminisce Over You (T.R.O.Y.)." The song was a tribute to the late "Trouble" T. Roy of Heavy D & The Boyz who passed away in 1990.

1994: Eazy-E began hosting a weekly radio program, *The Ruthless Radio Show*, on KKBT (The Beat) in Los Angeles. He was joined on the show by former N.W.A. member Yella.

1998: Rob Pilatus of the duo Milli Vanilli was found dead in a hotel room in Frankfurt, Germany. He had accidentally overdosed on a combination of alcohol and prescription pills.

2002: Cam'ron released his debut solo single, "Oh Boy" (featuring Juelz Santana). The track sampled "I'm Going Down" by Rose Royce. The song was nominated for a Grammy in the category of Best Rap Performance by a Duo or Group. Mariah Carey later recorded an answer record, "Boy (I Need You)."

2002: The documentary, *Tupac Shakur: Thug Angel, The Life Of An Outlaw*, was released. The film included interviews with Suge Knight, Snoop Dogg, Treach, Shock G and Big Syke. The highlight of the film was an interview with Shakur, at age 17, discussing his future.

2005: Kanye West abandoned an autograph session at the grand opening of the FTK boutique in Fresno, California, after a fight erupted between a fan and a security guard. Nearly 1,000 people were waiting in line at the time.

2011: Snoop Dogg revealed that he had turned down an offer from Simon Cowell to be a judge on the U.S. version of the television show, *The X Factor*.

2013: Method Man starred in the film, *The Mortician*. He portrayed an undertaker who befriended a young boy that was in danger.

2015: LL Cool J began hosting the Spike network series, *Lip Sync Battle*, which pitted celebrities against each other in a lip syncing competition.

APRIL 3

1989: Slick Rick released the hit single, "Children's Story." The comedy-styled song sampled "Think (About It)" by Lyn Collins and "Nautilus" by Bob James.

1989: MTV rejected the music video for "Straight Outta Compton" by N.W.A. due to its excessive violence.

1992: Kentucky Fried Chicken announced that they had hired MC Hammer as their television spokesman.

1997: Rap-rock group the Bloodhound Gang released the single, "Fire Water Burn." The track featured the chorus of the funk classic "The Roof Is On Fire" by Rock Master Scott & The Dynamic Three.

2001: Run-D.M.C. released their final album before the murder of Jam Master Jay. The album *Crown Royal* was only a moderate seller.

2003: A trio of hip hop artists – Ashanti, Ja Rule and Redman – performed a free concert in Long Island, New York, for the families of U.S. troops stationed overseas.

2008: Frosty Freeze (real name Wayne Frost) passed away at the age of 44 after battling an undisclosed illness. He was a member of the award-winning breakdancing group, Rock Steady Crew.

2008: Lil Jon launched his own line of bottled wines, Little Jonathan Winery.

2012: The quartet of Kanye West, Big Sean, Pusha T and 2 Chainz released the single, "Mercy." The track appeared on the compilation album *Cruel Summer*, which featured artists on Kanye West's record label, G.O.O.D. Music. The track prominently sampled "Dust A Sound Boy" by Super Beagle. The song sold more than three-million copies in the U.S. and was nominated for two Grammys in the categories of Best Rap Song and Best Rap Performance.

2013: A Burger King commercial featuring Mary J. Blige was criticized for its racial overtones. The ad for chicken wraps was quickly pulled by the burger chain. Both Burger King and Blige later apologized.

2013: To celebrate their fifth wedding anniversary, Jay-Z and Beyoncé traveled to the Communist country of Cuba. But the trip ignited a controversy in Washington, D.C., over whether or not the couple had broken federal law, which banned Americans from traveling to the Caribbean island nation except for educational or cultural purposes. Later, the U.S. Treasury Department declared the trip was legal and the couple had broken no laws. In response to the controversy, Jay-Z later released the song, "Open Letter."

2015: At a concert in Tallahassee, Florida, rapper Plies was thrown into the audience by a fan he had invited to come onstage. After the fan was escorted out of the building, the concert resumed despite an outbreak of fighting in the audience.

APRIL 4

2000: Big Punisher's album *Yeeeah Baby* was released two months after the rapper's sudden death. The album was highlighted by the tracks, "It's So Hard" (featuring Donell Jones) and "100%" (featuring Tony Sunshine).

2002: At age 15, Lil' Bow Wow dropped the "Lil" portion from his stage name.

2006: Marion "Suge" Knight filed for bankruptcy after he lost a lawsuit over the ownership of Death Row Records and was ordered to pay $107 million in damages.

2008: Jay-Z and Beyoncé were married in a private ceremony that was attended by a small number of friends and family. The wedding was held at Jay-Z's loft apartment in the Tribeca district of New York City. The couple had dated for six years.

2009: Nike introduced the Air Yeezy shoe in collaboration with rapper Kanye West. The limited edition shoes were priced at $215 a pair.

2009: Run-D.M.C. became the second rap act inducted into the Rock and Hall of Fame. Inducted were Darryl "D.M.C." McDaniels, Jason "Jam-Master Jay" Mizell and Joseph "DJ Run" Simmons. The surviving members of the group did not perform at the event. The event was staged at Public Hall in Cleveland.

2013: Beyoncé starred in a television commercial for Pepsi.

2014: An investment group that included Jennifer Lopez outbid Sean "Diddy" Combs to purchase the cable music network, Fuse TV. According to reports, Lopez's group offered a deal worth approximately $275 million in cash and equity.

APRIL 5

1964: Kid Coolout (birth name Christopher Reid) was born in the Bronx, New York. As a member of the popular hip hop duo Kid 'n Play, he first hit the charts in the late 1980s. Launching a successful acting career, he appeared in a series of popular *House Party* films.

1975: Juicy J (birth name Jordan Michael Houston) was born in Memphis, Tennessee. He was a founding member of the Southern hip hop group Three 6 Mafia, which released their breakthrough album in 2000, *When The Smoke Clears: Sixty 6, Sixty 1*. Juicy J also pursued a solo career, often in collaboration with Wiz Khalifa.

1996: Tupac Shakur was sentenced to 120 days in prison for violating the terms of his release while out on bail.

2002: Omar Epps and Heavy D co-starred in the Tim Allen comedy film, *Big Trouble*. The two rappers portrayed a pair of FBI agents in search of an errant nuclear bomb.

2006: Eminem filed for divorce from his wife, Kimberly Scott, just three months after the couple had reconciled and remarried. The couple were previously married from June 1999 to October 2001.

2007: The MTV reality show, *Adventures in HollyHood*, followed the members of the hip hop group Three 6 Mafia after their move from Memphis to Hollywood, California. The program ran for one season.

2010: A federal judge in Los Angeles dismissed a wrongful death lawsuit that was filed by the family of the Notorious B.I.G., which claimed that Los Angeles officials had covered up the police's involvement in the rapper's death. The long-running lawsuit had been filed in 2002.

2012: Aaliyah was the subject of an episode of the VH-1 program, *Behind The Music.*

2014: Pharrell Williams was the musical guest on *Saturday Night Live.* He performed "Happy" and "Marilyn Monroe."

2014: Hip hop producer and historian 9th Wonder (real name Patrick Douthit) was the subject of the documentary *The Hip-Hop Fellow*, which premiered at the Full Frame Documentary Film Festival in Durham, North Carolina. The film chronicled 9th Wonder's effort to assemble a hip hop archive at Harvard University. *The Hip-Hop Fellow* was a follow-up to the 2012 documentary, *The Wonder Year.*

APRIL 6

1990: A three-hour, pay-per-view concert, *Rapmania, A Salute To The 15th Anniversary Of Hip-Hop*, aired on cable television. The concert featured a number of classic hip hop acts including Tone Loc, Ice-T, Kurtis Blow, Melle Mel, Afrika Bambaataa, Heavy D & The Boys, Kool Moe Dee, Marley Marl, the Sugarhill Gang and others.

1999: Krayzie Bone released his first solo album, *Thug Mentality*. The million-selling album spawned the hits, "Thug Mentality" and "Paper."

1999: Nas released his third studio album, *I Am...*, which was originally planned as a double-album. The project spawned two singles: "Nas Is Like" and "Hate Me Now."

2003: K-Ci and JoJo were released from prison after paying a combined $650,000 bail. The brothers had been charged with tax evasion.

2007: Fergie of the Black Eyed Peas co-starred in the horror film, *Planet Terror.*

APRIL 7

1977: The German electronic-rock band Kraftwerk released the single, "Trans-Europe Express." The song greatly influenced a number of pioneering rappers in the late-1970s and was sampled by Afrika Bambaataa on his classic rap hit, "Planet Rock." The song was also embraced by early beatbox performers.

1992: The hip hop duo Das EFX released their debut album, *Dead Serious*. The influential album was highlighted by the hit singles, "They Want EFX," "Mic Checka" and "Straight Out The Sewer."

1995: Will Smith starred opposite Martin Lawrence in the feature film, *Bad Boys*. Both men portrayed police detectives in a narcotics division. The film was a box office hit and earned more than $140 million. Smith and Lawrence reunited for the 2003 sequel, *Bad Boys II.*

1998: The soundtrack of the film, *I Got The Hook-Up*, was released. The million-selling album featured tracks by a number of leading hip hop artists including Ol' Dirty Bastard, Ice Cube, Jay-Z, Soulja Slim, Master P, Mystikal and Snoop Doggy Dogg. The album was highlighted by the hit single, "I Got The Hook-Up!" by Master P featuring Sons Of Funk.

2011: Following a nationwide vote, Gold's Gym announced that the track "Stronger" by Kanye West was "the greatest workout song of all time." The other songs to reach the final four were "Lose Yourself" by Eminem, "Boom Boom Pow" by the Black Eyed Peas and "Welcome To The Jungle" by Guns N' Roses.

APRIL 8

1991: The British group Massive Attack released their debut album, *Blue Lines*. The critically-acclaimed album helped to define the "trip hop" genre which combined rap, reggae and electronic music. The album was highlighted by the tracks, "Unfinished Sympathy" and "Safe From Harm."

1998: Ice Cube directed and starred in the comedy-drama film, *Player's Club*. He portrayed a poverty-stricken pimp named Reggie. The film's hit soundtrack featured tracks by Ice Cube, Master P, DMX, Jay-Z and others.

1999: Kid Rock released his signature hit single, "Bawitdaba." The rap-rock track sampled "Rapper's Delight" by the Sugarhill Gang, "Making Cash Money" by Busy Bee and "Rocket In My Pocket" by Cerrone. The song was nominated for a Grammy in the category of Best Hard Rock Performance.

2003: Lil' Kim released the single, "Magic Stick" (featuring 50 Cent). The track sampled "It Be's That Way Sometimes" by Joe Simon. "Magic Stick" was original intended for 50 Cent's album *Get Rich Or Die Tryin'*. Lil' Kim and 50 Cent recorded a sequel to the song in 2008, "Wanna Lick (Magic Stick, Pt. 2)."

2006: Mary J. Blige was the musical guest on *Saturday Night Live*. She performed "Be Without You" and "Enough Cryin."

2009: Kanye West was parodied on *South Park*. On an episode titled "Fishsticks," a cartoon version of the rapper was the only person in America who didn't understand a joke told by the character, Jimmy.

2016: N.W.A. were inducted into the Rock and Roll Hall of Fame. Inducted were Eazy-E, Dr. Dre, Ice Cube, MC Ren and DJ Yella.

APRIL 9

1991: Ed O.G. & Da Bulldogs released the hit single, "I Got To Have It." The song sampled "Singing A Song For My Mother" by Hamilton Bohannon and "I Don't Want Nobody To Give Me Nothing (Open Up The Door I'll Get It Myself)" by James Brown.

1992: Dr. Dre released his first solo single after the breakup of N.W.A., "Deep Cover." Also known by its alternative title "187," the single marked the recording debut of guest artist Snoop Doggy Dogg. The track was included on the soundtrack album of the Laurence Fishburne film, *Deep Cover*.

1993: Tupac Shakur began a ten-day prison sentence after he was convicted of striking a fellow rapper with a baseball bat at a concert in Lansing, Michigan.

2005: MC Kenzie of the British pop/hip hop group Blazin' Squad published his autobiography, *Kenzie: My Life*.

2008: A DMX concert at the Lambda Chi Alpha fraternity house on the campus of Indiana University ended after just three songs. The performance was stopped after an unknown assailant unleashed either mace or pepper spray on the unruly crowd.

2014: Chicago rapper Blood Money (real name Mario Hess) was killed by gunfire at the age of 30. He was the cousin of rapper Chief Keef. Blood Money (also known as Big Glo) had signed with Interscope just two weeks before his death.

APRIL 10

1970: Q-Tip (birth name Kamaal Ibn John Fareed) was born in Queens, New York. A producer and rapper, he initially found success as a member of A Tribe Called Quest.

1985: The Beastie Boys began a two-month tour as the opening act for Madonna on her "The Virgin Tour." A mismatched pairing, the rap group was not well received by most of Madonna's audiences. The tour began at the Paramount Theatre in Seattle and ended on June 11 at Madison Square Garden in New York City.

1990: Public Enemy released their best-selling album, *Fear Of A Black Planet*. The album spawned the singles, "Fight The Power," "Welcome To The Terrordome," "911 Is A Joke," "Brothers Gonna Work It Out" and "Can't Do Nuttin' For Ya Man." The track "Fight The Power" was popularized by its prominent placement in the Spike Lee film, *Do The Right Thing*. The album sold two-million copies in the U.S. and was nominated for a Grammy in the category of Best Rap Performance by a Duo or Group.

1992: LL Cool J portrayed a former NFL player in his first televison series, *In The House*. The program co-starred Debbie Allen for the first season. The series ran for five seasons, one season on NBC and four seasons on UPN.

1999: TLC began a four-week run at number-one on the U.S. singles chart with "No Scrubs."

1999: Jay-Z released the Grammy-nominated hit single, "Big Pimpin'." The song, which was produced by Timbaland, featured the Southern hip hop duo UGK. Jay-Z and Timbaland were later sued over the use of a sample from a 1960 Egyptian song.

2002: Texas-born rapper Big Lurch murdered a female friend at her apartment in Los Angeles. He was allegedly high on PCP at the time and was found roaming the streets with blood all over his face and clothing. Although he pleaded not guilty by reason of insanity, he was convicted of murder and aggravated mayhem, and was sentenced to life in prison.

2014: Anthony "Treach" Criss of the group Naughty By Nature was arrested in Union City, New Jersey, after he tried to elude police. He was allegedly clocked going 55-mph in a 25-mph speed zone. He was charged with multiple counts and released after posting a $15,000 bond.

2015: Nelly was arrested after his tour bus was stopped by authorities in Putman County, Tennessee. After searching the vehicle, state troopers found a number of handguns as well as methamphetamine and marijuana. Nelly was released the following day after posting bail.

APRIL 11

1992: Markie Dee, a former member of the Fat Boys, released his first solo album, *Free*. The album was highlighted by the single, "Typical Reasons (Swing My Way)."

1997: Ice Cube and Jennifer Lopez starred in the horror film, *Anaconda*. The movie earned more than $135 million at the box office and spawned a number of sequels.

2006: Proof (real name DeShaun Dupree Holton) was killed in a nightclub shooting. He was shot four times at the CCC nightclub in Detroit. Keith Bender, a man shot by Proof during the altercation, died a week later. A childhood friend of Eminem, Proof was a member of the group D12.

2010: The reality series, *Brandy and Ray J: A Family Business*, debuted on the VH-1 network. The program starred Brandy Norwood, her brother Ray "Ray J" Norwood and their parents. A number of rappers appeared on the program including Shorty Mack, Timbaland, the Game, Rodney Jerkins, Tyrese, Flo Rida, Kelly Rowland, Ludacris and Gucci Mane. The series ran for two seasons.

2010: The reality series, *What Chilli Wants*, debuted on the VH-1 network. The program starred Rozonda "Chilli" Thomas of the group TLC and relationship advisor Tionna T. Smalls. The series ran for two seasons.

2012: Akon was the subject of an episode of the VH-1 program, *Behind The Music*.

2013: Reebok cancelled a shoe deal with rapper Rick Ross due to a controversy over song lyrics. On the track "U.O.E.N.O." by Atlanta rapper Rocko, Ross performed a rap about using the drug Molly (also known as MDMA) to date-rape a woman. Ross made a public apology the following day: "To every woman that has felt the sting of abuse, I apologize."

APRIL 12

1967: Mellow Man Ace (birth name Ulpiano Sergio Reyes) was born in Pinar del Río, Cuba, but was raised in New Jersey and California. He is best known for the 1989 hit single, "Mentirosa." He was also a member of the hip hop group DVX, which was renamed to Cypress Hill after his departure.

1988: Boogie Down Productions released their influential hit single, "My Philosophy." As one of the first socially and politically conscious songs in rap music, it would change the direction of the genre.

1997: The Fugees played the first of two fundraising concerts in Haiti. Unfortunately, the cost of staging the concerts exceeded the amount of money that was raised.

2005: The Black Eyed Peas released "Don't Phunk With My Heart," the debut single from their album, *Monkey Business*. The song's music video parodied a number of game shows from the 1970s and '80s.

2008: Gnarls Barkley were the musical guests on *Saturday Night Live*. They performed "Run (I'm A Natural Disaster)" and "Who's Gonna Save My Soul."

2010: Cali Swag District released the track, "Teach Me How To Dougie." The hit song spawned a major dance craze, "The Dougie," which took its name from rapper Doug E. Fresh. The dance was initially popularized by Dallas-based rapper Lil' Wil with the release of his 2007 single, "My Dougie."

2012: The program *Hip Hop POV* debuted on the MTV network. The show featured news, interviews and commentary, and was hosted by Amanda Seales, Charlamagne, Bu Thiam, Devi Dev and Sowmya Krishnamurthy. The program lasted just several episodes before it evolved into another series, *This Week In Jams*, which aired on the MTV2 network.

2012: Kanye West staged a surprise, free concert in Yerevan, the capital city of Armenia. West was visiting the country with his wife, Kim Kardashian, for a week-long vacation. Kardashian's father was of Armenian descent.

2015: British radio deejay Mike Allen passed away at the age of 63. From 1984 to 1987, he hosted a pioneering hip hop show on Capital Radio in London. He was also instrumental in organizing the UK Fresh '86 concert at Wembley Arena, which brought American rappers and break dancers to Britain.

APRIL 13

1985: Ty Dolla $ign (birth name Tyrone William Griffin, Jr.) was born in Los Angeles. Signed to Atlantic Records, he scored his breakthrough solo hit in 2013 with "Paranoid." His father, Tyrone Griffin, Sr., was a member of the R&B group Lakeside.

1985: Doug E. Fresh and the Get Fresh Crew released the hit single, "The Show." The track sampled the theme of the cartoon series, *Inspector Gadget*. In the original version of the song, Slick Rick sang a verse of the Beatles classic "Michelle," which he later removed due to copyright issues. "The Show" was later featured in the film, *New Jack City*.

1989: At the 3rd annual Soul Train Music Awards which were staged in Los Angeles, *He's The DJ, I'm The Rapper* by DJ Jazzy Jeff and the Fresh Prince won the award for Best Rap Album.

2001: Lil' Romeo released the hit single, "My Baby," from his debut album, *Lil' Romeo*. The track sampled "I Want You Back" by the Jackson 5. At age 11, Lil' Romeo became the youngest performer in history to top the *Billboard* pop chart, breaking the record set by Michael Jackson.

APRIL 14

1974: Da Brat (birth name Shawntae Harris) was born in Joliet, Illinois, and raised in Chicago. In 1994, her debut release, *Funkdafied,* became the first album by a solo, female hip hop artist to be certified platinum for sales of one-million copies.

2000: The documentary, *Freestyle: The Art Of Rhyme*, explored the rise of musical rhyming from the black church to the streets of New York City. The film featured a number MCs including Supernatural, Cut Chemist, Black Thought and Mos Def.

2001: Eve was the musical guest on *Saturday Night Live*. She performed "Let Me Blow Ya Mind" (with Gwen Stefani) and "Who's That Girl?"

2005: Civil rights pioneer Rosa Parks settled her lawsuit against OutKast and their label LaFace Records over the unauthorized use of her name in the hip hop duo's 1998 hit song, "Rosa Parks." Parks received an undisclosed financial settlement.

2005: Sean "Diddy" Combs sold 50-percent of his record label, Bad Boy Entertainment, to Warner Music Group for a reported $30 million. Combs continued to serve as the label's CEO.

2008: The reality program, *Miss Rap Supreme*, debuted on the VH-1 network. Created by *Ego Trip* magazine and hosted by MC Serch and Yo-Yo, the program pitted ten aspiring female rappers against each other for the opportunity to win a $100,000 grand prize. The series ran for eight episodes with Rece Steele selected as the winner. (Khia, the first contestant to be eliminated, was the only contestant to find commercial success.) A number of celebrity guests appeared on the program including Too $hort, Ghostface Killah, Missy Elliott, Roxanne Shanté and will.i.am.

2012: The Beastie Boys were inducted into the Rock and Roll Hall Fame. At the induction ceremony, the group performed "No Sleep Till Brooklyn," "The New Style," "So What'cha Want," "Rhymin & Stealin" and "Sabotage." The event was staged at Public Hall in Cleveland.

2013: Grammy-winning hip hop producer Patrick Douthit – better known as 9th Wonder – announced the establishment of the Hip-Hop Institute at North Carolina Central University.

APRIL 15

1983: *Flashdance* was the first Hollywood film to feature break dancing. The film included a 90-second scene that spotlighted Rock Steady Crew, a group of talented b-boys from the Bronx. The film helped to spawn a break dancing craze across the country.

1988: Latin rapper Gerardo (of "Rico Suave" fame) appeared in the Sean Penn film, *Colors*.

1989: Eric B. & Rakim scored their only top-40 crossover hit when they appeared as featured artists on the single "Friends" by R&B singer Jody Watley.

1990: The comedy program *In Living Color* premiered on the Fox network. The program served as a platform for performances by many of the leading names in hip hop including Shabba Ranks, Gang Starr, Public Enemy, Eazy-E, Heavy D & The Boyz and Naughty By Nature.

1991: Kool Moe Dee released the single, "Rise 'n' Shine" (featuring KRS-One and Chuck D). The track sampled "Outa-Space" by Billy Preston, "Stand!" by Sly & The Family Stone and "Little Old Money Maker" by the Meters.

1994: Ice-T co-starred in the action-thriller film, *Surviving The Game*. The rapper played the role of Jack Mason, a depressed homeless man who lost his wife and child.

1995: Montell Jordan began a seven-week run at number-one on the U.S. singles chart with "This Is How We Do It."

1995: Redman and Method Man released their first of many collaborative hits, "How High." The track was featured on the soundtrack of the hip hop documentary, *The Show*. A remixed version of the song was later included on their first collaborative album, *Blackout!*

1999: City Spud (real name Lavell Webb) of the St. Lunatics was arrested for his involvement in a violent robbery. He served a nine-year prison sentence. Before going to jail, he contributed to Nelly's breakthrough album, *Country Grammar*.

2000: Sisqó was the musical guest on *Saturday Night Live*. He performed "The Thong Song."

2003: The documentary, *50 Cent: The New Breed*, was released. This was the first project from G-Unit Films, a division formed by 50 Cent and Interscope Records.

2004: G-Unit member Lloyd Banks released his debut solo single, "On Fire." The track featured uncredited vocals by 50 Cent and was co-produced by Eminem. The song's music video included cameo appearances by fellow G-Unit members, the Game, 50 Cent and Young Buck.

2005: Philadelphia rapper Cassidy (real name Barry Reese) was involved in a shooting that left one man dead and two others injured. He was initially charged with murder. Convicted of involuntary manslaughter, he was sentenced to an 11½ to 23 month prison term. He spent eight-months behind bars.

2005: Wyclef Jean appeared in the first of four episodes of the hit NBC program, *Third Watch*. He portrayed a vicious gang leader named Marcel Hollis.

2011: A concert headlined by Pitbull and Yelawolf at Rutgers University ended in violence. Nearly 50,000 fans had attended the concert in New Brunswick, Jersey, as part of the annual day-long Rutgersfest, which marked the end of the school year. As a result of the incident, school officials permanently cancelled Rutgerfest.

2012: A hologram of Tupac Shakur "performed" at the Coachella Festival in Indio, California. Shakur's hologram was joined onstage by Snoop Dogg. A few days later, Suge Knight protested the fact that the Shakur hologram was not wearing a Death Row chain.

2014: Flavor Flav pleaded guilty to misdemeanor domestic violence charges in a Las Vegas courtroom. He was accused of assaulting his fiancee. The rapper reached a plea deal in order to avoid a trial. He was sentenced to one-year of probation and ordered to attend counseling sessions.

APRIL 16

1955: Pioneering rapper DJ Kool Herc (birth name Clive Campbell) was born in Kingston, Jamaica. He moved with his family to New York City at age 12. Often called the founder of hip hop music, he originated the practice of rapping over the instrumental "breaks" of records during the early-1970s. He based his technique on the toasting-style deejays of his native Jamaica.

1965: Gerardo (birth name Gerardo Mejía) was born in Ecuador but raised in California. He is best known for the 1991 hit single, "Rico Suave."

1984: Nearly eight-years before she would join the Black Eyed Peas, Fergie provided the voice of Sally in the Charlie Brown animated film, *It's Flashbeagle*. The following year, she provided the voice of Sally for the film, *Snoopy's Getting Married, Charlie Brown*.

1993: German eurodance group Culture Beat scored a worldwide hit with "Mr. Vain." The rapping in the song was provided by Jay Supreme.

1996: Master P released his breakthrough album, *Ice Cream Man*. The project spawned three singles, "Mr. Ice Cream Man," "Bout It Bout It Pt II" and "No More Tears." The album was released on Master P's own label, No Limit Records, and sold nearly two-million copies in the U.S.

1999: Sean "Puffy" Combs and two associates were charged in the assault of Steve Stoute, an executive at Interscope Records. Combs and Stoute were involved in a physical altercation on the previous day after arguing about a music video. A court later ordered Combs to attend anger management classes.

2002: Nelly released the single, "Hot In Herre." The track sampled "Bustin' Loose" by Chuck Brown, "There's A World" by Neil Young and "As Tears Go By" by Nancy Sinatra. A major hit, "Hot In Herre" won a Grammy in the category of Best Male Rap Solo Performance.

2014: Wu-Tang Clan-affiliated rapper Christ Bearer (real name Andre Johnson) cut off his own penis after jumping from the second-story balcony of his home in North Hollywood, California. He later admitted that he was under the influence of PCP and other drugs at the time.

2014: Drake was sued by the estate of the late jazz pianist Jimmy Smith over the unauthorized use of a 35-second spoken-word sample from the 1982 track "Jimmy Smith Rap." The sample was featured on Drake's hit song, "Pound Cake/Paris Morton Music 2."

APRIL 17

1957: Afrika Bambaataa (birth name Kevin Donovan) was born in the Bronx, New York. A rap pioneer with roots in funk and electronic music, he is best known for the hit, "Planet Rock." As the leader of the Universal Zulu Nation, he introduced the term "hip hop" in 1974. He declared that the "Four Elements" of hip hop were DJing, Breaking, Graffiti Artists and MCing.

1968: K-Solo (birth name Kevin Madison) was born in the Bronx, New York. After a stint in the hip hop group the Hit Squad, he pursued a solo career. Also known as Wolfgang Murder Mouth, he is best known for the hits, "Your Mom's In My Business" and "Spellbound."

1970: Redman (birth name Reginald Noble) was born in Newark, New Jersey. After signing with Def Jam Recordings, he released his debut album in 1992. He frequently collaborated with Method Man and was also a member of the rap supergroup Def Squad.

1982: Afrika Bambaataa & Soul Sonic Force released the pioneering hip hop classic, "Planet Rock." The track featured uncredited samples or interpolations from two songs by the German electronic group Kraftwerk, "Trans Europe Express" and "Numbers." Although the single was a major hit in New York City, where it sold nearly 700,000 copies, it failed to the reach the national top-40.

1990: After leaving N.W.A. the previous year over a royalty dispute, Ice Cube released the solo single, "AmeriKKKa's Most Wanted," which appeared on the album of the same name. The politically-charged song received only limited airplay at the time. The track sampled "Humpin'" by the Bar-Kays, "Let The Music Take Your Mind" by Kool & The Gang, "There It Is" by James Brown and "Advice" by Sly & The Family Stone.

1997: The crime drama series, *Players,* debuted on the NBC network. The program starred Ice-T, who played the role of Isaac "Ice" Gregory, an ex-convict who was hired by the FBI. The series ran for one season.

2001: J Records, a label owned by Clive Davis, released its first album, *Olivia* by Olivia Longott. The label would enjoy success with a number of R&B and hip hop acts including Alicia Keys, Lyric, O-Town, D'Angelo, Luther Vandross, Jamie Foxx and Monica.

2003: Harvard University co-sponsored the academic symposium, "All Eyez On Me: Tupac Shakur And The Search For The Modern Folk Hero."

2010: Ke$ha was the musical guest on *Saturday Night Live*. She performed "Tik Tok" and "Your Love Is My Drug."

2012: Kanye West revealed his feelings for Kim Kardashian in the song, "Cold" (featuring DJ Khaled). The song was originally titled "Theraflu" and was also known as "Way Too Cold."

2014: Stormey Ramdhan, the former girlfriend of Suge Knight, published the book, *My Life With The Knight*, which detailed the rap mogul's turbulent history while running the Death Row Records empire.

APRIL 18

1961: Grandmaster Caz (birth name Curtis Fisher) was born in the Bronx, New York. A hip hop pioneer, he was possibly the first person to incorporate spoken rhymes in rap music. He later joined the Cold Crush Brothers.

1967: Todd Terry was born in Brooklyn, New York. A rapper and producer, he enjoyed success in the U.K. with hits such as "Something Goin' On" and "Keep On Jumpin'."

1997: The estate of Tupac Shakur – led by his mother Afeni Shakur and attorney Richard S. Fischbein – filed a federal lawsuit against Death Row Records, Marion "Suge" Knight and the label's attorney, seeking damages of $150 million, back royalties and a formal accounting of the late rapper's music sales. According to *The Los Angeles Times*, despite selling more than $60 million worth of music in 1996, Shakur owed $4.9 million to Death Row Records at the time of his death.

1999: TLC was the subject of an episode of the VH-1 program, *Behind The Music*.

2003: Reebok introduced Jay-Z's first signature brand of athletic shoes, the S. Carter Collection. The rapper celebrated the launch with a personal appearance at a Foot Locker store in Philadelphia.

2005: Reebok stopped running a British television commercial starring 50 Cent after receiving complaints that the ad glamorized gun crimes. In the commercial, the rapper slowly counted to nine, a reference to the nine times he was shot during an attack in 2000.

2006: In the MTV top-10 ranking of "The Greatest MCs of All Time," Jay-Z topped the list at number-one. At number-two was Tupac Shakur.

2009: The Black Eyes Peas began a remarkable twelve-week run at number-one on the U.S. singles chart with "Boom Boom Pow."

2011: Rapper/producer David Banner teamed with British singers Estelle and Daley to record a single for Mercedes-Benz. The track, "Benz," was a reworked rendition of the final song recorded by Janis Joplin before her death in 1970, "Mercedes Benz."

2012: Nas was the subject of an episode of the VH-1 program, *Behind The Music*.

2013: Public Enemy was inducted into the Rock and Roll Hall of Fame. Inducted were Flavor Flav (real name William Drayton), Professor Griff (real name Richard Griffin), Terminator X (real name Norman Lee Rogers) and Chuck D (real name Carlton Ridenhour). After a long, rambling 20-minute speech by Flavor Flav – who joked about donating his clock to the Rock Hall – Public Enemy performed "Bring The Noise," "911 Is A Joke" and "Fight The Power."

APRIL 19

1965: Suge Knight (birth name Marion Hugh Knight, Jr.) was born in Compton, California. A prominent music mogul, he co-founded Death Row Records in 1991. An outspoken and often brash icon in the hip hop community, he was involved in several high-profile brushes with the law.

1994: Nas released his solo album, *Illmatic*. The album spawned five singles: "Halftime," "It Ain't Hard to Tell," "Life's A Bitch," "The World Is Yours" and "One Love." The album sold one-million copies in the U.S.

1999: The hip hop trio Sporty Thievz released the single "No Pigeons," which was a parody of TLC's hit "No Scrubs."

2000: Dr. Dre was sued by Lucasfilm Ltd., which was owned by filmmaker George Lucas, over the use of a trademarked sound – the THX Deep Note – which appeared at the beginning of the rapper's album, *Dr. Dre 2001*. The matter was settled out of court.

2008: KRS-One was injured during a stop on his "Stop The Violence" concert and speaking tour. During a nightclub performance in New Haven, Connecticut, the rapper suffered a broken hand after he was struck by a bottle that was thrown at the stage by a member of the audience. KRS-One was forced to cancel the next several dates of the tour.

2010: Guru (real name Keith Elam) of the duo Gang Starr passed away. He suffered a heart attack while battling cancer. Falling into a coma, he died two months later. He was 48-years-old.

2011: Albert "Prodigy" Johnson published the book, *My Infamous Life: The Autobiography Of Mobb Deep's Prodigy*.

2011: The Black Eyed Peas announced the creation of a school to teach video and music production skills. The Peapod Adobe Youth Voices music and multimedia academy opened in Manhattan.

2011: Dr. Dre won a lawsuit against WIDEawake/Death Row Records for selling digital copies of his 1992 hit album, *The Chronic*, without permission. He also claimed that his former label had not paid him any royalties for the album since 1996.

APRIL 20

1994: Bone Thugs-N-Harmony released their debut single, "Thuggish Ruggish Bone" (featuring Shatasha Williams). The track sampled "Mama Used To Say" by Junior. The song's music video featured an appearance by the group's early mentor, Eazy-E. The group's breakthrough hit, it sold two-million copies.

1999: Ma$e announced he was quitting his music career in order to follow God. The rapper became an ordained minister and took the name, Pastor Betha. In 2001, he established the Saving a Nation Endangered Ministries and held services in a hotel ballroom. But in 2004, he would return to his career as a rapper.

2001: Darryl "D.M.C." McDaniels published his autobiography, *King Of Rock: Respect, Responsibility, And My Life With Run-D.M.C.*

2008: VL Mike (real name Michael Allen) was shot and killed in New Orleans while exiting his vehicle. Before launching a solo career, he was a member of the Chopper City Boyz. He was 32-years-old.

2011: The Game was barred from entering Canada after customs officials accused the rapper of having ties to organized gangs. He was traveling to the country for the start of a concert tour.

2011: DJ Khaled released the track, "I'm On One" (featuring Drake, Rick Ross and Lil Wayne). This was Khaled's first top-40 pop hit. The song was nominated for a Grammy in the category of Best Rap/Sung Collaboration.

2012: Snoop Dogg teamed with country music legend Willie Nelson on the pro-marijuana single, "Roll Me Up And Smoke Me When I Die." Also appearing on the track were Kris Kristofferson and Jamey Johnson.

2012: Marion "Suge" Knight told a radio interviewer on KDAY in Los Angeles that Tupac Shakur could still be alive. The comment ignited a number of conspiracy theories.

2015: Big Sean broke up with girlfriend Ariana Grande, following an eight-month relationship.

APRIL 21

1998: Snoop Dogg starred in the drama film, *Da Game Of Life*. The film was written and produced by Snoop Dogg and Master P.

2001: Nick Cannon won the award for Favorite TV Actor at the 2001 Kids' Choice Awards which aired on the Nickelodeon network.

2006: The first annual Trinity International Hip Hop Festival was staged at Trinity College in Hartford, Connecticut. The guest speakers included Fab 5 Freddy and Charlie Ahern, the director of the hip hop film, *Wild Style*.

2014: Big Sean and Ariana Grande became the first rappers to perform at an official White House event when they took the stage at the annual Easter Egg Roll.

2014: Iggy Azalea released her debut album, *The New Classic*. The album spawned five singles: "Work," "Bounce," "Change Your Life," "Black Widow" and the smash hit "Fancy." The album earned four Grammy nominations in the categories of Best New Artist, Record of the Year, Best Rap Album and Best Pop Duo/Group Performance for track "Fancy."

2015: Brad "Scarface" Jordan published his autobiography, *Diary Of A Madman: The Geto Boys, Life, Death, And The Roots Of Southern Rap*.

APRIL 22

1978: DJ Drama (birth name Tyree Cinque Simmons) was born in Philadelphia. The rapper released his debut solo album in 2008, *Gangsta Grillz: The Album*. Also an entrepreneur, he co-founded the label, Aphilliates Music Group. He later joined the A&R department of Atlantic Records.

1990: Machine Gun Kelly (birth name Richard Colson Baker) was born in Houston but raised in suburban Cleveland. Signing with Bad Boys Records, MGK released his debut EP in 2012, *Half Naked & Almost Famous*. Also an actor, he made his film debut in the 2014 release, *Beyond The Lights*.

2007: Warren G and Da Brat were contestants on the fifth season of the VH-1 series, *Celebrity Fit Club*. Both rappers lost to former *Brady Bunch* actress Maureen McCormick.

2014: Fetty Wap released his debut single, "Trap Queen."A sizable hit, the song earned two Grammy nominations in the categories of Best Rap Song and Best Rap Performance. The song's music video was filmed in the rapper's hometown of Paterson, New Jersey.

2015: While still in bankruptcy court, 50 Cent announced that he would place his mansion up for sale. Located in Farmington, Rhode Island, the 51,000-square-foot dwelling was situated on 18 acres and boasted 21 bedrooms, 37 bathrooms and a large disco. The estate sold the following year for $8 million.

APRIL 23

1993: Former MTV veejays Ed Lover and Doctor Dré (not to be confused with Dr. Dre of N.W.A.) starred in the comedy film, *Who's The Man?* Lover and Dré portrayed a pair of barbers who became police officers. The film featured appearances by numerous hip hop artists including House Of Pain, Busta Rhymes, Cheryl "Salt" James, Bushwick Bill, Guru, Eric B., Kris Kross, Ice-T, Queen Latifah, KRS-One and Run-D.M.C.

1993: DJ Subroc (real name Dingilizwe Dumile) of the hip hop groups KMD and Constipated Monkey was killed while attempting to cross the Long Island Expressway. He was 19-years-old.

2008: Lil Wayne released the single, "A Milli." The track sampled "Don't Burn Down The Bridge" by Gladys Knight & The Pips, "Go Crazy (Remix)" by Young Jeezy and "I Left My Wallet In El Segundo (Vampire Mix)" by A Tribe Called Quest. The song sold more than two-million copies in the U.S.

2011: Nick Cannon began hosting a syndicated, weekly radio program, *Cannon's Countdown*.

2012: Wiz Khalifa was arrested at a Nashville hotel on marijuana charges. According to the police report, Khalifa was observed throwing a joint out of a window. He was in the city for a headlining performance at Vanderbilt University.

APRIL 24

1998: Rapper Ol' Dirty Bastard announced that he had changed his stage name to "Big Baby Jesus." A few months later, he had a change of heart and reverted to his previous name.

2000: Rapper 50 Cent was shot multiple times while sitting in a car outside of his grandmother's home in the South Jamaica neighborhood of Queens, New York. He was hospitalized for 13 days and suffered some permanent injuries. The alleged shooter was shot and killed the following month. Several years later, 50 Cent recalled the attack in his autobiography: "After I got shot nine times at close range and didn't die, I started to think that I must have a purpose in life.... How much more damage could that shell have done? Give me an inch in this direction or that one, and I'm gone."

2009: T.I. (real name Clifford Harris) pleaded guilty to charges of attempting to purchase unregistered machine guns and silencers. He was sentenced to one-year and a day in prison.

APRIL 25

1955: Coke La Rock was born in the Bronx, New York. Possibly the very first MC in rap, he was an essential part of Kool Herc's crew beginning in 1973.

1989: Oaktown's 357, a female rap group formed by MC Hammer, released their debut album, *Wild & Loose*. All but one of the nine tracks on the album were written by MC Hammer. The group would record one more album before disbanding.

1990: Cypress Hill released their fifth album, *Skull & Bones*. The two-disc set featured hip hop music on one disc and rap-metal on the other. The project was highlighted by the singles, "(Rap) Superstar," "(Rock) Superstar" and the double-sided hit "Highlife" / "Can't Get The Best Of Me."

1992: The duo Kris Kross began an eight-week run at number-one on the U.S. singles chart with "Jump."

1995: Method Man scored a hit with the medley, "I'll Be There For You"/"You're All I Need To Get By," which featured Mary J. Blige. The track was a remixed version of "All I Need," which was included on Method Man's debut album, *Tical*. The medley won a Grammy in the category of Best Rap Performance by a Duo or Group.

2000: The Ying Yang Twins released their first hit single, "Whistle While You Twurk."

2002: Lisa "Left Eye" Lopes of the group TLC died in an auto accident in the town of La Ceiba, Honduras. After driving off the road to avoid another car, she was thrown from her vehicle and died at the scene. She was 30-years-old.

2011: DMX was arrested for driving 102-mph in a 65-mph zone in Maricopa County, Arizona. He was also charged with driving on a suspended license.

2012: Brandy was the subject of an episode of the VH-1 program, *Behind The Music*.

2012: Ca$h Out released the single, "Cashin' Out."

2014: The single "See You Again" by Wiz Khalifa featuring Charlie Puth began a remarkable twelve-week run at number-one on the U.S. charts.

APRIL 26

1981: British rapper/soul singer Ms. Dynamite (birth name Niomi Arleen McLean-Daley) was born in Archway, London, England. Originally known as Lady Dynamite, she released her debut album in 2002, *A Little Deeper*.

1994: Adam Horovitz of the Beastie Boys pleaded "no contest" to a misdemeanor battery charge. The previous November, he had attacked a television cameraman from *Hard Copy* during a memorial service for actor River Phoenix. Horovitz was sentenced to 200 hours of community service and ordered to pay a $200 fine.

1994: OutKast released their debut album, *Southernplayalisticadillacmuzik*. The project helped to popularize Southern hip hop in the 1990s. The million-selling album spawned the singles, "Player's Ball," "Southernplayalisticadillacmuzik" and "Git Up, Git Out." Both members of OutKast – André 3000 and Big Boi – were still in their teens when the album was released.

1995: Ice Cube co-wrote and starred in the crime-comedy film, *Friday*. The rapper played the role of Craig Jones, a resident of the South Central section of Los Angeles who was framed for a crime he did not commit. The film spawned a number of sequels: *Next Friday*, *Friday After Next* and *Last Friday*.

2003: The Hip-Hop Summit Action Network staged an event at Cobo Hall in Detroit, which drew 13,000 participants. Among the speakers were Eminem, the Rev. Run and Doug E. Fresh. The theme of the summit was "Remix: Rebuilding, Refocusing, Reinvesting, Resurgence."

2006: Brooklyn-based rapper Gravy (real name Jamal Woolard) was shot in the rear end while enroute to the studios of New York City radio station, Hot 97. Despite his injuries, he arrived at the station for his scheduled interview. (Gravy was later selected to play the lead role in the film biography of the Notorious B.I.G., *Notorious*.)

2007: Snoop Dogg was scheduled to co-host the MTV Australian Music Video Awards, but was banned from entering the country after "failing a character test."

2011: Cee Lo Green was hired as one of the original judges on the television singing competition, *The Voice*. He left the program after season three in 2014, shortly after he was charged with giving a woman the drug ecstasy.

2013: Nas opened his own sneaker store in Las Vegas, 12AM: RUN. The shop was located in the Caesars Casino Linq district and stocked higher end sports shoes including a new line called High Rollers.

2015: Jimmy Winfrey (also known as Peewee Roscoe) fired multiple shots into two tour buses owned by Lil Wayne. Winfrey was in his Camaro on Interstate-285 in Atlanta when he fired at the buses, causing more than $20,000 in damages. He was charged with multiple counts including aggravated assault, criminal damage, possession of a firearm by a felon and criminal gang activity. He later pleaded guilty to a total of six charges and was sentenced to ten-years in prison.

APRIL 27

1999: The female R&B/hip hop group 702 released the single, "Where My Girls At?" The original version of the song was recorded by TLC who decided not to include it on their third album, *FanMail*.

2001: Mary J. Blige and rapper Q-Tip starred in the drama film, *Prison Song*. A number of other musical acts also appeared in the film including Fat Joe, N.O.R.E. and Snow.

2004: Jay-Z released his smash hit single, "99 Problems." In the much-analyzed second verse of the song, Jay-Z described an alleged real-life incident in which he was pulled over by police in New Jersey who nearly found the cocaine he had hidden in the sunroof of his car. The track was named the #2 song of the decade, 2000 to 2010, by *Rolling Stone* magazine and won a Grammy in the category of Best Rap Solo Performance. The original version of the song was recorded by Ice-T and included on his 1993 album, *Home Invasion*.

2004: D12 released their second album, *D12 World*. The album was highlighted by the tracks, "My Band," "How Come" and "American Psycho II" (featuring B-Real). This was the final album to feature D12 member Proof before his death in 2006.

2014: DJ E-Z Rock (real name Rodney Bryce) died after suffering a diabetic seizure. He was best known for his collaborative hit with Rob Base, "It Takes Two." He was 46-years-old.

APRIL 28

1966: Too $hort (birth name Todd Anthony Shaw) was born in the South Central district of Los Angeles. After releasing his debut album in 1983, he teamed with fellow rapper Freddie B to launch the record label, Dangerous Music.

1972: Violent J (birth name Joseph Bruce) was born in Berkley, Michigan. In the early-1990s, he teamed with Shaggy 2 Dope (birth name Joseph William Utsler) to form the horror-core hip hop group, Insane Clown Posse. The group's loyal fans are known as Juggalos.

1994: Warren G and Nate Dogg released the hit single, "Regulate." The track had originally appeared on the soundtrack of the film, *Above The Rim,* and was later included on Warren G's debut album, *Regulate...G Funk Era.* The song was built upon a sample of "I Keep Forgettin' (Every Time You're Near)" by Michael McDonald. "Regulate" was nominated for a Grammy in the category of Best Rap Performance By A Duo Or Group.

1998: Silkk The Shocker released the crossover hit single, "It Ain't My Fault." The track featured backing vocals by Mystikal.

1998: Big Pun released his debut solo album, *Capital Punishment.* The album featured the hit singles, "I'm Not A Player," "Still Not A Player" and "You Came Up." The million-selling album earned a Grammy nomination in the category of Best Rap Album.

2011: Chidera "Chiddy" Anamege set the world record for the longest freestyle rap. He rapped, non-stop, for a period of nine hours, 18 minutes and 22 seconds. He broke a record that had been set by Indianapolis-based rapper, M-Eighty.

2014: Ariana Grande released "Problem," the debut single from her second album, *My Everything.* The track featured a verse by Iggy Azalea and the backing vocals of Big Sean. The song's music video won the award for Best Pop Video at the MTV Video Music Awards.

APRIL 29

1967: Rapper and entertainment media mogul Master P (birth name Percy Robert Miller) was born in New Orleans. He is the founder and CEO of P. Miller Enterprises as well as the founder of No Limit Records (which was later renamed New No Limit Records, Guttar Music Entertainment and, finally, No Limit Forever Records). He is the brother of rappers C-Murder and Silkk the Shocker, and the uncle of Romeo Miller (Lil Romeo) and Cymphonique Miller.

1986: Whodini released their third album, *Back In Black.* The million-selling album was highlighted by the singles, "Funky Beat," "Growing Up" and "One Love."

1995: Tupac Shakur married his girlfriend Keisha Morris. The ceremony took place while he was serving a prison sentence at the Clinton Correctional Facility in New York. The marriage was annulled 10 months later.

2002: The VH-1 network aired the documentary, *Uprising: Hip-Hop & The L.A. Riots,* on the 20th anniversary of the violence that followed a jury's not guilty verdict in the Rodney King beating trial. A number of rappers were featured in the film including Eazy-E, Dr. Dre and Ice-T.

2003: 50 Cent released the single, "21 Questions" (featuring Nate Dogg). The track sampled elements of "It's Only Love Doing Its Thing." The song's music video featured appearances by G-Unit and Nate Dogg.

2010: Eminem released the gospel-influenced track, "Not Afraid." The single sold more than ten-million copies.

APRIL 30

1958: Wonder Mike (birth name Michael Anthony Wright) of the pioneering rap group, the Sugarhill Gang, was born in New York City.

1982: Lloyd Banks (birth name Christopher Charles Lloyd) was born in New Carrollton, Maryland, but raised in Queens, New York. A member of the hip hop group G-Unit, he often worked with longtime friends Tony Yayo and 50 Cent. Pursuing a solo career, Banks released his debut album in 2004, *The Hunger For More*.

1999: MTV filmed the special, *MTV's 25 Most Lame Videos*, which was hosted by Jon Stewart, Denis Leary, Chris Kattan and Janeane Garofalo. A total of three rap videos appeared in the top-10: "Ice Ice Baby" by Vanilla Ice, "Girl You Know It's True" by Milli Vanilli and "Rico Suave" by Gerardo. But when Vanilla Ice appeared on the program and was asked to destroy a copy of his music video, he instead smashed up the entire set with a baseball bat.

2000: Kid Rock and Joe C. portrayed cartoon versions of themselves on an episode of *The Simpsons*.

2008: Jay-Z signed a 10-year deal with Live Nation that was reportedly worth $150 million. The arrangement gave Live Nation a portion of Jay-Z's album and concert sales as well as access to his business ventures.

2008: Nick Cannon married Mariah Carey in a private ceremony at her $5 million estate on Windermere Island in the Bahamas. According to *People* magazine, Cannon's relatives were "upset they weren't invited and didn't even know about the wedding. They were shocked they had to hear about it secondhand." At the time, Cannon was 27 and Carey was 38. The marriage lasted six years.

2009: R&B singer Kelis filed for divorce from rapper Nas in a Los Angeles court. She was seven-months pregnant at the time. The couple had been together for seven years.

2011: Nick Cannon and Mariah Carey welcomed the birth of fraternal twins, Monroe and Moroccan.

▶ MAY

MAY 1

1990: The German electronic/dance group Snap! released the crossover hit single, "Ooops Up." The song was a reworked rendition of the Gap Band's 1980 hit, "I Don't Believe You Want To Get Up And Dance (Ooops!)." The song featured the vocals of Penny Ford and a rap by Turbo B. Penny Ford was also a backup singer on the Gap Band's recording of the song.

1991: The acoustic-based concert series, *Yo! Unplugged Rap*, debuted on MTV. The program was similar to the series, *MTV Unplugged*. The first episode of *Yo! Unplugged Rap* showcased performances by LL Cool J, De La Soul, MC Lyte and A Tribe Called Quest. The highlight of the evening was LL Cool J's rendition of "Mama Said Knock You Out."

1997: A car rental company in Beverly Hills, California, was forced to cancel an auction of a bullet-ridden door from the vehicle in which the Notorious B.I.G. had been killed. The police claimed they needed the door for evidence.

2002: Wyclef Jean starred in a television commercial for Virgin Mobile cell phones. He starred in a second Virgin Mobile commercial later that same year.

2004: Usher was the musical guest on *Saturday Night Live*. He performed "Yeah!" and "Burn."

2006: Big Hawk (real name John Edward Hawkins) was murdered in Houston. The rapper was shot and killed by an unknown assailant. A solo artist who released several albums, he was also a member of the rap collective, the Screwed Up Click. He was 36-years-old.

2009: Black Eyed Peas member will.i.am played the role of a teleporting mutant named John Wraith in the hit film, *X-Men Origins: Wolverine*. The film earned nearly $180 million in the U.S.

2013: Will Smith starred in the science fiction film, *After Earth*. Smith played the role of Prime Commander Cypher Raige, who led a battle against alien creatures. Raige's son was played by Smith's real-life son, 15-year-old Jaden. The script was written by the team of Gary Whitta and director M. Night Shyamalan, and was based on a storyline by Will Smith. Grossing approximately $86 million worldwide, it was one of Smith's least successful efforts

2013: Mac Daddy (real name James Christopher Kelly) of the teenage rap duo, Kris Kross, was found dead at his home in Atlanta. The Fulton County Medical Examiner's Office attributed the death to a fatal mixture of drugs. Kris Kross were best known for their 1992 hit single, "Jump."

MAY 2

1995: Ol' Dirty Bastard released the single, "Shimmy Shimmy Ya." The song's music video was a tribute to the television show, *Soul Train*.

1996: Ed Lover and Doctor Dré published the book, *Naked Under Our Clothes: Unzipped, Uncut, And Totally Unplugged*.

1997: R. Kelly played his first game as a member of the semi-pro basketball team, the Atlantic City Seagulls of the United States Basketball League. The 6-foot-2 Kelly was the team's shooting guard.

1997: Bone Thugs-N-Harmony released the crossover hit single, "Look Into My Eyes," from their album *The Art Of War*. The track also appeared on the soundtrack album of the film, *Batman & Robin*. The single sold more than one-million copies in the U.S.

2007: Soulja Boy released the chart-topping, crossover hit single, "Crank That (Soulja Boy)" which launched the popular Soulja Boy Dance. The track was nominated for a Grammy in the category of Best Rap Song. "Crank That (Soulja Boy)" was the first song to sell three-million digital copies in the U.S.

2008: P. Diddy was awarded a star on the Hollywood Walk of Fame. The name on the star read "Sean Diddy Combs."

2010: Kanye West portrayed a fictional rapper named Kenny West on the animated television series, *The Cleveland Show*.

2015: Offset (real name Kiari Cephus) of the hip hop group Migos was charged with battery and inciting a riot within a correctional facility. At the time, he was awaiting a trial on charges of drug and weapons violations. After he was denied bail multiple times, the rapper later accepted a plea bargain deal that resulted in five years of probation and a $1,000 fine.

2015: Wiz Khalifa was the musical guest on *Saturday Night Live*. He performed "We Dem Boyz" and was joined by Charlie Puth on "See You Again."

MAY 3

1971: Damon Dash was born in New York City. An entrepreneur and music industry heavyweight, he was Jay-Z's manager and business partner at both Rocawear clothing and Roc-A-Fella Records. Dash was credited with discovering Kanye West, Beanie Sigel and Cam'ron.

1986: Often called the original "Gangster of Hip Hop," Bronx-based rapper Just-Ice (real name Joseph Williams) released his influential album, *Back To The Old School*. Just-Ice was backed on the album by human beatbox Cool DMX and producer Kurtis Mantronik. The album was highlighted by the tracks, "Cold Gettin' Dumb" and "Latoya."

1990: Luke featuring 2 Live Crew released the politically-charged crossover single, "Banned In The U.S.A." The song was meant as a response to the many attacks against the embattled group for their 1988 album, *As Nasty As They Wanna Be*. The track borrowed the melody of Bruce Springsteen's rock anthem, "Born In The U.S.A."

2003: 50 Cent was the musical guest on *Saturday Night Live*. He performed "In Da Club" with G-Unit and "21 Questions" with G-Unit and Nate Dogg.

2006: Philant Johnson, a member of T.I.'s touring entourage, was shot and killed in a hail of gunfire. Following an after-party at Club Ritz in Cincinnati, T.I. and Yung Joc drove away in a van. While on Interstate-75, the vehicle was struck by multiple gunshots. Johnson was killed and three passengers were wounded. Neither T.I. nor Yung Joc was injured. The shooter, Hosea Thomas, was angry over being denied entry to the nightclub's VIP area, where the two rappers were sitting. At his 2008 trial, Thomas was found guilty of murder and five counts of felonious assault, and was sentenced to 66-years to life in prison.

2013: Lil Wayne was dropped as a spokesman by Mountain Dew in response to the rapper's controversial lyrics on the track, "Karate Chop" by Future.

MAY 4

1984: Ice-T made his acting debut as a nightclub MC in the comedy-drama film, *Breakin'*. Set in Los Angeles, the film helped to popularize break dancing. The film's soundtrack album spawned two hit singles "Breakin'... There's No Stopping Us" by Ollie & Jerry and "Ain't Nobody" by Rufus and Chaka Khan.

1996: Tupac Shakur and Ice-T were the musical guests on the Fox network program, *Saturday Night Special*. They performed "Only God Can Judge Me" and "You Don't Bring Me Flowers."

1999: Lauryn Hill released the single, "Everything Is Everything." The track featured a teenage John Legend on piano. The song was nominated for a Grammy in the category of Best Short Form Music Video.

1999: Will Smith released the hit single "Wild Wild West" from the film of the same name. The song was played during the film's closing credits. The track prominently sampled "I Wish" by Stevie Wonder and "Wild Wild West" by Kool Moe Dee, and featured guest vocals by Dru Hill.

MAY 5

1976: DJ and producer Hi-Tek (birth name Tony Cottrell) was born in Cincinnati, Ohio. In the late-1990s, he teamed with Talib Kweli to form the hip hop duo, Reflection Eternal.

1989: Chris Brown (birth name Christopher Maurice Brown) was born in Tappahannock, Virginia. After signing with Jive Records at age 15 in 2004, he recorded his first album the following year, *Chris Bown*. Also an actor, he made his film debut in 2007 with *Stomp The Yard*.

1992: Gang Starr released their third album, *Daily Operation*. The album was highlighted by the hit singles, "Ex Girl To Next Girl" and "Take It Personal."

1992: House Of Pain released the crossover single, "Jump Around." The track was produced by DJ Muggs of Cypress Hill and sampled "Harlem Shuffle" by Bob & Earl, "Popeye (The Hitchhiker)" by Chubby Checker and "Shoot Your Shot" by Junior Walker & The All Stars. The song's music video was mostly shot at the 1992 St. Patrick's Day parade in New York City.

1998: DMX released the B-side hit, "Ruff Ryders' Anthem," which appeared on his debut studio album, *It's Dark And Hell Is Hot*. This was one of the first hits produced by Swizz Beatz. Although the track was only a minor hit, it later became a hip hop classic.

2009: Eminem appeared on the cover of the Marvel comic book, *The Punisher*.

2012: Rihanna was the musical guest on *Saturday Night Live*. She performed "Birthday Cake," "Talk That Talk" and "Where Have You Been."

2014: Solange Knowles, the younger sister of Beyoncé, physically attacked Jay-Z in an elevator at the Standard Hotel in New York City. A video of the confrontation was leaked to the celebrity gossip website, TMZ.

MAY 6

1967: MC Serch (birth name Michael Berrin) of the group 3rd Bass was born in Queens, New York. Also a solo artist, he released his debut album in 1992, *Return Of The Product*.

1987: Meek Mill (birth name Robert Rihmeek Williams) was born in Philadelphia. He released his debut album in 2012, *Dreams And Nightmares*. That same year, he launched his own record label, Dream Chasers Records.

1995: TLC were the musical guests on *Saturday Night Live*. They performed "Creep" and "Red Light Special."

2003: Dr. Dre lost a copyright infringement lawsuit and was ordered to pay $1.5 million for using a sample of "Backstrokin'" by the Fatback Band on his 2000 track, "Let's Get High."

MAY 7

1991: Terminator X of Public Enemy released his debut solo album, *Terminator X & The Valley Of The Jeep Beets*. The album spawned two hit singles, "Homey Don't Play Dat" and "Buck Whylin'."

1993: Tag Team released their smash hit, "Whoomp! (There It Is)." The track sampled "I'm Ready" by Kano. The song was the best-selling single of 1993 and later became a staple at sporting events.

2010: Snoop Dogg was the featured vocalist on Katy Perry's smash hit, "California Gurls." The song was nominated for a Grammy in the category of Best Pop Collaboration with Vocals.

MAY 8

1992: Will Smith married songwriter/actress Sheree Zampino. They met in 1991 on the set of his sitcom, *The Fresh Prince Of Bel-Air*. The couple divorced in 1995. Zampino later married and divorced former NFL player, Terrell Fletcher.

2001: William Dail, the road manager for Insane Clown Posse, was arrested in Omaha, Nebraska. He allegedly choked a member of the audience for waving an Eminem t-shirt and throwing M&Ms at the stage. Dail later pleaded guilty to a disorderly conduct charge and was fined $100.

2001: The film, *Carmen: A Hip Hopera*, premiered on the MTV network. The film starred Beyoncé Knowles, Wyclef Jean, Mos Def, Rah Digga, Mekhi Phifer, Da Brat, Joy Bryant, Jermaine Dupri and Lil' Bow Wow. The musical film was an urban-style adaptation of Georges Bizet's classic 19th century opera, *Carmen*, that featured rap and R&B instead of traditional opera music.

2004: Snoop Dogg was the guest host on *Saturday Night Live*.

2005: Former *American Idol* contestant Fantasia Barrino provided the voice of fictional singer Clarissa Wellington on the animated television series, *The Simpsons*. On an episode titled "A Star Is Torn," Barrino performed the song, "Hush, Little Baby."

2007: Bone Thugs-N-Harmony released their seventh album, *Strength & Loyalty*. The album spawned the singles, "I Tried" (featuring Akon) and "Lil Love" (featuring Bow Wow and Mariah Carey).

2007: DJ Jazzy Jeff released his best-selling solo album, *The Return Of The Magnificent*. The album was a follow-up to his 2002 release, *The Magnificent*.

2008: Snoop Dogg made his first of several appearances on the popular, daytime soap-opera, *One Life To Live*. He appeared on the program again in 2010 and 2013.

2012: Tyrese Gibson published the book, *How To Get Out Of Your Own Way*.

2012: 2 Chainz released his debut solo single, "No Lie" (featuring Drake).

2015: The media reported that Beyoncé and Jay-Z had purchased a mansion in New Orleans for $2.6 million. The actual sale had occurred the previous January.

MAY 9

1970: Ghostface Killah (birth name Dennis Coles) was born in Staten Island, New York. A member of the groundbreaking group the Wu-Tung Clan, he also pursued a solo career and released his debut album in 1996, *Ironman*.

1990: Jay Berman, the president of the RIAA, announced the introduction of a standardized black and white "warning sticker" to be placed on albums with explicit content. The stickers read "Parental Advisory, Explicit Lyrics." The stickers were a reaction to complaints about rap albums such as 2 Live Crew's *As Nasty As They Wanna Be* as well as a number of heavy metal releases.

1998: Puff Daddy and guitarist Jimmy Page were the musical guests on *Saturday Night Live*. The duo performed the track, "Come With Me."

2001: Shyne (real name Moses Levi) was sued for $6 million in a civil case after allegedly assaulting a 32-year-old man during a basketball game at a gym in New York City.

2005: The single "Feel Good Inc." by electronic Brit Pop band Gorillaz was released. The hit featured rap verses by De La Soul.

2005: Flavor Flav was one of ten celebrities that appeared on the first season of the British reality series, *The Farm*. He was the third contestant eliminated from the show.

2009: Ciara was the musical guest on *Saturday Night Live*. She performed "Never Ever" and was joined by Justin Timberlake on "Love Sex Magic."

2015: Waka Flocka Flame was forced to cancel a tour of Australia after he was barred from entering the country due to arrests on firearm and drug charges.

MAY 10

1967: Young MC (birth name Marvin Young) was born in London, England, but raised in Queens, New York. He is best known for his Grammy-winning hit, "Bust A Move."

1971: Craig Mack was born in Queens, New York. He originally recorded under the stage name MC EZ. Signing with Puff Daddy's record label Bad Boy Entertainment, Mack is best known for the 1994 hit single, "Flava In Ya Ear."

1985: The musical-drama film, *Rappin'*, was released. Starring Mario Van Peebles, Eriq La Salle and Melvin Plowden, the film followed the exploits of an ex-convict who joined forces with a break dancer to battle a greedy developer. In a subplot, Van Peebles' character competed in a rapping contest. Also appearing in the film were the Force M.D.'s, Eugene Wilde and Ice-T.

1988: The female hip hop trio J. J. Fad released the single, "Supersonic." The song was nominated for a Grammy in the category of Best Rap Performance.

1991: Chubb Rock released the hit, "Treat 'Em Right." The song sampled "Love Thang" by First Choice and "There Was A Time" by Dee Felice Trio. "Treat 'Em Right" was later sampled by K'naan on his debut single "ABCs."

2003: Sean Paul and Wayne Wonder were the musical guests on *Saturday Night Live*. Sean Paul performed "Get Busy" and Wayne Wonder performed "No Letting Go."

2003: Chingy released his debut single, "Right Thurr." The Southern-style rap song appeared on his debut album, *Jackpot*.

2005: The documentary, *Public Enemy: It Takes A Nation, The First London Invasion Tour 1987*, was released. The film chronicled the arrival of the East Coast gangsta rap group in the U.K.

2005: 50 Cent released the single, "Just A Lil Bit." The song's music video featured cameo appearances by a number of artists from G-Unit.

2013: Kendrick Lamar served as the "Celebrity Principal for the Day" at Mount Pleasant High School in Providence, Rhode Island.

2014: Sean "Puffy" Combs received an honorary Ph.D. in humanities from Howard University at the school's spring commencement ceremony. Combs had attended the university for two years before launching his music career.

MAY 11

1988: Ace Hood (birth name Antoine McColister) was born in Port St. Lucie, Florida. The rapper is best known for his hits, "Hustle Hard" and "Bugatti."

1993: Onyx released their hit single, "Slam." The track sampled "The Champ" by the Mohawks and "Rich Kind Of Poverty" by Sam & Dave. The heavy metal band Biohazard released a remixed version of "Slam" which was titled, "Slam (Bionyx remix)."

2001: Marlon Brando (real name Marlon Bryant) of the hip hop group Sporty Thievz was killed in the Bronx, New York. He was fatally struck by a van as he exited a delicatessen. He was 22-years-old.

2002: Eminem was the musical guest on *Saturday Night Live*. He was joined by Proof for a performance of "Without Me."

2007: Shop Boyz released the single, "Party Like A Rockstar." The track sampled the heavy metal song "Crazy Train" by Ozzy Osbourne. The track was nominated for a Grammy in the category of Best Rap Performance by a Duo or Group.

2010: Mad Cobra was shot three times by robbers near his home in Braeton, Jamaica. He survived the wounds. The following week, his home was targeted by gunmen.

2011: Common recited a short poem at a White House event which was billed as "An Evening of Poetry." The rapper appeared at the invitation of Michelle Obama.

2011: Flavor Flav of Public Enemy published his autobiography, *The Icon The Memoir*.

2015: The highest-ranked hip hop album on *Spin* magazine's list of "The 300 Best Albums of the Past 30 Years" was *Enter The Wu-Tang (36 Chambers)* by Wu-Tang Clan, which landed at #2. (The number-one album was *Nevermind* by grunge-rock group, Nirvana.)

2015: Kanye West received an honorary Ph.D. from the Art Institute of Chicago during the school's spring commencement ceremony. Years earlier, West had attended both Chicago State University and the American Academy of Art, but dropped out at age 20.

MAY 12

2006: Fergie of the Black Eyed Peas portrayed a lounge singer in the hit film, *Poseidon*. She also performed two songs on the film's soundtrack album, "Won't Let You Fall" and "Bailamos."

2007: The rap-metal group Linkin Park were the musical guests on *Saturday Night Live*. They performed "What I've Done" and "Bleed It Out."

2012: Usher was the musical guest on *Saturday Night Live*. He performed "Scream" and "Climax."

2012: Vanilla Ice hosted the launch of the Mr. Freeze Reverse Blast roller coaster at Six Flags Over Texas. Later that day, he gave a free concert at the park.

2015: Reverend Run (real name Joseph Simmons) of Run-D.M.C. published his autobiography, *It's Like That: A Spiritual Memoir*.

MAY 13

1968: PMD (birth name Parrish J. Smith) of the group EPMD was born in Brentwood, New York. As a solo artist, he released his first album in 1994, *Shade Business*.

1977: Pusha T (birth name Terrence Thornton) was born in the Bronx, New York. Before launching a solo career, he was a member of the hip hop duo Clipse, along with his brother Gene "No Malice" Thornton. The two men also formed their own label, Re-Up Records, and their own clothing line, Play Cloths. In 2015, Kanye West appointed Pusha T as the president of the record company, G.O.O.D. Music.

1992: Sister Souljah created a media firestorm when she told *The Washington Post*, "If black people kill black people every day, why not have a week and kill white people?" President Bill Clinton criticized her comment and said, "If you took the words 'white' and 'black,' and you reversed them, you might think David Duke was giving that speech."

2014: Gucci Mane (real name Radric Davis) pleaded guilty to a federal firearms charge after he was arrested for carrying a weapon as a convicted felon. He was sentenced to 39-months in prison.

MAY 14

1966: Fab Morvan (full name Fabrice Morvan) was born in Paris, France. He was a member of the disgraced duo Milli Vanilli. He later pursued a solo career and worked as a deejay at KIIS-FM in Los Angeles.

1988: The members of the Liverpool football team scored a top-10 U.K. hit with a rap song, "Anfield Rap (Red Machine In Full Effect)," just ahead of a championship match against Wimbledon. Written by Mary Byker of Pop Will Eat Itself, rapper Derek B. and Liverpool F.C. midfielder Craig Johnston, the song parodied a number of rap hits including "Rock The Bells" by LL Cool J and "I Know You Got Soul" by Eric B. & Rakim. Despite scoring a hit song, Liverpool lost the FA Cup final to Wimbledon.

1993: Big Daddy Kane and Tone Loc co-starred the Mario Van Peebles-produced film, *Posse*. A Western set in 1898, Kane played a gambler named Father Time and Loc was a member of the Buffalo Soldiers in the U.S. Army's 10th Cavalry Regiment.

2002: Cam'ron released his third solo album, *Come Home With Me*. The album spawned three singles, "Oh Boy," "Hey Ma" and "Daydreaming." This was Cam'ron's biggest-selling album of his career.

2012: George Clinton's lawsuit against the Black Eyed Peas was settled out of court. The funk star had accused the Black Eyes Peas of using unauthorized samples of his 1979 track "(Not Just) Knee Deep" in the remixes of their hit "Shut Up."

2013: Before he became a rapper, Jay DatBull was a talented high school football star named Jay Harris. But he was stripped of his football scholarship by the University of Michigan after the school learned that Harris had posted a number of profanity-laced rap videos on YouTube, some of which showed him smoking marijuana. According to Harris, it was a mutual decision to abandon the scholarship. A few months later, Harris had a change of heart and decided to play football for ASA College in Brooklyn.

2014: Kanye West married Kim Kardashian in a ceremony that was held at Fort di Belvedere in Florence, Italy. Bruce Jenner walked Kardashian down the aisle while Andrea Bocelli sang his international hit, "Con te Partiró." It was the first marriage for West and the third marriage for Kardashian. The couple paid more than $300,000 to rent the 400-year-old fortress.

MAY 15

1961: Melle Mel (birth name Melvin Glover) was born in the Bronx, New York. The rapper and songwriter was a member of the pioneering hip hop group, Grandmaster Flash and the Furious Five. He was the first rapper to call himself an "MC."

1991: Puerto Rican-born hip hop dancer Buck 4 (real name Gabriel Marcano) was killed in New York City at the age of 27. He was a member of the award-winning break dancing group, Rock Steady Crew.

1994: Tricia Rose, a professor of Africana Studies at Brown University, wrote the first academic book on the subject of hip hop, *Black Noise: Rap Music And Black Culture In Contemporary America*.

2004: J-Kwon was the musical guest on *Saturday Night Live*. He performed "Tipsy."

2004: The first annual Breakin' Convention was staged at Sadler's Wells Theatre in London. The international three-day event was established by rapper and choreographer Jonzi D.

2004: Birdman (real name Bryan "Baby" Williams) teamed with Lugz to launch a line of athlete shoes.

2007: Kurupt co-starred in the action film, *Half Past Dead 2*. The rapper portrayed a prison inmate named Twitch.

2008: Kanye West was selected as the winner of MTV's annual "Hottest MCs in the Game."

2011: M-Bone (real name Monte Ray Talbert) of the hip hop group Cali Swag District was murdered in Inglewood, California, at the age of 22. He was shot twice in the head while sitting in a parked car. A passenger was uninjured. M-Bone's group, Cali Swag District, had scored a hit the previous year with the track, "Teach Me How To Dougie."

2013: Jimmy Iovine and Dr. Dre donated $70 million to the University of Southern California in order to establish the Jimmy Iovine and Andre Young Academy for Arts, Technology and the Business of Innovation. The program created a degree that combined elements of business, marketing, product development, design and classic liberal arts. The first class of 25 students entered the program in the fall of 2014.

MAY 16

1960: Hip hop pioneer Lovebug Starski (birth name Kevin Smith) was born in the Bronx, New York. A DJ and record producer, he came to prominence as the DJ at the famed Dance Fever nightclub, which was featured in the 1985 film, *Krush Groove*. Lovebug Starski's first single, "Positive Life," was released in 1981.

1972: Special Ed (birth name Edward Archer) was born in Brooklyn, New York, of Jamaican descent. He released his breakthrough album at age 16, *Youngest In Charge*. He later teamed with Buckshot and Masta Ace to form the hip hop group, the Crooklyn Dodgers.

1981: The Sugarhill Gang was the second-ever hip hop act to perform on the syndicated music program, *Soul Train*. The group performed "8th Wonder."

1990: After his departure from N.W.A. the previous year over a royalty dispute, Ice Cube released the solo album, *AmeriKKKa's Most Wanted*. Mostly produced by Public Enemy's famed production team, the Bomb Squad, the politically-charged album spawned the hit singles, "AmeriKKKa's Most Wanted," "Who's The Mack?" and "Endangered Species (Tales From The Darkside)." One of the seminal "gangsta rap" albums of the 1990s, it sold more than one-million copies in the U.S.

2000: Eminem released the smash hit single, "The Real Slim Shady," the debut track from his album *The Marshall Mathers LP*. It was his first single to top the British charts. The song's lyrics mentioned a number of celebrities including Tom Green, Tommy Lee, Will Smith, Christina Aguilera and Britney Spears. The single won a Grammy in the category of Best Rap Solo Performance.

2015: Rihanna was the musical guest on *Saturday Night Live*. She performed "Bitch Better Have My Money" and "American Oxygen." This was her fifth appearance on the program.

2015: Queen Latifah portrayed blues legend Bessie Smith in the HBO production *Bessie*. The film earned four Primetime Emmy Awards.

2015: Jay-Z performed B-sides and rare tracks at the Terminal 5 concert club in Manhattan. The free event was billed as "TIDAL X: Jay-Z B-Sides" and was staged for the subscribers of the TIDAL music streaming service. Although just one concert was originally scheduled, a second show was added.

MAY 17

2003: Beyoncé was the musical guest on *Saturday Night Live*. She performed "Dangerously In Love" and was joined by Jay-Z on "Crazy In Love."

2003: *MC Battle*, a hip hop competition hosted by Carson Daly and La La Anthony, aired on MTV. In the American Idol-like contest, aspiring MCs competed against each other. The contestants were judged by Kevin Liles, Ludacris and Method Man.

2008: Usher was the musical guest on *Saturday Night Live*. He performed "This Ain't Sex" and was joined by Young Jeezy on "Love In This Club."

2015: Chinx (real name Lionel Pickens) was murdered in Queens, New York, at the age of 31. A victim of a drive-by shooting, he was killed while in his Porsche. A passenger in the vehicle was also shot but survived. The rapper was a member of the Rockaway Riot Squad and French Montana's Coke Boys.

MAY 18

1967: Rob Base (birth name Robert Ginyard) was born in Harlem, New York. He formed a duo with DJ E-Z Rock and recorded the often-sampled crossover hit, "It Takes Two." As a solo artist, Rob Base released his debut album in 1989, *The Incredible Base*.

1984: Sitcom actor Gary Coleman attempted a career in rap music with the single, "The Outlaw And The Indian."

1996: Bone Thugs-N-Harmony began an eight-week run at number-one on the U.S. singles chart with "Tha Crossroads."

2003: Beyoncé released the single, "Crazy In Love," which featured her future husband Jay-Z. The track sampled "Are You My Woman (Tell Me So)" by the Chi-Lites. The song won two Grammys in the categories of Best R&B Song and Best Rap/Sung Collaboration. The song's music video won three awards at the MTV Music Video Awards.

2009: Dolla (real name Roderick Anthony Burton II) was shot and killed at Beverly Center shopping mall in Los Angeles. He was 21-years-old. The Atlanta-based rapper was originally a member of the hip hop group, Da Razkalz Cru, during which time he was known as Bucklyte. He later scored his first solo hit with the track, "Who The Fuck Is That?"

2010: Nas collaborated with reggae artist Damian Marley on the album, *Distant Relatives*. The project spawned the singles, "As We Enter," "Strong Will Continue" and "My Generation." The album's proceeds went to a project in Africa.

2013: Kanye West was the musical guest on *Saturday Night Live*. He performed "Black Skinhead" and "New Slaves." This was his fifth appearance on the program.

2013: The single "Can't Hold Us" by Macklemore and Ryan Lewis featuring Ray Dalton began a five-week run at number-one on the U.S. charts.

MAY 19

1981: Yo Gotti (birth name Mario Mims) was born in Memphis. Previously known as Lil Yo, he released his debut album in 1996, *Youngsta's On A Come Up*.

1996: Cypress Hill appeared on the animated television series, *The Simpsons*. On the episode titled Homerpalooza, the group performed two songs, "Throw Your Set In The Air" and "Insane In The Brain."

1998: Soulja Slim released his debut studio album, *Give It 2 'Em Raw*. The album featured guest vocals by C-Murder, Master P, Snoop Dogg, Silkk The Shocker and others. The album was highlighted by the singles, "From What I Was Told" and "Street Life."

2003: Camoflauge (real name Jason Eugene Johnson) was shot to death in his native city of Savannah, Georgia. After his death, the 21-year-old rapper's album, *I Represent*, hit the R&B charts.

2007: The VH-1 network aired a biography of Lisa "Left Eye" Lopes, *The Last Days Of Left Eye*. The film focused on her final days which were spent at a spiritual retreat in Honduras.

2013: Chuck D was the featured speaker at Adelphi University's spring graduation commencement where he received an honorary doctorate. He was a 1994 graduate of the university.

2015: Pitbull launched his own music channel on Sirius XM Radio. His channel, Globalization Radio, featured various forms of dance, rap and electronic music.

MAY 20

1972: Busta Rhymes (birth name Trevor Tahiem Smith, Jr.) was born in Brooklyn, New York. He was given his stage name by Chuck D of Public Enemy. Originally a member of the Leaders Of The New School, Busta Rhymes began his solo career in 1996 with the release of the album, *The Coming*.

1984: Carlton Douglas Ridenhour, later known as Chuck D of Public Enemy, earned his Bachelor's of Fine Arts degree from Adelphi University in Garden City, New York. While attending Adelphi, he worked at the student radio station, WBAU 90.3 FM.

1991: DJ Jazzy Jeff & The Fresh Prince released the crossover hit single, "Summertime." The track sampled "Summer Madness" by Kool & The Gang and "Funky President (People It's Bad)" by James Brown. The song won a Grammy in the category of Best Rap Performance by a Duo or Group.

1993: Fat Joe released his debut solo single, "Flow Joe." The track sampled "Get Out Of My Life, Woman" by Lee Dorsey and "The Long Wait" by Morton Stevens.

1993: Dr. Dre released the single, "Fuck Wit Dre Day (And Everybody's Celebratin')," which featured vocals by Snoop Doggy Dogg. The diss song attacked Dr. Dre's former N.W.A. bandmate Eazy-E as well as Tim Dog and Luther Campbell.

2000: Kid Rock was the musical guest on *Saturday Night Live*. He performed "American Bad Ass" and "Only God Knows Why."

2006: Nelly Furtado was the musical guest on *Saturday Night Live*. She performed "Maneater" and was joined by Timbaland on "Promiscuous."

2014: Toni Braxton published her autobiography, *Unbreak My Heart: A Memoir*.

MAY 21

1972: The Notorious B.I.G. (birth name Christopher George Latore Wallace) was born in New York City. His other stage names included Biggie, Biggie Smalls, the King of New York and Frank White. ("B.I.G." stood for Business Instead of Game.) In 1994, he married singer Faith Evans. He was murdered in 1997 at the age of 24.

1974: Havoc (birth name Kejuan Muchita) of the duo Mobb Deep was born in Queens, New York. Mobb Deep, which also included Prodigy, released their breakthrough album in 1995, *The Infamous*.

1991: Chubb Rock released the hit album, *The One*. The project spawned three hit singles: "Treat 'Em Right," "Just The Two Of Us" and "The Chubbster."

1991: Shabba Ranks released his first major-label album, *Raw As Ever*. The album spawned a pair of hits: "Housecall" (featuring Maxi Priest) and "The Jam" (featuring KRS-One). The album won a Grammy in the category of Best Reggae Album.

1996: A popular San Francisco radio station, KMEL 106.1, lifted its ban on playing the music of Oakland rapper, Too $hort.

1999: Bugz (real name Karnail Pitts) of the hip hop group D12 was killed in Detroit. He was fatally shot during a dispute over a water pistol. He was 21-years-old.

2009: Jay-Z announced that he had left Def Jam Recordings. Still owing one more album to the label, he reportedly bought out his contract for $5 million. He also announced a deal with Live Nation to establish Roc Nation, a combination record label, music publishing company and management agency.

MAY 22

1967: MC Eiht (birth name Aaron Tyler) was born in Compton, California. He was the leader of the West Coast hip hop group, Compton's Most Wanted. Also an actor, he appeared in the 1993 film, *Menace II Society*.

1989: In an interview with *The Washington Times*, Professor Griff of Public Enemy made the incendiary statement, "Jews are responsible for the majority of the wickedness in the world." Following a media storm, Griff was fired from the group by Chuck D.

1989: Young MC released the crossover top-10 single, "Bust A Move." The track prominently sampled "Found A Child" by Ballin' Jack. The song featured singer Crystal Blake and bassist Flea of the funk-rock group, Red Hot Chili Peppers. The single won a Grammy in the category of Best Rap Performance.

1994: Masta Killa of the group Wu-Tang Clan reportedly punched music journalist Cheo Coker in the eye. Masta Killa was unhappy with the illustrations that were used in an article about the group in *Rap Pages* magazine.

2001: Milwaukee-based rapper Coo Coo Cal released the single, "My Projects."

2003: Big DS (real name Marlon Fletcher) of the group Onyx died after a battle with cancer. He appeared on Onyx's debut album, *Bacdafucup*, and later released one solo album. He was 31-years-old.

2010: Massachusetts-born rapper Souleye (real name Mario Treadway) married rock singer Alanis Morissette in a ceremony at their home in Los Angeles.

2012: Young Buck received an 18-month prison sentence after he was convicted of possessing firearms and ammunition as a convicted felon. The IRS had discovered a loaded weapon in his Nashville home during a raid. The IRS was attempting to reconcile a $334,000 tax debt owed by the rapper.

2012: DJ and producer Baauer released the track, "Harlem Shake." The song was initially ignored until the following February when a music video appeared on YouTube. The song quickly raced up the music charts and spawned a dance craze of the same name. Reaching number-one, it was the first instrumental song to top the *Billboard* pop chart in 27 years. The "Harlem Shake" dance was invented in 1981 and was originally called "The Albee." Then in 2001, a dancer performed the Harlem Shake in the music video for "Let's Get It" by rapper G. Dep.

2012: The game show *Hip Hop Squares* debuted on the MTV2 network. The program was hosted by Peter Rosenberg and employed the same format as the long-running, celebrity game show, *Hollywood Squares*. Dozens of rappers appeared on the program including Biz Markie, Childish Gambino, Common, DJ Khaled, Fat Joe, Ghostface Killah, Method Man, Machine Gun Kelly and Nick Cannon.

MAY 23

2000: Eminem released his third album, *The Marshall Mathers LP*. It was issued with two different covers. The album spawned four singles, "The Real Slim Shady," "The Way I Am," "Stan" and "I'm Back." Another track, "Kim," reflected his anger toward his wife, Kim Mathers. The album sold more than eleven-million copies in the U.S. The sequel album, *The Marshall Mathers LP 2*, was released in 2013.

2008: Slick Rick, who spent five-years in prison on various charges related to a 1990 double shooting, was granted a full and unconditional pardon by New York Governor David Paterson.

2012: Will Smith reprised his role as a government agent involved with extraterrestrial life forms in the film, *Men In Black III*.

MAY 24

1967: Heavy D (birth name Dwight Arrington Myers) was born in Mandeville, Jamaica. Relocating to Mount Vernon, New York, in the early 1970s, he later formed the hip hop group, Heavy D & The Boyz. Beginning with 1987's *Living Large*, he recorded five albums with the group, and later pursued a solo career. He passed away in 2011 at the age of 44.

1974: M.C. Brains (birth name James DeShannon Davis) was born in Cleveland, Ohio. He is best known for his 1992 hit, "Oochie Coochie." He later recorded as M.C. Brainz and then Brainz Davis.

1989: G-Eazy (birth name Gerald Earl Gillum) was born in Oakland, California. Also known as Young Gerald, he released his breakthrough album in 2014, *These Things Happen*.

1994: Aaliyah released her debut album, *Age Ain't Nothing But A Number*. She was 15-years-old at the time. The album spawned six singles beginning with "Back & Forth" and "At Your Best (You Are Love)." The album sold three-million copies in the U.S.

2002: The documentary *Biggie And Tupac* was released. The British film examined the deaths of rappers, the Notorious B.I.G. and Tupac Shakur, as well as the East Coast/West Coast hip hop rivalry.

2006: British rapper M.I.A. was banned from entering the U.S. The daughter of a Tamil Tiger rebel, she blamed the decision on the political nature of her song lyrics.

2009: Just two days before he was scheduled to begin a prison sentence, T.I. staged what was described as a "farewell concert" at the Philips Arena in Atlanta.

2011: Luther Campbell (a.k.a. Uncle Luke) came in fourth place in the race for mayor of Miami-Dade County. He captured 11-percent of the vote.

2011: *XXL* magazine named "Nothin' But A 'G' Thang" by Dr. Dre featuring Snoop Dogg the best rap song of the 1990s. The remixed version of "It's All About The Benjamins" by Puff Daddy came in second place.

2013: DJ Jazzy Jeff and the Fresh Prince reunited on the BBC program *The Graham Norton Show* and performed the theme song of *The Fresh Prince Of Bel-Air*.

MAY 25

1973: Daz Dillinger (birth name Delmar Drew Arnaud) was born in Long Beach, California. Originally known as Dat Nigga Daz, he was a member of the duo, Tha Dogg Pound. He released his debut solo album in 1998, *Retaliation, Revenge And Get Back*.

1979: JT Money (birth name Jeff Thompkins) was born in Miami. A member of the hip hop group Poison Clan, he later pursued a solo career and scored his biggest hit with the 1989 single, "Who Dat."

1996: An 18-year-old Kobe Bryant took 17-year-old singer and actress Brandy to his high school senior prom in suburban Philadelphia. Later in the year, he returned the favor and appeared on her television show, *Moesha*.

2004: Kanye West released "Jesus Walks," the fourth single from his debut album, *The College Dropout*. The Christian-themed track was built upon a sample of "Walk With Me" by the ARC Choir. West released three different music videos for the track. The song won a Grammy in the category of Best Rap Song.

2005: The Black Eyed Peas released their fourth album, *Monkey Business*. The album spawned the hit singles, "Don't Phunk With My Heart," "Don't Lie," "My Humps" and "Pump It." The album sold more than three-million copies in the U.S.

2007: The film, *I Tried*, explored the notion of what could have happened if the members of Bone Thugs-N-Harmony had never crossed paths with their early mentor, Eazy-E. The film was set in Los Angeles and starred Layzie Bone, Krayzie Bone and Wish Bone.

2014: Waka Flocka Flame and his girlfriend Tammy Rivera secretly eloped. At the time, the couple starred on the VH-1 series, *Love & Hip Hop: Atlanta*.

2015: SMS Promotions, a boxing and entertainment company started by 50 Cent in 2012, filed for Chapter 11 bankruptcy. According to court filings, the company owed between $100,000 and $500,000 to creditors.

MAY 26

1975. Soul and hip hop performer Lauryn Hill was born in South Orange, New Jersey. Nicknamed "Miss Hill" and "L. Boogie," she is also an actress and producer. After enjoying success as a member of the Fugees, she emerged as a solo artist.

1980: Kurtis Blow released the groundbreaking hip hop single, "The Breaks." This was the first 12-inch rap single to be certified gold for sales of one-million copies. It was also the second-ever 12-inch single to be certified platinum.

1993: A film depicting the violent, urban culture of the South Central district of Los Angeles, *Menace II Society*, featured rappers MC Eiht, Pooh-Man, Saafir and Too $hort.

1998: Black Star released their debut single, "Definition." The duo consisted of Mos Def and Talib Kweli.

2002: Rappers Mos Def, Da Brat and MC Lyte appeared in the award-winning action film, *Civil Brand*.

2004: Fantasia was voted the Season 3 winner of *American Idol*. For her final song, she performed "I Believe" by Tamyra Gray. Fantasia also recorded the song as her debut single, which topped the pop charts.

2005: Nelly and D12 appeared in the Adam Sandler comedy film, *The Longest Yard*.

2007: Sean Kingston released his debut single, the chart-topping hit, "Beautiful Girls." The track sampled "Stand By Me" by Ben E. King. The song's music video featured an appearance by rapper Lil Mama. Many radio stations in the U.S. banned the song because it mentioned the word "suicide."

2014: DJ Father Shaheed of the New Jersey hip hop group Poor Righteous Teachers was killed in a motorcycle crash. He was 45-years-old.

2015: Boosie Badazz became violently ill less than two-minutes into his concert at Webster Hall in New York City and was forced to leave the stage. He had suffered a diabetes-related health issue and was without his medication.

MAY 27

1971: Lisa "Left Eye" Lopes (birth name Lisa Nicole Lopes) was born in Philadelphia. She was a major star in the 1990s as part of the trio, TLC. She died in an auto accident at the age of 30.

1975: André 3000 (birth name André Lauren Benjamin) was born in Atlanta. Best known as a member of the hip hop duo OutKast, he also pursued a solo career. Also an actor, he portrayed Jimi Hendrix in the film, *All Is By My Side*.

1975: Jadakiss (birth name Jason Phillips) was born in Yonkers, New York. A successful solo artist, he was also a member of the group LOX and the hip hop collective Ruff Ryders.

1994: Florida-based rap group 69 Boyz released their debut single, "Tootsee Roll."

1996: Run-D.M.C. released their best-selling album, *Raising Hell*. Produced by Rick Rubin, it was the first hip hop album to top the R&B charts. Embraced by MTV, the album spawned four hits, "My Adidas," "You Be Illin'," "It's Tricky" and a duet with the rock group Aerosmith, "Walk This Way." The album sold more than two-million copies in the U.S.

1997: Puff Daddy and Faith Evans released the smash hit single, "I'll Be Missing You" (featuring 112). The song was a tribute to fallen rapper, the Notorious B.I.G. The track prominently sampled "Every Breath You Take" by the Police.

1998: The comedy-crime film, *I Got The Hook-Up*, was released. The film starred a number of hip hop artists including Master P, Ice Cube, C-Murder and Snoop Dogg. This was the first theatrical release by Master P's label, No Limit Records.

2009: Tega (real name Ortega Henderson) died of gunshot wounds eleven days after he was attacked during a robbery at his home in St. Louis. He was 25-years-old. Tega was a member of Nelly's St. Lunatics crew.

2011: Gil Scott-Heron, nicknamed the Godfather of Rap, passed away at the age of 62. He died of an undisclosed illness in a New York City hospital after returning from a European trip. He had been in poor health for some time. A Chicago-born soul and jazz musician, Scott-Heron was also a "spoken word" performer whose vocal style greatly influenced early rap music.

MAY 28

1968: Chubb Rock (birth name Richard Simpson) was born in Kingston, Jamaica. Later moving to New York City, he scored a string of hits in the 1990s including "The Chubbster" and "Treat 'Em Right."

1999: Jay-Z released the single, "Jigga My Nigga." The track appeared on the compilation album, *Ryde Or Die Vol. 1*, and as a hidden track on Jay-Z's album, *Vol. 3... Life and Times of S. Carter*.

2004: The comedy film *Soul Plane* was released. The movie starred Kevin Hart and featured a number of R&B and hip hop performers including Method Man, Mo'Nique, Lil John, Snoop Dogg and the Ying Yang Twins.

2008: Rapper 50 Cent co-starred along with Val Kilmer and Sharon Stone in the action film, *Street Of Blood*. The film was set in New Orleans during Hurricane Katrina, with 50 Cent portraying a police detective named Stan Johnson.

2014: Apple announced its acquisition of Beats Music and Beats Electronics, which were founded by Dr. Dre and Jimmy Iovine. Apple paid $3 billion for the two companies: $400 million in Apple stock and $2.6 billion in cash.

MAY 29

1984: The Art Of Noise, one of the pioneers of modern electronic music, released the single, "Close (To The Edit)." The song was a remixed version of their earlier hit, "Beat Box." Both songs were embraced by the break dancing community. The music video for "Close (To The Edit)" featured a punk rocker and three musicians in tuxedos symbolically destroying old-fashioned musical instruments.

1986: Run-D.M.C. released the single, "My Adidas." The song was meant as a celebration of the group's trademark footwear – white Adidas sneakers with no shoelaces.

1989: The single "Back To Life" by Soul II Soul featuring Caron Wheeler was released. With its hip hop beats, the soul-based track was a hit in both the U.S. and in the group's native county, England.

1990: The anti-violence hip hop anthem, "We're All In The Same Gang," was released. The track was produced by Dr. Dre and featured a number of artists including MC Hammer, Body & Soul, King Tee, Def Jef, Tone Loc, Michel'le, Young MC, Oaktown's 357, Above The Law, Ice-T, J.J. Fad, as well as members of N.W.A. and Digital Underground.

2005: Ice Cube starred in the action film, *xXx: State Of The Union*. Ice Cube played the role of Lt. Darius Stone, a former U.S. Navy SEAL officer. Xzibit also appeared in the film.

2006: The hip hop music show, *Sucker Free* (also known as *Sucker Free Daily*), debuted on the MTV2 network. The program experienced various incarnations before it was rebranded *This Week In Jams*.

2009: Tone Loc collapsed and passed out while performing on a stage at the Capt'n Fun Beach Club in Pensacola Beach, Florida. He blamed the health scare on heat exhaustion.

2011: Sean Kingston was severely injured in a jet ski accident near Miami Beach, Florida. He suffered a fractured wrist and jaw. A female passenger was also injured. The watercraft had struck the Palm Island Bridge, which connected Palm Island with the MacArthur Causeway.

MAY 30

1974: Big L (birth name Lamont Coleman) was born in Harlem, New York. The rapper was the victim of a drive-by shooting at the age of 24 in 1999.

1980: Remy Ma (birth name Reminisce Smith) was born in the Bronx, New York. Originally known as Remy Martin, she was a member of Big Punisher's rap group, Terror Squad. She later pursued a solo career and released her debut album in 2006, *There's Something About Remy: Based On A True Story*.

1987: A riot broke out at the final stop of the Beastie Boys' *Licensed To Ill* tour, which took place at the Royal Court Theatre in Liverpool, England. Shortly after Beastie Boys member Ad-Rock began throwing cans of beer from the stage, violence erupted and a canister of tear gas was fired into the audience. The concert lasted just 12 minutes. Ad-Rock was arrested the following day on charges of assault.

1994: Da Brat released her debut single, "Funkdafied." The track sampled "Between The Sheets" by the Isley Brothers.

2008: A $2.4 million mansion in the Long Island town of Dix Hills owned by 50 Cent burned down. The blaze was described as "suspicious" by the town's fire chief. Several people were in the home at the time including 50 Cent's ex-girlfriend and their 10-year-old son, all of whom suffered smoke inhalation.

MAY 31

1964: Frost (birth name Arturo Molina, Jr.) was born in Windsor, California. Previously known as Kid Frost, he was a pioneering West Coast break dancer and DJ.

1971: DJ Casper (birth named Willie Perry, Jr.) was born in Chicago. He is best known for the 1990 hit, "Cha Cha Slide," which spawned a dance craze.

1985: The Fresh Fest tour began a successful 50-date run across the U.S. The lineup included Whodini, Run-D.M.C., Grandmaster Flash and LL Cool J.

1986: Waka Flocka Flame (birth name Juaquin James Malphurs) was born in Queens, New York, but was raised in the suburban Atlanta community of Riverdale. He broke through as a solo artist with the 2010 album, *Flockaveli*.

1988: Boogie Down Productions released their influential debut album, *Criminal Minded*. The group consisted of KRS-One, D-Nice and Scott La Rock. One of the first "gangsta rap" albums, it was highlighted by the tracks, "South Bronx," "The Bridge Is Over" and "9mm Goes Bang." Scott La Rock was murdered just one-month after the album was released.

1991: Azealia Banks (full name Azealia Amanda Banks) was born in Harlem, New York. After adopting the stage name Miss Bank$, she signed with XL Recordings at age 17. In 2011, she released her debut single, "212."

1994: Nas released the single, "The World Is Yours" (featuring Pete Rock). The track sampled "I Love Music" by Ahmad Jamal and "It's Yours" by T La Rock. The song's music video was a tribute to the gangster film, *Scarface*.

1995: In an attack against gangsta rap, Senate Majority Leader Bob Dole accused Time Warner of profiting from music that glorified violence. "We have reached the point where our popular culture threatens to undermine our character as a nation," Dole said in a speech.

1996: Oakland-based rapper Seagram (real name Seagram Miller) was killed in a drive-by shooting at the age of 26. The murder went unsolved.

1996: The Fugees released their best-known single, a remake of Roberta Flack's 1973 soul classic, "Killing Me Softly." The track – which featured Lauryn Hill on lead vocals – was produced by the members of the Fugees and A Tribe Called Quest. The Fugees had originally wanted to record a dramatically different version of the song, which they reworked as "Killing Them Softly." The single won a Grammy in the category of Best R&B Performance by a Duo or Group.

2008: The single "Lollipop" by Lil Wayne featuring Static Major began a four-week run at number-one on the U.S. charts.

2010: J. Cole released the single, "Who Dat." The song's music video was shot in his hometown of Fayetteville, North Carolina, and featured members of the marching band from E.E. Smith High School and cheerleaders from Fayetteville State University.

▶ JUNE

JUNE 1

1977: Saigon (birth name Brian Daniel Carenard) was born in Spring Valley, New York. He is best known for his 2011 debut album, *The Greatest Story Never Told.* Also an actor, he appeared on the HBO television series, *Entourage.*

1996: Steven Stancell published the first-ever rap encyclopedia, *Rap Whoz Who: The World Of Rap Music, Performers, Producers & Promoters.* Stancell was a music columnist for *The New York Beacon.*

1999: The all-girl, teenage hip hop trio Blaque released their debut album, *Blaque.* The album was highlighted by the hits, "808," "Bring It All To Me" (featuring JC Chasez of *N Sync) and "I Do."

1999: Ja Rule released his debut studio album, *Venni Vetti Vecci.* The album spawned five singles beginning with "Holla Holla" and "Daddy's Little Baby." The album sold one-million copies in the U.S.

2000: A major exhibition, "Hip-Hop Nation," was unveiled at the EMP Museum in Seattle. It ran until May 2003.

2004: The documentary, *Dirty States Of America: The Untold Story Of Southern Hip Hop*, was released.

2010: Nicki Minaj released the single, "Your Love." The track prominently sampled "No More I Love You's" by Annie Lennox. This was Minaj's first crossover top-40 hit as a solo artist. In the song's music video, Michael Jai White appeared as Minaj's love interest.

2011: Eminem filed a lawsuit in a German court against Audi. He claimed that the German automaker featured a song in an online commercial that sounded very much his hit, "Lose Yourself." The suit was later settled out of court.

2012: Kanye and Jay-Z closed their Paris concert at the Palais Omnisports de Paris-Bercy stadium by performing the song "Niggas In Paris" a total of 11 times over 50 minutes.

2014: South Korean rapper Psy made history when his video for "Gangnam Style" became the first ever in YouTube history to reach two-billion views. The clip was released in July 2012.

2014: After months of rumors, G-Unit reunited for a performance at Hot 97's Summer Jam 2014, which was staged at MetLife Stadium in New Jersey.

JUNE 2

1979: Sony of Japan introduced the Walkman, a portable cassette player. The device allowed consumers to carry their music with them.

1995: A series of "Live 8" charity concerts were staged in 11 cities around the world. In Philadelphia, the lineup included an all-star cast of rock and hip hop artists including the Black Eyed Peas, Alicia Keys, Kanye West, Linkin Park with Jay-Z, DJ Jazzy Jeff & Will Smith, Bon Jovi and Maroon 5. In London, the lineup included Snoop Dogg, Ms. Dynamite, Dido, Coldplay and Pink Floyd.

1998: 50 Cent made his recording debut when he appeared as a guest vocalist on the single, "React," by the hip hop group Onyx. The track was a minor hit on R&B radio.

2010: Ice Cube co-starred in the TBS network sitcom, *Are We There Yet?* In addition to portraying the role of Terrence Kingston, he was also the co-executive producer of the series.

JUNE 3

1973: Tek (birth name Tekomin B. Williams) was born in Brooklyn, New York. Teaming with Steele to form the rap duo Smif-N-Wessun, he released his debut album in 1993, *Enta Da Stage*. He was also a member of the hip hop collective, Boot Camp Clik. After converting to Islam, he changed his name to El-Amin.

1991: Authorities in Britain seized 5,000 copies of N.W.A.'s album, *Efil4zaggin*, from a warehouse near London. According to Scotland Yard, the record was banned under the Obscene Publications Act.

1993: Lords Of The Underground released their single, "Chief Rocka." The track sampled several songs including "Twine Time" by Alvin Cash & The Crawlers and "Drum Pan Sound" by Reggie Stepper. "Chief Rocka" was included on the group's debut album, *Here Come The Lords*.

1997: The Wu-Tang Clan released their highly-anticipated third album, *Wu-Tang Forever*. The double-album spawned three singles, "Triumph," "It's Yourz" and "Reunited." The project featured guest appearances by Wu-Tang affiliates Streetlife, Cappadonna, 4th Disciple, True Master and Tekitha. The album was nominated for a Grammy in the category of Best Rap Album.

2000: Eminem was arrested and charged with felony possession of a concealed weapon after he got into an argument with an employee of the group, Insane Clown Posse. In June 2001, he pleaded "no contest" to the charges and was sentenced to one-year of probation.

2001: At age 11, Lil' Romeo released the top-10 album, *Lil' Romeo*. The album spawned the hit singles, "My Baby" and "The Girlies."

2008: Verna Griffin, the mother of Dr. Dre, published the autobiography, *Long Road Outta Compton: Dr. Dre's Mom On Family, Fame And Terrible Tragedy*.

2008: The documentary, *2 Turntables And A Microphone: The Life And Death Of Jam Master Jay*, examined the career of the successful DJ and explored the mystery surrounding his death.

2009: The Black Eyed Peas released their fifth studio album, *The E.N.D. (The Energy Never Dies)*. The album spawned six singles, "Boom Boom Pow," "I Gotta Feeling," "Meet Me Halfway," "Imma Be," "Rock That Body" and "Missing You." The album won a Grammy in the category of Best Pop Vocal Album.

2010: Queen Latifah published her autobiography, *Put On Your Crown: Life-Changing Moments On The Path To Queendom*.

2010: André 3000 of OutKast performed the Beatles classic "All Together Now" in a Nike television commercial. The 60-second spot aired during the first game of the 2010 NBA finals between the Los Angeles Lakers and the Boston Celtics.

2012: Nicki Minaj cancelled her headlining appearance at the annual Hot 97 Summer Jam hip hop festival, which was staged at the MetLife Stadium in East Rutherford, New Jersey. She pulled out of the event after a Hot 97 deejay made disparaging comments about her single, "Starships." Two of Minaj's labelmates, DJ Khaled and Busta Rhymes, also cancelled their sets.

2014: 50 Cent released his fifth album, *Animal Ambition: An Untamed Desire To Win*. All 11 of the album's tracks were released as singles beginning with "Don't Worry 'Bout It."

JUNE 4

1970: Devin the Dude (birth name Devin Copeland) was born in Pontiac, Michigan. Signed to Rap-A-Lot Records, he released his debut album in 1998, *The Dude*.

1988: The Fat Boys released a remake of the 1960s pop-rock standard, "The Twist." Backed by Chubby Checker – who topped the charts with his version of the song – the Fat Boys retitled the song, "The Twist (Yo!, Twist)."

1991: MC Trouble passed away after suffering heart failure following an epileptic seizure. She was the first female rapper signed to Motown Records. She was 20-years-old.

1992: The hip hop duo Kris Kross released their second single, "Warm It Up," which was the follow-up to their debut smash, "Jump." The single sold more than one-million copies in the U.S.

1996: The 2Pac single, "How Do U Want It" (featuring K-Ci & JoJo), was posthumously released. The track sampled "Body Heat" by Quincy Jones. The song topped the pop charts and was nominated for a Grammy in the category of Best Rap Performance by a Duo or Group. One of the B-side tracks was a remixed version of "California Love." Another B-side track, "Hit 'Em Up," was one of the most famous diss tracks in rap history. The track criticized Shakur's former friend, the Notorious B.I.G. The song was recorded in response to Biggie's 1995 track "Who Shot Ya?," which was released two-months after Shakur had been shot and robbed in Manhattan.

1996: Nas released the hit single, "If I Ruled The World (Imagine That)," which was a reworked version of Kurtis Blow's 1985 hit, "If I Ruled The World." Nas was backed on the song by Lauryn Hill.

2002: Eminem published his autobiography, *Angry Blonde*.

2002: Wyclef Jean and nine other protesters were arrested at a rally in New York City and charged with disorderly conduct. Jean was angry about a proposed $1.2 billion reduction in spending on public education. Also in attendance at the rally were P. Diddy, Jay-Z, Alicia Keys, LL Cool J and Erykah Badu.

2003: Pharrell Williams signed a longterm licensing agreement with Reebok. The deal created the Ice Cream brand of athletic shoes and the Billionaire Boys Club line of men's apparel.

2010: Sean "Diddy" Combs co-starred in the comedy film, *Get Him To The Greek*. Combs portrayed Sergio Roma, the president of a fictional label, Pinnacle Records. The film grossed more than $90 million in the U.S.

2014: Dr. Dre paid $40 million to purchase an 18,298-square-foot home in Brentwood, California. The four-acre estate had previously belonged to New England Patriots quarterback Tom Brady and his wife, supermodel Gisele Bündchen. The rapper would sell the home less than one year later.

JUNE 5

1971: Marky Mark (birth name Mark Robert Michael Wahlberg) was born in Boston, A former member of New Kids On The Block, he launched a solo career as the leader of the rap group, Marky Mark and the Funky Bunch, and scored crossover hits with "Good Vibrations" and "Wild Side."

1976: Aesop Rock (birth name Ian Matthias Bavitz) was born in North Port, New York. A rapper and producer, he emerged from the alternative hip hop scene of the 1990s. He was a member of the groups, the Weathermen, Hail Mary Mallon and the Uncluded.

1992: The hip hop comedy film, *Class Act*, starred both members of the duo, Kid 'n Play.

1995: Shaggy released the single, "Boombastic." A worldwide hit, the song enjoyed popularity after it was featured in a commercial for Levi's clothing. The track sampled "Baby Let Me Kiss You" by King Floyd.

2001: D12, a Detroit hip hop group featuring Eminem, released their debut single, "Purple Pills." The track received little radio airplay due to its many drug and sexual references. A heavily censored version of the song was retitled, "Purple Hills."

2001: The St. Lunatics – a hip hop group that included Nelly – released their debut album, *Free City*. The album was highlighted by the tracks, "Summer In The City," "Here We Come" and "Midwest Swing." The album was issued one-year after Nelly had released his breakthrough solo album, *Country Grammar*.

2004: Jennifer Lopez and Marc Anthony were married in a secret ceremony at her estate in Beverly Hills, California. The couple had first met in 1998 when Anthony was starring in Paul Simon's Broadway show, *The Capeman*. The couple performed together for the first time at the Grammy Awards ceremony in February 2005.

2011: Turk, a former member of the New Orleans group the Hot Boys, released his first solo album, *Young & Thuggin'*. The top-10, million-selling album spawned the hit singles, "It's In Me" and "Freak Da Girls."

2014: The television series, *Power*, made its debut on the Starz network. The program was produced by 50 Cent, who also appeared in the series as a drug dealer named Kanan.

2014: The Beastie Boys won their lawsuit against Monster Energy over the unauthorized use of the group's music in an online advertisement. The group was asking for $2.4 million but was awarded $1.7 million by a jury in a Manhattan federal court.

JUNE 6

1974: Young Bleed (birth name Glenn Clifton, Jr.) was born in Baton Rouge, Louisiana. The Southern-style rapper is best known for his 1998 album, *My Balls And My Word.*

1990: Federal Court Judge Jose Gonzalez ruled that the rap album, *As Nasty As They Wanna Be* by 2 Live Crew, had violated local "community standards" and was therefore "obscene." He wrote in his ruling: "The Philistines are not always wrong, nor are the guardians of the First Amendment always right." The ruling made it a felony to sell the album to a minor in three Florida counties. Eventually, Judge Gonzalez's ruling was overturned by the 11th Circuit Court of Appeals.

1995: The Notorious B.I.G. released a remixed version of "One More Chance," which became a top-10 crossover hit. The original version of the track was included on his debut album, *Ready To Die.*

2000: DMX released the single, "Party Up (Up In Here)." It was the biggest pop hit of his career.

2003: Ludacris made his first appearance in the Fast & Furious franchise when he co-starred in the third film of the series, *2 Fast 2 Furious*. He portrayed a former street racer and race organizer named Tej Parker. Ludacris would reprise his role in three more films. Also appearing in the film was rapper Tyrese Gibson.

2006: Ice Cube formed his own label, Lench Mob Records, and released the solo album, *Laugh Now, Cry Later*. It was his first album in six-years. The album was highlighted by the tracks, "Why We Thugs" and "Go To Church" (featuring Snoop Dogg and Lil Jon), and sold more than one-million copies in the U.S.

2006: Yung Joc released his debut album in 2006, *New Joc City*. The album spawned three singles, "It's Goin' Down," "I Know You See It" and "1st Time."

2012: British rapper Ben Drew (a.k.a. Plan B) wrote and directed the crime film, *Ill Manors*. He had written the film script at age 21. He also co-wrote the film's music score and topped the U.K. charts with the film's soundtrack album.

2014: JayAre (real name Cahron Childs) of the hip hop group Cali Swag District died after suffering a heart attack at the age of 25. JayAre's group, Cali Swag District, had scored a hit in 2010 with the track, "Teach Me How To Dougie." He was the second member of the group to die unexpectedly.

JUNE 7

1956: Musician and record executive Antonio "L.A." Reid was born in Cincinnati. In the 1980s, he was a member of the R&B group, the Deele. After the group disbanded, he teamed with bandmate Kenneth "Babyface" Edmonds to form LaFace Records. Later, he was the CEO of Arista Records, then the Island Def Jam Music Group and finally Epic Records. He was also a judge on the U.S. version of *X Factor* for two seasons.

1990: Iggy Azalea (birth name Amethyst Amelia Kelly) was born in Sydney, Australia. Drawn to hip hop, she moved to the U.S. at age 16 to further her music career. After signing with Grand Hustle Records in 2012, she was mentored by the label's owner, T.I. Releasing her debut studio album in 2014, *The New Classic*, she enjoyed quick stardom with hit singles such as "Work" and "Fancy."

1991: Fetty Wap (birth name Willie Maxwell II) was born in Paterson, New Jersey. The rapper released his breakthrough single in 2014, "Trap Queen."

1994: Warren G released his debut album, *Regulate...G Funk Era*. The album spawned three singles, "Regulate" (with Nate Dogg), "This D.J." and "Do You See." The album earned two Grammy nominations.

2004: Ludacris was given an honorary "key to the city" by the mayor of Atlanta.

2005: Nelly released the single, "Grillz" (featuring Paul Wall and Ali & Gipp), from his compilation album, *Sweatsuit*. The track sampled "Soldier" by Destiny's Child. The song was nominated for a Grammy in the category of Best Rap Performance by a Duo or Group.

2010: The VH-1 network staged the 7th annual Hip Hop Honors ceremony. The inductees included 2 Live Crew, J. Prince, Jermaine Dupri, Luther "Uncle Luke" Campbell, Master P, Organized Noise and Timbaland. The event was staged at the Hammerstein Ballroom in Manhattan and was hosted by Craig Robinson.

2010: A year after he pleaded guilty to assaulting his girlfriend Rihanna, Chris Brown was banned from entering the U.K. The rapper was forced to cancel scheduled concerts in England, Scotland and Ireland.

2011: DMX was the subject of an episode of the VH-1 program, *Behind The Music*.

2012: Lil Phat (born Melvin Vernell III) was murdered. The rapper was shot and killed inside a parking deck at an Atlanta hospital. He was 19-years-old. He was best known for his appearance on the 2008 hit, "Independent" by Webbie.

2014: The single "Fancy" by Iggy Azalea featuring Charli XCX began a seven-week run at number-one on the U.S. charts.

2015: New Jersey State Police arrested 61 people outside the annual Hot 97 Summer Jam concert, which was held at MetLife Stadium in East Rutherford. Hundreds of people who attempted to enter the sold-out concert clashed with police.

JUNE 8

1964: Rob Pilatus (full name Robert Pilatus) was born in Munich, Germany. He was a member of the disgraced duo Milli Vanilli. A break dancer and former model, he was also a backing singer for the group Wind during their appearance on the musical competition, the Eurovision Song Contest.

1983: Whodini released their debut album, *Whodini*. The album was highlighted by the singles, "Magic's Wand" and "The Haunted House Of Rock." Formed in 1981, the Brooklyn-based group was managed by Russell Simmons, the brother of Joseph "DJ Run" Simmons of Run-D.M.C.

1984: One of the first movies to embrace hip hop culture and music, *Beat Street*, was released. The project was based on a script written by journalist Steven Hager, "Looking For The Perfect Beat." The film was set in the South Bronx and followed the lives of an MC, b-boy and graffiti artist. A number of real life rappers appeared in the film including DJ Kool Herc, the Treacherous Three, Doug E. Fresh, the Magnificent Force and Grandmaster Melle Mel & The Furious Five.

1990: The owner of E-C Records, a record store in Fort Lauderdale, was arrested for selling copies of the album, *As Nasty As They Wanna Be* by 2 Live Crew, to a minor and was charged with a felony. He was convicted at an October trial and fined $1,000.

1993: Fu-Schnickens released the single, "What's Up Doc? (Can We Rock)" featuring NBA star Shaquille O'Neal. The basketball player was asked to perform on the song after he publicly stated that Fu-Schnickens was his favorite group.

2004: Hip hop supergroup the Terror released their biggest hit, the chart-topping single, "Lean Back" (featuring Fat Joe and Remy). The remixed version of the track featured Eminem, Lil Jon and Ma$e. The single earned a Grammy nomination in the category of Best Rap Performance by a Duo or Group.

2004: Ciara released her debut single, "Goodies" (featuring Petey Pablo). The track was an answer song to "Freak-A-Leek" by Petey Pablo. The chart-topping single gave Ciara a pair of nicknames, the First Lady and the Princess of Crunk&B.

JUNE 9

1989: Brandy released her second album, *Never Say Never*. The album spawned several hits and sold more than five-million copies in the U.S. The album earned four Grammy nominations. One of the tracks, "The Boy Is Mine" won a Grammy in the category of Best R&B Performance by a Duo or Group with Vocal.

1989: LL Cool J released his third album, *Walking With A Panther*. The million-selling album was highlighted by the hits, "Going Back To Cali," "I'm That Type O Guy," "Jingling Baby," "Big Ole Butt" and "One Shot At Love."

1992: Pete Rock & CL Smooth released one of the most celebrated albums in rap music history, *Mecca And The Soul Brother*. The album was highlighted by the tracks "Straighten It Out," "Lots Of Lovin'" and a tribute to the late Trouble T-Roy, "T.R.O.Y. (They Reminisce Over You)."

2007: The single "Umbrella" by Rihanna featuring Jay-Z began a seven-week run at number-one on the U.S. charts.

2007: Fabolous released the single, "Make Me Better" (featuring Ne-Yo). The song's music video featured Puerto Rican actress and singer Roselyn Sanchez.

2015: Pumpkinhead (real name Robert Alan Diaz) died during surgery at the age of 39. The Brooklyn-based rapper released several albums including *Orange Moon Over Brooklyn*.

JUNE 10

1967: The Human Beat Box (birth name Darren Robinson) was born in Queens, New York. In 1982, he co-founded the groundbreaking rap group, the Fat Boys. Also known as Buffy and DJ Doctor Nice, he pioneered a percussive vocal style called beatboxing. He died in 1995 at the age of 28.

1968: The D.O.C. (birth name Tracy Lynn Curry) was born in Dallas. Also known as Doc-T and the Diggy Diggy Doc, he was a member of the hip hop group Fila Fresh Crew. He also wrote a number of tracks for N.W.A.

1973: Faith Evans (full name Faith Renée Evans) was born in Florida but raised in Newark, New Jersey. She was the first female performer to sign with Bad Boy Entertainment, a label owned by Sean "Puff Daddy" Combs. She married the Notorious B.I.G. in 2004.

1990: The members of the rap group 2 Live Crew were arrested at the Club Futura nightclub in Hollywood, Florida, on obscenity charges after performing songs from their controversial album, *As Nasty As They Wanna Be*. A series of highly-publicized court cases examined whether the album was obscene and not protected by the First Amendment of the U.S. Constitution. Although a Federal court had declared that the album was obscene, the 11th Circuit Court of Appeals later overturned the ruling. Consequently, all of the charges against 2 Live Crew were later dropped.

1993: 2Pac released the single, "I Get Around." The track sampled "Computer Love" by Zapp, "Step In The Arena" by Gang Starr and "Impeach The President" by the Honey Drippers.

2008: Grandmaster Flash published his autobiography, *The Adventures Of Grandmaster Flash: My Life, My Beats*.

2011: British rapper Plan B appeared in a commercial for Hewlett-Packard's Beats Audio laptop.

2014: The city of Houston officially declared the day, "Drake Day." The city's mayor presented the rapper with an award at a ceremony before an Astros game at Minute Maid Park.

2015: Rick Ross was arrested on a charge of marijuana possession while driving his Bentley in Fayette County, Georgia. He had been stopped by a deputy for a window tint violation. He was released after posting a $2,400 bond.

JUNE 11

1968: The Lady of Rage (birth name Robin Yvette Allen) was born in Farmville, Virginia. The rapper recorded several collaborations at Death Row Records and is best known for her solo hit, "Afro Puffs."

1987: Rapper and actor Dappy (birth name Costadinos Contostavlos) was born in Camden, London, England. He was the lead singer of the hip hop trio, N-Dubz.

2005: The Tupac Amaru Shakur Center for the Arts opened in Stone Mountain, Georgia. The facility was founded by the late rapper's mother, Afeni Shakur, and focused on promoting the study of music, drama, dance and creative writing.

2011: Lil Wayne was sued by producers Juan and Oscar Salinas, better known as Play-N-Skillz, for $1 million over the rapper's hit, "Got Money." The Texas-based brothers claimed they were never compensated for their work on the track.

JUNE 12

1989: Public Enemy released the single, "Fight The Power." The song was far more aggressive and militant than most of the hip hop music of the era and helped to define the "gangsta rap" genre. The song was further popularized by its prominent placement in Spike Lee's film, *Do The Right Thing*. As the group's signature hit, Public Enemy would close all of their concerts with the song.

1995: Luther Campbell of 2 Live Crew filed for Chapter 11 bankruptcy in the U.S. District Court of Miami. The previous year, he lost a court case and was ordered to pay a $1.6 million judgement.

2003: KRS-One published the book, *Ruminations*.

2004: Snoop Dogg was banned from the annual Hot 97 Summer Jam for throwing chairs into the audience and dissing fellow performers R. Kelly and Ja Rule. Snoop Dogg was invited to perform at the festival in 2014 after a ten-year absence.

2007: Plies released the single, "Shawty" (featuring T-Pain). The track sampled "Fantasy" by Earth, Wind & Fire. The song's music video featured appearances by Rick Ross, Rich Boy, Lil Duval, Elgin James and Jevon Kearse.

2008: R. Kelly was found not guilty by a Chicago jury on all 14 charges of child pornography. Kelly and the alleged underage victim denied that they were the couple in a video that was shown in court.

2009: The Beastie Boys performed in public for the very last time when they took the stage at the Bonnaroo Music and Arts Festival in Tennessee.

2011: Kidd Kidd (real name Curtis Stewart) was shot six times while sitting in a vehicle, which was parked in front of his mother's home in New Orleans. He survived his injuries.

2012: Jimmy "The Henchman" Rosemond admitted his involvement in the 1994 shooting and robbery of Tupac Shakur at Quad Recording Studios, according to *The Village Voice*. Shakur had accused Rosemond of the assault in the lyrics of the song, "Against All Odds."

2013: Kanye West and Kim Kardashian welcomed the birth of their first child, a daughter named North West.

JUNE 13

1989: The group DC Talk released the first Christian rap album to be certified Gold in the U.S. with sales of 500,000 copies, *DC Talk*. The music video for one of the album's tracks, "Heavenbound," received airplay on the BET program, *Rap City*.

1999: Bad Meets Evil, a hip hop duo consisting of Eminem and Royce da 5'9", released the EP, *Hell: The Sequel*. The album spawned the singles, "Fast Lane" and "Lighters." The EP sold more than one-million copies in the U.S.

2003: Master P co-starred in the Harrison Ford action film, *Hollywood Homicide*.

2006: Busta Rhymes released his seventh studio album, *The Big Bang*. The chart-topping album spawned four singles, "Touch It," "I Love My Bitch," "New York Shit" and "In The Ghetto."

2006: Yung Joc released his debut solo single, "It's Goin' Down." In the song's music video, the actors performed a dance popularized by Yung Joc, "The Joc-In" (also called "The Motorcycle"). The song was nominated for a Grammy in the category of Best Rap Song.

2013: MC Supreme (real name Dewayne Coleman) was killed in a traffic accident along the Pacific Coast Highway in Malibu, California. He was sitting in a parked car that was struck by a pickup truck. He was 47-years-old. A female passenger in Coleman's vehicle was injured.

2014: Kanye West was booed by the audience during his entire performance at the Bonnaroo Arts and Music Festival in Tennessee. He was also booed during his previous Bonnaroo appearance in 2008, when he was nearly two-hours late for his headlining set.

2014: Ice Cube co-starred in the action-comedy film, *22 Jump Street*. He played the role of an undercover police officer named Captain Dickson. Queen Latifah and Diplo also appeared in the film. A box office smash, the movie earned more than $330 million.

JUNE 14

1991: Disgraced duo Milli Vanilli appeared in a television commercial for Carefree Sugarless Bubble Gum. In the spot, the two members pretended to sing Italian opera but stopped when the record began skipping.

1997: The single "I'll Be Missing You" by Puff Daddy and Faith Evans featuring 112 began an eleven-week run at number-one on the U.S. charts.

1997: *Wu-Tang Forever* by the Wu-Tang Clan became the first rap album to reach number-one on the British charts. *Hello Nasty* by the Beastie Boys was the second album.

2010: Eve was the subject of an episode of the VH-1 program, *Behind The Music*.

2011: Hip hop supergroup Random Axe released their only album, *Random Axe*. The group consisted of Guilty Simpson, Sean Price and producer Black Milk. The trio had previously performed together on a 2008 track by Guilty Simpson, "Run."

2012: The entourages of Drake and Chris Brown were involved in a massive brawl at the W.i.P. nightclub in Manhattan. During the melee, NBA star Tony Parker was struck in the eye by a shard of glass. Drake, Brown, Parker and a number of other celebrities were at the club to celebrate the birthday of Ne-Yo's manager, Javon Smith. In the wake of the fight, the nightclub's owners sued the two rappers for $16 million and Parker sued the club for $20 million.

2014: Eve married British race car driver Maximillion Cooper. The couple were married at a ceremony in Ibiza, Spain.

JUNE 15

1969: Ice Cube (birth name O'Shea Jackson) was born in the South Central section of Los Angeles. After a brief stint in the group C.I.A., he joined the groundbreaking gangsta rap outfit, N.W.A. After enjoying a successful solo career, he later turned to acting.

1981: Kurtis Blow released his second album, *Deuce*. The album did not produce any radio hits.

1987: A concert at the Portland Memorial Coliseum featuring Run-D.M.C. and the Beastie Boys was nearly cancelled due to concerns by local police groups. The authorities feared a repeat of the gang violence at Run-D.M.C.'s concert in Long Beach, California, the previous year. To alleviate fears, police installed metal detectors at the facility's 12 entrances.

1989: Punk rock legend Dee Dee Ramone quit his group, the Ramones, and attempted a career as a rapper. Changing his name to Dee Dee King, he released the rap album, *Standing In The Spotlight*. It sold poorly.

1995: Bone Thugs-N-Harmony released "1st Of Tha Month," the first single from their hit album, *E. 1999 Eternal*. The track sampled "I Just Wanna Be Your Girl" by Chapter 8 and "Sexual Healing" by Marvin Gaye. The single was nominated for a Grammy in the category of Best Rap Performance by a Duo or Group.

1996: The Beastie Boys hosted the first annual Tibetan Freedom Concert. The two-day event was staged at Golden Gate Park in San Francisco and raised $800,000. The proceeds were donated to the Milarepa Fund. Among the performers were the Beastie Boys, A Tribe Called Quest, Cibo Matto, Red Hot Chili Peppers, Biz Markie, De La Soul, the Fugees and the Skatalites.

1999: Naughty By Nature released the single, "Jamboree" (featuring Zhané). The track sampled "I'm Always Dancin' To The Music" by Benny Golson, "On Your Face" by Earth, Wind & Fire and "Holiday" by Naughty By Nature. The song's music video featured a cameo appearance by NBA player Shaquille O'Neal.

2000: Flesh-n-Bone (real name Stanley Howse) of Bone Thugs-N-Harmony was convicted of assault with a firearm and after he threatened an acquaintance with an AK-47 in December 1999. After pleading guilty, the rapper was sentenced to 12-years in a California state prison. He was released after serving eight-years.

2006: Jay-Z called for a boycott of Cristal after the managing director of the champagne's maker lamented the fact that his product was popular among rappers.

2008: Kanye West was booed during his performance at the Bonnaroo Festival after he arrived nearly two-hours late for his headlining set, which started at 4:30 A.M. He was also pelted by bottles and glow sticks. Days after the show, West wrote on his blog: "This Bonnaroo thing is the worst insult I've ever had in my life. This is the most offended I've ever been."

2009: Rapper Tru Life (real name Roberto Guzman Rosado, Jr.) and his brother attacked two men in a Manhattan apartment building, injuring one of the men and killing the other. While Tru Life pleaded guilty to charges of second-degree gang assault, his brother pleaded guilty to first-degree manslaughter. Tru Life was sentenced to eight-years in prison and his brother received a ten-year sentence.

2010: Drake released his first full-length studio album, *Thank Me Later*. The chart-topping album spawned the hit singles, "Over," "Find Your Love," "Miss Me" and "Fancy." The album sold nearly two-million copies in the U.S.

2012: Mary J. Blige appeared in the hit comedy film, *Rock Of Ages*.

2015: Killer Mike of the rap group Run The Jewels announced his candidacy in the special election for an open seat in the 55th District of the Georgia State House of Representatives, which covered parts of Atlanta. He was ruled ineligible to run after missing the deadline to formally file his candidacy.

2015: After performing two songs at a wrestling event in Cleveland, Machine Gun Kelly was attacked by one of the wrestlers on the bill, Kevin Owens, because of the rapper's affiliation with rival wrestler John Cena. Machine Gun Kelly was unhurt.

2015: Sprite announced the introduction of the "Obey Your Verse" collection of cans and bottles, which featured the printed hip hop lyrics of Drake, Nas, Rakim and the Notorious B.I.G.

JUNE 16

1969: MC Ren (birth name Lorenzo Jerald Patterson) was born in Compton, California. After writing half the tracks on Eazy-E's debut album *Eazy-Duz-It*, MC Ren was asked to join N.W.A. Later pursuing a solo career, he released his debut EP in 1992, *Kizz My Black Azz*.

1971: Tupac Shakur (previously known as Lesane Parish Crooks) was born in Harlem, New York. He occasionally used the stage names of Makaveli and 2Pac. He began his music career as an MC and dancer for the hip hop group, Digital Underground. Signing with Death Row Records as a solo artist in 1995, he enjoyed a brief but influential career. He was murdered in 1996.

1982: The pop/dance duo Wham! released the early rap hit, "Wham Rap! (Enjoy What You Do)." The single failed to chart when it was initially released but managed to reach the British top-10 the following year when it was reissued. In the U.S., the song failed to reach the top-40 but still received a healthy amount of club and radio airplay.

1985: Austrian-born singer Falco released the rap-styled pop single, "Rock Me Amadeus." A worldwide hit, the track was sung in German. An English language version of the song was later released.

1997: Will Smith released his first solo single, "Men In Black," which was included on the soundtrack of the film of the same name. The song was heard during the film's closing credits. The track was built upon a sample from "Forget Me Nots" by Patrice Rushen and featured backing vocals by Coko of the group SWV. The song earned a Grammy Award in the category of Best Rap Solo Performance.

2003: The Atlanta-based hip hop duo YoungBloodZ released the single, "Damn!" (featuring Lil Jon).

2003: The Black Eyed Peas released the hit single, "Where Is The Love?" It was the group's first single to feature Fergie. The track earned two Grammy nominations.

2004: Method Man and Redman starred in the Fox sitcom, *Method & Red*. The series ran for 12 episodes.

2004: Chuck D was the keynote speaker at the first National Hip-Hop Political Convention, which was held in Newark, New Jersey. The event was scheduled to start on Tupac Shakur's birthday and to end on the Juneteenth holiday.

2008: Will Smith starred in the superhero-comedy film, *Hancock*. In the film, Smith portrayed John Hancock, an alcoholic with a number of superhero powers. The film grossed more than $600 million.

2009: Drake released "Best I Ever Had," the first single from his EP, *So Far Gone*. A surprise hit, the track initially appeared on his third mixtape. The track earned two Grammy nominations and was named the "Hot Rap Song" of the year by *Billboard* magazine.

2013: Public Enemy was given an honorary "key to the city" by the mayor of Durham, North Carolina.

JUNE 17

1961: Guru (birth name Keith Edward Elam) was born in Boston. He co-founded the hip hop duo Gang Starr in 1987. He died in 2010 at the age of 48.

1974: Krayzie Bone (birth name Anthony Henderson) was born in Cleveland. In addition to his success as a member of Bone Thugs-N-Harmony, he pursued a solo career beginning in 1999 with the release of the million-selling album, *Thug Mentality*.

1975: Arabian Prince (birth name Kim Nazel) was born in Compton, California. A founding member of N.W.A., he left the group in 1988 shortly before the release of the album, *Straight Outta Compton*. Also a producer, he oversaw J.J. Fad's hit "Supersonic." He was not mentioned in the 2015 film biography of N.W.A.

1987: A scheduled concert by Run-D.M.C. and the Beastie Boys at the Seattle Civic Arena was cancelled and forced to relocate to another venue. Although 3,800 tickets had already been sold for the concert, the backup venue had seating for only 2,800. An employee of the Seattle Civic Arena told *The Seattle Post-Intelligencer*, "There are ample predictions of real trouble in the neighborhood."

2009: Notable graffiti artist Iz the Wiz (real name Michael Martin) passed away at the age of 51. He was featured in the documentary, *Style Wars*.

2012: As a gift for father's day, Beyoncé bought her husband Jay-Z a brand-new jet airplane. The model Challenger 850 aircraft retailed at the time for more than $40 million.

JUNE 18

1975: Silkk The Shocker (birth name Vyshonne King Miller) was born in New Orleans. Originally called "Silkk," he added "The Shocker" to his name following the release of his debut album in 1996. He is the brother of rappers Master P and C-Murder and is the uncle of Romeo Miller (also known as Lil' Romeo) and Cymphonique Miller.

1990: Acuff-Rose Music, a Nashville-based music publishing company, sued 2 Live Crew for recording an unlicensed version of the song, "Oh, Pretty Woman." The landmark lawsuit worked its way through various courts. Eventually, the U.S. Supreme Court ruled that 2 Live Crew's rendition was a commercial parody that qualified under the rule of "fair use" and did not violate the copyright held by the publishing company.

1991: The hip hop trio 3rd Bass released the crossover hit single, "Pop Goes The Weasel." The track sampled "Sledgehammer" by Peter Gabriel and several other songs. The song's music video featured singer Henry Rollins who portrayed rapper Vanilla Ice.

1996: LL Cool J released the hit single, "Loungin." The song appeared on his sixth album, *Mr. Smith*, as well as on the soundtrack of the film, *Good Burger*. The track sampled "Nite And Day" by Al B. Sure!

2003: Jay-Z and his business partners opened the first of several "40/40" sports bars. The upscale tavern was located in the Flatiron District of New York City.

2005: The first annual Brooklyn Hip-Hop Festival was founded by Wes Jackson. It was staged in the Williamsburg neighborhood. The event was headlined by Brand Nubian and Little Brother, and also featured Leela James, Medina Green, Ge-ology and Amir. In 2006, Ralph McDaniels began hosting the festival.

2010: Rick Ross (real name William Leonard Roberts II) was sued by Los Angeles-based rapper and drug kingpin, "Freeway" Ricky Ross, who asked for $10 million in damages. Rick Ross was accused of committing copyright infringement by borrowing Ricky Ross' name and public reputation. Rick Ross won the case in 2013 on First Amendment grounds.

2010: Lil Boosie was indicted on federal charges of first-degree murder. He was found not guilty at a trial in May 2012.

2010: Eminem released his seventh studio album, *Recovery*. The album spawned four singles, "Not Afraid," "Love The Way You Lie," "No Love" and "Space Bound." The album was nominated for a Grammy in the category of Album of the Year and won a Grammy in the category of Best Rap Album. The album sold four-million copies in the U.S., making it the best seller of 2010.

2013: Kanye West released his sixth solo album, *Yeezus*. An electronic album that employed synthesizers, the project was a departure from West's hip hop roots. The album spawned two singles, "Black Skinhead" and "Bound 2."

2013: Questlove of the Roots published his autobiography, *Mo' Meta Blues: The World According To Questlove*.

JUNE 19

1970: D-Nice (birth name Derrick Jones) was born in the Bronx, New York. A member of Boogie Down Productions, he later pursued a solo career. In 1988, D-Nice discovered Kid Rock and helped the rap-rocker get signed by Jive Records.

1983: Macklemore (birth name Ben Haggerty) was born in Seattle. Formerly known as Professor Macklemore, he teamed with producer Ryan Lewis in 2009 to form a hip hop duo. In 2012, Macklemore & Ryan Lewis issued their self-financed independent album, *The Heist*. A surprise hit, the project spawned five singles, most notably "Thrift Shop." As a result of the album's success, the duo won four Grammys.

1984: The nationally-syndicated hip hop program *Graffiti Rock* aired its first and only episode. Hosted by journalist Michael Holman, the program featured performances by Run-D.M.C., the New York City Breakers, Shannon, Kool Moe Dee and Special K of the Treacherous Three.

1991: Bushwick Bill of the Geto Boys lost one of his eyes after convincing his girlfriend to shoot him during a domestic squabble. A photo of the injured rapper was featured on the cover of the group's next album, *We Can't Be Stopped*.

1998: Hip hop artists Missy Elliott, Erykah Badu and Queen Latifah joined the 57-date Lilith Fair music festival. The tour began in Portland, Oregon.

2001: Sisqó released his second solo album, *Return Of Dragon*, which spawned the hit singles, "Can I Live" and "Dance For Me."

2001: D12, a Detroit hip hop group featuring Eminem, released their debut album, *Devil's Night*. The album spawned three singles, "Purple Pills," "Ain't Nuttin' But Music" and "Fight Music." This was the first release on Eminem's label, Shady Records.

2001: Fabolous released his debut solo single, "Can't Deny It" (featuring Nate Dogg). The track sampled "Ambitionz Az A Ridah" by 2Pac and "Shook Ones Part II" by Mobb Deep.

2001: At the first annual BET Awards, the winners were: Eve for Best Female Hip-Hop Artist and Jay-Z for Best Male Hip-Hop Artist. The ceremony was staged at the Paris Las Vegas hotel and casino in Las Vegas.

2003: G-Man (real name Jason Phillips) of the British hip hop group So Solid Crew was sentenced to four-years in prison for possessing a loaded handgun.

2004: Rapper T.I. was on a work-release program from prison when he jumped onto the stage at the annual Hot 107.9 Birthday Bash in Atlanta. Wearing an orange jumpsuit, he began a free-style rap that targeted his rival, Lil Flip, who had criticized T.I.'s decision to start calling himself "The King of the South" the previous year.

2012: Meek Mill released the controversial single, "Amen." Within weeks of its release, a pastor in Mill's hometown of Philadelphia described the song's lyrics as blasphemous and called for a boycott of the track. After Mill made a public apology, the pastor called off his boycott.

2014: A musical inspired by the songs of Tupac Shakur, *Holler If Ya Hear Me*, opened on Broadway. The $8 million production was produced by his mother, Afeni Shakur, and starred Saul Williams. The musical featured 21 songs by the fallen rapper.

JUNE 20

1975: Loon (birth name Chauncey Lamont Hawkins) was born in Harlem, New York. Signing with Bad Boy Records, he released his debut solo album in 2003, *Loon*, and was the featured artist on a pair of top-10 hits by P. Diddy. After converting to Islam in 2009, Loon adopted the name Amir Junaid Hawkins.

1993: J-Dee (real name Dasean Cooper), a member of the Los Angeles gangsta rap trio Da Lench Mob, was charged with the murder of his girlfriend's roommate. He was later convicted of the crime and sentenced to 29-years to life in prison. J-Dee has repeatedly denied any involvement in the crime.

2000: Afroman released his second album, *Because I Got High*. The album's title track was a sleeper hit that didn't receive widespread airplay until late-2001. The track was nominated for a Grammy and was featured in several films.

2006: Jibbs released his debut single, "Chain Hang Low." The song is built around the melody of a 19th century folk song, "Do Your Ears Hang Low?" (which is also known as "Turkey In The Straw").

2007: Ludacris guest starred on an episode of *The Simpsons*, titled "You Kent Always Say What You Want."

2008: British rapper Ben Drew (a.k.a. Plan B) co-starred in the film drama, *Adulthood*. He portrayed a hoodlum named Dabs. The film was a sequel to the 2006 release, *Kidulthood*.

2009: Ludacris staged a launch party for his new cognac, Conjure, at an outdoor park in the city of Bordeaux, France. The rapper introduced the brand in conjunction with Norwegian spirits maker Birkedal Hartmann Cognac.

2009: At the annual 107.9 FM Birthday Bash at Philips Arena in Atlanta, rapper Plies threw $50,000 into the audience to promote his new single, "Plenty Money."

2013: Jennifer Lopez was awarded a star on the Hollywood Walk of Fame.

2015: Thieves broke into Chris Brown's mansion in Los Angeles. After holding the singer's aunt at gunpoint, they rummaged through the house and stole $50,000. At the time of the robbery, Brown was in Hollywood hosting an ESPY party.

JUNE 21

1968: DJ Scratch (birth name George Spivey) of EPMD was born in Brooklyn, New York.

1970: Pete Rock (birth name Peter Phillips) was born in the Bronx, New York. As a member of the hip hop duo Pete Rock & CL Smooth, he is best known for the hit single, "They Reminisce Over You (T.R.O.Y.)." He later enjoyed a successful career as a producer.

1984: The synthpop/R&B song, "Breakin'... There's No Stopping Us" by Ollie & Jerry became a hit after it was featured in the break dance film, *Breakin'*.

1984: *The New York Times* ran an article about the risk of serious injury from break dancing. The article quoted a Chicago surgeon who had treated five break dancers for broken arms.

1994: Bone Thugs-N-Harmony, a Cleveland-based hip hop group, released their debut EP, *Creepin On Ah Come Up*. The group consisted of Krayzie Bone, Bizzy Bone, Layzie Bone, Wish Bone and Flesh-n-Bone. The album was highlighted by the singles, "Foe Tha Love Of $" and the breakthrough hit, "Thuggish Ruggish Bone."

2014: Rick Ross was forced to cancel a concert in Detroit due to numerous threats. When he arrived on the grounds of Chene Park Amphitheater for Summer Jamz 17, Ross was met by a large group of people who would not let his pass.

JUNE 22

1962: Schoolly D (birth name Jesse Bonds Weaver, Jr.) was born in Philadelphia. Often called the first gangsta rapper, he released his debut album in 1985, *Schoolly D*. A single from the album, "P.S.K. What Does It Mean?," is often considered the first gangsta rap song.

1988: Big Daddy Kane released the single, "Ain't No Half-Steppin'" from his debut album, *Long Live The Kane*. The track sampled "Blind Alley" by the Emotions.

1993: Cypress Hill released the single, "Insane In The Brain." A crossover hit, it became the group's signature song. The track was intended as a diss song aimed at rival rapper Chubb Rock. The track sampled "Good Guys Only Win In The Movies" by Mel and Tim, "Son Of A Preacher Man" by Dusty Springfield and three other songs. "Insane In The Brain" earned a Grammy nomination in the category of Best Rap Performance by a Duo or Group.

2000: The daily dance competition, *Sisqó's Shakedown*, debuted on MTV. Hosted by rapper Sisqó and featuring deejay Funkmaster Flex from Direct Effect, the series was filmed at Mission Beach in San Diego. The winning dancer earned a prize of $10,000.

2004: The Black Eyed Peas released the hit single, "Let's Get It Started." The track appeared on the 2004 re-issue of the album, *Elephunk*. The track won a Grammy in the category of Best Rap Performance by a Duo or Group. This was the first track to sell 500,000 digital copies in the U.S.

2004: Jadakiss released his second solo album, *Kiss Of Death*. The album spawned three singles, "Time's Up," "Why?" and "U Make Me Wanna."

2009: Chris Brown pleaded guilty to a felony charge of assault with the intent of doing great bodily injury. He had been arrested the previous January for allegedly assaulting his girlfriend, Rihanna. In a plea deal, he was sentenced to 1,400 hours of labor-oriented community service, five years of formal probation and one year of domestic violence counseling. He was also ordered to stay at least 50 yards from Rihanna, unless it was a music industry event.

2009: Internet gossip blogger Perez Hilton got into an altercation with Black Eyed Peas member will.i.am and his entourage outside of the Cobra nightclub in Toronto.

2011: Cee Lo Green debuted his shortlived, late-night talk show on the Fuse network, *Talking To Strangers*.

2013: The single "Blurred Lines" by Robin Thicke featuring T.I. and Pharrell Williams began a remarkable twelve-week run at number-one on the U.S. charts.

2015: Sean "Diddy" Combs was involved in a physical altercation with a football coach at UCLA. The confrontation occurred after Diddy complained about how his 21-year-old son, Justin Combs, was treated by the coach at a practice session. Despite his arrest on suspicion of felony assault and other related charges, Diddy was cleared of the more serious charges.

JUNE 23

1978: Memphis Bleek (birth name Malik Cox) was born in Brooklyn, New York. Signed to Roc-A-Fella Records, he was featured on a number of Jay-Z tracks before releasing his debut solo album in 1999, *Coming Of Age*. He later founded his own label, Get Low Records.

1992: Three members of MC Hammer's touring crew were injured during a drive-by shooting at Roosevelt Park in Albuquerque, New Mexico. The shooting took place after a charity softball game between firemen and the rapper's crew.

2009: The Black Eyed Peas released the smash hit single, "I Gotta Feeling." The digital-only track sold nearly nine-million copies in the U.S. and was the first track to sell one-million digital copies in the U.K. The song won a Grammy in the category of Best Pop Performance by a Duo or Group with Vocals.

2011: Missy Elliott revealed that she was battling Graves' Disease, an autoimmune disorder. She was diagnosed with the condition in 2008.

2014: The reality series, *CeeLo Green's The Good Life*, debuted on TBS. The program was cancelled after six episodes.

JUNE 24

1997: Wyclef Jean of the Fugees released his debut solo album, *The Carnival*. The album sold two-million copies in the U.S. and spawned the singles, "We Trying To Stay Alive," "To All The Girls," a cover of the Cuban folk standard "Guantanamera" and the Grammy-nominated "Gone Till November."

2003: At the third annual BET Awards, the winners were: Missy Elliot for Best Female Hip-Hop Artist and 50 Cent for Best Male Hip-Hop Artist. The ceremony was staged at the Kodak Theater in Hollywood.

2003: The Black Eyed Peas released their breakthrough album, *Elephunk*. The group's third album, it was the first to feature Fergie. The album spawned the hit singles, "Where Is The Love?," "Shut Up," "Hey Mama" and "Let's Get It Started." The album sold more than three-million copies in the U.S.

2004: DMX (real name Earl Simmons) and an accomplice attempted to steal a car from a parking lot at JFK Airport in New York City. According to the car's owner, the rapper identified himself as an FBI agent who was commandeering the vehicle. After DMX failed in his robbery attempt, he took off in his own SUV and crashed through a toll gate without paying. When Port Authority Police arrested rapper, they found crack cocaine in his vehicle. DMX was taken to Elmhurst Hospital Center for an examination before he was booked.

2006: Beyoncé released the single, "Déjà Vu," which featured her future husband Jay-Z. The song was nominated for a Grammy in three categories.

2007: T.I. was involved in a scuffle with Ludacris' manager Chaka Zulu during a charity luncheon at the Sunset Tower Hotel in Los Angeles, which was hosted by an executive of Warner Music Group. Among those in attendance at the event were Brandy, Yung Joc, Musiq, Twista and Omar Epps.

2008: At the ninth annual BET Awards, the winners were: Missy Elliot for Best Female Hip-Hop Artist and Kanye West for Best Male Hip-Hop Artist. The ceremony was staged at the Shrine Auditorium in Los Angeles.

2014: Olivia Longott published her autobiography, *Release Me: My Life, My Words*.

2015: Rap mogul Rick Ross was arrested at his home in Fayette County, Georgia, by the U.S. Marshals Service. He was charged with aggravated assault, kidnapping and aggravated battery in an incident involving his groundskeeper.

2015: Hit record producer Scott Storch filed for bankruptcy. A one-time multi-millionaire who owned a $10 million mansion in Miami, Storch had worked with dozens of top artists including 50 Cent, Beyoncé, Tupac Shakur, Snoop Dogg, Dr. Dre, Nas and Lil Wayne.

JUNE 25

1968: Candyman (birth name Candell Manson) was born in Los Angeles. He is best known for his 1990 hit, "Knockin' Boots."

1988: The disgraced lip-syncing duo Milli Vanilli released their debut single, "Girl You Know It's True." The single was a worldwide hit and sold one-million copies in the U.S. The song was originally recorded in 1987 by Maryland-based hip hop group, Numarx.

1996: Jay-Z released his debut album, *Reasonable Doubt*. The album spawned the singles, "Dead Presidents," "Ain't No Nigga," "Can't Knock The Hustle" and "Feelin' It." The critically-acclaimed album sold one-million copies in the U.S.

2000: Eminem was the first solo rap artist to score a number-one album on the British charts. *The Marshall Mathers LP* topped the U.K. chart for two non-consecutive weeks.

2002: Nelly released his hit solo album, *Nellyville*. The album spawned six singles, "#1," "Hot In Herre," "Dilemma," "Air Force Ones," "Work It" and "Pimp Juice." The album earned three Grammy nominations and sold nearly seven-million copies in the U.S.

2002: Nelly released the single, "Dilemma" (featuring Kelly Rowland), from his debut solo album, *Nellyville*. The track sampled "Love, Need And Want You" by Patti LaBelle. "Dilemma" would also appear on Rowland's debut solo album, *Simply Deep*. The song won a Grammy in the category of Best Rap/Sung Collaboration.

2014: Beyoncé and Jay-Z launched their successful "The On The Run" tour. The co-headlining stadium tour earned nearly $110 million over 21 shows, with 19 stops in North America and two in Europe. Tickets ranged in price from $40 to $275. The tour was promoted with a video which featured the married couple as gangsters Bonnie and Clyde.

2015: Silentó released his debut single, the pop/rap hit "Watch Me (Whip/Nae Nae)." The song's video consisted of dancers performing the whip, the Nae Nae, the Crank That and the Stanky Legg. Silentó later recorded a remixed version of the track for the Nickelodeon cable network.

2015: Tyga allegedly got into a fight with the management at the Envogue Genèv nightclub in Geneva, Switzerland, after he arrived late for a concert and performed for only 10 minutes.

JUNE 26

1970: Irv Gotti (birth name Irving Domingo Lorenzo, Jr.) was born in Queens, New York. A prolific producer, he worked with a number of leading artists including Jay-Z, Ja Rule, Foxy Brown, Jennifer Lopez, Fat Joe, Vanessa Carlton and Ashanti. In 1999, Gotti started his own label, The Inc. Records (which was originally called Murder Inc.).

2002: The television film, *Play'd: A Hip Hop Story*, chronicled a fictional East Coast rapper named Jaxx who was convinced to move to the West Coast. The film starred Rashaan Nall and Toni Braxton.

2005: Trey Songz released his debut album, *I Gotta Make*. The album spawned the singles, "Gotta Make It" and "Gotta Go."

2007: At the eighth annual BET Awards, T.I. won the award for Best Male Hip-Hop Artist. The ceremony was staged at the Shrine Auditorium in Los Angeles.

2011: At the12th annual BET Awards, the winners were: Nicki Minaj for Best Female Hip-Hop Artist and Kanye West for Best Male Hip-Hop Artist. The ceremony was staged at the West Shrine Auditorium in Los Angeles.

2012: Rapper and producer Mike Scala ran in the Democratic primary for New York's 5th Congressional district. He lost to the incumbent, Congressman Gregory Meeks.

2012: Just eleven days after a violent melee at a Manhattan nightclub between the entourages of Drake and Chris Brown, a promoter approached *The New York Post* with an offer to pay each of the two men $1 million if they would step into the ring and settle their beef in a boxing match.

2015: Professor Griff of Public Enemy published the book, *Acapella Revolution*.

JUNE 27

1986: Run-D.M.C. made a guest appearance at an Adidas outlet in a Baltimore mall. But when more than 13,000 youth converged on the store, the mall was forced to close.

1988: The Fat Boys filed a $5 million lawsuit against the Miller Beer Company after the beermaker ran commercials that featured three overweight rappers in Fat Boys-style Davy Crockett hats. The Fat Boys claimed they had turned down an offer to appear in the Miller Lite commercial which also starred comedian Joe Piscopo.

1991: Denise "Dee" Barnes, the host of the Fox network hip hop show *Pump It Up!,* sued rapper Dr. Dre of N.W.A. after he allegedly assaulted her. She filed a $22.7 million lawsuit against Dr. Dre for assault as well as "libel, slander and infliction of emotional distress." She would later settle the suit out of court.

1993: HoodShock – a free, afternoon rap concert in Harlem – was marred by injuries. Hundreds of concertgoers started a stampede after hearing a gunshot and firecrackers. The outdoor event featured the Fugees and drew 15,000 people.

2000: Nelly released his debut studio album, *Country Grammar*. The hit album spawned the singles, "Country Grammar (Hot Shit)," "E.I.," "Ride Wit Me" and "Batter Up." Nelly's group, the St. Lunatics, appeared on the album. The album sold more than nine-million copies in the U.S.

2006: At the seventh annual BET Awards, the winners were: Missy Elliot for Best Female Hip-Hop Artist and T.I. for Best Male Hip-Hop Artist. The ceremony was staged at the Shrine Auditorium in Los Angeles.

2010: At the 11th annual BET Awards, the winners were: Nicki Minaj for Best Female Hip-Hop Artist and Drake for Best Male Hip-Hop Artist. The ceremony was staged at the Shrine Auditorium in Los Angeles.

2010: Pioneering New York-based rapper and graffiti artist Rammellzee passed away at the age of 49. He was featured in the 1983 film, *Wild Style*.

2010: Snoop Dogg was banned from performing at the Parkpop festival in the Hague, Netherlands. According to authorities, he was removed from the lineup in keeping with a family-friendly environment.

2014: Following a concert at the 2014 SuperJam at the Greensboro Coliseum, Rick Ross was arrested for failing to appear in court for a 2013 drug arrest. He was released after paying $1,000 bail.

2015: Three surviving members of N.W.A. – Ice Cube, DJ Yella and MC Ren – reunited at the BET Experience concert in Los Angeles, shortly before the release of the film, *Straight Outta Compton*. It was their first performance in 26 years.

2015: DMX was arrested just hours before a scheduled concert at Radio Music City Hall in New York City on charges of failure to pay child support. According to court records, he owed $400,000 in back child support.

JUNE 28

1983: Herbie Hancock released the early hip hop classic, "Rockit." Backed by deejay Grandmixer D. ST., the jazz-rooted Hancock mixed electronic music and industrial beats with the new art of record scratching. The song's award-winning music video featured a team of dancing robots.

1986: Following a concert by Run-D.M.C. at the Civic Arena in Pittsburgh, concertgoers roamed through the downtown district, where they assaulted dozens of pedestrians and broke numerous windows. In all, 27 people were arrested and 22 were treated for injuries.

1988: Public Enemy released their breakthrough album, *It Takes A Nation Of Millions To Hold Us Back*. The album was highlighted by the tracks, "Rebel Without A Pause," "Don't Believe The Hype," "Black Steel In The Hour Of Chaos," a song about crack cocaine, "Night Of The Living Baseheads," and a song that originally appeared in the 1987 film *Less Than Zero*, "Bring The Noise." The album sold nearly two-million copies in the U.S.

1992: Mary J. Blige released her widely-acclaimed debut solo album, *What's The 411?* The album spawned six singles including "You Remind Me" and "Real Love."

1994: Da Brat released her debut album, *Funkdafied*. It was the first solo album by a female hip hop artist to be certified Platinum by the RIAA with sales of more than one-million copies. The album spawned the hit singles, "Funkdafied," "Fa All Y'all" and "Give It 2 You."

1994: A concert by Tupac Shakur at the Robin Hood Dell East in Philadelphia was cancelled by the city's mayor. His chief of staff told *The Philadelphia Inquirer* that Shakur's music was not "consistent with the family-based entertainment that the city wants to provide" at the city-owned venue.

2005: The Fugees reunited at the 2005 BET Awards. The group performed a number of their hits including, "Ready Or Not," "Fu-Gee-La" and "Killing Me Softly."

2005: At the fifth annual BET Awards, the winners were: Remy Ma for Best Female Hip-Hop Artist and Kanye West for Best Male Hip-Hop Artist. The ceremony was staged at the Kodak Theater in Hollywood.

2009: The television program *Tiny and Toya* debuted on the BET network. Starring best friends Tameka "Tiny" Cottle-Harris and Antonia "Toya" Carter, the docu-drama chronicled their personal and working lives in the Atlanta music community. At the time, Cottle-Harris (a former member of the group Xscape) was engaged to rapper T.I., while Carter was divorced from Lil Wayne. The program ran for two seasons.

2009: At the tenth annual BET Awards, the winners were: M.I.A. for Best Female Hip-Hop Artist and Little Wayne for Best Male Hip-Hop Artist. The ceremony was staged at the Shrine Auditorium in Los Angeles.

2011: A full-sized wax figure of Alicia Keys was unveiled at Madame Tussauds in New York City. The singer was in attendance for the unveiling ceremony.

2011: Big Sean released his debut studio album, *Finally Famous*. The album spawned the singles, "My Last," "Marvin & Chardonnay" and "Dance (A$$)."

2012: R. Kelly published his autobiography, *Soulacoaster: The Diary Of Me*.

2013: Sisqó appeared on the television reality series, *Celebrity Wife Swap*. He swapped partners for one week with Ecuadorian-born rapper Gerardo of "Rico Suave" fame.

2015: At the 16th annual BET Awards, the winners were: Nicki Minaj for Best Female Hip-Hop Artist and Kendrick Lamar for Best Male Hip-Hop Artist. The ceremony was staged at the Microsoft Theatre in Los Angeles.

JUNE 29

1972: DJ Shadow (birth name Joshua Paul Davis) was born in San Jose, California. He is best known for his debut album, *Endtroducing*.

1992: The hip hop program, *The Grind*, debuted on MTV. The program, which featured music videos, was originally hosted by Eric Nies and DJ Jackie Christie. The show ran until November 1997.

1994: Shortly before his 19th birthday, Curtis Jackson (later known as 50 Cent) was arrested for his involvement in the sale of a small amount of cocaine to an undercover police officer. When his home was searched three weeks later, he was arrested and charged with additional drug counts after authorities found crack cocaine and heroin. Sentenced to three-to-nine years in prison, he served just seven-months after agreeing to enter a boot camp-style institution in Beaver Dams, New York.

1998: The Black Eyed Peas released their debut album, *Behind The Front*. The album was highlighted by the single, "Joints & Jam," which featured the lead vocals of Ingrid Dupree. Fergie would not join the group until 2002.

2002: Nelly began a seven-week run at number-one on the U.S. singles chart with "Hot In Herre."

2002: At the second annual BET Awards, the winners were: Missy Elliot for Best Female Hip-Hop Artist and Ja Rule for Best Male Hip-Hop Artist. The ceremony was staged at the Kodak Theater in Hollywood.

2003: The trio of Nelly, P. Diddy and Murphy Lee released the single, "Shake Ya Tailfeather." The track was featured on the soundtrack of the film, *Bad Boys II*, as well as on Lee's debut album, *Murphy's Law*. The song won a Grammy in the category of Best Rap Performance by a Duo or Group.

2004: At the fourth annual BET Awards, the winners were: Missy Elliot for Best Female Hip-Hop Artist and Jay-Z for Best Male Hip-Hop Artist. The ceremony was staged at the Kodak Theater in Hollywood.

2008: Faith Evans, the widow of the Notorious B.I.G., published her autobiography, *Keep The Faith: A Memoir*.

2011: Missy Elliott was the subject of an episode of the VH-1 program, *Behind The Music*.

2012: Romeo Miller (also known as Lil' Romeo) co-starred in the Tyler Perry comedy film, *Madea's Witness Protection*.

2012: Chris Brown released his fifth album, *Fortune*. The chart-topping album spawned the hits, "Strip" (featuring Kevin McCall), "Turn Up The Music," "Sweet Love," "Till I Die," "Don't Wake Me Up" and "Don't Judge Me."

2012: Lauryn Hill pleaded guilty to a charge of tax evasion for not paying federal taxes from 2005 to 2007. After facing a maximum of three-years in prison, she was sentenced to three-months behind bars, three-months of supervised home detention and one-year of probation.

2014: At the 15th annual BET Awards, the winners were: Nicki Minaj for Best Female Hip-Hop Artist and Drake for Best Male Hip-Hop Artist. The ceremony was staged at the Microsoft Theatre in Los Angeles.

2014: Bow Wow dropped his stage name and asked to be called by his birth name, Chad Moss.

JUNE 30

1979: Matisyahu (birth name Matthew Paul Miller) was born in West Chester, Pennsylvania. He combined rap, rock and reggae with Jewish themes, and is best known for his 2005 hit, "King Without A Crown."

1984: Fantasia (full name Fantasia Monique Barrino), the winner of Season 3 of *American Idol*, was born in High Point, North Carolina.

1997: Puff Daddy released the hit single, "It's All About The Benjamins," featuring Lil' Kim, the LOX and the Notorious B.I.G. (An earlier version of the track appeared on DJ Clue's 1996 mixtape, *Holiday Holdup*.) The track sampled "I Did It For Love" by Love Unlimited. Puff Daddy also released a rock version of "Benjamins" which was titled, "It's All About The Benjamins (Rock Remix)," which featured Tommy Stinson, Fuzzbubble, Rob Zombie and Dave Grohl.

1997: Lil' Kim released the single, "Ladies Night (Not Tonight Remix)," which featured Da Brat, Missy "Misdemeanor" Elliott, Angie Martinez, and Lisa "Left Eye" Lopes. The track appeared on the soundtrack of the film, *Nothing To Lose*. The original version of "Not Tonight" appeared on Lil' Kim's debut solo album, *Hard Core*.

1998: The rap supergroup Def Squad released the album, *El Niño*. The group consisted of Redman, Erick Sermon and Keith Murray. The album produced only one single, "Full Cooperation."

1998: Ol' Dirty Bastard was shot by masked robbers at his Brooklyn apartment. The thieves made off with cash and jewelry.

1999: Will Smith starred in the big screen adaptation of the 1960s television western, *Wild Wild West*. Smith portrayed the character of Captain James T. West. The film earned more than $220 million at the box office. Smith also scored a hit with the track, "Wild Wild West."

2006: Juvenile performed for members of the U.S. military at the Marine Corps Base on the island of Oahu, Hawaii. He was the headliner at a free concert that featured a number of rock and country music acts including Staind, Molly Hatchet and .38 Special. After the concert, Juvenile flew to South Korea to entertain U.S. troops at several military bases.

2008: Soulja Boy announced a partnership with Yum Shoes to release a signature line of athletic shoes.

2009: 50 Cent teamed with Right Guard to create the product, "Pure 50 Body Spray."

2009: R&B/hip hop performer Jeremih released his debut album, *Jeremih*. While enrolled at Columbia College Chicago, Jeremih teamed with record producer Mick Schultz to write and record the album's tracks. After auditioning the songs for Def Jam Recordings, Jeremih was signed to the label on the same day. The album spawned the top-10 crossover single, "Birthday Sex."

2009: *Vibe* magazine announced it was shutting down after 16 years. The publication was sold the following year.

2013: At the 14th annual BET Awards, the winners were: Nicki Minaj for Best Female Hip-Hop Artist and Kendrick Lamar for Best Male Hip-Hop Artist. The ceremony was staged at the Shrine Auditorium in Los Angeles.

2014: Chris Brown released the single, "New Flame." There were two versions of the song, one featuring Usher and Rick Ross and the other featuring only Ross.

2015: Turk, a member of the New Orleans hip hop group the Hot Boys, settled his lawsuit against his label, Cash Money Records. The rapper claimed he did not receive royalties because the label had failed to copyright the 34 songs he had written or co-written. Terms of the deal were not disclosed. Turk had originally asked for a judgement of $1.3 million.

▶ JULY

JULY 1

1956: Pioneering deejay Disco King Mario was born in the Bronx, New York. Although he never released a record during his career, he greatly influenced the hip hop movement in the 1970s. He also mentored early rappers such as Afrika Bambaataa and Busy Bee Starski. Disco King Mario died with little fanfare in 1994.

1971: Missy "Misdemeanor" Elliot (birth name Melissa Arnette Elliott) was born in Portsmouth, Virginia. Before launching a successful solo career, she was a member of the all-female R&B group, Sista, and the hip hop collective, the Swing Mob.

1976: Plies (birth name Algernod Lanier Washington) was born in Fort Myers, Florida. The rapper is best known for his 2007 hit, "Shawty." He also co-founded the label, Big Gates Records

1982: Grandmaster Flash and the Furious Five released their groundbreaking rap single, "The Message." This was the first hip hop hit to embrace social commentary. Grandmaster Flash – who rejected his label's request to record the song – did not appear on the track except for the spoken outro. Instead, the song featured the vocals of songwriter Ed "Duke Bootee" Fletcher who traded verses with Melle Mel. The track is one of the most sampled songs in the history of rap music.

1988: *Hip Hop Connection*, the first major hip hop magazine in Britain, published its first issue. Chris Hunt was the magazine's editor. The monthly magazine printed its final issue in 2009.

1991: The Geto Boys released the crossover hit single, "Mind Playing Tricks On Me." The track sampled "Hung Up On My Baby" by Isaac Hayes.

1991: Before he was known as RZA, rapper and producer Robert Diggs performed under the stage name Prince Rakeem and released a solo EP for Tommy Boy Records, *Ooh I Love You Rakeem*.

1992: Def Jam Recordings co-founder Russell Simmons launched the HBO comedy series, *Def Comedy Jam*. The program was a showcase for African-American comedians such as Martin Lawrence, Chris Tucker and Bernie Mac.

1997: Sean "Puff Daddy" Combs released his debut album, *No Way Out*. The album spawned five singles: "Can't Nobody Hold Me Down," "I'll Be Missing You," "It's All About The Benjamins," "Been Around The World" and "Victory." The album sold more than seven-million copies in the U.S. and earned five Grammy nominations, winning an award in the category of Best Rap Album.

1997: Missy "Misdemeanor" Elliott released her debut solo single, "The Rain (Supa Dupa Fly)." The track sampled "I Can't Stand The Rain" by Ann Peebles. A number of rappers made cameo appearances in the song's music video including Timbaland, Yo-Yo, Lil' Kim, Puff Daddy, Total, 702, Da Brat and Lil' Cease.

1998: Sean "Puff Daddy" Combs released the single, "Come With Me," which was featured on the soundtrack of the film, *Godzilla*. Instead of using a traditional sample, the song featured legendary rock guitarist Jimmy Page who recreated his performance from Led Zeppelin's 1975 hit track, "Kashmir." Both men appeared in the song's music video.

2011: Antonio "L.A." Reid was hired as the Chairman and CEO of Epic Records. He was previously the Chairman of the Island Def Jam Music Group.

2012: At the 13th annual BET Awards, the winners were: Nicki Minaj for Best Female Hip-Hop Artist and Drake for Best Male Hip-Hop Artist. The ceremony was staged at the Shrine Auditorium in Los Angeles.

2014: Ja Rule published his autobiography, *Unruly: The Highs And Lows Of Becoming A Man*.

2014: Trey Songz released his sixth studio album, *Trigga*. The chart-topping album featured a number of guest vocalists including Nicki Minaj, Justin Bieber, Mila J, Ty Dolla $ign and Juicy. The album spawned several singles including "Na Na," "Foreign" and "Touchin, Lovin."

2015: Rihanna became the first artist in history to sell 100 million digital tracks, according to a report in *Billboard* magazine.

JULY 2

1970: Monie Love (birth name Simone Gooden) was born in London, England. A member of the hip hop group Native Tongues, Love is best known for her 1990 solo hit, "It's A Shame (My Sister)." Her brother is techno producer Dave Angel.

1970: Spice 1 (birth name Robert L. Green, Jr.) was born in Corsicana, Texas. The rapper's name stands for "Sex, Pistols, Indo, Cash, and Entertainment." Discovered by Too $hort, Spice 1 released his breakthrough album in 1992, *Spice 1*.

1990: Vanilla Ice released his smash hit, "Ice Ice Baby." It was the first hip hop song to top *Billboard* magazine's pop chart. "Ice Ice Baby" was built upon the prominent bass line from "Under Pressure" by David Bowie and Queen. Following legal threats, Bowie and Queen were both given songwriter credits.

1991: Slick Rick released his second album, *The Ruler's Back*. The album was recorded while the rapper was out on bail and was released after he returned to prison. Not as popular as his debut release, the album spawned the hit single, "I Shouldn't Have Done It."

1991: The Geto Boys released their best-selling album, *We Can't Be Stopped*. The cover of the album featured a gruesome photo of member Bushwick Bill after he was shot in the eye.

1996: Nas released the album, *It Was Written*. The album spawned the singles, "If I Ruled The World (Imagine That)," "Street Dreams" and "The Message." For the album, Nas adopted the mafioso persona, Nas Escobar. This was Nas' best-selling album of his career with sales of more than four-million copies in the U.S.

1997: Will Smith starred opposite Tommy Lee Jones in the blockbuster, science fiction/comedy film, *Men In Black*. Smith and Jones portrayed government agents who worked with extraterrestrial life forms on Earth. The film was based on Lowell Cunningham's "The Men In Black" comic book series. The film grossed over half a billion dollars. Smith also recorded two songs for the film's soundtrack album.

2007: "My Humps" by the Black Eyed Peas topped *Rolling Stone* magazine's list of "the 20 Most Annoying Songs" of all time.

JULY 3

1976: A trio of New York-based graffiti artists – CAINE, MAD 103 and FLAME ONE – were the first to paint an entire subway train. The three artists dubbed their work "The Freedom Train" in tribute to the nation's bicentennial on the following day. It took several hours of work to paint the entire train which was parked at a yard in Queens.

1989: MC Lyte released the single, "Cha Cha Cha." The track sampled "Rockin' It" by the Fearless Four.

1990: Slick Rick shot two men – his cousin and a bystander – after a simmering dispute. Jumping into his car and fleeing from police, he eventually drove into a tree. Charged with attempted murder, assault, the use of a firearm and criminal possession of a weapon, the rapper pleaded guilty. He spent five-years in prison before being released in 1997.

1993: Memphis-based hip hop duo 8Ball & MJG released their breakthrough album, *Comin' Out Hard*.

1994: The mockumentary, *Fear Of A Black Hat*, was released. The film offered a satirical look at the rise of hip hop music through the adventures of a fictional gangsta rap group, N.W.H. (Niggaz With Hats).

1995: The members of TLC filed for bankruptcy protection. The group claimed $1 million assets and $3.5 million of liabilities, despite selling 11 million copies of their hit album, *CrazySexyCool*, the previous year.

1996: Will Smith starred in the blockbuster, science fiction film, *Independence Day*. Smith portrayed a cigar-smoking Marine pilot named Captain Steven Hiller who battled space aliens.

1996: Lil' Kim was released from prison after serving 10-months of a year-long sentence. She had been convicted of perjury after lying to a federal grand jury in an effort to protect her friends, following a shooting incident that involved the entourage of rival rapper, Foxy Brown. Lil' Kim was picked up from prison in a Rolls-Royce.

2001: Ja Rule released the single, "Livin' It Up" (featuring Case). The track sampled "Do I Do" by Stevie Wonder. The song was featured in the film, *Friday After Next*.

2002: Will Smith reprised his role as a government agent who worked with extraterrestrial lifeforms living on Earth for the film, *Men In Black II*. Biz Markie appeared in the film as a beatboxing alien.

2002: Lil' Bow Wow starred in the comedy film, *Like Mike*. The rapper portrayed a teenage orphan named Calvin Cambridge who was signed to an NBA team as a walk-on player. Lil' Bow Wow recorded the song, "Basketball," for the film's soundtrack album.

2012: Rappers Snoop Dogg, Wiz Khalifa and Teairra Marí starred in the comedy-stoner film, *Mac & Devin Go To High School*.

2014: Brooklyn rapper Bobby Shmurda was arrested and charged with felony criminal possession of a weapon. He was released after posting a $10,000 bond. He was arrested for a second time later that year and charged with conspiracy to commit murder.

JULY 4

1986: Run-D.M.C. and Aerosmith released the pioneering rap-rock collaboration, "Walk This Way." At the time, Run-D.M.C. were at the top of their game while Aerosmith were in a career slump. The duet was the idea of Run-D.M.C.'s producer, Rick Rubin. A surprise hit, the song was embraced by both MTV and radio. Run-D.M.C. had previously employed elements of rock music on early hits such as "Rock Box" and "King Of Rock." In the music video for "Walk This Way," Aerosmith singer Steven Tyler broke down a symbolic wall that separated the rock and rap genres.

1992: Sir Mix-A-Lot began a five-week run at number-one on the U.S. singles chart with "Baby Got Back."

1995: The Junior M.A.F.I.A. released their debut single, "Player's Anthem" (featuring the Notorious B.I.G.). The track sampled "You Are What I'm All About" by the New Birth and "La Di Da Di" by Slick Rick & Doug E. Fresh.

1996: Tupac Shakur performed on stage for the very last time. He was the headlining act at the House of Blues in Los Angeles. Also on the bill were Snoop Dogg and Tha Dogg Pound. Shakur would be murdered just two months later.

1998: Ol' Dirty Bastard was caught stealing a pair of $50 shoes from a Sneaker Stadium outlet in Virginia Beach, Virginia. When he failed to show up for a scheduled court appearance, an arrest warrant was issued.

2006: Young Dro released the single, "Shoulder Lean" (featuring T.I.). The track sold two-million copies in the U.S.

2006: Bow Wow starred in the crime-action film, *The Fast And The Furious: Tokyo Drift*. The rapper portrayed a high school student in Japan named Twinkie who has a penchant for drag racing.

2011: Nick Cannon was the host of the annual Nathan's Hot Dog Eating Contest in Atlantic City, New Jersey. The winner of the event ate 62 hot dogs in just 10 minutes.

2013: Nicki Minaj staged a launch party on a cruise ship along the Hudson River in New York to introduce her new drink, Myx Fusions. Not only was she the product's spokesperson but she was also a co-owner of the company. Bottles of the beverage have been featured in several of her music videos including "High School," "Up In Flames," "Anaconda" and her duet with DJ Khaled, "I Wanna Be With You."

2013: Jay-Z released the album, *Magna Carta... Holy Grail*. The album spawned the singles, "Holy Grail," "Tom Ford" and "Part II (On The Run)," and featured guest appearances by Nas, Rick Ross, Justin Timberlake, Frank Ocean and Beyoncé. The album was nominated for six Grammys and sold more than two-million copies.

2013: Jay-Z released the single, "Holy Grail" (featuring Justin Timberlake). The track featured elements of "Smells Like Teen Spirit" by Nirvana. "Holy Grail" was nominated for two Grammys and won the award in the category of Best Rap/Sung Collaboration.

2015: Ariana Grande was filmed licking a tray of donuts that was sitting on top of a display case at Wolfee Donuts in Lake Elsinore, California. The security camera footage also captured her saying, "I hate Americans. I hate America." After the incident went public, she cancelled an upcoming concert. She blamed the cancellation on "wisdom teeth." She later apologized for her actions: "Seeing a video of yourself behaving poorly, that you have no idea was taken, is such a rude awakening, that you don't know what to do. I was so disgusted with myself."

JULY 5

1969: RZA (birth name Robert Fitzgerald Diggs) was born in Brooklyn, New York. A founding member of the groundbreaking group the Wu-Tung Clan, he was also a member of the hip hop groups Furthermore and Gravediggaz, where he was known as the RZArector. Also a producer and solo artist, he released albums under the names RZA and Bobby Digital. RZA is the cousin of both Ol' Dirty Bastard and GZA.

1977: Royce da 5'9" (birth name Ryan Daniel Montgomery) was born in Detroit. In addition to his successful solo career, he was a member of Slaughterhouse, PRhyme and Bad Meets Evil (with Eminem). Also a songwriter, he wrote music for Dr. Dre and Sean "Diddy" Combs.

1988: Rick James released the single "Loosey's Rap," which featured rappers Roxanne Shanté and Big Daddy Kane.

1993: Us3 released the single, "Cantaloop (Flip Fantasia)." The song combined jazz and hip hop, and was built around a sample of "Cantaloupe Island" by Herbie Hancock.

1994: Warren G released the crossover hit single, "This D.J." The track sampled "Curious" by Midnight Star, "Juicy Fruit" by Mtume and "Paid In Full" by Eric B and Rakim. "This D.J." was nominated for a Grammy in the category of Best Rap Solo Performance.

2004: Rapper the D.O.C. and his girlfriend Erykah Badu celebrated the birth of their daughter, Puma Curry.

2005: Kanye West released the single, "Gold Digger," featuring Jamie Foxx. The track sampled "I Got A Woman" by Ray Charles. A massive hit, it topped the pop charts for a ten-week span. The song was nominated for a Grammy in the category of Record of the Year and won a Grammy for Best Rap Solo Performance. The song sold more than five-million copies in the U.S.

2010: Big Boi of OutKast released the solo album, *Sir Lucious Left Foot: The Son Of Chico Dusty*. The album spawned the singles, "Shutterbugg" and "Follow Us."

2011: Eminem's album, *Recovery*, became the first in history to sell one-million digital copies in the U.S. The album was released in June 2010.

2011: Bad Meets Evil, a hip hop duo consisting of Eminem and Royce da 5'9", released the hit single, "Lighters" (featuring Bruno Mars).

JULY 6

1970: Inspectah Deck (birth name Jason Hunter) was born in Brooklyn, New York, but raised in nearby Staten Island. A member of the groundbreaking hip hop group the Wu-Tung Clan, he also pursued a solo career beginning with the 1999 album, *Uncontrolled Substance*.

1975: 50 Cent (birth name Curtis James Jackson III) was born in Queens, New York. After he was discovered by Eminem in 2002, 50 Cent quickly became an international star. Also a successful entrepreneur, he launched various business ventures including his own label, G-Unit Records. His stage name was inspired by a Brooklyn robber named Kelvin Martin, who was nicknamed "50 Cent."

2001: Lil' Kim (real name is Kimberly Jones) was sentenced to one year and one day in prison and fined $50,000 after she was convicted of perjury. She had been accused of lying to a federal grand jury in an effort to protect her friends following a shooting incident near the studios of radio station, Hot 97 in New York City.

2011: Ice Cube was the subject of an episode of the VH-1 program, *Behind The Music*.

JULY 7

1987: Eric B. & Rakim released their groundbreaking debut album, *Paid In Full*. The album brought the use of sampling to the forefront in hip hop and was highlighted by the tracks, "Eric B. Is President," "I Ain't No Joke," "Paid In Full" and the hip hop classic "I Know You Got Soul." The album would sell one-million copies in the U.S.

1998: Ma$e released the hit single, "Lookin' At Me" (featuring Puff Daddy). The track appeared on his debut album, *Harlem World*.

1998: Lauryn Hill released her solo single, "Doo Wop (That Thing)." A smash hit, the single appeared on her groundbreaking album, *The Miseducation of Lauryn Hill*. The song won two Grammys in the categories of Best Female R&B Vocal Performance and Best R&B Song.

2010: Three 6 Mafia released their hit single, "Stay Fly," which featured Young Buck and the duo 8Ball & MJG. The track sampled "Tell Me Why Has Our Love Turned Cold" by Willie Hutch. The single appeared on the million-selling album, *Most Known Unknown*.

2012: KMG the Illustrator (real name Kevin Michael Gulley) passed away after collapsing in his home. He co-founded the gangsta rap group, Above The Law, in 1989. He was 43-years-old.

2015: Rapper Big Frieddia, the star of the Fuse network reality show *Queen Of Bounce*, published the autobiography, *God Save The Queen Diva!*

2015: Young Thug (real name Jeffery Lamar Williams) was accused of threatening to shoot a security guard at a mall in Dunwoody, Georgia.

JULY 8

1988: From his second album, LL Cool J released the single, "I Need Love." The song was his first crossover pop hit, peaking in the top-20. The track is considered the very first "rap ballad" hit.

1995: TLC began a seven-week run at number-one on the U.S. singles chart with "Waterfalls."

2001: The Notorious B.I.G. was the subject of an episode of the VH-1 program, *Behind The Music*.

2003: Eminem purchased a mansion in the suburban Detroit community of Rochester Hills for $4.8 million. The home was previously owned by the CEO of K-Mart.

2006: The single "Promiscuous" by Nelly Furtado featuring Timbaland began a six-week run at number-one on the U.S. charts.

2008: Ludacris signed a lucrative endorsement deal with AT&T to appear in several television commercials for the communications giant.

2011: The documentary, *Beats, Rhymes & Life: The Travels Of A Tribe Called Quest*, was released. Directed by Michael Rapaport, the film examined the career of the alternative hip hop group.

2013: Wiz Khalifa married model Amber Rose after a two-year relationship. Rose would file for divorce in September 2014.

2014: Iggy Azalea released the single, "Black Widow" (featuring Rita Ora). The song was originally intended for Katy Perry's album, *Prism*. The track sold more than three-million copies in the U.S.

JULY 9

1998: A security guard was arrested for allegedly firing a gun into the air after a large fight broke out during an Xzibit/Big Punisher concert at the Industry nightclub in Pontiac, Michigan.

2000: Queen Latifah was the subject of an episode of the VH-1 program, *Behind The Music*.

2002: Styles P of the hip hop group the LOX released his debut album, *A Gangster And A Gentleman*. The album was highlighted by the tracks, "Good Times" and "The Life."

2007: Timbaland released his second solo single, "The Way I Are" (featuring Keri Hilson and D.O.E.). The song's music video featured an extra verse by Timbaland's brother, Sebastian. The track sold three-million copies in the U.S.

2009: Latin hip hop DJ Ivan Sanchez published his autobiography, *It's Just Begun*.

2013: Treach of the group Naughty By Nature starred in the science fiction/action film, *Atlantic Rim*. He portrayed the pilot of a submarine.

2013: Insane Clown Posse topped *GQ* magazine's list of "The worst rappers of all time."

JULY 10

1962: Play (birth name Christopher Martin) was born in Queens, New York. As a member of the popular hip hop duo, Kid 'n Play, he first hit the charts in the late 1980s. Launching a successful acting career, he appeared in a series of popular *House Party* films.

1987: The Fat Boys released the crossover single, "Wipe Out." The track was a remake of the 1963 surf-rock classic by the Surfaris. The Fat Boys' version featured the backup vocals of another surf-rock group, the Beach Boys.

2005: Sandra Denton, the "Pepa" in the rap group Salt-n-Pepa, was a member of the cast on the fifth season of the MTV reality show, *The Surreal Life*. The series ran for thirteen episodes.

2011: DJ Paul and Juicy Jay of the rap group Three 6 Mafia were two of the eight contestants on the VH-1 cooking competition, *Famous Food*. DJ Paul was declared the winner of the eight-episode series.

2012: Kanye West made his first appearance on the reality show, *Keeping Up With The Kardashians*.

2013: Master P (real name Percy Miller) was the first hip hop artist inducted into the Louisiana Music Hall of Fame.

2015: 50 Cent lost a civil lawsuit in a Manhattan court over the release of a 13-minute sex video that featured Lastonia Leviston, the mother of one of Rick Ross' children. After a five-week trial, Leviston was awarded a total of $7 million – $2.5 million for using her image without permission, $2.5 million for infliction of emotional distress and another $2 million in punitive damages. 50 Cent had allegedly purchased the video from Leviston's former boyfriend.

2015: Hussein Fatal (born Bruce Edward Washington, Jr.) died in an auto accident at the age of 42. He was a passenger in a vehicle that went off the road in Banks Country, Georgia. A member of the hip hop group Outlawz, he gained notoriety for his work with Tupac Shakur.

JULY 11

1974: Lil' Kim (birth name Kimberly Denise Jones) was born in Brooklyn, New York. Nicknamed "Queen Bee," she was discovered by the Notorious B.I.G. and earned her nickname "Lil" because of her diminutive 4-foot-11 height. She also worked with Biggie in the hip hop group, Junior M.A.F.I.A.

1982: Lil' Zane (birth name Zane Copeland, Jr.) was born in Yonkers, New York, but raised in Atlanta. He is best known for the hit single, "Callin' Me" (featuring 112). In 2003, he changed his stage name to Zane.

1991: Cypress Hill released the double-sided hit single, "The Phuncky Feel One" / "How I Could Just Kill A Man."

1997: The rap duo Timbaland & Magoo (Timothy "Timbaland" Mosley and Melvin "Magoo" Barcliff) released the single, "Up Jumps da Boogie" (featuring Missy Elliott and Aaliyah). It was the duo's biggest hit.

2009: The Black Eyes Peas began a remarkable thirteen-week run at number-one on the U.S. singles chart with "I Gotta Feeling." Ironically, they knocked their previous hit, "Boom Boom Pow," out of the number-one spot.

2011: H.P. Bulmer, a British brewer of hard cider, hired rapper Plan B to star in an advertising campaign for a new product.

2013: A full-sized wax figure of Rihanna was unveiled at Madame Tussauds in New York City.

2014: Philadelphia rapper Meek Mill received a three-to-six month prison sentence for multiple violations of his parole in the wake of his 2008 weapon and drug convictions. He was previously sentenced to 11 to 23 months behind bars but released on probation in 2009 after serving eight-months.

2014: Eminem was the first rapper to headline a concert at London's massive Wembley Stadium, which seats 90,000 people. Dr. Dre made a surprise appearance.

2015: The annual Brooklyn Hip-Hop Festival celebrated its tenth year. Headlined by Common, the festival also featured Mobb Deep, Lion Babe, Freeway, Charles Hamilton, Foxy Brown, Astro Kid and others.

JULY 12

1970: Black Rob (birth name Robert Ross) was born in Harlem, New York. Signing with Bad Boy Records, the rapper appeared as a guest artist on a number of hit singles before releasing his solo album in 1999, the million-selling *Life Story*.

1973: Magoo (birth name Melvin Barcliff) was born in Norfolk, Virginia. After a stint in the rap duo Timbaland & Magoo, Magoo became a successful songwriter and worked with artists such as Missy Elliott and Ginuwine.

1977: Sylk-E. Fyne (birth name La'Mar Lorraine Johnson) was born in Los Angeles. She is best known for her 1998 hit, "Romeo And Juliet."

1984: The BBC television network aired the documentary, *Beat This: A Hip-Hop History*. Directed by Dick Fontaine, the film explored early hip hop culture and featured pioneering rappers such as DJ Kool Herc, Afrika Bambaataa, the Cold Crush Brothers, Jazzy Jay, Brim Fuentes, Grandmaster Caz and the Dynamic Rockers.

1991: Ice Cube made his acting debut in the crime-drama film, *Boyz N The Hood*. Set in the South Central district of Los Angeles, the film explored the topics of race, violence and relationships. Ice Cube portrayed a gangbanger named Darin "Doughboy" Baker.

1993: Redman released the single, "Time 4 Sum Aksion." The track sampled "Tramp" by Lowell Fulson, "How I Could Just Kill A Man" by Cypress Hill, "Mama Said Knock You Out" by LL Cool J and several other songs.

1994: Above The Law released their third album, *Uncle Sam's Curse*. The album was highlighted by the tracks, "Return Of The Real Shit" and the gangsta rap classic "Black Superman." This was their final album on Ruthless Records before they were dropped by the label.

2001: Sean "Puffy" Combs co-starred in the comedy-crime film, *Made*. Combs portrayed a criminal named Ruiz.

2003: The single "Crazy In Love" by Beyoncé featuring Jay-Z began an eight-week run at number-one on the U.S. charts.

2013: Eminem became the first person in the world to gain 60 million friends on Facebook.

JULY 13

1985: Run-D.M.C. was the only hip hop act to perform at the Live Aid charity concert. Their seven-and-a-half-minute performance at JFK Stadium in Philadelphia consisted of two songs, "Jam Master Jay" and "King Of Rock." Run-D.M.C. later mentioned the concert in the lyrics of their hit, "My Adidas."

1988: British rapper and actress Tulisa (birth name Tula Paulinea Contostavlos) was born in London, England. Before pursuing a solo career, she was a member of the group, N-Dubz. She was also a judge on the British version of *The X Factor*.

1989: Singer-songwriters Mark Volman and Howard Kaylan of the rock group the Turtles sued De La Soul for using an unlicensed sample. A looped sample from the Turtles' 1969 hit "You Showed Me" was used on De La Soul's track "Transmitting Live From Mars." Volman and Kaylan asked for $2.5 million but settled the suit for $1.7 million.

1993: Kris Kross released the debut single, "Alright," from their second album, *Da Bomb*. The million-selling single featured reggae singer Super Cat on the chorus.

2004: Jadakiss released the crossover hit single, "Why" (featuring Anthony Hamilton). The controversial protest song was banned by a number of radio stations due to its lyrics which blamed President George W. Bush for the 9/11 terrorist attacks.

2005: A tour bus carrying members of Eminem's entourage flipped over on a Missouri highway. Stat Quo and DJ Alchemist were both on the vehicle. While Stat Quo suffered minor injuries, Alchemist suffered broken ribs and a collapsed lung.

2012: Young Buck was sentenced to an 18-month prison term on weapons charges. He entered prison in August 2012 and was released in October 2013.

2015: Just three days after losing a multi-million dollar lawsuit in a sex tape controversy, rapper 50 Cent filed for Chapter 11 bankruptcy. He claimed debts of more than $32 million.

JULY 14

1975: Tameka "Tiny" Cottle-Harris (birth name Tameka Pope) was born in College Park, Georgia. She was a member of the 1990s group Xscape. She married rapper T.I. in 2010. Her father and uncle were members of the soul group the Tams, who were best known for their 1964 hit, "What Kind Of Fool (Do You Think I Am)."

1975: Taboo (birth name Jaime Luis Gómez) of the Black Eyed Peas was born in Los Angeles. He joined an early incarnation of the group in 1995 as the replacement for Dante Santiago.

2004: Flavor Flav was a member of the cast on the third season of the MTV reality show, *The Surreal Life*. During the filming of the show, Flav began a relationship with another cast member, model Brigitte Nielson. The program ran for ten episodes.

2008: Global Music Group announced that it had purchased Death Row Records from Marion "Suge" Knight. The New York-based company paid an auction price of $24 million.

2015: DMX was sentenced to six-months in prison for failing to pay $400,000 in past-due child support.

JULY 15

1976: Jim Jones (birth name Joseph Guillermo Jones II) was born in the Bronx, New York. The rapper began his career as a member of the hip hop collective the Diplomats (also known as Dipset), and later teamed with Cam'ron to launch Diplomat Records. Jones released his debut album in 2004, *On My Way To Church*.

1986: *Raising Hell* by Run-D.M.C. became the first hip hop album to be certified platinum by the R.I.A.A., with sales over one-million copies.

1990: Hip hop dancer Trouble T Roy (real name Troy Dixon) of the hip hop group Heavy D & The Boyz passed away at the age of 22. He suffered fatal injuries during a tour stop in Indianapolis.

1997: A single by the Notorious B.I.G., "Mo Money Mo Problems" (featuring Puff Daddy and Ma$e), was released. One of the most influential hits of the rap era, it topped the pop charts nearly six-months after Biggie's death. The track sampled "I'm Coming Out" by Diana Ross and "Only You (Bad Boy Remix)" by 112 featuring the Notorious B.I.G. and Ma$e. The single was nominated for a Grammy in the category of Best Rap Performance by a Duo or Group.

1997: Missy "Misdemeanor" Elliott released her first solo album, *Supa Dupa Fly*. The album spawned four singles, "The Rain (Supa Dupa Fly)," "Sock It 2 Me," "Beep Me 911" and "Hit Em Wit Da Hee."

1999: Dr. Dre filed a lawsuit against his former labels, Priority Records and Death Row Records, over the release of the album, *The Chronic 2000*. The rapper claimed that he owned the trademark of the term, "the chronic."

2001: Poetic (real name Anthony Ian Berkeley) passed away after battling cancer for two years. The Trinidadian-born rapper – alternately known as Grym Reaper and Too Poetic – was a member of the groups, Gravediggaz and the Brothers Grym. He was 36-years-old.

2004: Will Smith starred in the science fiction film, *I, Robot*. Smith played Del Spooner, a Chicago police detective in the year 2035. The film grossed more than $300 million worldwide.

2008: Farnsworth Bentley, a rapper and former assistant to Sean Combs, began hosting the MTV reality series, *From G's to Gents*. The contestants competed to transform themselves into sophisticated and productive men. The series, which was created by Jamie Foxx, ran for two seasons.

2008: Nas released his ninth album, which he had intended to call *Nigger*. But after public outcries from Jesse Jackson, Al Sharpton and the NAACP as well as commentators on the Fox network, Nas dropped the name and instead released the album without a title. The untitled album spawned two singles, "Hero" and "Make The World Go Round." The album was nominated for a Grammy in the category of Best Rap Album.

2012: Ice-T and Andy Baybutt directed the documentary, *Something From Nothing: The Art Of Rap*. The film explored the process of creating hip hop music.

2012: South Korean rapper Psy released the international smash hit, "Gangnam Style." The song reached the number-one spot on more than 30 worldwide music charts. The song's music video was the first to reach one-billion views on YouTube.

2015: Thieves broke into a safe at Chris Brown's home in Tarzana, California, and escaped with $50,000 in cash. According to reports, Brown suspected that the burglary was an inside job.

JULY 16

1991: Marky Mark and the Funky Bunch, a group headed by Mark Wahlberg of New Kids On The Block, released the crossover rap hit, "Good Vibrations." The female singer on the chorus was Loleatta Holloway.

1992: Actor Charlton Heston recited the lyrics of the controversial Ice-T song "Cop Killer" at Time Warner's annual shareholders meeting at the Beverly Wilshire Hotel in Los Angeles. Many of the attendees appeared shocked by the song's lyrics. Heston and representatives from various national police groups attended the meeting to protest and condemn the song. In response, Time Warner's CEO Gerald M. Levin argued: "For a company like ours to have meaning... we must help ensure that the voices of the powerless, the disenfranchised, those at the margins are heard."

1992: Das EFX released the single, "Mic Checka." The track sampled "Think 73'" by James Brown.

1993: The German eurodance group Real McCoy scored an international hit with "Another Night." The track featured rapping by Olaf "O-Jay" Jeglitza.

1995: Queen Latifah was the victim of a carjacking in Harlem. Two teenagers stole her BMW and shot her boyfriend in the stomach. Both teens were later arrested.

1996: Chicago-based hip hop trio Do Or Die released the single, "Po Pimp" (featuring Twista). The single was originally issued by a small independent label before catching the attention of Rap-a-Lot Records.

2000: Public Enemy was the subject of an episode of the VH-1 program, *Behind The Music*.

2005: Young Jeezy released the single, "Soul Survivor" (featuring Akon). The song's music video was inspired by the film, *Paid In Full*.

2011: LMFAO began a six-week run at number-one on the U.S. singles chart with "Party Rock Anthem."

2012: Drake purchased a mansion in Calabasas, California, for $7.7 million.

2012: Nas released his eleventh album, *Life Is Good*. Nas wrote the album's introspective tracks shortly after his divorce from Kelis. The album spawned four singles: "Nasty," "The Don," "Daughters" and "Cherry Wine." The album was nominated for a Grammy in the category of Best Rap Album.

JULY 17

1973: Solé (birth name Tonya Michelle Johnston) was born in Kansas City, Missouri. She is best known for her 1999 solo hit, "4.5.6." She was married to singer Ginuwine from 1993 to 2015.

2004: The first "Rock The Bells" hip hop festival was staged in the city of San Bernardino, California. The lineup at the debut event included Supernatural, Redman, Sage Francis, Fantastik 4our, DJ Mark Luv, DJ Icy Ice, DJ Abel, DJ Nu-Mark of Jurassic 5 and a reunited Wu-Tang Clan. The festival continued in various locations around the world.

2006: Ludacris released the single, "Money Maker" (featuring Pharrell Williams). The song won a Grammy in the category of Best Rap Song. Ludacris appeared in the song's music video without his longtime, trademark cornrow hairstyle.

2009: New York graffiti artist Iz the Wiz (real name Michael Martin) passed away. He was featured in the 1983 documentary, *Style Wars*. After battling kidney failure – possibly from longterm exposure to aerosol paint – he suffered a fatal heart attack.

2009: Jermaine Dupri and Janet Jackson broke up after a seven-year relationship.

2012: Ms. Melodie (real name Ramona Parker) passed away at the age of 43. The former wife of KRS-One, she was a member of Boogie Down Productions. She scored her first hit in 1988 with the single, "Hype."

2013: Jay-Z and Justin Timberlake began their co-headlining tour which was dubbed "The Legends of the Summer Stadium Tour." The 14-date tour began in Toronto and closed in Miami, and grossed approximately $70 million.

JULY 18

1975: British rapper M.I.A. (birth name Mathangi "Maya" Arulpragasam) was born in the Hounslow section of London, England. She released her debut album in 2005, *Arular*, and is best known for her 2008 hit, "Paper Planes."

1987: Jeremih (birth name Jeremih Felton) was born in Chicago. He is best known for his 2009 debut single, "Birthday Sex."

1991: Ice-T debuted his side project, Body Count. The heavy metal band joined the lineup of the Lollapalooza Festival, which began at the Compton Terrace amphitheater in Tempe, Arizona, and ended on August 28 in Enumclaw, Washington. Half of Ice-T's set consisted of his rap hits while the other half featured his rock-oriented material with Body Count.

2000: Common released the single, "The Light," a love song which was written for his girlfriend at the time, Erykah Badu. The track sampled "Open Your Eyes" by Bobby Caldwell and "You're Gettin' A Little Too Smart" by the Detroit Emeralds. The track was nominated for a Grammy in the category of Best Rap Solo Performance.

2006: Fergie of the Black Eyed Peas released her debut single, "London Bridge." The chart-topping song was also featured on the soundtrack of the film, *Neighbors*. The track sampled "Down To The Nightclub" by Tower Of Power. The song's music video was filmed in the Woolwich district of London and featured cameo appearances by the other members of the Black Eyed Peas.

2012: B.G. (real name Christopher Dorsey) of the New Orleans hip hop group the Hot Boys was sentenced to 14-years in prison after he was convicted on charges of gun possession and witness tampering. In 2009, he had been arrested in Covington, Louisiana, after police discovered three guns (two of which were reported stolen), a number of loaded magazines and illegal drugs in his vehicle.

2015: R&B/hip hop performer Jeremih was arrested on his birthday for driving under the influence. The singer is best known for his 2009 hit, "Birthday Sex."

JULY 19

1986: The UK Fresh '86 festival was staged at Wembley Arena in London. The event featured electronic and hip hop music. Hosted by radio deejay Mike Allen, the lineup included Grandmaster Flash, Lovebug Starski, Sir Mix-A-Lot, Afrika Bambaataa, Mantronix, World Class Wreckin' Cru, Roxanne Shanté and others.

1986: During and after a concert by Run-D.M.C. at Madison Square Garden in New York City, 18 people were arrested on charges of theft.

1996: Nate Dogg was found not guilty by a Long Beach Superior Court jury of the armed robbery of a check cashing store.

2001: Ol' Dirty Bastard received a two-to-four year sentence after he was convicted of possessing crack cocaine and marijuana. Police had stopped the rapper's vehicle after he ran a red light in Los Angeles.

2005: Nelly purchased a minority stake in the Carolina Bobcats NBA team. As part of the deal, he also became a part-owner of the Charlotte Sting WNBA team and C-SET (the Carolinas Sports Entertainment Television network).

2008: DMX was arrested for providing a false name after receiving treatment at Mayo Clinic in Scottsdale, Arizona. According to Sheriff Joe Arpaio, the rapper fraudulently registered as Troy Jones and racked up a $7,500 medical bill. He was charged with theft of services and identity theft.

JULY 20

1968: Kool G Rap (birth name Nathaniel Thomas Wilson) was born in Queens, New York. In the 1980s, he was a member of the pioneering hip hop groups, the Juice Crew and Kool G Rap & DJ Polo.

1990: Candyman released the crossover hit single, "Knockin' Boots," from his debut album, *Ain't No Shame In My Game*. The song sampled "Ooh Boy" by Rose Royce and "Tonight Is The Night" by Betty Wright. Tone Loc appeared in the song's music video.

1992: Oakland-based rapper Paris left Tommy Boy Records (which at the time was a subsidiary of Warner Brothers Records) after the two labels refused to release his controversial album, *Sleeping With The Enemy*. The album contained a pair of controversial tracks: "Bush Killa" which was about the revenge killing of President George H. W. Bush and "Coffee, Donuts & Death" which was about killing police officers. Paris reached a financial arrangement with Warner Brothers and later released the album on his own label, Scarface Records.

1993: Cypress Hill released their second album, *Black Sunday*. The album was highlighted by the hit singles, "When The Shit Goes Down," "Lick A Shot," the Grammy-nominated "I Ain't Goin' Out Like That" and their signature track "Insane In The Brain." The album sold more than three-million copies in the U.S.

1995: Flavor Flav broke both of his arms in a motorcycle accident in Milan, Italy.

1998: Will Smith released his debut solo single, "Just The Two Of Us," which was a reworked rendition of the 1981 hit by Bill Withers and Grover Washington, Jr. The song's music video examined the relationships between fathers and sons and featured Will Smith's real life son, Trey.

2004: Sean "P. Diddy" Combs helped to launch the Citizen Change campaign in order to sign up new voters in support of presidential candidate John Kerry in his race against George W. Bush. The campaign's slogan was "Vote or Die."

2010: Usher was the subject of an episode of the VH-1 program, *Behind The Music*.

2011: Jay-Z and Kanye West released the single, "Otis." The track prominently sampled "Try A Little Tenderness" by Otis Redding. "Otis" was nominated for two Grammys and won an award in the category of Best Rap Performance.

2015: Christopher "Fresh Kid Ice" Wong Won of 2 Live Crew published his autobiography, *My Rise 2 Fame*.

JULY 21

1989: During a performance by Milli Vanilli at the Lake Compounce amusement park in Connecticut, a pre-recorded backing track began skipping, over and over, during the song, "Girl You Know It's True." Eventually, the lip-syncing duo walked off the stage.

1989: Spike Lee's award-winning film, *Do The Right Thing*, was released. The film focused on the racial tensions in the Bedford-Stuyvesant section of Brooklyn. The song, "Fight The Power" by Public Enemy, was played at various times throughout the film and later emerged as an anthem in the black community. Both the film and the song were considered controversial at the time. Public Enemy would record a new version of the track for their 1990 album, *Fear Of A Black Planet*.

1998: Producer and record label owner Jermaine Dupri released his debut album, *Life In 1472*. The album was highlighted by the tracks, "Money Ain't A Thang" and "The Party Continues."

2000: Rap duo Insane Clown Posse staged their first annual Gathering of Juggalos. The event was held at the Expo Center in Novi, Michigan, and drew more than 7,000 attendees.

2001: Lauryn Hill performed an acoustic concert at the MTV studios in New York City for an episode of the hit program, *MTV Unplugged*. Her performance was far more soul-oriented than her debut solo album, *The Miseducation Of Lauryn Hill*. The concert was later issued on the million-selling album, *MTV Unplugged No. 2.0*.

2003: British hip hop deejay and recording artist Goldie published his autobiography, *Nine Lives*.

2008: Kid Rock was sentenced to one year of probation and fined $1,000 for his part in a fight the previous year at a Waffle House restaurant in suburban Atlanta. He pleaded "no contest" to one count of simple battery after four other charges were dropped.

JULY 22

1973: Petey Pablo (birth name Moses Mortimer Barrett III) was born in Greenville, North Carolina. He is best known for the 2001 hit single "Raise Up" which appeared on his debut, Grammy-nominated album, *Diary Of A Sinner: 1st Entry*.

1987: LL Cool J released his second album, *Bigger And Deffer (BAD)*. The album featured the hit singles, "I Need Love," "Go Cut Creator Go" and "I'm Bad." The best-selling album of his career, it sold more than three-million copies in the U.S.

1996: The Smokin' Grooves Tour kicked off a 33-date trek across the U.S. with a performance in Sacramento, California. The music festival featured a lineup of rap and reggae acts that included Busta Rhymes, Spearhead, Cypress Hill, A Tribe Called Quest, the Fugees and Ziggy Marley & The Melody Makers.

2002: Dr. Evil, as portrayed by Mike Myers, performed a parody of Jay-Z's hit "Hard Knock Life (Ghetto Anthem)" in the Austin Powers comedy film, *Goldmember*.

2003: Sean "P. Diddy" Combs announced on *The Howard Stern Show* that he wanted to purchase the New York Knicks. He explained, "I'm publicly puttin' it out there, because they're not taking my calls."

2005: 50 Cent was sentenced to two years of probation as the result of a scuffle during a 2004 performance at the Hippodrome nightclub in Springfield, Massachusetts. After being struck in the head by a water bottle, he allegedly jumped into the audience and chased after the bottle thrower. The rapper was initially charged with multiple counts of assault and battery.

2008: The mayor of Houston proclaimed the day, "Trae Day," in honor of rapper Trae tha Truth for his outstanding work in the community.

JULY 23

1990: 2 In A Room released the 12-inch single, "Wiggle It." It was the duo's only top-40 U.S. hit.

1991: The hip hop group Main Source released their influential debut album, *Breaking Atoms*. The album is notable for the recording debut of Nas who appeared on the track, "Live At The Barbeque." The album was highlighted by the hits, "Just Hangin' Out" and "Looking At The Front Door."

1993: Tupac Shakur starred opposite Janet Jackson in the romance-drama film, *Poetic Justice*. Shakur played a postal clerk named Lucky. (Ice Cube was the original choice for the role.) Rappers Tone Loc and Q-Tip also appeared in the film.

1996: Freak Nasty released the single, "Da' Dip." The single sold more than one-million copies.

2009: Nick Cannon was named the host of the television singing competition, *America's Got Talent*, starting with the fourth season of the program.

2013: The members of the duo Kid 'n Play reprised their starring roles in the film sequel, *House Party 5: Tonight's The Night*.

2014: The live music program, *SoundClash*, debuted on VH-1. Hosted by deejay and producer Diplo, the program brought together three performers from three different musical genres onto the same stage. The first episode featured Lil Wayne, Fall Out Boy and London Grammar. The program's executive producer was Ahmir "Questlove" Thompson.

2015: Flavor Flav announced that he was putting up the $2 million bail to free Brooklyn rapper Bobby Shmurda, who was being held in Rikers Island on various charges including conspiracy to commit murder.

JULY 24

1963: The Real Roxanne (birth name Adelaida Martinez) was born in Brooklyn, New York. She is best known for recording an answer record to UTFO's "Roxanne, Roxanne." She later scored a U.K. hit with the single, "Bang Zoom (Let's Go-Go)."

1990: 2 Live Crew released their fourth album *Banned In The U.S.A.*, which was the very first album that featured an RIAA "Parental Advisory" warning sticker.

1990: MC Hammer released the film, *Please Hammer, Don't Hurt 'Em: The Movie*. In the film, Hammer returned to his hometown of Oakland to battle a druglord who hired children to peddle drugs.

1997: MTV aired a musical special by NBA player and rapper Shaquille O'Neal. The program, *Shaq Session*, featured the Los Angeles Lakers star performing songs from his album, *You Can't Stop The Reign*.

2008: Abkco Music filed a lawsuit against Lil Wayne over the song, "Playing With Fire." The music publisher charged that the track was based on a song by the Rolling Stones, "Play With Fire." As a result of the suit, "Playing With Fire" was deleted from the digital version of the album.

2009: Jay-Z released the single, "Run This Town," which featured Rihanna and Kanye West. The track sampled "Someday In Athens" by the 4 Levels Of Existence. "Run This Town" won two Grammys in the categories of Best Rap Song and Best Rap/Sung Collaboration.

2010: Percy Miller (also known as Lil' Romeo) launched his own clothing line, College Boyys.

2010: Drake was sued for copyright infringement over his track, "Best I Ever Had." Playboy Enterprises claimed that the song used an unauthorized sample of the 1975 hit, "Fallin' In Love" by Hamilton, Joe Frank & Reynolds.

2011: Mary J. Blige was the subject of an episode of the VH-1 program, *Behind The Music*.

2015: The reality series, *Kingin' With Tyga*, debuted on the MTV2 network. The program starred Compton-born rapper Tyga.

JULY 25

1963: Rapper and activist Sister Souljah (birth name Lisa Williamson) was born in the Bronx, New York.

1995: Bone Thugs-N-Harmony released their hit album, *E. 1999 Eternal*. The album was released four months after the death of the group's mentor, Eazy-E. The album spawned three singles, "1st Of Tha Month," "East 1999" and the group's signature hit, "Tha Crossroads." The chart-topping, Grammy-nominated album sold five-million copies in the U.S.

1995: At 25-years-old, Jay-Z released his debut solo single, "In My Lifetime." The CD single was issued by a small label, Payday Records. The track sampled "Oh Baby" by Aretha Franklin and two songs by Soul II Soul, "Back To Life" and "Get A Life."

2005: Nick Cannon released the pro-life single, "Can I Live." The track was included on an album he had intended to release later that year, *Stages*. But with his acting career in full swing, the album was shelved.

2008: Xzibit played the role of FBI special agent Mosley Drummy in the feature film, *The X-Files: I Want To Believe*. The film earned nearly $70 million in the U.S.

2008: Dr. Dre and Jimmy Iovine joined forces to create a line of high-end headphones, Beats by Dre. The first model was initially priced at $349.

2014: Brooklyn rapper Bobby Shmurda released the top-10 crossover hit, "Hot Nigga," which spawned the Shmoney dance craze. The track sold one-million copies in the U.S.

JULY 26

1988: Salt-n-Pepa released their second album, *A Salt With A Deadly Pepa*. The album featured the hits, "Shake Your Thang," "Get Up Everybody (Get Up)" and a remake of the rock standard "Twist And Shout."

1994: Sean "Diddy" Combs issued the first record on his new Bad Boy label, "Flava In Ya Ear" by rapper Craig Mack. LL Cool J and Busta Rhymes were featured on the song's remix. The hit track was nominated for a Grammy in the category of Best Rap Solo Performance.

1994: The Lady of Rage released the single, "Afro Puffs." The track sampled "Love That Will Not Die" by Johnny "Guitar" Watson. "Afro Puffs" was included on the soundtrack of the film, *Above The Rim*.

1994: DJ Train (real name Clarence Lars) died of smoke inhalation. Concerned that some of his family members might be trapped in a burning house, he ran into the structure and collapsed after reaching the living room. A close associate of Eazy-E, DJ Train worked with a number of artists at Ruthless Records including MC Ren and J. J. Fad. He was also a member of the hip hop group, CPO (Capital Punishment Organization).

2005: Trey Songz released his debut album, *I Gotta Make It*, which featured guest appearances by Aretha Franklin, Twista and Juvenile. The album spawned the singles, "Gotta Make It" and "Gotta Go." Trey Songz had previously used the stage name, the Prince of Virginia.

JULY 27

1999: Sandra Denton, the "Pepa" of Salt-n-Pepa, married Treach (real name Anthony Criss) of the group Naughty By Nature.

1999: The New Orleans hip hop group the Hot Boys released their debut album, *Guerrilla Warfare*. The million-selling album was highlighted by the tracks, "We On Fire" and "I Need A Hot Girl." The group consisted of Juvenile, B.G., Lil Wayne and Turk.

2004: Hip hop supergroup the Terror released their second album, *True Story*. The album was highlighted by the chart-topping hit, "Lean Back." Another track, "Bring 'Em Back," featured the vocals of deceased rappers, Big L and Big Pun.

2010: Trey Songz released "Bottoms Up," the debut single from his fourth album, *Passion, Pain & Pleasure*. Featuring Nicki Minaj on backing vocals, the single was Songz's biggest hit to date. Two weeks before its official release date, the song was intentionally leaked onto the internet.

JULY 28

1974: Afroman (birth name Joseph Edgar Foreman) was born in the South Central section of Los Angeles. He is best known for his Grammy-nominated hit song, "Because I Got High."

1990: Soulja Boy (birth name DeAndre Cortez Way) was born in Chicago but raised in Atlanta. He is best known for his debut single, "Crank That (Soulja Boy)," which became a hit on MySpace a few months before he was signed to a record label. In 2004, he formed his own label, Stacks on Deck Entertainment.

1990: "Turtle Power" by Partners In Kryme was the first rap single to reach number-one on the British charts. Other previous British number-one hits that featured elements of hip hop included "I Feel For You" by Chaka Khan, "Dub Be Good To Me" by Beats International and "Pump Up The Volume" by MARRS.

1991: Following a concert by MC Hammer in the city of Penticton, British Columbia, more than 2,000 youths looted nearby businesses, smashed store windows and overturned several cars. The riot began with 20 concertgoers throwing rocks at a police officer who was directing traffic.

1992: Grand Puba released the single, "360 Degrees (What Goes Around)." The track sampled "Don't Burn Down The Bridge" by Gladys Knight & The Pips and "Tramp" by Otis Redding and Carla Thomas.

1999: LL Cool J starred in the science fiction film, *Deep Blue Sea*. He portrayed a cook on a top-secret military base that was attacked by genetically-modified sharks.

2005: Nick Cannon launched the popular MTV improvisational comedy series, *Nick Cannon Presents: Wild 'N Out*. Cannon hosted and produced the program. A number of hip hop performers appeared on the first season of the show including Lil Wayne, Lil Scrappy, Trillville, Cassidy, Biz Markie, Common, the Ying Yang Twins, Kanye West, T.I. and P$C.

2009: 50 Cent and Val Kilmer starred in the action-drama film, *Streets Of Blood*. Both men portrayed New Orleans police detectives in the aftermath of Hurricane Katrina.

2011: After staging what was described as a risque performance at the Reggae Sumfest in Jamaica, Nicki Minaj was fined $1,000 by local authorities.

JULY 29

1997: Bone Thugs-N-Harmony released the album, *The Art Of War*. The project was highlighted by the singles, "Look Into My Eyes" and "If I Could Teach The World." (A sequel to the album, *The Art Of War: World War III*, was released in 2013.)

2003: Jam Master Jay of Run-D.M.C. released the instructional DVD, *Scratch DJ Academy: Semester 01*.

2008: T.I. released the single, "Whatever You Like." The track sampled "Redemption (Theme From Rocky II)" by Bill Conti. A major hit, the song topped the pop charts for five weeks.

2010: Mark Wahlberg was awarded a star on the Hollywood Walk of Fame.

2011: Eminem was one of the three headliners at the Osheaga Music and Arts Festival in Montreal, Canada. He was the first rap act to headline the annual event. The three-day festival also featured Cypress Hill, Janelle Monáe, Shad and Kid Koala.

2011: Lil Wayne and his label UMG Records were sued for $15 million by a Georgia production company, Done Deal Enterprises. The plaintiffs claimed that Lil Wayne's hit track, "BedRock," borrowed elements from a song of the same name that was recorded in 2009 by rapper Blue Marley. The suit was settled in October 2012.

2013: DMX filed for Chapter 11 bankruptcy in a Manhattan court. He claimed just $50,000 of assets but millions of dollars of debt, including $1.24 million owed in child support.

2014: Rapper DJ Paul, a founding member of the hip hop group Three 6 Mafia, appeared on the television reality series, *Celebrity Wife Swap*. He swapped partners for one week with NFL player Plaxico Burress.

JULY 30

1991: Jibri Wise One released the hit single, "The House The Dog Built."

1991: Leaders Of The New School – a hip hop group that included Busta Rhymes – released the single, "The International Zone Coaster." The track sampled "Lowdown" by Boz Scaggs, "Jeepers Creepers" by the Dave Brubeck Quartet, "Cussin', Cryin' And Carryin' On" by Ike & Tina Turner and "You Better Think" by Rasputin's Stash.

1996: The hip hop duo UGK released the album, *Ridin' Dirty*. Despite receiving little airplay due to its raunchy lyrics, it was the duo's best-selling album with sales of two-million copies.

1999: DMX turned himself into police after a search of his New Jersey home netted an illegal weapon. He was released from jail after posting a $50,000 bond.

2007: Lil Wayne was selected as the winner of MTV's annual "Hottest MCs in the Game."

2010: Rapper T.I. married his girlfriend of nine years, Tameka "Tiny" Cottle (birth name Tameka Pope), formerly of the popular 1990s R&B group, Xscape.

2011: Pitbull was given an honorary "key to the city" by the mayor of Kodiak, Alaska.

2013: DMX filed for Chapter 11 bankruptcy. He claimed assets of less than $50,000 but between $1 million and $10 million in debts. His application was later dismissed by a bankruptcy court.

JULY 31

1968: D-Dot (birth name Deric Michael Angelettie) was born in Brooklyn, New York. A rapper and prolific music producer, he worked with dozens of artists including 50 Cent, Kanye West, Lil' Kim, Nicki Minaj, the Notorious B.I.G., Puff Daddy and Ma$e. In 1998, D-Dot was named the Producer of The Year by NARAS.

2009: Baatin (real name Titus Glover) of the hip hop group Slum Village was found dead in his home. After experiencing health problems in 2003, he was fired from the group. He subsequently launched a solo career under the name, Baatin The Slumlord. He reunited with Slum Village a year before his death. He was 35-years-old.

2009: While performing the song "Best I Ever Had Drake" during a concert in Camden, New Jersey, Canadian-born rapper Drake fell and exasperated an existing knee injury. Several weeks later, he underwent surgery to repair a torn ligament in his knee.

2009: Jay-Z was added to the lineup of the All Points West Music and Arts Festival in Jersey City, New Jersey, as the replacement for the Beastie Boys who canceled their appearance following the illness of member Adam Yauch. Also on the bill were Q-Tip, the Pharcyde and Organized Konfusion.

2010: Mary J. Blige launched her own perfume, My Life. The name was taken from the title of her second album. The fragrance was launched in collaboration with the beauty product company, Carol's Daughter, and was sold exclusively on the Home Shopping Network. The following year, Blige introduced a second perfume, My Life Blossom, and a line of designer sunglasses, Melodies by MJB.

2010: The single "Love The Way You Lie" by Eminem featuring Rihanna began a seven-week run at number-one on the U.S. charts.

2010: R&B singer Alicia Keys married hip hop producer and performer Swizz Beatz (real name Kasseem Dean) at a ceremony on the French island of Corsica.

2015: Drake released the hit single, "Hotline Bling." The song's music video was financed by Apple Inc. and initially aired only on Apple Music. The track sold more than three-million copies in the U.S.

▶ AUGUST

AUGUST 1

1960: Chuck D (birth name Carlton Douglas Ridenhour) of Public Enemy was born in Queens, New York. The outspoken rapper co-founded Public Enemy at age 26.

1960: Professor Griff (birth name Richard Griffin) of Public Enemy was born in Hempstead, New York. In the group, he was referred to as the Minister of Information.

1963: Coolio (birth name Artis Leon Ivey, Jr.) was born in Monessen, Pennsylvania. A rapper, producer and professional chef, he is best known for his 1995 hit, "Gangsta's Paradise."

1981: MTV debuted on cable television with the video "Video Killed The Radio Star" by the Buggles. It would be several years before the music video network began airing videos by rap artists in regular rotation.

1988: DJ Jazzy Jeff & The Fresh Prince released the Freddy Krueger-inspired hit single, "A Nightmare On My Street." After the producers of *The Nightmare On Elm Street* film series sued the rap duo, the song's music video was never released. Additionally, the duo was forced to add a disclaimer sticker to the cover of the album, *He's The DJ, I'm The Rapper*, which informed buyers that the song was "not authorized, licensed, or affiliated with *The Nightmare On Elm Street* films."

1988: Salt-n-Pepa released the crossover hit single, "Shake Your Thang." The song was based on the 1969 soul hit "It's Your Thing" by the Isley Brothers and sampled "Funky President" by James Brown.

1988: The first issue of *The Source* was published by students at Harvard University, originally as a free newsletter. After relocating from Boston to New York in the early-1990s, the magazine was published on a monthly basis.

1989: The FBI sent a letter of complaint to Brian Turner, the head of Priority Records, over the controversial track, "Fuck Tha Police" by N.W.A. The federal law enforcement agency was concerned that the song could promote violence against police officers.

1993: *Murder Dog* magazine published its first issue. Young "D" Boyz was featured on the front cover. The magazine was founded by photographer Black Dog Bone.

1995: Raekwon released his debut solo album, *Only Built 4 Cuban Linx...*, which featured Ghostface Killah as the "guest star." The project included multiple dialogue samples from the John Woo film, *The Killer*. The album spawned four singles: "Heaven & Hell," "Criminology," "Ice Cream" and "Rainy Dayz." The sequel album, *Only Built 4 Cuban Linx... Pt. II*, was released in 2009.

1997: *XXL* magazine published its debut issue. The first issue was released with two different covers, one featuring Jay-Z and the other with Master P.

2003: The documentary film, *Beef*, examined the various "beefs" and feuds in rap music since the early-1980s and how these public battles helped to fuel record sales. Among the beefs that were chronicled in the film: 50 Cent vs. Murder Inc.; KRS-One vs. MC Shan; Tru Life vs. Mobb Deep; Kool Moe Dee vs. Busy Bee Starski; Common vs. Ice Cube; Jay-Z vs. Nas; and Tupac Shakur vs. the Notorious B.I.G. The sequel, *Beef II*, was released in 2004, and was followed by the BET program, *Beef: The Series*.

2005: The mayor of Long Beach, California, officially declared the week of August 1 to 6, "Warren G Week."

2008: Master P was given an honorary "key to the city" by the mayor of Memphis.

2015: When Snoop Dogg was stopped by authorities at the Italian border, he was carrying $422,000 in cash. Under European law, a maximum amount of 10,000 Euros (worth about $11,000 at the time) of undeclared cash could be transported across a border.

2015: Travi$ Scott (real name Jacques Webster) was arrested at the Lollapalooza festival in Chicago. Just two-minutes into his performance, the rapper instructed the audience to jump over a barricade in front of the stage. During the ensuing melee, one female fan was trampled. Police and security staff rushed onto the stage and ordered Scott to end his performance. He performed just one song.

2015: Dr. Dre announced the release of what he described as his "final album." The album, *Compton*, was made available exclusively on iTunes the following week.

AUGUST 2

1980: The New York City borough of Queens declared the day, "Kurtis Blow Day."

1988: Rob Base and DJ E-Z Rock released the crossover hit, "It Takes Two." The song sampled "Think (About It)" by Lyn Collins and "Space Dust" by the Galactic Force Band. "It Takes Two" became one of the most sampled songs of the rap era.

2010: Canadian-born rapper Drake launched the annual OVO Fest in Toronto. Staged at the Molson Canadian Amphitheatre and hosted by Drake, the first year's lineup included Bun B, Young Jeezy, Fabolous, Kardinal Offishall, Jay-Z and Eminem.

AUGUST 3

1971: DJ Spinderella (birth name Deidra Muriel Roper) of the rap trio Salt-n-Pepa was born in New York City. She had replaced original member Latoya Hanson one-year after the group had formed in 1986.

1987: The single "Pump Up The Volume" by MARRS was released. The hit track got its title from a vocal sample of "I Know You Got Soul" by Eric B. & Rakim. This was the only single released by the group, which was a studio-only project formed by members of Colourbox and A. R. Kane. In all, "Pump Up The Volume" sampled nearly 30 songs.

1993: The hip hop duo Kris Kross released their second album, *Da Bomb*. The album was highlighted by the tracks, "Alright," "I'm Real" and featuring Da Brat, "Da Bomb." The album was harder edged than their debut release and sold more than one-million copies in the U.S.

1995: Snoop Dogg called out the East Coast while on stage at the second annual Source Awards. Unhappy with the audience's reaction after he won an award, he angrily asked: "The East Coast ain't got no love for Dr. Dre and Snoop Dogg?" The members of the audience responded with a loud "No!"

2001: D12 and Esham were both kicked off the Warped Tour after a backstage fight during a stop in Camden, New Jersey. Allegedly, the members of D12 were unhappy with the lyrics of Esham's song "Chemical Imbalance," which criticized Eminem. Esham suffered multiple injuries in the scuffle.

2003: Beyoncé released the single, "Baby Boy" (featuring Sean Paul). The song appeared on Beyoncé's debut solo album, *Dangerously In Love*, as well as on Sean Paul's Grammy-winning album, *Dutty Rock*. The track contained an interpolation of "No Fear" by O.G.C.

2010: The IRS raided the Nashville home of Young Buck in an attempt to reconcile a $334,000 tax debt owed by the rapper. During the raid, IRS agents discovered a loaded weapon. In 2012, he accepted a plea deal and agreed to an 18-month prison sentence.

2012: After changing his stage name to Snoop Lion, the former Snoop Dogg performed for the first time under his new moniker at a concert in Toronto. He was given his new stage name by Bunny Wailer. (In 2013, he changed his name back to Snoop Dogg.)

2015: Two men were shot and seriously injured following an argument at a concert headlined by J. Cole and Big Sean. The shootings occurred in the parking lot of the PNC Bank Arts Center in Holmdel, New Jersey.

2015: A full-sized wax figure of Nicki Minaj was unveiled at Madame Tussauds in Las Vegas.

AUGUST 4

1971: Yo-Yo (birth name Yolanda Whitaker) was born in Compton, California. A protege of rapper Ice Cube, she is best known for the 1991 single, "You Can't Play With My Yo-Yo."

1992: Arrested Development released the single, "People Everyday." Dionne Farris was a guest vocalist on the song. The track sampled "Tappan Zee" by Bob James and the chorus of "Everyday People" by Sly & The Family Stone.

1994: Faith Evans married the Notorious B.I.G. just nine days after the couple had met for the first time.

1994: Bobby Shmurda (birth name Ackquille Jean Pollard) was born in Brooklyn, New York. He is best known for the track "Hot Nigga," which spawned the Shmoney dance craze.

1998: Snoop Dogg released his third album, *Da Game Is To Be Sold, Not To Be Told*. The album marked a departure from his gangsta rap roots. After leaving Death Row Records, this was his first album on Master P's No Limit Records. The album spawned two singles, "Still A G Thang" and "Woof." The album did not sell as well as his releases on Death Row.

1999: "Weird Al" Yankovic released a parody of Puff Daddy's hit "It's All About The Benjamins" which was reworked as "It's All About The Pentiums."

2003: Styles (full name Davis Styles) of the hip hop trio, Lox, was released from prison after a ten-month and eight-day stint for stabbing a man in the buttocks. His last 30 days were spent in solitary confinement. After his release from the Valhalla Correctional Facility, he immediately returned to the recording studio.

2008: The reality series, *I Want To Work For Diddy*, debuted on the VH-1 network. On the program, contestants battled for a position as an assistant at Sean John, a fashion company owned by Sean "Diddy" Combs. The program ran for two seasons.

2010: Hip hop artists Chris Brown, T.I. and Idris Elba co-starred in crime-thriller film, *Takers*.

2011: Snoop Dogg was one of the three headliners at the Osheaga Music and Arts Festival in Montreal, Canada. The three-day event also featured Common, Aloe Blacc and the Weeknd.

2014: Nicki Minaj released the smash hit single, "Anaconda." The track sampled "Baby Got Back" by Sir Mix-A-Lot. The single was nominated for a Grammy in the category of Best Rap Song.

2015: Luther Campbell of 2 Live Crew published his second autobiography, *The Book Of Luke: My Fight For Truth, Justice, And Liberty City*.

2015: Two people were shot dead and three others were injured at a party in Toronto hosted by Drake. The shootings occurred at the OVO Fest after-party at the Muzik Nightclub.

AUGUST 5

1998: LL Cool L co-starred in the slasher film, *Halloween H20: 20 Years Later*. The rapper portrayed Ronny Jones, a security guard who refused to die despite being stabbed and shot.

2005: Beanie Sigel was released from a federal prison after spending nearly a year behind bars on a weapons conviction.

2010: Wyclef Jean of the Fugees submitted a formal application to run for the presidency of the country of Haiti. He was ruled ineligible after not meeting the requirement of Haitian residency for the previous five-years.

AUGUST 6

1978: Freeway (birth name Leslie Edward Pridgen) was born in Philadelphia. Signed to Roc-A-Fella Records, he worked with Jay-Z and Beanie Sigel. Freeway also joined Sigel in the group, State Property. Later pursuing a solo career, Freeway released his debut solo album in 2003, *Philadelphia Freeway*.

1988: MTV debuted its first rap-oriented series, *Yo! MTV Raps*. The program was originally intended as a one-time special. The first video to air was "Follow The Leader" by Eric B. & Rakim. The two-hour daily series showcased the growing hip hop scene and was originally hosted by Fab 5 Freddy. Later, it was hosted by the team of Doctor Dré (not to be confused with N.W.A. co-founder Dr. Dre) and Ed Lover. Graffiti artist Dr. Revolt created the show's distinctive logo. The popular program ran until August 17, 1995.

1989: Despite making a promise not to perform "Fuck Tha Police" at the Joe Louis Arena in Detroit, the members of N.W.A. had a change of heart. But as soon as the group began playing the song, police rushed the stage and put an end to the concert. Allegedly, N.W.A. were never paid for their performance.

1991: P.M. Dawn released their debut album, *Of The Heart, Of The Soul And Of The Cross: The Utopian Experience*. The group was headed by brothers Attrell and Jarrett Cordes, who were known by their stage names, Prince Be and DJ Minutemix. After the album's first single, "A Watcher's Point of View," was mostly ignored by radio, the group enjoyed success with the follow-up single, "Set Adrift On Memory Bliss." The album sold more than one-million copies in the U.S.

1991: Salt-n-Pepa released the crossover million-selling hit single, "Let's Talk About Sex." The track sampled "I'll Take You There" by the Staple Singers and "Kool Is Back" by Funk, Inc.

1993: Robert Townsend directed and starred in the super-hero comedy film, *The Meteor Man*. The project featured appearances by Luther Vandross, Naughty by Nature, Cypress Hill, Big Daddy Kane and Another Bad Creation.

2001: N.E.R.D., a hip hop group formed by Pharrell Williams and Chad Hugo, released their debut album *In Search Of...* The project was issued only in Europe. Unhappy with the album, the duo re-recorded the tracks with the rock group Spymob and released the updated version of the album in 2002.

2004: LL Cool J announced the introduction of his own fashion line, the James Todd Smith clothing collection. He wore some of the clothing in the music video for his single, "Headsprung."

2005: Bow Wow released the single, "Like You" (featuring singer Ciara). The track sampled "I'm Leaving You Again" by New Edition. This was Bow Wow's biggest pop hit of his career.

2012: British rapper Dizzee Rascal performed at the opening ceremonies of the 2012 Summer Olympics in London, alongside a number of pop and rock acts including Paul McCartney, the Arctic Monkeys and Mike Oldfield.

AUGUST 7

1990: Deee-Lite released the crossover dance hit, "Groove Is In The Heart." Q-Tip of A Tribe Called Quest performed the rap verse in the song.

1995: LL Cool J married Simone Johnson. The rapper first began dating his future wife when he was just 19-years-old.

1997: Big Pun released his debut single, "I'm Not A Player." The track sampled "Darlin' Darlin' Baby (Sweet Tender Love)" by the O'Jays. Big Pun later released a remixed version of "I'm Not A Player" which was retitled, "I'm Still Not A Player."

2001: Marion "Suge" Knight was released from a federal prison in Oregon after serving more than half of a nine-year sentence.

2003: The reality program, *InsideOUT: ODB On Parole*, debuted on the VH-1 network. The series followed Ol' Dirty Bastard after the completion of his two-year prison stint as he struggled to restart his career.

2007: UGK (Underground Kingz) released the album, *Underground Kingz*. The project was recorded after the release of member Pimp C from prison. The album featured an all-star cast of rappers including Rick Ross, OutKast, Z-RO, T.I., Talib Kweli, Jazze Pha, Kool G Rap, Big Daddy Kane, Slim Thug, Dizzee Rascal, Too $hort, Middle Fingaz and Three 6 Mafia as well as Charlie Wilson of the Gap Band. The album spawned the hit singles, "The Game Belongs To Me" and "International Players Anthem (I Choose You)."

2010: M.I.A. invited members of the audience to join her onstage at the Big Chill music festival in Herefordshire, England. After hundreds of fans rushed forward, the overwhelmed members of security were forced to clear the stage. Ultimately, the event's organizers ordered M.I.A. to end her performance. Local reports claimed that two security officers were injured during the melee.

2014: Rihanna and Eminem began the first stop of their three-date co-headlining "Monster Tour." The stadium tour landed in the cities of Los Angeles, Detroit and East Rutherford, New Jersey.

2015: Dr. Dre released his long-awaited third solo album, *Compton*. He was inspired to record the project during the filming of the N.W.A. biopic *Straight Outta Compton*. The album spawned two singles, "Talking To My Diary" and "Talk About It." Originally issued only as a digital album, it was the first digital-only album to top the British charts.

AUGUST 8

1962: Kool Moe Dee (birth name Mohandas Dewese) was born in Manhattan, New York. He co-founded the Treacherous Three in the late-1970s. Later pursuing a solo career, he scored a hit with the single, "Wild Wild West."

1967: Positive K (birth name Darryl Gibson) was born in the Bronx, New York. He is best known for the hits, "I Got A Man" and a duet with MC Lyte "I'm Not Havin' It."

1980: Chain Reaction was the first hip hop dance act to perform in a Hollywood film. The New York City-based street troupe appeared in the Olivia Newton-John film, *Xanadu*. Chain Reaction introduced the "locking" and "popping" styles of urban dance to the big screen.

1995: Coolio released the single, "Gangsta's Paradise" (featuring L.V.). The track sampled "Pastime Paradise" by Stevie Wonder. The song appeared on the soundtrack of the film *Dangerous Minds* as well as on Coolio's album *Gangsta's Paradise*. The track was the top-selling U.S. single of 1995 and won a Grammy in the category of Best Rap Solo Performance.

2000: Shaggy released the hit album, *Hot Shot*. The album spawned four singles: "It Wasn't Me," "Angel," "Luv Me, Luv Me" and "Dance & Shout / Hope." The album sold six-million copies in the U.S.

2000: Lil' Bow Wow released his debut single, "Bounce With Me." The track sampled "Love Serenade (Part II)" by Barry White.

2001: Big Ed (real name Edward Lee Knight) passed away at the age of 30 after battling throat cancer. Also known as Big Ed The Assassin, he released only one solo album during his career, *The Assassin*. He was also a member of TRU (The Real Untouchables).

2003: LL Cool J starred in the big screen remake of the 1970s television crime show, *S.W.A.T.* The rapper portrayed a police officer named Deacon Kaye.

2011: Jay-Z and Kanye West teamed up to record the album, *Watch The Throne*. The project spawned seven singles: "H•A•M," "Otis," "Lift Off," "Niggas In Paris," "Why I Love You," "Gotta Have It" and "No Church In The Wild." Guest vocalists on the project included Beyoncé, The-Dream, Frank Ocean and Mr Hudson. The album earned seven Grammy nominations.

2012: Young Jeezy (real name Jay Wayne Jenkins) was named the Senior Vice President of A&R at Atlantic Records.

2015: Ruckus (real name Sean Price) died during his sleep at his apartment in Brooklyn, New York. The rapper was a member of the hip hop groups, Heltah Skeltah, Boot Camp Clik and Random Axe. Also a solo artist, he released his debut album in 2005, *Monkey Barz*. He was 43-years-old.

AUGUST 9

1959: Pioneering rapper Kurtis Blow (birth name Kurt Walker) was born in Harlem, New York. In 1979, he was the first rapper signed to a major label. He later became an ordained minister.

1988: N.W.A. released the controversial single, "Fuck Tha Police." The lyrics of the protest song were written as a parody of a court trial with Dr. Dre as the judge.

1990: Brandon "B-Doggs" Mitchell of the New York-based new jack swing group Wreckx-n-Effect was shot and killed. He was 20-years-old.

1994: The Notorious B.I.G. released his debut solo single, "Juicy." The track sampled "Juicy Fruit" by Mtume. The autobiographical track chronicled the rapper's life from poverty to riches.

1996: Graffiti artist Jean-Michel Basquiat was the subject of the feature film, *Basquiat*. In the film, Jeffrey Wright portrayed Basquiat while David Bowie played the role of Andy Warhol.

2004: Lil John hosted a launch party in New York City for his new beverage, Crunk!!! Energy Drink.

2004: Lil Kim was given an honorary "key to the city" by the mayor of Miami.

2009: Snoop Dogg was a guest contestant on an episode of the game show, *Who Wants To Be A Millionaire?* He won $50,000 for his charity, the Snoop Youth Football League.

2010: Eminem released the hit single, "Love The Way You Lie" (featuring Rihanna). The song's music video starred Dominic Monaghan and Megan Fox, and examined the subject of domestic violence. The single earned five Grammy nominations. (Rihanna later recorded a sequel which was titled, "Love The Way You Lie (Part II)," for her album, *Loud*.)

2011: Drake released the hit single, "Headlines." The song's music video featured appearances by the Weeknd, T-Minus, Noah "40" Shebib, Boi-1da and Kromatik.

2011: Jay-Z topped *Forbes* magazine's fifth annual Hip-Hop Cash Kings list by earning $37 million over the previous year. Sean "Diddy" Combs came in second place.

2015: Tyga gave his girlfriend Kylie Jenner a $320,000 white Ferrari for her 18th birthday. (A number of news sources later claimed that Tyga actually leased the vehicle.)

AUGUST 10

1968: Michael Bivins (full name Michael Lamont Bivins) was born in Boston, Massachusetts. He was a member of the new jack swing / hip hop trio, Bell Biv DeVoe. The group had been formed by members of the R&B boy band New Edition.

1970: Q-Tip (birth name Jonathan Davis) was born in Queens, New York. In 1985, he co-founded the hip hop group, A Tribe Called Quest. Following the breakup of the group in 1998, he pursued a solo career. After converting to Islam, he changed his name to Kamaal Ibn John Fareed.

2010: Brooklyn-based rapper Lil' Kim launched a promotional campaign as the spokesperson for Three Olives Vodka.

AUGUST 11

1961: DJ Disco Wiz (birth name Luis Cedeño) was born in the Bronx, New York. He is considered the first Latino hip hop deejay.

1973: DJ Kool Herc, who has been credited as the first rapper, hosted his very first block party. He performed for a crowd of 300 people in the recreation room of an apartment building on Sedgwick Avenue in the Bronx.

1978: Mac Daddy (birth name James Christopher Kelly) was born in Atlanta. As a member of the teenage rap duo Kris Kross, he scored a smash hit in 1992 with "Jump." The members of the duo were known for wearing their clothes backwards. He died in 2013 at the age of 34.

1989: In the wake of the popularity of the MTV program *Yo! MTV Raps*, the BET network introduced the two-hour series, *Rap City*. The program consisted of music videos, artist interviews and live performances. The series featured a number of hosts including Chris Thomas (nicknamed "The Mayor of Rap City"), Hans Dobson (nicknamed "Prime"), Prince Dejour, Joe Clair, Leslie Segar (nicknamed "Big Lez"), Big Tigger, Mad Linx, J-Nicks and Q-45. The show was cancelled after a 19-year run in 2008.

2004: André 3000 of the hip hop group OutKast was voted "the best-dressed man in the world" by *Esquire* magazine.

2007: Sean Kingston began a four-week run at number-one on the U.S. singles chart with "Beautiful Girls"

AUGUST 12

1988: Public Enemy performed a free concert for the inmates at Rikers Island in New York City. Ironically, four years later Public Enemy member Flavor Flav would spend nine-weeks behind bars at Rikers Island for a probation violation and driving with a suspended license.

1988: Graffiti artist Jean-Michel Basquiat passed away at the age of 27. The Brooklyn-born tagger began his career as part of the graffiti duo, SAMO, before he emerged as a more serious artist. His work was later displayed in galleries and museums. He was found dead from a heroin overdose at his art studio.

1997: Puff Daddy released the single, "Been Around The World" (featuring the Notorious B.I.G and Ma$e). The track sampled "Let's Dance" by David Bowie and "Feelin' Good" by Roy Ayers, and featured an interpolation of "All Around The World" by Lisa Stansfield. The song's music video featured appearances by Quincy Jones, Vivica A. Fox, Wyclef Jean and Jennifer Lopez.

1997: Hollywood Records, which was owned by Disney, recalled an album by Insane Clown Posse on the same day it was released. The label was unhappy with the lyrics of the duo's album, *The Great Milenko*, which were not consistent with Disney's family-friendly image. Hollywood also cancelled Insane Clown Posse's 25-date tour and terminated their recording contract.

2001: Mr. Cheeks released his debut solo single, "Lights, Camera, Action!" The track sampled "Keep On Truckin'" by Eddie Kendricks. Mr. Cheeks was previously a member of the hip hop group, Lost Boyz.

2003: 50 Cent released the remixed version of the track, "P.I.M.P.," which featured Snoop Dogg, Lloyd Banks and Young Buck.

2005: Singers Mark Wahlberg, Tyrese, André 3000 and Garrett Hedlund starred in the action film, *Four Brothers*. The film grossed more than $90 million in the U.S.

2006: Busta Rhymes attacked a man who allegedly spit on his car, following a performance at the AmsterJam festival. The rapper was arrested by New York City police the following week and charged with assault.

2007: Flavor Flav was the guest of honor on an episode of *The Comedy Central Roast*. Katt Williams was the "roastmaster" and the guests included Brigitte Nielsen, Ice-T, Snoop Dogg, Jimmy Kimmel, Carrot Top, Lisa Lampanelli, Jeff Ross, Patton Oswalt, Greg Giraldo and Sommore.

2008: Mike Jones and Trae the Truth were involved in a physical altercation at the annual Ozone Awards in Houston. The brief melee occurred backstage shortly before the start of the ceremony.

AUGUST 13

1971: Tragedy Khadafi (birth name Percy Chapman IV) was born in Queens, New York. He was originally known as Intelligent Hoodlum. A rapper and producer, he has worked with dozens of artists including DJ Krush, Cormega, Marley Marl, Nas, Mobb Deep and Capone-N-Noreaga.

1984: A team of break dancers performed at the closing ceremony of the Summer Olympics in Los Angeles. As Lionel Richie sang his hit "All Night Long," he was joined by 200 break dancers on the massive stage. One of the dancers was a young Cuba Gooding, Jr.

1985: Doug E. Fresh and MC Ricky D (better known as Slick Rick) released the B-side hit, "La Di Da Di." It appeared on the flip side of the single, "The Show." The song has been heavily sampled over the years and was later recorded by Snoop Dogg as "Lodi Dodi."

1986: MC Hammer released his debut solo album, *Feel My Power*. The album was issued on Hammer's own label, Bustin' Records, and was a regional hit on the West Coast. After he signed with Capitol Records, the album was re-released in 1988 with three additional tracks and was retitled, *Let's Get It Started*. The album sold more than two-million copies and spawned the hit, "Turn This Mutha Out."

1991: Cypress Hill released their debut album, *Cypress Hill*. The album spawned the singles, "Hand On The Pump," "Pigs," "Latin Lingo" and the double-sided hit, "The Phuncky Feel"/ "How I Could Just Kill A Man." The influential album sold more than two-million copies.

2005: Dem Franchize Boyz released the single, "I Think They Like Me" (featuring Jermaine Dupri, Da Brat and Bow Wow). The track sampled the group's previous hit, "White Tee."

AUGUST 14

1969: Boss (birth name Lichelle Laws) was born in Detroit. She is best known for her 1993 hits, "Deeper" and "Recipe Of A Hoe." She also worked with Krayzie Bone on his solo album, *Thug On Da Line*.

1987: The Fats Boys starred in the comedy film, *Disorderlies*. The film's soundtrack included a number of rap and rock tracks including the Fat Boys remake of the Beatles hit, "Baby, You're A Rich Man."

1987: Latin rapper Gerardo (of "Rico Suave" fame) appeared in the comedy film, *Can't Buy Me Love*. He portrayed a high school jock named Ricky.

2001: C-Murder (real name Cory Miller) was charged with attempted murder after he was accused of firing a gun outside of Club Raggs in Baton Rouge, Louisiana. The incident was sparked by a doorman's request to search the rapper. Just five-months later, C-Murder would be charged with the death of a teenager in Harvey, Louisiana.

2011: Flavor Flav was an emcee at the twelfth annual Gathering of the Juggalos, which was staged in the town of Cave-In-Rock, Illinois. The musical acts at the festival included Juvenile, Ice Cube, Xzibit, Busta Rhymes, Mystikal, Lil Jon, MC Hammer, Vanilla Ice, Paris and George Clinton and Parliament-Funkadelic.

2012: Cornell University announced the appointment of Afrika Bambaataa as a visiting scholar. The three-year appointment was made by the university's music department in conjunction with the library's Hip Hop Collection.

2015: The N.W.A. biographical film *Straight Outta Compton* was released. The film starred Jason Mitchell as Eazy-E, O'Shea Jackson, Jr., as Ice Cube, Corey Hawkins as Dr. Dre, Aldis Hodge as MC Ren, Neil Brown, Jr., as DJ Yella and Paul Giamatti as N.W.A.'s manager Jerry Heller. The hit film grossed more than $200 million in box office receipts and was the most successful musical biopic in history.

2015: A solo album by Chinx, *Welcome To JFK*, was released three months after his death. The album spawned the hit single, "On Your Body."

AUGUST 15

1990: Ca$h Out (birth name John-Michael Hakim Gibson) was born in Columbus, Georgia, but raised in Atlanta. The rapper is best known for his 2012 hit single, "Cashin' Out."

1995: Nipsey Hussle (birth name Ermias Asghedom) was born in Los Angeles. The rapper is best known for his series of popular mixtapes.

2006: 50 Cent published his autobiography, *From Pieces To Weight: Once Upon A Time In Southside Queens*.

2006: Rich Boy released his debut single, "Throw Some D's." The track sampled "I Call Your Name" by Switch. The single sold one-million copies in the U.S.

2008: The hip hop group, the GS Boyz, released the single, "Stanky Legg." The song launched a popular dance craze.

AUGUST 16

2000: Pioneering rapper Kurtis Blow was ordained a minister. He preached his "Hip Hop Church" services at various churches around the country.

2000: Eminem filed for divorce from wife, Kim Mathers, and requested joint custody of their 4-year-old daughter. The couple had been married for 14-months.

2005: During an appearance on *The Today Show*, Sean "P. Diddy" Combs announced that he was dropping the "P" from his stage name and wanted to be known as "Diddy."

2011: Macklemore and Ryan Lewis released the single, "Can't Hold Us" (featuring Ray Dalton). The track was nominated for a Grammy in the category of Best Music Video. The video was filmed at 16 different locations on two continents.

2012: Nelly was one of the artist coaches on the CW Network talent program, *The Next: Fame Is At Your Doorstep*. He was joined by three other coaches: Gloria Estefan, John Rich and Joe Jonas. The series ran for one season.

2015: Rapper and actor Lamar Davenport was charged with the murder of his girlfriend E'Dena Hines, the step-granddaughter of legendary actor Morgan Freeman. Police claimed that Davenport stabbed Hines while in front of her apartment building in New York City.

AUGUST 17

1969: Posdnuos (birth name Kelvin Mercer) of the rap trio De La Soul was born in the Bronx, but raised in East Massapequa, New York.

1986: A hip hop concert headlined by Run-D.M.C. at the Long Beach Arena was marred by widespread gang violence. More than a dozen members of the audience were stabbed and gunshots were fired from both the front and rear of the 14,000 seat venue. At least 42 victims were treated by local hospitals. Also appearing on the bill were Whodini, LL Cool J and two other acts. A Run-D.M.C. concert that had been scheduled for the following night at the Hollywood Palladium was cancelled.

1995: The final episode of *Yo! MTV Raps* aired on the MTV network. Guests on the program included Rakim, KRS-One, Chubb Rock, MC Serch, Craig Mack and Erick Sermon of EPMD. The episode was highlighted by a freestyle rap session. The show's demise was partly fueled by an anti-MTV protest by the members of Naughty By Nature.

1997: The duo Milli Vanilli was the subject of the first-ever episode of the VH-1 series, *Behind The Music*.

2002: The single "Dilemma" by Nelly featuring Kelly Rowland began a remarkable ten-week run at number-one on the U.S. charts. Ironically, Nelly had knocked his previous single, "Hot In Herre," out of the number-one spot.

2004: The rap supergroup, 213, released their only album, *The Hard Way*. The trio was formed in 1990 by Snoop Dogg, Warren G and Nate Dogg. The top-10 album spawned the hits, "Groupie Luv" and "So Fly."

2010: Jay-Z topped *Forbes* magazine's fourth annual Hip-Hop Cash Kings list by earning $63 million over the previous year. Sean "Diddy" Combs followed in second place.

2010: Lil Wayne released the single, "Right Above It" (featuring Drake). The track sampled "Hail Mary" by Tupac Shakur. "Right Above It" was later used as the opening theme of the HBO series, *Ballers*. The track sold more than two-million copies in the U.S.

2010: Waka Flocka Flame released the single, "No Hands" (featuring Roscoe Dash, Wale and Roscoe Dash). The track sold three-million copies.

AUGUST 18

1969: Everlast (birth name Erik Francis Schrody) was born in Valley Stream, New York. He teamed with DJ Lethal and Danny Boy to form the hip hop group House Of Pain, best known for their 1992 hit "Jump Around." Later pursing a solo career under the names Everlast and Whitey Ford, he scored a rock-rap hit in 1998 with "What It's Like."

1969: Masta Killa (birth name Elgin Turner) was born in Brooklyn, New York. The final person to join the original lineup of the Wu-Tang Clan, he was also the last member of the group to record a solo album. He later adopted the name, Jamel Irief.

1977: Pioneering rap deejay Grand Wizard Theodore introduced the technique of "scratching" a record during a performance at the Sparkle Club in New York City. According to *The Guardian* newspaper, Theodore scratched with the single, "Bongo Rock" by the Incredible Bongo Band.

1986: A scheduled hip hop concert at the Hollywood Palladium – headlined by Run-D.M.C. and featuring Whodini and LL Cool J – was cancelled. Authorities feared a repeat of the widespread gang violence that occurred the previous night when the three rap acts appeared at the Long Beach Arena.

1990: Soul II Soul were forced to cancel the remainder of their tour after members of the group were injured in a traffic accident enroute to a concert near Chicago. According to police, the group's tour bus struck the rear of another bus, which set off a chain reaction accident that involved four more vehicles and caused 31 injuries.

1994: Ini Kamoze released the single, "Here Comes The Hotstepper." The chart-topping track combined rap with reggae and sampled several songs including "The Champ" by the Mohawks and "La Di Da Di" by Slick Rick & Doug E. Fresh.

1998: Detroit rap-rocker Kid Rock released his smash album, *Devil Without A Cause*. The album took the rap-rock genre to a new level and spawned six singles, "Welcome 2 The Party (Ode 2 The Old School)," "I Am The Bullgod," "Bawitdaba," "Cowboy," "Only God Knows Why" and "Wasting Time." The album sold ten-million copies in the U.S.

2013: Nas organized an online fundraiser that collected nearly $65,000 for a father-of-nine who had lost his home in a fire.

2014: The reality series *Atlanta Exes* debuted on VH-1. The program followed the ex-wives of various celebrities in the entertainment field. The cast featured Tameka Raymond (ex-wife of singer Usher), Christina Johnson (ex-wife of singer Cee Lo Green), Monyetta Shaw (former fiancee of singer Ne-Yo), Sheree Buchanan (ex-wife of NFL player Ray Buchanan) and Torrei Hart (ex-wife of comedian and actor Kevin Hart).

2015: The three members of the Atlanta-based hip hop trio, Migos, were arrested. Following a concert at Georgia Southern University, police noticed a strong smell of marijuana coming from the group's touring vans. After a short investigation, all three members of Migos and 12 members of their entourage were arrested for the possession of marijuana, the possession of firearms within a school safety zone, the possession of firearms during the commission of a crime and the possession of firearms by convicted felons.

AUGUST 19

1969: Nate Dogg (birth name Nathaniel Dwayne Hale) was born in Clarksdale, Mississippi. A pioneer of West Coast rap, he worked with a number of leading hip hop artists including Warren G, Dr. Dre, Eminem, Tupac Shakur, Westside Connection, Snoop Dogg, 50 Cent, Ludacris and Xzibit, and was a member of the rap group 213. He passed away in 2011 after suffering a series of strokes.

1970: Fat Joe (birth name Joseph Antonio Cartagena) was born in the Bronx, New York. He was a member of the hip hop groups, D.I.T.C. and Terror Squad, and also enjoyed a successful solo career. In 1992, he founded his own record label, Terror Squad Entertainment.

1989: Rapper and actor Percy Romeo Miller, Jr. – also known as Lil' Romeo, Romeo and Maserati Rome – was born in New Orleans. He is the son of music mogul Master P.

1997: MC Hammer, who had filed for bankruptcy protection in 1996, sold his mansion in Fremont, California, for $5.3 million. The house had been valued at $9 million.

2003: Ludacris released the single, "Stand Up" (featuring Shawna). The song's music video featured cameo appearances by Chingy, 2 Chainz, Katt Williams, Scooter Braun, Tyra Banks, Lauren London and Kanye West, who produced the track. The song was nominated for a Grammy in the category of Best Rap Solo Performance.

2005: 50 Cent sued a Philadelphia car dealership for using his trademarked name in an advertisement without permission. Filing the lawsuit in federal court, he asked for damages of at least $1 million.

2009: Pitbull was given an honorary "key to the city" by the mayor of his hometown, Miami. The Cuban-American rapper has often called himself "Mr. 305," a reference to Miami's area code.

AUGUST 20

1965: KRS-One (birth name Lawrence "Krisna" Parker) was born in the Bronx, New York. Also known as Teacha, he teamed with DJ Scott La Rock to form the hip hop group, Boogie Down Productions. In 1993, KRS-One released the solo album, *Return Of The Boom Bap*.

1977: Lil' Cease (birth name James Lloyd) was born in Brooklyn, New York. A member of the hip hop group Junior M.A.F.I.A., he also released a solo album in 1999, *The Wonderful World Of Cease A Leo*.

1989: Kirko Bangz (birth name Kirk Jerel Randle) was born in East Houston, Texas. The rapper is best known for his 2012 hit, "Drank In My Cup."

1990: Geffen Records announced it would not distribute an album by Houston-based rap group the Geto Boys due to the controversial lyrics of two tracks, "Mind Of A Lunatic" and "Assassins." Geffen released a statement which read in part: "The Geto Boys album glamorizes and possibly endorses violence, racism and misogyny [which] compels us to encourage Def American to select a distributor with a greater affinity for this musical expression." In response, Rick Rubin of Def American Records ended his relationship with Geffen and signed a distribution deal with Warner Brothers Records.

1996: Silkk The Shocker released his debut album, *The Shocker*. At the time he was known as "Silkk." The album featured his brothers, Master P and C-Murder.

1996: Ginuwine released his debut single, "Pony." The R&B/hip hop track was produced by Timbaland.

2002: Erykah Badu released the single, "Love Of My Life (An Ode To Hip-Hop)" (featuring Common). The track appeared on the soundtrack of the film, *Brown Sugar*. The song was nominated for three Grammys and won an award in the category of Best R&B Song.

2010: Bow Wow and Ice Cube starred in the comedy film, *Lottery Ticket*. Bow Wow portrayed the winner of a $370 million lottery ticket who was overwhelmed by people asking him for money. Rappers Naturi Naughton and T-Pain also appeared in the film.

2011: Machine Gun Kelly was arrested for organizing a flash mob in the food court of a mall in the suburban Cleveland community of Strongsville. With several hundred fans in attendance, the rapper jumped on a table and started performing. He was charged with misdemeanor disorderly conduct.

AUGUST 21

1984: Whodini released the single, "Friends," which reached the top-10 on the R&B charts. The single's B-side, "Five Minutes Of Funk," was also a hit.

2001: Jay-Z released the single, "Izzo (H.O.V.A.)." The diss song targeted rappers Nas and Prodigy. The track sampled "I Want You Back" by the Jackson 5. The song's music video featured appearances by Damon Dash, Eve, Nelly, Kanye West, Destiny's Child, Trina and OutKast.

2012: Trey Songz released the chart-topping album, *Chapter V*. The album spawned the singles, "Heart Attack," "2 Reasons," "Simply Amazing" and "Never Again."

2012: Busta Rhymes gave away his ninth studio album, *Year Of The Dragon*, as a free download on Google Play.

2013: Rick Ross introduced his new Belaire Rose sparkling wine at the Gotha Club in Cannes, France.

2014: Al Roker, a host on the NBC program *The Today Show*, criticized Nicki Minaj's video for "Anaconda." The veteran weatherman stated: "It's just vile."

AUGUST 22

1966: GZA (birth name Gary Grice) was born in Brooklyn, New York. The oldest member of the groundbreaking group the Wu-Tung Clan, he also enjoyed a successful solo career. Before joining the Wu-Tang Clan, he recorded under the name, the Genius.

2000: Violence broke out during the Source Hip-Hop Music Awards in Pasadena, California. Only five of the fifteen awards had been presented when multiple brawls erupted throughout the audience. Dozens of police officers stormed the venue and the rest of the ceremony was cancelled. No one was arrested.

2004: The documentary, *Just To Get A Rep*, examined the relationship between graffiti artists and rap music.

2007: Snoop Dogg, Big Pun, Ice-T and Fat Joe starred in the horror film, *Urban Menace*. Snoop Dogg portrayed a crazed preacher who targeted a crime syndicate.

2007: A total of five hip hop superstars – 50 Cent, T.I., Jay-Z, Kanye West and Sean "P. Diddy" Combs – performed together on the same stage during Screamfest, which took place at Madison Square Garden in New York.

2007: Houston-based rapper Lil Flip was hired as the spokesman for Lucky Nites Golden Liqueur.

2008: Da Brat pleaded guilty to a charge of aggravated assault and was sentenced to three-years in prison, seven-years of probation and 200-hours of community service. The previous year, she had struck a female employee in the face with a bottle of rum during an argument at the Studio 72 nightclub in Atlanta. She was released from prison after serving nearly two-years of her sentence.

2014: Concert promoter Eric Johnson died after he was shot five times while backstage at a concert headlined by Wiz Khalifa. The shooting occurred at the Shoreline Amphitheatre in Irvine, California. The murder went unsolved.

AUGUST 23

1985: The British hip hop movie, *Electro Rock*, made its premiere in London. The concert film was shot at the Hippodrome the previous March at a concert billed as "Hip Hop at the Hippodrome" and featured the best of British hip hop as well as a few American acts.

1986: Sky Blu (birth name Skyler Austen Gordy) of LMFAO was born in Los Angeles. He formed the duo in 2006 with his uncle, Redfoo. In 2011, LMFAO scored a major hit with the track, "Party Rock Anthem." Sky Blu is the grandson of Motown Records founder, Berry Gordy, Jr.

1996: Bone Thugs-N-Harmony released their signature hit, "Tha Crossroads." The track sampled "Make Me Say It Again Girl" by the Isley Brothers. The song explored the afterlife and was dedicated to the group's mentor, Eazy-E. The song's music video opened with the female vocal group, Tré, performing a traditional spiritual, "Mary Don't You Weep." The single won a Grammy in the category of Best Rap Performance by a Duo or Group.

1998: Atlanta-based hip hop duo OutKast released the single, "Rosa Parks," which was a tribute to the civil rights pioneer. A year later, Parks filed a lawsuit against OutKast and their label, LaFace Records, charging trademark infringement. The case was settled in 2005 with OutKast and others paying Parks an undisclosed settlement.

2013: Snoop Lion (also known as Snoop Dogg) surprised his fans by releasing a reggae album, *Reincarnated*. He had recorded the project after experiencing a spiritual renewal while visiting Jamaica. The album spawned four singles, "Here Comes The King," "Lighters Up," "No Guns Allowed" and "Ashtrays And Heartbreaks." The album was nominated for a Grammy in the category of Best Reggae Album.

2015: Wiz Khalifa was detained by custom agents at LAX airport in Los Angeles after riding a two-wheel electric scooter inside the facility.

AUGUST 24

1985: Run-D.M.C. appeared on the long-running television program, *American Bandstand*. The group performed two songs including "Jam-Master Jammin'."

1991: Naughty By Nature released their crossover hit single, "O.P.P." The track sampled "ABC" by the Jackson 5 and "Synthetic Substitution" by Melvin Bliss.

1993: *Vibe* magazine was launched by hit producer Quincy Jones and Time-Warner. Focusing on R&B and hip hop music, the magazine featured Snoop Doggy Dogg on the cover of the first issue. Before the official launch, a test issue was released the previous year.

1997: M.C. Hammer was the subject of the second-ever episode of the VH-1 series, *Behind The Music*.

1999: Puff Daddy released the album, *Forever*. The album was highlighted by the single, "Satisfy You," featuring R. Kelly.

1999: Rap-metal band Limp Bizkit released the hit single, "Nookie." The song was allegedly written about the ex-girlfriend of the band's singer, Fred Durst.

2004: Nearly five years after abandoning his rap career to become a Christian preacher, Ma$e returned to music and released his third album, *Welcome Back*. The album's title track was based on the theme of the popular 1970s television sitcom, *Welcome Back, Kotter*.

2010: Fantasia was the subject of an episode of the VH-1 program, *Behind The Music*.

2014: Marion "Suge" Knight was shot six times – once in the arm and five times in the stomach – at a party hosted by Chris Brown. The event was held at the 1 OAK nightclub in West Hollywood. Two other clubgoers were also shot. Witnesses claimed that Chris Brown was the intended target of the gunmen.

AUGUST 25

1966: Terminator X (birth name Norman Rogers) of the group Public Enemy was born in Long Island, New York. After he left the group in 1999, he replaced by DJ Lord.

1992: Wreckx-N-Effect released the crossover hit single, "Rump Shaker." The track featured the guest vocals of Teddy Riley, who was the brother one of the group's members, Markell Riley. The track sampled "Darkest Light" by Lafayette Afro Rock Band, "Midnight Theme" by Manzel, "Scratchin'" by the Magic Disco Machine and "Blues & Pants" by James Brown. MTV banned the music video for "Rump Shaker."

1992: Mary J. Blige released the single, "Real Love." It was her first top-10 crossover hit. The track sampled "Top Billin'" by Audio Two.

1995: *The Show*, a documentary about the rise of hip hop music, made its premiere. Narrated by Russell Simmons, the film featured a number of pioneering rap artists including Afrika Bambaataa, the Notorious B.I.G., Kurtis Blow, Sean "Puffy" Combs, Snoop Doggy Dogg, Dr. Dre, Warren G, Kid Capri, LL Cool J, Craig Mack, Method Man, Melle Mel, Naughty By Nature, Raekwon, Run-D.M.C., Slick Rick, Tha Dogg Pound, the Twinz, Whodini and the Wu-Tang Clan. The film's soundtrack album was released by Def Jam Recordings.

1998: Lauryn Hill released her solo album, *The Miseducation Of Lauryn Hill*. The album, which was recorded at Tuff Gong Studios in Jamaica, spawned three singles: "Ex-Factor," "Everything Is Everything" and the number-one pop hit, "Doo Wop (That Thing)." Hill was nominated for ten Grammys and won five awards including Best New Artist, Best R&B Song, Best Female R&B Vocal Performance and Best R&B Album. Additionally, *The Miseducation Of Lauryn Hill* was the very first rap album to earn a Grammy in the prestigious category of Album of the Year. The album sold more than eight-million copies in the U.S.

1998: Tatyana Ali – Will Smith's co-star in *The Fresh Prince Of Bel Air* – released the album, *Kiss The Sky*. A surprise success, the album spawned the top-10 U.S. hit "Daydreamin'" and the British hit "Boy You Knock Me Out."

1999: Rappers LL Cool J and Omar Epps starred in the crime-thriller film, *In Too Deep*. While LL Cool J portrayed a crime boss nicknamed "God," Epps played a young police officer. Several other hip hop artists appeared in the film including Nas, Shyheim Franklin, Michie Mee and Sticky Fingaz.

2001: A small airplane carrying Aaliyah and eight others crashed during takeoff from an airport in the Bahamas. Everyone aboard the Cessna 402B was killed. The singer had flown to the Carribean country in order to film a music video for her upcoming single, "Rock The Boat." Aaliyah's family later filed lawsuits against Virgin Records, Blackhawk International Airways and others.

2006: Both members of OutKast, André 3000 and Big Boi, starred in the musical film, *Idlewild*. The film was set in the fictional Depression-era town of Idlewild, Georgia. Several other musical performers appeared in the film including Terrence Howard, Patti LaBelle, Macy Gray and Ben Vereen. OutKast also recorded the film's soundtrack album.

2011: During an outdoor concert in Alaska, Mos Def announced he was abandoning his stage name of "Mos Def" the following year and would instead be known as Yasiin Bey.

AUGUST 26

1976: The pioneering Los Angeles street dance troupe, the Lockers, appeared on an episode of the 1970s sitcom, *What's Happening!!* One of the program's stars – Fred Berry who played the role of "Rerun" – was a member of the Lockers.

1981: The first music video to feature break dancing was released. The clip for "Through Being Cool" by the New Wave rock band Devo featured street dancers from Los Angeles. At the time, break dancing was sometimes called "down rocking."

1986: Big K.R.I.T. (birth name Justin Scott) was born in Meridian, Mississippi. The rapper released his breakthrough album in 2012, the self-produced *Live From The Underground*.

2001: Petey Pablo released the single "Raise Up." The track sampled "Enta Omri" by Hossam Ramzy.

2012: Meek Mill announced the launch of his own record label, Dream Chasers Records. The label's roster included Louie V. Gutta, Lee Mazin, Goldie and Lil Snupe. (Lil Snupe was murdered in June 2013.)

2015: Tyler, The Creator (real name Tyler Gregory Okonma) was banned from entering the United Kingdom for a period of three-to-five years. The U.K. Home Office refused entry to the rapper, citing lyrics which "foster[ed] hatred with views that seek to provoke others to terrorist acts."

AUGUST 27

1977: Ma$e (birth name Mason Durell Betha) was born in Jacksonville, Florida, but raised in the Harlem borough of New York City. He enjoyed a successful solo career beginning with his 1997 debut album, *Harlem World*. Finding religion and becoming a Christian minister in 1999, he abandoned his music career for the next five-years.

1987: DJ Scott La Rock of the hip hop group Boogie Down Productions was murdered at the age of 25. He was shot in the neck while driving away from the Highbridge Projects in the South Bronx after trying to mediate a disagreement between his friends and residents of the housing complex. Although two suspects were arrested for the murder, both men were later acquitted of the charges. La Rock was killed just one month after the release Boogie Down Productions' debut album, *Criminal Minded*.

1988: EPMD released their debut single, "Strictly Business," from the album of the same name. The track sampled "I Shot The Sheriff" by Eric Clapton, "Jungle Boogie" by Kool & The Gang and "Long Red" by Mountain. Although the song was not a big hit upon its release, "Strictly Business" became a hip hop classic.

1991: After allegedly assaulting Dee Barnes, the host of the hip hop program *Pump It Up!*, Dr. Dre of N.W.A. pleaded no contest in a Los Angeles courtroom. He was sentenced to 240-hours of community service and two-years of probation and fined $2,513. Additionally, he was ordered to produce an anti-violence public service announcement.

1992: Redman released his debut single, "Blow Your Mind." The track sampled "The Payback" by James Brown, "Theme From The Black Hole" by Parliament, "Computer Love" by Zapp and several other songs.

1996: OutKast released their second album, *ATLiens*. The album spawned the singles, "Elevators (Me & You)," "ATLiens," and "Jazzy Belle." The album sold more than two-million copies in the U.S.

1996: Aaliyah released her second album, *One In A Million*. The album spawned six singles beginning with "If Your Girl Only Knew" and "One In A Million." The album sold three-million copies in the U.S.

2000: Ice-T was the subject of an episode of the VH-1 program, *Behind The Music*.

2012: Macklemore and Ryan Lewis released the single, "Thrift Shop." The smash hit was the fourth single from their debut studio album, *The Heist*. The track sold more than ten-million copies in the U.S.

2013: Eminem released the hit single, "Berzerk." The Rick Rubin-produced track sampled "The Stroke" by Billy Squier and two Beastie Boys songs also produced by Rubin, "The New Style" and "(You Gotta) Fight For Your Right (To Party!)."

2015: Fetty Wap was given an honorary "key to the city" by the mayor of Paterson, New Jersey.

2015: Macklemore & Ryan Lewis released the single, "Downtown," which featured pioneering rappers Eric Nally, Melle Mel, Kool Moe Dee and Grandmaster Caz.

AUGUST 28

1991: Chuck D filed a $5 million lawsuit against a San Francisco brewery over the use of his voice in a radio advertisement for St. Ides malt liquor. Ironically, Chuck D had publically condemned malt liquor in the Public Enemy song, "One Million Bottlebags."

1996: The Westside Connection released their debut single, "Bow Down." The West Coast group consisted of Ice Cube, WC and Mack 10.

2001: The documentary, *Tupac Shakur: Before I Wake*, was released five years after the rapper's brutal murder in Las Vegas. The film focused on his final years and was mostly based on the observations of his personal bodyguard, Frank Alexander.

2002: One day after television talk show host Bill O'Reilly spearheaded a protest against Pepsi for hiring Ludacris, the soda maker backed down and pulled the rapper's television spots. The company issued a statement which read in part: "We have a responsibility to listen to our customers – and we've heard from a number of people that they were uncomfortable with our association with this artist."

2005: Marion "Suge" Knight was shot in the leg at a party hosted by Kanye West, following the MTV Video Awards ceremony. Knight was sitting at a VIP table in the Red Room nightclub inside the Shore Club hotel in Miami Beach, when a man started shooting. Although the gunman fired six shots, no one else was injured.

2009: DJ AM (real name Adam Michael Goldstein) of the rap-rock group, Crazy Town, was found dead in his New York City apartment from a suspected drug overdose. Crazy Town scored their biggest hit in 2000 with the single, "Butterfly." He was 36-years-old.

2012: The song "Reach For The Stars" by will.i.am was broadcast from the planet Mars back to Earth, a distance of 350 million miles. The Black Eyed Peas member had been asked by NASA to record a song for a mission involving the Curiosity Rover, which had landed on the Red Planet. This was the first time that a song had been beamed from a planet in our solar system back to Earth.

2012: TobyMac (also known as Momentum) became the first Christian rap artist to top *Billboard* magazine's top-200 sales chart. The album, *Eye On It*, also won a Grammy in the category of Best Contemporary Christian Music Album.

2013: Kanye West released the single, "Bound 2." The track featured former Gap Band singer Charlie Wilson and sampled "Bound" by Ponderosa Twins Plus One and "Sweet Nothin's" by Brenda Lee. The song's controversial music video featured a topless Kim Kardashian on a motorcycle.

2014: Snoop Dogg posted photos of himself in whiteface makeup, a blond wig and oversized gold-toned reading glasses on Instagram. Calling himself "Todd," he promoted a fictitious dating website.

2015: The reality series *Kingin' With Tyga* debuted on the MTV2 network.

2015: Kevin Gates kicked an 18-year-old woman in the chest during a concert in Lakeland, Florida, after she reportedly touched the rapper's leg. He was arrested and charged with battery. Gates later released a song about the incident, "The Truth."

2015: Lil Wayne staged the first annual Lil Weezyana Fest in his hometown of New Orleans. Among the performers at the festival were Master P, Mia X, Drake and a reunited Hot Boys (without B.G. who was in prison at the time).

AUGUST 29

1981: Frankie Smith was the first artist to perform a rap song on the long-running television program, *American Bandstand*. He performed his hit at the time, "Double Dutch Bus." A week later, the Sugarhill Gang appeared on the program and performed "Rapper's Delight."

1993: The sitcom, *Living Single*, debuted on the Fox network. The series starred Queen Latifah as Khadijah James, one of six single friends who resided in a Brooklyn apartment building. The program ran for five seasons. Queen Latifah also wrote and performed the show's theme song, "We Are Living Single."

1995: Junior M.A.F.I.A., a hip hop group organized and mentored by the Notorious B.I.G., released their debut album, *Conspiracy*. The album spawned the singles, "Player's Anthem," "I Need You Tonight" and "Get Money." One of the group's members, Lil' Kim, later launched a successful solo career.

1998: The Miami Hip-Hop Fest '98 was staged at the AT&T Amphitheater at Bayfront Park.

2004: Foxy Brown got into a fight with a pair of manicurists in New York City over a $20 bill. She was charged with misdemeanor assault and attempted assault, and was later sentenced to three-years of probation. But after violating the terms of her probation, she was sentenced to one-year in prison. She served her time at Rikers Island.

2004: 50 Cent was booed off the stage at the annual Reading Festival in England. After enduring a barrage of bottles and other projectiles from the audience, he ended his performance after 25 minutes. He was one of two acts at the music festival that were booed off the stage.

2005: Kanye West appeared on the cover of *Time* magazine. The headline read: "Defying the Rules of Rap, Kanye Goes His Own Way: Why He's the Smartest Man in Pop Music."

2006: Jerry Heller, who co-founded Ruthless Records with rapper Eazy-E, published the book, *Ruthless: A Memoir*.

2011: Michael Eric Dyson, a professor at Georgetown University, began teaching the course, *Sociology of Hip Hop: Jay-Z*. Dyson is the author of more than two-dozen books including the Tupac Shakur biography *Holler If You Hear Me* and *Know What I Mean?: Reflections On Hip-Hop*.

AUGUST 30

1998: The Miami-based hip hop duo L'Trimm released the single, "Cars With The Boom." The female duo was formed by teenage rappers Lady Tigra and Bunny D.

2002: Treach of Naughty By Nature starred in the action film, *Love And A Bullet*. He portrayed a contract killer named Malik Bishop who had a change of heart about his career.

2007: The reality show, *Celebrity Rap Superstar*, debuted on MTV. The program featured eight celebrity contestants who were taught how to rap. The series was hosted by Kevin Hart and Liz Hernandez, and featured three judges, Darryl "D.M.C." McDaniels, Da Brat and radio deejay Big Boy. The winner of the competition was Sharisse "Shar" Jackson, who is best known for playing the role of Niecy Jackson on the UPN sitcom, *Moesha*.

2011: After Rick Ross released his 2010 top-10 album, *Teflon Don*, he was sued by Memphis rapper Teflon Don (real name Donald Askey, Jr.) for trademark infringement and unfair competition. Also named in the lawsuit were DJ Khaled and various record companies.

2012: Hip hop mogul Chris Lighty fatally shot himself following a heated argument with his estranged wife. The founder of Violator Management, he worked with a number of leading artists including Sean "Diddy" Combs, Busta Rhymes, Ja Rule, 50 Cent and Mariah Carey. Lighty was 44-years-old.

2015: A smiling Taylor Swift presented her one-time adversary, Kanye West, with the Michael Jackson Video Vanguard Award at the MTV Video Music Awards. The gesture was meant to symbolize the end of any animosity between the two performers, following West's actions at the 2009 WMAs when he grabbed an award from the hands of the startled Swift.

AUGUST 31

1959: Pioneering rapper Fab 5 Freddy (birth name Frederick Brathwaite) was born in Brooklyn, New York. Also an artist, he was a member of the graffiti group, the Fabulous 5. In 1981, he was mentioned in the lyrics of the Blondie hit, "Rapture," and also appeared in the song's music video. Later, he was the original host of the music video show, *Yo! MTV Raps*.

1963: Pioneering West Coast rapper Egyptian Lover (birth name Greg Broussard) was born in Los Angeles. A successful club DJ who often performed for thousands of people, he was also a member of the groups, Radio Crew and Uncle Jamm's Army. He recorded his debut solo album in 1984, *On The Nile*.

1980: Joe Budden was born in Jersey City, New Jersey. In addition to his membership in the hip hop group Slaughterhouse, he pursued a solo career. He is best known for the 2003 solo hit, "Pump It Up" as well as for his appearance on the VH-1 reality show, *Love & Hip Hop*.

1983: The music video for "All Night Long" by Lionel Richie was one the first clips to feature hip hop-style street dancers.

1995: Long before Plies was a successful rapper, he was a talented football player named Nod Washington who attended Miami University (of Ohio) on a football scholarship. Playing the wide receiver position, he made 36 career receptions for 347 yards.

1997: Tombstone (real name Paul O'Neal) was shot to death. A member of the Cleveland hip hop group, Gaveyard Shift, he was killed near his home. He was 23-years-old.

1998: Rudy Pardee, a co-founder of the West Coast electronic/rap group L.A. Dream Team, died at the age of 41 in a scuba-diving accident near Catalina Island in Southern California.

1998: The police in the city of Pontiac, Michigan, called for a ban on rap music concerts as part of a citywide ban of what they described as "violent music."

2007: 50 Cent released the single, "Ayo Technology" (featuring Justin Timberlake). The track was nominated for a Grammy in the category of Best Rap Song.

2009: Trey Songz released his third album, *Ready*. The album spawned six singles, "Successful," "I Need A Girl," "LOL :-)," "I Invented Sex," "Neighbors Know My Name" and his first ever top-10 pop hit "Say Aah."

2014: The documentary, *ATL: The Untold Story Of Atlanta's Rise In The Rap Game*, premiered on the VH-1 network. The film was initially screened at the Rialto Center for the Arts in Atlanta.

2015: The talk show, *Girl Code Live*, debuted on MTV. It was hosted by rapper Awkwafina and media personalities Carly Aquilino and Nessa.

▶ SEPTEMBER

SEPTEMBER 1

1984: A 9-year-old Fergie, who would later join the Black Eyes Peas, began her first season of the popular Disney children's program, *Kids Incorporated*. She was a cast member for the first six seasons of the series.

1995: Sugar Shaft (real name Anthony Hardin) of the militant rap group, X Clan, died from complications of AIDS.

1998: *Blaze* magazine published its first issue. Method Man was featured on the cover. The magazine was published by the editors of *Vibe*.

1998: Fat Joe released his third album, *Don Cartagena*. The album spawned the singles, "Don Cartagena" (featuring Puff Daddy) and "Bet Ya Man Can't (Triz)" (featuring Big Pun, Cuban Link and Triple Seis).

2007: Percy Miller (also known as rapper Master P) published the business and motivational book, *Guaranteed Success*.

2010: Rapper T.I. and his wife were arrested in West Hollywood on suspicion of possessing methamphetamine. Just five-months earlier, T.I. had completed a seven-month prison stint on a weapons charge. The couple were released after posting a $20,000 bond. A federal judge later sentenced T.I. to an eleven-month prison sentence.

2012: Jay-Z teamed with Budweiser to launch the annual Made in America Festival. The two-day event was staged in Philadelphia and featured a lineup of rock and hip hop acts including Jay-Z, Pearl Jam, Drake, Run-D.M.C., Skrillex, Calvin Harris, D'Angelo, Janelle Monáe, Drake, Chris Cornell, DJ Shadow, the Hives and Rita Ora.

SEPTEMBER 2

1984: The first major U.S. hip hop tour of rappers and break dancers, the New York City Fresh Fest, kicked off in Greensboro, North Carolina. The 27-date tour featured Run-D.M.C., Kurtis Blow, Whodini, the Fat Boys, Newcleus, Kurtis Blow and others. Swatch Watches paid $300,000 for the sponsorship rights.

1993: Snoop Dogg and his bodyguard McKinley Lee were arrested for the shooting death of Philip Woldemariam. Both men were placed under house arrest until their trial, which began on November 27, 1995, and lasted nearly three-months. Snoop Dogg and his bodyguard were both acquitted of the murder.

1997: Master P released the solo album, *Ghetto D*, which was issued by his own label, No Limit Records. The album was highlighted by the hit singles, "I Miss My Homies" and "Make 'Em Say Uhh!" Selling more than three-million copies in the U.S., the album was the biggest of Master P's career.

2005: Kanye West caused a firestorm during an NBC telethon for the victims of Hurricane Katrina. While standing next to actor Mike Myers, West said: "George Bush doesn't care about black people." The phrase was later used as the title of a song by Houston hip hop group, K-otix.

2012: The two surviving members of Run-D.M.C. – Joseph Simmons and Darryl McDaniels – reunited after 13-years for a performance at Jay-Z's Made in America Festival in Philadelphia.

2014: The University of Calgary offered a course in "Rap Linguistics," which analyzed the evolution and impact of the language used by rappers such as Jay-Z, Eminem and Kanye West.

SEPTEMBER 3

1975: Redfoo (birth name Stefan Kendal Gordy) was born in Los Angeles. He formed the duo LMFAO in 2006 with his nephew Sky Blu. In 2011, LMFAO scored a massive hit with the track, "Party Rock Anthem." Redfoo is the youngest son of Motown Records founder, Berry Gordy, Jr.

1990: Vanilla Ice released his breakthrough album, *To The Extreme*. The album was highlighted by the tracks, "Play That Funky Music" and the smash hit "Ice Ice Baby." The album topped the charts for 16-weeks and sold seven-million copies in the U.S.

1995: Junior M.A.F.I.A., a hip hop group organized and mentored by the Notorious B.I.G., released the single, "Get Money." The million-selling track was the group's biggest hit.

1997: The hip hop duo BLACKstreet recorded an acoustic concert at the Brooklyn Academy of Music in New York City for an episode of the hit series, *MTV Unplugged*.

2004: Rappers Queen Latifah, Ja Rule and Eve starred in the comedy film, *The Cookout*. Of the three rappers, only Ja Rule returned for the 2011 sequel, *The Cookout 2*.

2014: Legendary rock performer Lou Reed surprised the music community by writing a glowing review of Kanye West's album, *Yeezus*, on the website, thetalkhouse.com.

SEPTEMBER 4

1981: Beyoncé (birth name Beyoncé Giselle Knowles) was born in Houston, Texas. She broke into music as a member of the 1990s R&B group, Destiny's Child. In 2003, she pursued a solo career with the release of her hit album, *Dangerously In Love*. She married Jay-Z in 2008.

1991: A Tribe Called Quest released their second album, *The Low End Theory*. The album spawned three singles, "Check The Rhime," "Jazz (We've Got)" and "Scenario."

1991: Funk-rock band Red Hot Chili Peppers released the rap-styled single, "Give It Away." The song was the group's first top-10 hit in the U.K. and won a Grammy in the category of Best Hard Rock Performance With Vocals.

2001: Before he was a rapper, Wale (real name Olubowale Akintimehin) began attending Robert Morris University in Pittsburgh on a football scholarship. Playing the running back position, he later transferred to Virginia State and then Bowie State.

2002: Nelly starred in the action-drama film, *Snipes*. The rapper portrayed a musical performer named Prolifik.

2015: A tour bus transporting Lil Durk was hit by gunfire before a concert at the Theater of Living Arts in Philadelphia. The incident, which was triggered by an argument, left a 20-year-old man dead. A suspect was captured by police.

SEPTEMBER 5

1981: The Sugarhill Gang were the second musical act to perform a rap song on the long-running television program, *American Bandstand*. The trio performed "Rapper's Delight" and "8th Wonder."

1991: MC Hammer released the crossover hit single, "2 Legit 2 Quit." The song's 15-minute music video cost nearly $3 million to make and included dozens of cameo appearances by athletes and musicians such as James Brown, Mark Wahlberg, Eazy-E, Queen Latifah and Milli Vanilli. The song was featured in the film, *The Addams Family*.

1994: Long before Rick Ross was a successful hip hop mogul, he was a student named William Leonard Roberts II who attended a historically black college, Albany State University in Columbus, Georgia. Earning an athletic scholarship, he played on the school's football team as an offensive lineman for two-years. While in college, he majored in Criminal Justice and worked for a time as a correctional officer.

2012: Dr. Dre topped *Forbes* magazine's sixth annual Hip-Hop Cash Kings list by earning $110 million over the previous year. Sean "Diddy" Combs came in second place

2015: 50 Cent announced that he was nearly finished building a mansion in an unnamed country in Africa.

2015: N.W.A. landed on *Billboard* magazine's Hot 100 for the very first time. The track "Straight Outta Compton" debuted on the chart a full 27-years after its initial release.

2015: Usher secretly married his manager, Grace Miguel. The couple were planning to wed in a small ceremony in front of friends and family but instead decided to elope.

SEPTEMBER 6

1977: N.O.R.E. (birth name Victor Santiago, Jr.) was born in Queens, New York. Previously known as Noriega, he began his career as a member of the hip hop duo, Capone-N-Noreaga.

1978: Foxy Brown (birth name Inga DeCarlo Fung Marchand) was born in Brooklyn, New York. She released her debut album in 1996, *Ill Na Na*. She was also a member of the hip hop group, the Firm.

1983: Marion "Suge" Knight began his first semester at El Camino College, which he attended on a football scholarship. A defensive player for the team, Knight was victorious in his first game, helping to beat Cerritos College by a score of 13 to 10. Then in 1985, he transferred to the University of Nevada, Las Vegas, where he played football for an additional two-years.

1985: Webbie (birth name Webster Gradney, Jr.) was born in Baton Rouge, Louisiana. He is best known for the 2008 hit "Independent" which featured Lil Phat and Lil Boosie.

1989: The MTV Music Video Awards introduced a new category, Best Rap Video. The first year's winner was "Parents Just Don't Understand" by DJ Jazzy Jeff & The Fresh Prince.

1997: The crime film, *First Time Felon*, featured a number of rappers including Anthony "Treach" Criss, Sandra "Pepa" Denton and Omar Epps.

2000: Pras Michel of the Fugees starred in the urban action film, *Turn It Up*. He played the role of a fictional Brooklyn hip hop artist named Diamond. The film also featured Ja Rule, Faith Evans and Jason Statham.

2013: Jay-Z sold half of his small share in the Brooklyn Nets NBA basketball team to Jason Kidd for a reported $500,000. The other half was purchased by an existing owner.

SEPTEMBER 7

1963: Eazy-E (birth name Eric Lynn Wright) of the rap group N.W.A. was born in Compton, California. Nicknamed the Godfather of Gangsta Rap, he also co-founded the successful label, Ruthless Records. He died in 1995 at the age of 30.

1987: *Street Frogs*, the first television cartoon series to feature rap music, was part of a 90-minute syndicated program called *The Comic Strip*. The music for *Street Frogs* was provided by Mr. Rhymes, D. St., Doug E. Fresh and Melle Mel. The series ran for 25 episodes.

1991: *Hammerman*, a weekly cartoon television series based on rapper M.C. Hammer, debuted on ABC. Hammer performed the Saturday morning program's theme song and also served as the show's host. The series ran for 13 episodes.

1993: NBA star Shaquille O'Neal released his debut single, "(I Know I Got) Skillz." A surprise hit, it was featured on his first album, *Shaq Diesel*.

1993: Erick Sermon of the hip hop group EPMD scored a solo hit with the single, "Stay Real." The track was included on his debut album, *No Pressure*.

1996: After attending the Mike Tyson-Bruce Seldon fight at the MGM Grand in Las Vegas, Tupac Shakur and Marion "Suge" Knight were on their way to Club 662, a nightclub owned by Death Row Records. As they were sitting in traffic, the two men were struck by a hail of gunfire that came from a nearby vehicle. While Knight was merely grazed, Shakur was struck by four of the bullets. At the hospital, the members of Shakur's group, Outlawz, guarded the injured rapper. After sustaining extensive internal injuries, Shakur died six-days later. The shooter was never brought to justice.

2012: Nicki Minaj announced the introduction of her first fragrance, Pink Friday. The product was released in collaboration with Elizabeth Arden.

2015: Dex Osama (real name Byron Cox) was shot and killed at the Crazy Horse strip club in his hometown of Detroit. A fight between two groups of men that began inside the club continued into the parking lot and ended in gunshots.

SEPTEMBER 8

1983: The German documentary, *Breakin' 'n' Enterin'*, was released. The film chronicled the early West Coast hip hop scene, and starred Ice-T, Shabba-Doo, Kid Frost and Michael Chambers.

1987: Wiz Khalifa (birth name Cameron Jibril Thomaz) was born in Minot, North Dakota, and later settled in Pittsburgh. The rapper enjoyed his breakthrough success in 2010 with the album, *Rolling Papers*. He scored the biggest hit of his career in 2014 with the rap ballad, "See You Again."

1987: The original version of "Push It" by Salt-n-Pepa was released as a B-side track on the 12-inch remixed version of the group's hit, "Tramp." But after "Push It" began garnering airplay on pop and R&B stations, a remixed version of the song was released as a single the following year.

1989: Keef Cowboy (real name Keith Wiggins) of pioneering hip hop group Grandmaster Flash and The Furious Five died as the result of crack cocaine abuse. He was 29-years-old.

1990: Kid 'n Play were the subject of a Saturday morning cartoon series on NBC, *Kid 'n Play*. The program featured both live-action and cartoon segments. The cartoon versions of the duo were voiced by actors Christopher Hooks and Brian Stokes Mitchell. The series ran for one season.

1997: LL Cool J published his autobiography, *I Make My Own Rules*.

1998: Chuck D of Public Enemy published the book, *The Power: Rap, Race, And Reality*.

1998: Fat Joe and Big Pun were both arrested on assault and robbery charges for allegedly striking a man with a baseball bat and stealing his gold chain. The incident occurred the previous July during the Puerto Rican Day Parade in New York City. After the victim refused to testify in court, the charges were dropped.

2000: The documentary, *Backstage: A Hard Knock Life*, was released. Produced by Damon Dash, the film chronicled the 1999 "Hard Knock Life Tour," which featured a lineup that included Jay-Z, Method Man, Ja Rule, DMX and Redman.

2001: The Midwest rap group Strik 9ine released the hit single, "Dansin' Wit Wolvez."

2003: Ginuwine (real name Elgin Baylor Lumpkin) married rapper Solé (real name Tonya M. Johnston) at a ceremony in the Cayman Islands. The couple divorced in 2015.

2006: Sean "Diddy" Combs reached an out-of-court settlement with Richard "Diddy" Dearlove, a London producer and singer. Dearlove had been using the stage name "Diddy" since 1992, when he released a remix of the Blondie track, "Atomic." Combs agreed not to call himself Diddy in the U.K. and to pay a cash settlement of $200,000 in court costs and damages.

2008: 50 Cent launched his own PlayStation2 video game, *50 Cent: Bulletproof*. He decided to produce his own game after rejecting an offer to provide the voice of the lead character on *Grand Theft Auto: San Andreas*.

2009: 50 Cent published a book about how to overcome adversity, *The 50th Law*.

2009: Snoop Dogg was named the Creative Chairman of Priority Records.

2009: Jay-Z released the album, *The Blueprint 3*. This was the third release in the "Blueprint" trilogy. The album spawned six singles beginning with "D.O.A. (Death of Auto-Tune)," "Run This Town" and "Empire State Of Mind." Mostly recorded in Hawaii, it was Jay-Z's 11th number-one album. The album sold two-million copies in the U.S.

2009: British rapper Speech Debelle (real name Corynne Elliot) won the prestigious Mercury Prize for her debut album, *Speech Therapy*.

2009: Raekwon released his fourth solo album, *Only Built 4 Cuban Linx... Pt. II*. The critically-acclaimed album spawned five singles beginning with "New Wu." The album featured numerous guests including Beanie Sigel, Busta Rhymes, Slick Rick, Lyfe Jennings and members of the Wu-Tang Clan and Jadakiss.

2010: The world's first Hip Hop Studies Program was introduced at McNally Smith School of Music, located in St. Paul, Minnesota. The academic program consisted of 45 credit hours over three-semesters and included courses such as "DJ Techniques" and "Language of Rap and Spoken Word."

2011: Steve Stoute, a former executive at Interscope and Sony Records and an artist manager who worked with Mary J. Blige and Nas, published the book, *The Tanning Of America: How Hip-Hop Created A Culture That Rewrote The Rules Of The New Economy*.

SEPTEMBER 9

1970: Dray (birth name Andre Weston) of the hip hop duo Das EFX was born in Queens, New York. He was also known as Krazy Drayz.

1977: Soulja Slim (birth name James Adarryl Tapp, Jr.) was born in New Orleans. He was murdered in 2003 at the age of 23.

1998: Former Geto Boys member Bushwick Bill filed a $20 million lawsuit against three record companies, a comedy club and several individuals who he claimed had assaulted him. The alleged incident occurred in August 1998 at the Jus Joking Comedy Cafe in Houston.

1999: The MTV Music Video Awards introduced a new category, Best Hip-Hop Video. The first year's winner was "Intergalactic" by the Beastie Boys.

2002: Missy Elliott released the single, "Work It." The track sampled "Heart Of Glass" by Blondie, "Peter Piper" by Run-D.M.C., "Request Line" by Rock Master Scott & The Dynamic Three and "Take Me To The Mardi Gras" by Bob James. This was the biggest hit of Elliott's career.

2003: Dizzee Rascal won the prestigious Mercury Prize for his debut album, *Boy In Da Corner*.

2006: Justin Timberlake began a seven-week run at number-one on the U.S. singles chart with "SexyBack."

2006: Lupe Fiasco released his debut album, *Lupe Fiasco's Food & Liquor*. The album spawned four singles, "Kick, Push," "I Gotcha," "Daydreamin'" and "The Emperor's Soundtrack." The album earned four Grammy nominations, winning an award in the category of Best Urban/Alternative Song for the track "Daydreamin'."

2008: LL Cool J released his final studio album at Def Jam Recordings, *Exit 13*. The title referred to the 13-album contract that the rapper had signed with the label while still a teenager. The album was highlighted by the hits, "Cry" and "Baby."

2013: After losing 140 pounds, rapper Biz Markie became the spokesman for a zero-calorie soda, Zevia. The company celebrated the announcement by putting his face on a special edition soda can.

2015: Citystylez (real name Lavell Boyd) was murdered in St. Louis. He was shot multiple times by unknown suspects while sitting in his vehicle. He was 32-years-old. A 10-year-old bystander was also injured.

2015: Kool DJ AJ (real name Aaron Gerald O'Bryant) passed away after battling stomach cancer. A one-time concert promoter, the pioneering deejay worked with Kurtis Blow and Busy Bee Starski in the late-1970s and into the 1980s. He is best known for the track, "AJ Scratch," which appeared on Kurtis Blow's 1984 album, *Ego Trip*.

2015: Jimmy Fallon and Justin Timberlake teamed up on *The Tonight Show* for a performance that was dubbed "History of Rap, Part 6," which consisted of a medley of 23 rap songs over a six-minute period, beginning with "Fiesta" by R. Kelly and ending with "(You Gotta) Fight For Your Right (To Party!)" by the Beastie Boys.

SEPTEMBER 10

1968: Big Daddy Kane (birth name Antonio Hardy) was born in Brooklyn, New York. The rapper and actor began his music career in 1986 as a member of the Juice Crew.

1988: A total of nine people were arrested, four of whom were charged with murder, following an outbreak of violence that left one person dead and 14 injured at a rap concert at the Nassau Coliseum in Uniondale, New York. The "Jam '88" concert featured a number of hip hop acts including Kool Moe Dee, Doug E. Fresh, Eric B. & Rakim and Big Daddy Kane.

1990: *The Fresh Prince Of Bel-Air* was the first sitcom on a major television network to feature a rapper in the lead role. The series, which starred Will Smith, ran for six seasons on NBC. Smith also performed the show's theme song.

2001: G-Unit rapper Lloyd Banks was shot two times after he left a nightclub in the Jamaica section of Queens, New York. He managed to walk to a nearby hospital.

2004: Will Smith starred in the animated DreamWorks film, *Shark Tale*. Smith provided the voice of a fish named Oscar.

2010: Joaquin Phoenix starred in the pseudo-documentary, *I'm Still Here*, which chronicled his "retirement" from acting for a career in hip hop music. The comedy film was directed by Casey Affleck.

2015: British rapper Professor Green published his autobiography, *Lucky*.

SEPTEMBER 11

1977: Ludacris (birth name Christopher Brian Bridges) was born in Champaign, Illinois. After a stint as a deejay at Hot 97.5 in Atlanta, he pursued a recording career. Beginning with his major-label debut album *Back For The First Time*, Ludacris was at the forefront of the Dirty South movement. As an actor, he played the role of Tej Parker in four *Fast & Furious* films. Ludacris is a distant cousin of comedian Richard Pryor.

2000: Shaggy released the single, "It Wasn't Me" (featuring Rikrok). The track sampled "Smile Happy" by War.

2001: Jay-Z released his sixth album, *The Blueprint*. The album spawned four singles: "Izzo (H.O.V.A.)," "Girls, Girls, Girls," "Jigga That Nigga" and "Song Cry." The critically-acclaimed album sold nearly three-million copies in the U.S.

2001: Mary J. Blige released the single, "No More Drama." The track sampled "Nadia's Theme" (the theme song of the CBS soap opera, *The Young And The Restless*). The song's music video featured cameo appearances by Mariah Carey and Sean "P. Diddy" Combs.

2004: The single "Goodies" by Ciara featuring Petey Pablo began a seven-week run at number-one on the U.S. charts.

2005: André 3000 of OutKast co-starred in the crime-thriller film, *Revolver*. He portrayed a loan shark named Avi.

2007: The documentary, *Notorious B.I.G.: Bigger Than Life*, was released. The film featured never before seen footage of the fallen rapper as well as interviews with Method Man, P. Diddy, Easy Mo Bee, Matty C, E-40 and Raekwon.

2007: Chris Brown released the hit single, "Kiss Kiss." The track was featured on his second album, *Exclusive*. In the song's music video, Brown portrayed two roles – a nerd and a jock – with both characters competing for the attention of an attractive woman.

2007: 50 Cent released his third album, *Curtis*. The album spawned three commercial singles, "Straight To The Bank," "Ayo Technology" and "I'll Still Kill." The album sold nearly two-million copies in the U.S.

2008: Taboo of the Black Eyed Peas and Michelle Williams of Destiny's Child were two of the judges on the short-lived television series, *MTV's Top Pop Group*.

2008: Kanye West and his bodyguard/road manager Don "Don C." Crowley were arrested at the Los Angeles International Airport after a physical altercation with members of the paparazzi.

2009: Jay-Z headlined a charity concert on the 8th anniversary of the 9/11 attacks. Among the performers who joined Jay-Z were his wife Beyoncé, Kanye West, Mary J. Blige, Rihanna and John Mayer. The event was staged at Madison Square Garden in support of the New York Police & Fire Widows' and Children's Benefit Fund. The "Answer The Call" concert was also broadcast on the Fuse network.

2009: Mary J. Blige co-starred in the romantic-comedy film, *Tyler Perry's I Can Do Bad All By Myself*. Blige portrayed a bartender.

2010: Nick Cannon adopted the persona of "Slick Nick" for the track, "I'm A Slick Rick." The song was a response to Eminem's frequent attacks of Cannon and his then-wife Mariah Carey. (Cannon later released a second Slick Nick track, "Nick's Story," which was a freestyle rap version of Slick Rick's hit "Children's Story.")

2015: T.I. changed his stage name to TIP. His first release under his new name was the EP, *Da' Nic*.

SEPTEMBER 12

1977: 2 Chainz (birth name Tauheed Epps) was born in College Park, Georgia. Formerly known as Tity Boi, he enjoyed his first success as a member of the hip hop duo, Playaz Circle. He later pursued a solo career and released his debut album in 2012, *Based On A T.R.U. Story*.

1986: An early hip hop tour across Europe – the Raising Hell Tour – opened at the Hammersmith Odeon in London. The concert was headlined by Run-D.M.C. and featured Whodini, LL Cool J and the Beastie Boys.

2000: LL Cool J released his eighth album, *G.O.A.T. (Greatest Of All Time)*. The album spawned two singles, "Imagine That" and "You And Me." This was his only album that topped the pop charts.

2004: Snoop Dogg released the single, "Drop It Like It's Hot" (featuring Pharrell). The track sampled "White Horse" by Laid Back. The single was nominated for two Grammys in the categories of Best Rap Song and Best Rap Performance by a Duo or Group.

2006: The husband-and-wife team of Jennifer Lopez and Marc Anthony starred in the film, *El Cantante*. In the biographical film, Anthony portrayed the late salsa singer, Héctor Lavoe, while Lopez played the singer's wife.

2006: DJ Webstar & Young B released the single, "Chicken Noodle Soup" (featuring the Voice of Harlem). The track spawned a popular dance craze of the same name.

2006: "Weird Al" Yankovic released the single, "White & Nerdy," which was a parody of "Ridin'" by Chamillionaire and Krayzie Bone. A top-10 hit, the track appeared on Yankovic's album, *Straight Outta Lynwood*.

2006: Sean "Diddy" Combs released the single, "Come To Me" (featuring Nicole Scherzinger).

2008: 50 Cent and Donnie Wahlberg co-starred in the crime-thriller film, *Righteous Kill*. While 50 Cent portrayed a drug dealer, Wahlberg played a police detective.

2009: When Taylor Swift attempted to accept the award for the best female video at the MTV Video Music Awards, Kanye West jumped onto the stage and grabbed the statuette. A shocked Swift watched as West grabbed the microphone and said, "I'm sorry, but Beyoncé had one of the best videos of all time." West's comments were met with complete silence from the audience. Swift had regained her composure when she returned to the podium later in the evening. Over the next few weeks, West was criticized in the press, with even the president chiming in on the matter.

2012: Beanie Sigel entered prison after he was convicted of failing to file tax returns for the years of 2003 to 2005. He pleaded guilty and was sentenced to 25-months behind bars.

2012: British rapper Ben Drew (a.k.a. Plan B) co-starred in the action film, *The Sweeney*. He portrayed a police officer, Detective Constable George Carter.

2015: Ice Cube walked off the stage after performing just five songs at the Queen Mary in Long Beach, California. He ended his performance in response to several fights that had broken out in the audience. Ice Cube was the headliner at the concert.

SEPTEMBER 13

1978: Swizz Beatz (birth name Kasseem Dean) was born in the Bronx, New York. Originally a DJ and rapper, he later emerged as a prolific and successful producer in the hip hop and R&B fields. After his initial success with Cassidy, Swizz Beatz produced Beyoncé, DMX, T.I., Busta Rhymes and others. In 2009, he was the featured artist on Jay-Z's Grammy-winning single, "On To The Next One." He also founded his own label, Full Surface Records.

1988: MC Lyte released the first-ever solo rap album by a female, *Lyte As A Rock*. The project was highlighted by the tracks, "Lyte As A Rock" and "Paper Thin."

1993: Dr. Dre released the single, "Let Me Ride," which featured Jewell and Snoop Dogg. The song prominently sampled "Mothership Connection (Star Child)" by Parliament. The music video for "Let Me Ride" featured an appearance by Dr. Dre's former N.W.A. bandmate, Ice Cube. (The following year, Dr. Dre and Ice Cube would record the duet, "Natural Born Killaz.")

1994: The Notorious B.I.G. released his debut album, *Ready To Die*. The first release on Sean "Puffy" Combs' label, Bad Boy Records, the album spawned three singles, "Juicy," "Big Poppa" and "One More Chance." The album sold four-million copies in the U.S.

1996: Tupac Shakur died of massive internal bleeding at the University Medical Center of Southern Nevada. The official cause of death was listed as respiratory failure and cardiopulmonary arrest. He had been shot six-days earlier while sitting in a vehicle on a Las Vegas street.

2002: Rappers Ice Cube and Eve co-starred in the comedy film, *Barbershop*. A surprise hit, the film earned $77 million at the box office. (Ice Cube and Eve returned for the 2004 sequel, *Barbershop 2: Back In Business*, and were joined in the film by Queen Latifah.)

2002: LL Cool J released the top-10 hit single, "Luv U Better." Marc Dorsey sang backup vocals on the track.

2005: Anthony "Treach" Criss co-starred in the Steven Seagal crime-action film, *Today You Die*. In the film, Treach portrayed an inmate named Ice Kool.

2006: Fergie released her debut album, *The Dutchess*. The album was a smash hit that spawned a total of five top-5 pop singles, "London Bridge," "Big Girls Don't Cry," "Glamorous," "Fergalicious" and "Clumsy." The album sold more than four-million copies in the U.S.

2008: Lil Wayne was the musical guest on *Saturday Night Live*. He performed "Got Money" and "Lollipop."

2009: A day after Kanye West grabbed a statuette from the arms of Taylor Swift at the MTV Video Music Awards, he offered an apology during an appearance on *The Jay Leno Show*. After he was asked, "Have you had a tough day?," West replied, "It's been extremely difficult.... My entire life, I've only wanted to give and do something that I felt was right. And I immediately knew in the situation that it was wrong, and it wasn't a spectacle or just – you know, it's actually someone's emotions, you know, that I stepped on."

2010: Jay-Z and Eminem co-headlined the first of two concerts at Yankee Stadium in the Bronx. The highlight of the evening was a duet performance of "Renegade." The concert was one of just four dates on a two-city tour. The other two shows were staged in Detroit.

2011: Jay-Z and Kanye West released the single, "Niggas In Paris." The track sampled "Baptizing Scene" by Reverend W.A. Donaldson and featured dialogue from the 2007 film, *Blades Of Glory*. The single won a Grammy in the category of Best Rap Performance.

SEPTEMBER 14

1973: Nas (birth name Nasir bin Olu Dara Jones) was born in Brooklyn, New York. A successful solo artist, he released his first album in 1994, *Illmatic*. His father is jazz musician Olu Dara.

1990: LL Cool J released his fourth album, *Mama Said Knock You Out*. The album spawned the hits, "To Da Break Of Dawn," "The Boomin' System," "Around The Way Girl," "6 Minutes Of Pleasure" and "Mama Said Knock You Out." The Grammy-winning album sold more than two-million copies in the U.S.

1999: Eve released her debut album, *Let There Be Eve... Ruff Ryders' First Lady*. The project spawned the singles, "Gotta Man" and "Love Is Blind." The chart-topping album sold two-million copies in the U.S.

2003: The teen sitcom *Romeo!* premiered on the Nickelodeon network. The program, which starred Lil' Romeo and his father Master P, followed the exploits of a family musical group, the Romeo Show. The series ran for 53 episodes over three seasons.

2010: Wiz Khalifa released the single, "Black And Yellow," which appeared on his breakthrough album, *Rolling Papers*. The song's title referred to the team colors of the Pittsburgh Steelers. The song's music video featured various scenes of Pittsburgh.

2010: Trey Songz released his fourth studio album, *Passion, Pain & Pleasure*. The album spawned the singles, "Can't Be Friends," "Love Faces," "Unusual" and his biggest hit to date, "Bottoms Up."

2013: Jay-Z and Beyoncé performed their 2003 hit "Crazy In Love" at the wedding reception of LeBron James and his longtime girlfriend Savannah Brinson. The reception was held at the Grand Del Mar Hotel in San Diego.

2015: Rihanna introduced a line of sportswear and sneakers in collaboration with Puma.

SEPTEMBER 15

1992: Actor David Faustino who played the role of Bud Bundy on the sitcom, *Married... With Children*, attempted a career as a rapper. Using the name D' Lil, he released the album, *Balistyx*. The album sold poorly.

1993: Lisa "Left Eye" Lopes was arrested for fighting with police at the Georgia Dome in Atlanta. She was charged with disorderly conduct, criminal trespass and battery against a police officer. She received a 12-month suspended sentence and was ordered to perform community service and receive alcohol counseling.

2000: Hip hop artists Master P and Sticky Fingaz co-starred in the drama film, *Lockdown*.

2003: Eve starred in the UPN network sitcom, *Eve*. She played the role of Michelle "Shelly" Williams, a modern career woman who yearned for love. The series ran for three seasons.

2006: Run-D.M.C. was sued by the rock group, the Knack, for allegedly sampling their number-one hit, "My Sharona," on the trio's 1987 track, "It's Tricky." Although the three-year statute of limitations had long passed, members of the Knack claimed they were unaware of the rap song. The suit was settled out of court.

2009: The Black Eyed Peas began their "The E.N.D. World Tour" with a performance in Japan. In all, the group would play 115 shows over the next year.

2009: The tribute film, *Big Pun: The Legacy*, was released. The documentary included interviews with Snoop Dogg, DMX, Bone Thugs-N-Harmony, Method Man, Xzibit, Swizz Beatz, DJ Skribble, Chino XL, Redman, Sticky Fingaz, Ghostface Killah, Raekwon, Killer Mike and others.

2012: Frank Ocean was the musical guest on *Saturday Night Live*. He performed "Thinkin Bout You" and "Pyramids."

2015: Two former members of Danity Kane, Aubrey O'Day and Shannon Bex, told New York City radio station Power 105.1 that despite recording a pair of platinum-selling albums and going on successful tours, they were in debt. They blamed their financial state on their producer, Sean "Diddy" Combs.

SEPTEMBER 16

1979: Flo Rida (birth name Tramar Lacel Dillard) was born in Carol City, Florida. He scored his breakthrough hit in 2008 with the smash single, "Low."

1979: The Sugarhill Gang released the pioneering rap single, "Rapper's Delight." The song was built upon an instrumental break from the track, "Good Times" by Chic. The first major hit of the rap era, it barely made it into the top-40 charts despite selling millions of copies. The record was mostly sold in independent record stores and non-traditional outlets such barbershops. The 12-inch version of the song clocked in at nearly 15-minutes.

1988: The members of Run-D.M.C. starred in the urban crime film, *Tougher Than Leather*. Directed by Rick Rubin, the film followed the rap trio as they searched for their friend's killer. Also appearing in the film were Rubin, Slick Rick and the Beastie Boys. The film premiered around same time as the release of Run-D.M.C.'s fourth album which was also titled, *Tougher Than Leather*.

1995: Tupac Shakur signed with Death Row Records, which at time featured a roster that included Daz Dillinger, Lady of Rage, Snoop Dogg, Nate Dogg, RBX, the D.O.C. and Dr. Dre. Shakur's move to the label would mark the start of a rivalry between Death Row and Bad Boy Entertainment.

2000: *The Slim Shady Show*, an animated series, debuted on Eminem's internet channel. The series ran for 26 episodes.

2012: Kirko Bangz released the hit song "Drank In My Cup," which appeared on his mixtape, *Progression 2: A Young Texas Playa*. The track's official remix featured 2 Chainz and Juelz Santana.

2013: The syndicated program, *The Queen Latifah Show*, made its debut. The television talk show ran for two seasons.

2014: Sean "Diddy" Combs purchased a newly constructed 17,000-square-foot mansion in Holmby Hills, California. He paid nearly $40 million. The estate included a 3,000-square-foot guest house.

SEPTEMBER 17

1966: Doug E. Fresh (birth name Douglas E. Davis) was born in Christ Church Parish, Barbados, and raised in the Bronx, New York. Nicknamed the Original Human Beat Box, he often worked with pioneering rapper Slick Rick and scored hits such as "La Di Da Di" and "The Show."

1991: The group WC and the Maad Circle Before – which included Coolio before he became a solo artist – released the album, *Ain't A Damn Thang Changed*. The group's leader, WC, later formed the gangsta rap supergroup, Westside Connection, along with Ice Cube and Mack 10.

1999: Eminem was sued by his mother for $10 million. She claimed that he made slanderous comments about her which resulted in emotional distress and financial harm.

2002: British rapper Ms. Dynamite (real name Niomi Arleen McLean-Daley) won the prestigious Mercury Prize for her debut album, *A Little Deeper*.

2002: Eminem released the smash hit single, "Lose Yourself." The song was written and recorded on the set of the film, *8 Mile*, between takes. This was Eminem's first number-one hit on the U.S. pop charts. The song won an Academy Award in the category of Best Original Song and two Grammys in the categories of Best Rap Song and Best Rap Solo Performance. The track was included on the soundtrack album, *Music From And Inspired By The Motion Picture 8 Mile*.

2005: The single "Gold Digger" by Kanye West featuring Jamie Foxx began a remarkable ten-week run at number-one on the U.S. charts.

2008: The film, *Days Of Wrath*, featured a number of hip hop artists including Kurupt, Slim Thug, Rick Ross and David Banner.

2015: Sir Mix-A-Lot won a copyright lawsuit in a Washington state federal court. His former songwriting partner, David Ford (a.k.a. DJ Punish), claimed he had co-written a number of songs including "Baby Got Back" and "Anaconda." Judge Robert S. Lasnik ruled against Ford, who had missed the three-year statute of limitations.

SEPTEMBER 18

1967: Ricky Bell (birth name Ricardo Bell) was born in Boston, Massachusetts. He was the lead singer of the new jack swing / hip hop trio, Bell Biv DeVoe. The group had been formed by members of the R&B boy band New Edition. Also a solo artist, he released his debut album in 2000, *Ricardo Campana*.

1969: Cappadonna (birth name Darryl Hill) was born in Staten Island, New York. He joined the Wu-Tang Clan upon the death of Ol' Dirty Bastard. Cappadonna was initially called the group's "Unofficial Tenth Member." He made his first recording as a Wu-Tang Clan affiliate on Raekwon's solo hit, "Ice Cream."

1974: Xzibit (birth name Alvin Nathaniel Joiner) was born in Detroit but raised in Albuquerque, New Mexico. Best known as the host of the MTV program *Pimp My Ride*, the rapper launched a solo career in the mid-1990s and appeared as a featured vocalist on a number of rap hits.

1979: Clinton Sparks was born in Boston. The DJ, songwriter and producer worked with a wide variety of artists including Akon, Rick Ross, Ludacris, Tyrese Gibson and T-Pain. He also hosted the syndicated radio show, *Get Familiar w/ Clinton Sparks*.

1984: British rapper Dizzee Rascal (birth name Dylan Mills) was born in London, England. He scored a number of chart-topping hits in the U.K. including "Shout," "Dance Wiv Me," "Bonkers," "Holiday" and "Dirtee Disco."

2009: Speech of the group Arrested Development published the book, *What Is Success? How To Be Successful God's Way*. He wrote the book under the name of Speech Thomas.

2011: The VH-1 network aired the documentary, *Planet Rock: The Story Of Hip Hop And The Crack Generation*, which was narrated by Ice-T. A number of rappers appeared in the controversial film including Snoop Dogg, B-Real of Cyprus Hill and two members of the Wu-Tang Clan, RZA and Raekwon.

2012: Common published his autobiography, *One Day It'll All Make Sense*.

2012: Wyclef Jean published his autobiography, *Purpose: An Immigrant's Story*. In the book, he made the allegation that his group, the Fugees, broke up due to his romantic relationship with bandmate Lauryn Hill.

2012: Flo Rida released the single, "I Cry." The track prominently sampled "Piano In The Dark" by Brenda Russell. The song's dramatic music video chronicled the rapper's return to his childhood neighborhood in Carol City, Florida.

2015: Trick Daddy (real name Maurice Young) filed for Chapter 11 bankruptcy. He reported $430,000 in assets and almost $650,000 in debts.

SEPTEMBER 19

1980: Kurtis Blow performed on the first night of a two-night stint as the opening act for reggae legend Bob Marley at Madison Square Garden.

1982: A British rapper of Nigerian descent, Skepta (birth name Joseph Junior Adenuga) was born in Tottingham, North London, England. He was one of the originators of the Grime-style rap movement and was a co-founder of the record label, Boy Better Know.

2000: DJ Casper released the hit single, "Cha-Cha Slide." The song spawned a popular line dance. When DJ Casper originally wrote the song in 1998, he called it "The Casper Slide Part 1." Eventually, he released a second version of the song called "The Casper Slide Part 2." Finally, he teamed with M.O.B. Music Publishing to record a third rendition of the song which was titled, "Cha-Cha Slide." That version was released by Universal Records.

2000: OutKast released the single, "B.O.B." ("Bombs Over Baghdad"). Despite being banned from many urban and top-40 radio stations due to its lyrics, the song was praised by music critics.

2003: Beyoncé and Cuba Gooding, Jr., starred in the musical comedy, *The Fighting Temptations*. Beyoncé portrayed a lounge singer who was convinced to join a gospel choir.

2005: K-Ruger (real name Alfredrick Williams) died in Los Angeles. Signed to Def Jam by Jay-Z, the Houston-based rapper was recording his debut album at the time of his death.

2009: The four original members of the Goodie Mob – Cee Lo Green, Khujo, T-Mo and Big Gipp – staged their first reunion concert in more than 20 years. They performed at the Masquerade concert hall in Atlanta.

2013: Chris Brown co-starred in the 3-D dance film, *Battle Of The Year*. The film was based on director Benson Lee's 2008 documentary, *Planet B-Boy*.

2013: Beyoncé and Jay-Z – who together earned an estimated $95 million – were named the top-earning celebrity couple of the year by *Forbes* magazine.

2014: Big Sean released the single, "I Don't Fuck With You" (featuring E-40). The track sampled "Say You Love Me One More Time" by D.J. Rogers.

SEPTEMBER 20

1988: Rob Base and DJ E-Z Rock released their debut album, *It Takes Two*. The album was highlighted by the tracks, "It Takes Two," "Joy And Pain" and the club hit, "Get On The Dance Floor." *It Takes Two* was one of the best-selling rap albums of the 1980s.

1999: Ice-T joined the cast of the popular crime-drama series, *Law & Order: Special Victims Unit*. He played the role of Detective Odafin "Fin" Tutuola.

2003: Water Water (real name Jerel Allaine Spruill) of the hip hop act, the Spooks, died in a car crash just outside of Washington, D.C. The Spooks scored their biggest hit in 2000 with the single, "Things I've Seen." He was 30-years-old.

2004: The video game, *Def Jam: Fight For NY*, was released. The game was issued by Electronic Arts and featured a number of rappers including Method Man, Redman, Lil' Kim, Snoop Dogg, Fat Joe, Joe Budden, Xzibit, N.O.R.E., Ice-T, Ludacris, Busta Rhymes, Flavor Flav and Sean Paul.

2005: The Black Eyed Peas released the hit single, "My Humps." The track's co-writer, will.i.am, had originally intended to give the composition to the Pussycat Dolls. The song was criticized in the press for its bawdy lyrics.

2011: Cheetah Vision, a film production company launched by 50 Cent, released its first project, *Set Up*. The action-thriller film starred 50 Cent, Bruce Willis and Ryan Phillippe.

2014: HBO aired a concert special by Beyoncé and Jay-Z from their "The On the Run" tour. The program featured performances from two concerts in Paris.

SEPTEMBER 21

1968: David Jolicoeur of the rap trio De La Soul was born in Brooklyn, New York. He later adopted the stage name, Trugoy the Dove.

1974: Trick Daddy (birth name Maurice Samuel Young) was born in Miami. He released the best-selling album of his career in 2001, *Thugs Are Us*, which spawned the hit, "I'm A Thug."

1984: American-born, Nigerian rapper Wale (birth name Olubowale Victor Akintimehin, later changed to Ralph Folarin) was born in Washington, D.C.

1990: MC Hammer released the crossover hit single, "Pray." The track sampled "When Doves Cry" by Prince and "We Care A Lot" by Faith No More.

1999: Hip hop supergroup the Terror released their debut album, *The Album*. The group consisted of Big Pun, Fat Joe, Armageddon, Triple Seis, Prospect and Cuban Link.

1999: Mariah Carey teamed with Jay-Z on the hit single, "Heartbreaker." It was the first time that Carey had recorded a track with a hip hop artist. Due to contractual issues, a cartoon rendition of Jay-Z was used in the song's music video.

1999: 50 Cent released his debut single, "Thug Love." He was backed on the track by the members of Destiny's Child. But just two days before he planned to film a music video, he was shot a total of nine times. As a result, Columbia Records decided not to release his album, *Power Of The Dollar*.

2001: In the wake of the 9/11 attacks, a benefit concert, *America: A Tribute To Heroes*, was staged ten-days later. Among the 21 artists who performed at the somber event were Wyclef Jean, Alicia Keys and Stevie Wonder. The evening closed with all the performers taking the stage to sing "America The Beautiful."

2003: DMX published the book, *E.A.R.L.: The Autobiography Of DMX*.

2010: Nas teamed with rocker Carlos Santana to record a remake of the 1980 heavy metal hit by AC/DC, "Back In Black." The track appeared on Santana's solo album, *Guitar Heaven: The Greatest Guitar Classics Of All Time*.

2011: Antonio "L.A." Reid began his first of two seasons as a judge on the U.S. version of the talent show, *X Factor*. (During a 2015 public appearance in Cannes, France, he said that the program was the "worst thing I've ever done.")

2015: Drake teamed with Chef Susur Lee to open Fring's, an Asian-themed restaurant in Toronto. In attendance on the opening night were Jayden Smith and Serena Williams.

SEPTEMBER 22

1992: Public Enemy's music video for the song, "Hazy Shade Of Criminal" was banned by MTV due to "offensive" images and lyrics. The video network had previously banned the group's music video, "By The Time I Get To Arizona," for its portrayal of violence toward public officials in Arizona.

2002: During a speech in Texas, Vice President Dan Quayle attacked the record industry for selling rap music that promoted violence and asked that Interscope Records withdraw the album, *2pacalypse Now* by Tupac Shakur. Quayle visited the state on behalf of the family of a murdered Texas trooper whose killer was listening to the album while driving a stolen pickup truck when he was pulled over by the officer. Quayle blasted gangsta rap and stated: "There is absolutely no reason for a record like this to be published by a responsible corporation."

2006: The late Jam Master Jay of Run-D.M.C. was the recipient of a Lifetime Achievement Award at the Berklee College of Music. Darryl "D.M.C." McDaniels presented the award, which was accepted by Jay's mother, Connie Mizell.

2009: LL Cool J began his long-running starring role on the crime-drama television series, *NCIS: Los Angeles*. He portrayed Senior Field Agent Sam Hanna, a former Navy SEAL.

2011: A full-sized wax figure of Fergie was unveiled at Madame Tussauds in Las Vegas. The singer was on hand for the unveiling ceremony.

2014: Pharrell Williams began his first season as a judge on the television singing competition, *The Voice*.

2015: Sean "Diddy" Combs topped *Forbes* magazine's ninth annual Hip-Hop Cash Kings list by earning $60 million over the previous year. Jay-Z came in second place.

SEPTEMBER 23

1972: Jermaine Dupri (full name Jermaine Dupri Mauldin) was born in Asheville, North Carolina. A rapper and producer, he began his career in the entertainment field at the age of 12 as a dancer for the rap group Whodini. He later launched his own successful record label, So So Def Recordings, and oversaw the careers of Kris Kross and Xscape. He also worked with Usher, Destiny's Child, Lil' Bow Wow, Mariah Carey and others.

1999: Lil Wayne released his debut solo single, "Tha Block Is Hot" (featuring Juvenile and B.G.).

2000: Lil' Romeo sang the theme song of the animated series, *Static Shock*. The program ran on the WB Network for four seasons.

2003: OutKast released their classic double-album, *Speakerboxxx/The Love Below*. The project was promoted as two separate solo albums: *Speakerboxxx* by Big Boi and *The Love Below* by André 3000. The project was highlighted by a pair of number-one pop singles, "Hey Ya!" and "The Way You Move," as well as the top-10 hit, "Roses." (The smash single, "Hey Ya," was released on the same day as the album.) The double-album earned six Grammy nominations and won three awards, and sold more than more than five-million copies in the U.S.

2005: A number of hip hop artists starred in the comedy-drama film, *Roll Bounce*. Set in a 1970s roller rink, the film featured rappers Bow Wow, Nick Cannon and Brandon T. Jackson. Darryl "D.M.C." McDaniels portrayed a deejay named D.J. Smooth Dee.

2008: T.I. released the single, "Live Your Life" (featuring Rihanna). This was the biggest hit of T.I.'s career. The song's music video chronicled his rise to fame and featured an appearance by actress Sandra Bullock. The song won numerous awards and was included in the 2009 film, *The Hangover*.

2012: Ne-Yo was the subject of an episode of the VH-1 program, *Behind The Music*.

2014: Model Amber Rose filed for divorce from rapper Wiz Khalifa, citing irreconcilable differences. The couple had been married for one year.

2014: Dr. Dre topped *Forbes* magazine's eighth annual Hip-Hop Cash Kings list by earning a whopping $620 million over the previous year. Most of the fortune came from the sale of his Beats headphones to Apple. Jay-Z and Sean "Diddy" Combs tied for second place.

SEPTEMBER 24

1990: Luther Campbell of 2 Live Crew settled a lawsuit with *Star Wars* filmmaker George Lucas over the rapper's use of the stage name, Luke Skyywalker. Lucas had asked for $300 million in damages in the federal trademark infringement lawsuit, but agreed to a reported $300,000 payment in an out of court settlement.

1990: Monie Love released the Grammy-nominated hit single, "Monie In The Middle."

1995: Both Suge Knight and P. Diddy attended Jermaine Dupri's birthday party at the Platinum House in Atlanta. During a massive fight at the nightclub, Death Row Records employee Jake Robles was shot and killed. The incident added fuel to the East Coast versus West Coast rap war.

2002: Def Jam Recordings co-founder Russell Simmons published his autobiography, *Life And Def: Sex, Drugs, Money + God*.

2006: Atlanta-based rapper Unk released the track, "Walk It Out," from his album, *Beat'n Down Yo Block!*

2013: Sean "Diddy" Combs topped *Forbes* magazine's seventh annual Hip-Hop Cash Kings list by earning $50 million over the previous year. Jay-Z came in second place.

2013: Drake released his third studio album, *Nothing Was The Same*. The album spawned several singles beginning with "Started From The Bottom." The album was nominated for a Grammy in the category of Best Album and sold nearly two-million copies in the U.S.

SEPTEMBER 25

1968: Will Smith (birth name Willard Carroll Smith, Jr.) was born in Philadelphia. Taking the stage name, the Fresh Prince, he teamed with DJ Jazzy Jeff to release a series of crossover rap albums beginning in 1986. As an actor, he starred in the television sitcom, *The Fresh Prince of Bel-Air*. He later emerged as a major box-office draw in films such as *Independence Day* and *Men In Black*.

1980: T.I. (birth name Clifford Joseph Harris, Jr.) was born in Atlanta. Nicknamed "The King of the South," he enjoyed a successful solo career. He also founded the hip hop group, Pimp Squad Click (P$C) and was the CEO of his own label, Grand Hustle Records.

1983: Childish Gambino (birth name Donald McKinley Glover) was born in Southern California but raised in Stone Mountain, Georgia. Although he is a successful rapper who was nominated for two Grammys in 2014, he is best known as an actor. He played the role of college student Troy Barnes on the quirky sitcom, *Community*.

2000: The hip hop video and news series, *Direct Effect*, debuted on MTV. The program was later rebranded *Sucker Free*, which aired on MTV2 in 2006. MTV was hoping to launch a replacement for their landmark series, *Yo! MTV Raps*.

2001: The film *Welcome To Death Row* was released. The documentary chronicled the rise and fall of the influential West Coast hip hop label.

2004: Eminem released the hit single, "Just Lose It," the debut track from his album, *Encore*. An international smash hit, it topped the charts in a number of countries. The song's music video parodied Michael Jackson and other celebrities including Madonna and MC Hammer. The video was briefly banned by BET.

2007: Lil Mama released the single, "G-Slide (Tour Bus)," which spawned a popular dance craze. The song was based on the popular children's nursery rhyme, "The Wheels On The Bus."

2008: Busta Rhymes was barred from entering the United Kingdom due to "unresolved convictions" in New York City. He was enroute to London for a scheduled concert at the Royal Albert Hall on a bill with John Legend and Guillemots. The ban was later lifted.

2009: Nick Cannon was named the chairman of TeenNick at Nickelodeon. In his new role, he was in charge of program development.

2011: L.A. Sunshine of the pioneering hip hop group, the Treacherous Three, published his autobiography, *A True Story: The Real Accounts*.

2014: T.I. was given an honorary "key to the city" by the mayor of Jackson, Mississippi.

2014: OZ (real name Walter Josef Fischer), the most prolific graffiti artist in Germany, died after he was struck by a subway train. He claimed to have made more than 120,000 tags during his lifetime. He was 64-years-old.

2015: Fetty Wap released his debut album, *Fetty Wap*. The album spawned the singles, "Trap Queen," "679," "My Way" and "Again." The album earned two Grammy nominations.

SEPTEMBER 26

1973: Ras Kass (birth name John Austin IV) was born in the Watts section of Los Angeles. In addition to his solo career, he was a member of the hip hop supergroup, the HRSMN.

1995: The Goodie Mob released their debut single, "Cell Therapy." A pioneering example of Southern rap, the track appeared on their highly-acclaimed album, *Soul Food*.

2000: Lil' Bow Wow released his debut album at age 13, *Beware Of Dog*. The album spawned four singles: "Bounce With Me," "Bow Wow (That's My Name)," "Puppy Love" and "Ghetto Girls." The album sold more than one-million copies in the U.S.

2002: Jennifer Lopez released the single, "Jenny From The Block" which featured two members of the LOX, Jadakiss and Styles P. The autobiographical track sampled "Heaven And Hell Is On Earth" by 20th Century Steel Band and "South Bronx" by Boogie Down Productions. The song's music video featured Lopez and her boyfriend at the time, Ben Affleck.

2004: Vanilla Ice was one of ten celebrities on the first season of the British reality series, *The Farm*. He was the next-to-last contestant eliminated from the show.

2005: Beanie Sigel was cleared of an attempted murder charge by a jury in Pennsylvania. He had been charged with the 2003 shooting of a man outside of a strip club in Philadelphia. This was Sigel's second trial on the charge after the jury in the first trial was deadlocked.

2005: The VH-1 network staged the 2nd annual Hip Hop Honors ceremony. The second year inductees included Big Daddy Kane, Grandmaster Flash and the Furious Five, Ice-T, LL Cool J, the Notorious B.I.G. and Salt-n-Pepa. The event was hosted by Russell Simmons and his brother Reverend Run, and was staged at the Hammerstein Ballroom in Manhattan.

2006: Ludacris released the album, *Release Therapy*. The album spawned the singles, "Money Maker," "Grew Up A Screw Up," "Runaway Love," "Girls Gone Wild" and "Slap." The album won a Grammy in the category of Best Rap Album.

2013: Drake released the innovative, seven-minute track "Pound Cake/Paris Morton Music 2," which featured Jay-Z. Drake and his record company were later sued by the estate of jazz pianist Jimmy Smith over the unauthorized use of a 35-second spoken-word sample that was featured in the song.

2015: Fetty Wap broke his leg in a motorcycle accident in Paterson, New Jersey. He received three traffic citations including driving without a license and driving without insurance. The rapper had slammed his motorcycle into the path of an oncoming car.

SEPTEMBER 27

1973: Ras Kass (birth name John Austin IV) was born in Los Angeles. Best known as a solo artist, he was also a member of two hip hop groups, the HRSMN (with Canibus, Killah Priest and Kurupt) and Golden State Warriors (with Xzibit and Saafir).

1980: Kurtis Blow was the first hip hop act to appear on the syndicated music program, *Soul Train*. He performed the song, "The Breaks." The other two musical guests on the program were L.T.D. and Seventh Wonder.

1989: The Belgian group Technotronic scored a worldwide hit with the eurodance/hip hop track, "Pump Up The Jam."

1994: Brandy released her debut album, *Brandy*. The album sold four-million copies in the U.S. and spawned the crossover hits, "Best Friend," "I Wanna Be Down," a duet with Wanya Morris of Boyz II Men, "Brokenhearted," and the Grammy-nominated "Baby."

1994: Common released the single, "I Used To Love H.E.R." (At the time, he was known as Common Sense.) The song sampled "The Changing World" by George Benson and was a tribute to rap music. The song's music video featured Common's home in Chicago.

2005: Sean "Diddy" Combs starred in the crime-drama film, *Carlito's Way: Rise To Power*. He portrayed a gangster named Hollywood Nicky.

2005: Houston-based rapper Paul Wall released his second album, *The Peoples Champ*. The chart-topping album was highlighted by the tracks, "They Don't Know," "Girl," "Drive Slow" and "Sittin' Sidewayz."

2009: Professor Griff of Public Enemy published the book, *Analytixz: 20 Years Of Conversations And Enter-Views*.

2011: J. Cole released his debut studio album, *Cole World: The Sideline Story*. The project spawned four singles, "Who Dat," "Work Out," "Can't Get Enough" and "Nobody's Perfect." The album sold one-million copies in the U.S.

2011: Kanye West published the book, *Glow In The Dark*.

2014: Jay-Z headlined the third annual Global Citizen Festival in New York City. Staged in Central Park, the free six-hour event was organized to help the effort to end global poverty. Also on the bill were the Roots, Alicia Keys, fun, Sting, No Doubt, Carrie Underwood and Tiësto.

2014: Ariana Grande was the musical guest on *Saturday Night Live*. She performed "Break Free" and was joined by the Weeknd on "Love Me Harder."

SEPTEMBER 28

1991: Public Enemy was the musical guest on *Saturday Night Live*. This marked the first time a gangsta rap act appeared on the program. The group performed "Can't Truss It" and "Bring The Noise."

1999: The duo of Method Man and Redman released their debut album, *Blackout!* The album spawned three hit singles, "Tear It Off," "Da Rockwilder" and "Y.O.U."

2004: Ja Rule released the single, "Wonderful" (featuring R. Kelly and Ashanti). This was Ja Rule's first number-one single in the U.K.

2004: Ciara released her debut album, *Goodies*. The album spawned four singles: "Goodies," "1, 2 Step," "Oh" and "And I." The album sold three-million copies in the U.S. and earned a Grammy nomination in the category of Best Rap/Sung Collaboration for the track "1, 2 Step."

2009: Wyclef Jean began attending classes at the Berklee College of Music with the goal of earning a Bachelor's degree in music. The 39-year-old performer had dropped out of college after his first semester at age 18 in order to pursue a career in music.

2010: Rapper and activist Sister Souljah published the best-selling book, *Midnight: A Gangster Love Story*.

2012: When the Barclays Center opened in Brooklyn, Jay-Z was the first attraction booked at the new venue. He sold out an astounding eight concerts over a nine-day period.

2015: Chris Brown was denied a visa to enter Australia for an upcoming tour due to a domestic violence conviction. He was forced to cancel his One Hell Of A Night tour, which was scheduled to start in late-December. His last performance in the country was in 2012.

SEPTEMBER 29

1969: DeVante Swing (birth name Donald Earle DeGrate, Jr.) was born in Hampton, Virginia. A producer, songwriter and rapper, he is best known as the leader of the group Jodeci. He also formed his own record label, Swing Mob, and signed a number of hip hop acts including Missy Elliott, Ginuwine, Playa and Stevie J.

1980: Kurtis Blow released his debut album, *Kurtis Blow*. The pioneering album was highlighted by the tracks, "Rappin' Blow, Pt. 2," a remake of the rock hit "Takin' Care Of Business" and the groundbreaking hip hop standard "The Breaks."

1998: Jay-Z released the album, *Vol. 2... Hard Knock Life*. The album spawned four singles: "Money, Cash, Hoes," "Nigga What, Nigga Who (Originator 99)," "Can I Get A..." and the biggest hit of his career, "Hard Knock Life (Ghetto Anthem)." The album sold more than five-million copies in the U.S. and was his first to top the charts.

1998: The hip hop duo Blackstar released the album, *Mos Def & Talib Kweli Are Black Star*. The album spawned two singles, "Definition" and "Respiration." Both rappers later pursued solo careers but continued to collaborate on various projects.

2001: Alicia Keys was the musical guest on *Saturday Night Live*. She performed "Fallin'" and "A Woman's Worth."

2007: Kanye West was the musical guest on *Saturday Night Live*. He performed a medley of "Stronger" and "Good Life" and a medley of "Champion" and "Everything I Am."

2008: The VH-1 network issued its list of the top-100 rap songs of all time. The top three songs were: #3 "Nuthin' But A 'G' Thang" by Dr. Dre; #2 "Rapper's Delight" by the Sugarhill Gang; and #1 "Fight The Power" by Public Enemy.

2011: Sylvia Robinson, the co-founder of Sugarhill Records, passed away at the age of 75. A former R&B singer who scored hits with "Love Is Strange" and "Pillow Talk," she teamed with her husband Joe Robinson to start a label in 1967, All-Platinum Records. After changing the name of the label to Sugarhill Records in 1979, the couple helped to craft a number of pioneering rap classics beginning with "Rapper's Delight" by the Sugarhill Gang. The label's other hip hop acts included the Sequence, Grandmaster Flash and the Furious Five, the Treacherous Three, Funky Four Plus One and Spoonie Gee. Another of the label's acts, West Street Mob, featured Sylvia Robinson and her son, Joey.

2012: The BET network presented the seventh annual *BET Hip Hop Awards*. Among the winners were: "HYFR" by Drake featuring Lil Wayne for Best Hip Hop Video; Kendrick Lamar for Lyricist of the Year; 2 Chainz for Rookie of The Year; and Rakim for the I Am Hip-Hop Icon Award. The event was hosted by Mike Epps, and was staged at the Atlanta Civic Center. Also at the ceremony, 50 Cent and Fat Joe ended their feud and appeared on stage together.

2015: Sotheby's of London auctioned two handwritten lyric sheets by the late rapper Tupac Shakur. He had written both songs while in prison. One of the manuscripts contained the lyrics of his songs, "Tradin' War Stories" and "Ambitionz Az A Ridah," which appeared on his 1996 album, *All Eyes On Me*.

2015: Drake became the fourth musical act to place a total of 100 tracks on *Billboard* magazine's Hot 100 chart.

SEPTEMBER 30

1984: T-Pain (birth name Faheem Rashad Najm) was born in Tallahassee, Florida. A prolific rapper and R&B-styled singer who appeared on dozens of hits, he released his debut album in 2005, *Rappa Ternt Sanga*. He is also the founder of the label, Nappy Boy Entertainment.

1996: BLACKstreet released the single, "No Diggity" (featuring Dr. Dre and Queen Pen). None of the group's members believed the song would be a hit. The track sampled "Grandma's Hands" by Bill Withers. "No Diggity" won a Grammy in the category of Best R&B Performance by a Duo or Group with Vocals. The song returned to the U.K. music charts in 2013.

1998: New York graffiti artist Dondi White (real name Donald J. White) died at age 37 from complications of AIDS. Launching his work on the subway trains of New York City during the 1970s, he later took his talent to the traditional art canvas.

2003: Kanye West released his debut single, "Through The Wire." Remarkably, West recorded the track while his jaw was wired shut, just two weeks after he was seriously injured in an auto accident. The track sampled "Through The Fire" by Chaka Khan. The song was nominated for a Grammy in the category of Best Rap Solo Performance.

2013: Canadian-born rapper Drake was named the "global ambassador" of the NBA team, the Toronto Raptors.

2013: Nelly recorded a tribute song to the late funk star, Rick James. The track, "Rick James" (featuring T.I.) was included on Nelly's album, *M.O.*

2015: Nas (real name Nasir Jones) and eight others received the W.E.B. Du Bois Medal for Social Justice Work from Harvard University. Nas told the audience: "This is the thing I want kids to see. This is a light that I like on me. This is what I hope kids from my neighborhood can see, and want to be. I hope I can be a great role model for those kids."

2015: Kanye West made headlines when he announced his plans to run for president in 2020. He made the announcement at the MTV Video Music Awards ceremony in Los Angeles.

▶ OCTOBER

OCTOBER 1

1991: The first issue of *Rap Pages* was published. Ice Cube appeared on the cover of the magazine wearing a Lench Mob cap. The magazine was priced at $2.95.

1991: Public Enemy released their fourth album, *Apocalypse 91... The Enemy Strikes Black*. The million-selling album was highlighted by the tracks, "Bring The Noise," "Can't Truss It" and "Shut 'Em Down."

1992: Double XX Posse released the hit single, "Not Gonna Be Able To Do It." The track sampled "Ballin' Jack" by Never Let 'Em Say and "Batuki" by Buster Williams.

1999: Ice Cube starred alongside Mark Wahlberg and George Clooney in the satirical war film, *Three Kings*. Ice Cube played the role of Staff Sergeant Chief Elgin, who was stationed in Iraq shortly after the end of the First Gulf War. The film grossed nearly $108 million.

2001: Philadelphia 76ers player Allen Iverson announced he was ending his rap music career. Reportedly, NBA commissioner David Stern was unhappy with the controversial lyrics of one of Iverson's songs.

2001: Just 19-years-old at the time, the Game was shot five times while at his apartment in Compton, California. During his long recuperation, he decided to become a rapper and spent several months listening to classic rap albums.

2005: Kanye West was the musical guest on *Saturday Night Live*. He performed a medley of "Gold Digger" and "Touch The Sky" and teamed with Adam Levine to perform "Heard 'Em Say."

2006: The four original members of the Goodie Mob – Cee Lo Green, Khujo, T-Mo and Big Gipp – reunited on a stage for the first time in more than seven years.

2007: The Southern hip hop duo Playaz Circle released the single, "Duffle Bag Boy" (featuring Lil Wayne). The duo consisted of Dolla Boy and Tity Boi (who later changed his stage name to 2 Chainz). The track appeared on the album, *Supply & Demand*.

2009: Lady Gaga and Kanye West announced they were cancelling their much anticipated "Fame Kills" co-headlining tour. Neither of the two performers offered any explanation for the cancellation.

2010: New York City filmmaker Lyle Owerko published a book on the history of the portable boombox, *The Boombox Project: The Machines, The Music, And The Urban Underground*.

2010: British rapper Tinie Tempah released his debut album, *Disc-Overy*. The album spawned a pair of number-one U.K. hits, "Pass Out" and "Written In The Stars."

2011: Kanye West debuted a fashion line of women's clothing, DW Kanye West.

2014: Too $hort was found with a gun in his bag when he passed through a checkpoint at the Bob Hope Airport in Burbank. He was charged with misdemeanor possession of a loaded handgun in a public place.

2014: The documentary film, *Nas: Time Is Illmatic*, was issued on the 20th anniversary of the release of the rapper's classic album, *Illmatic*. The film made its premiere at the Tribeca Film Festival the previous April.

2015: Childish Gambino was booed at the Cambridge Hotel in Newcastle, Australia. Concertgoers were angry because the rapper had spent nearly the entire show deejaying instead of taking the microphone. He performed only one song during the entire concert.

2015: The film documentary, *Stretch And Bobbito: Radio That Changed Lives*, chronicled how a pair of pioneering, late-night deejays on WKCR 89.9 FM brought hip hop music to the airwaves of New York City. Their program was launched in 1990 and went off the air in 1998.

OCTOBER 2

1969: Paperboy (birth name Mitchell Charles Johnson) was born in San Diego but raised in Oakland. He is best known for his 1993 hit single, "Ditty."

1984: Afrika Bambaataa & The Soul Sonic Force made their concert debut in Britain with a performance in Birmingham, England.

1990: The Geto Boys released their controversial gangsta rap album, *The Geto Boys*. The group's label Def Jam Recordings was forced to switch distributors after Geffen Records refused to release the album due to the lyrics of two tracks, "Mind Of A Lunatic" and "Assassins."

1991: MC Hammer offered a $50,000 reward for the safe return of Michael Jackson's signature glove which was stolen from the Motown Museum in Detroit. Jackson had worn the white sequined glove during his *Thriller* tour.

1993: Cypress Hill were the musical guests on *Saturday Night Live*. Ignoring multiple warnings not to smoke marijuana during their performance, member DJ Muggs lit up a joint during the group's second song, "I Ain't Goin' Out Like That." The group also performed "Insane In The Brain." Cypress Hill were subsequently banned from the program.

1998: Brooklyn-based graffiti artist DONDI (real name Donald Joseph White) died at the age of 37 from AIDS. One of the most influential artists in New York City, he began his work in the mid-1970, often as a member of TOP crew and CIA (Crazy Inside Artists). His work was later exhibited in European art galleries.

2001: Black Eyed Peas co-founder will.i.am released his first solo album, *Lost Change*, which was the soundtrack of a film of the same name. The album was highlighted by the track, "I Am."

2001: Michael Jackson provided uncredited backing vocals on the remixed version of "Girls, Girls, Girls" by Jay-Z. The track sampled "There's Nothing In This World That Can Stop Me From Loving You" by Tom Brock and featured an interpolation of "High Power Rap" by Disco Dave and the Force Of The 5 MCs.

2001: Ja Rule released his third studio album, *Pain Is Love*. The album spawned three singles, "Livin' It Up," "Always On Time" and "Down Ass Bitch." The best-selling album of his career, it sold more than three-million copies in the U.S. In 2012, Ja Rule released a sequel album, *Pain Is Love 2*.

2004: Nelly was the musical guest on *Saturday Night Live*. He performed "Na-NaNa-Na" and was joined by Jaheim on "My Place."

2007: Kanye West released the single, "Good Life" (featuring T-Pain). The track sampled "P.Y.T. (Pretty Young Thing)" by Michael Jackson. The song sold more than two-million copies in the U.S. and won a Grammy in the category of Best Rap Song.

2007: 50 Cent published his autobiography, *50 X 50: 50 Cent In His Own Words*.

2007: Soulja Boy released his debut album, *Souljaboytellem.com*, which was highlighted by the smash hit, "Crank That (Soulja Boy)." Other hits from the million-selling album included "Soulja Girl," "Yahhh!" and "Donk."

2007: Trey Songz released his second album, *Trey Day*, which was highlighted by the hit single, "Can't Help But Wait." The track was also included on the soundtrack album of the film, *Step Up 2: The Streets*.

2009: Radio deejay Mr. Magic (real name John Rivas) passed away at the age of 53 after suffering a heart attack. He was the first person to host a rap program on a commercial radio station in New York City when his *Rap Attack* show debuted on WBLS-FM in April 1983.

2010: Kanye West was the musical guest on *Saturday Night Live*. This was his fourth appearance on the program. He performed "Power" and was joined by Pusha T on "Runaway."

OCTOBER 3

1971: Black Thought (birth name Tariq Luqmaan Trotter) was born in Philadelphia. The lead MC of the Roots, he co-founded the hip hop group with drummer Ahmir "Questlove" Thompson.

1975: Talib Kweli (birth name Talib Kweli Greene) was born in Brooklyn, New York. After forming the hip hop duo Black Star with fellow rapper Mos Def, Kweli later enjoyed a successful solo career.

2000: OutKast released the single, "Ms. Jackson." The track sampled "Strawberry Letter 23" by the Brothers Johnson. The song won a Grammy in the category of Best Rap Performance by a Duo or Group.

2002: Money Ray (real name Eric Hoskins) of the pioneering rap group, the Cold Crush Brothers, passed away from cancer at the age of 38.

2008: Hit producer and songwriter Johnny "J" (real name Johnny Lee Jackson) died at the age of 39 after he fell or jumped from an upper floor in a Los Angeles prison. He was serving a three-year jail sentence at the time. He was best known for his work with Tupac Shakur on the albums, *Me Against The World* and *All Eyez On Me*. Johnny "J" also released one solo album, *I Gotta Be Me*.

2009: Jay-Z was selected as the winner of MTV's annual "Hottest MCs in the Game."

2014: The Weeknd began a six-week run at number-one on the U.S. singles chart with "The Hills."

2015: Model and rapper Amber Rose gave a speech in Los Angeles in which she publically forgave her ex-husband Wiz Khalifa and ex-boyfriend Kanye West for demeaning comments they allegedly made about her.

OCTOBER 4

1957: Russell Simmons was born in Queens, New York. An entrepreneur and producer, he co-founded Def Jam Recordings. At Def Jam, Simmons teamed with Rick Rubin to work with a number of pioneering hip hop acts including LL Cool J, the Beastie Boys, Public Enemy and Run–D.M.C. Simmons later started a clothing company, Phat Farm. Russell's brother, Rev. Run, is a member of Run-D.M.C.

1982: Grandmaster Flash and the Furious Five released their pioneering debut album, *The Message*. The album was highlighted by the tracks, "It's Nasty," "Scorpio" and the hip hop standard "The Message."

1987: Before he became a giant in the hip hop world, Marion "Suge" Knight attempted a career in professional football. On this date, he played his first of two games for the Los Angeles Rams as a replacement player during the infamous player strike. The Rams lost to the New Orleans Saints by the score of 37 to 10.

1993: The hip hop duo, Illegal, released the single, "We Getz Buzy" (featuring Erick Sermon). The duo consisted of Jamal Phillips and Malik Edwards. The track sampled several songs including "Impeach The President" by the Honey Drippers.

2002: William Bratton, the newly appointed Police Chief of Los Angeles, announced a public crackdown on graffiti artists. He declared that he would "make graffiti a top priority for all officers."

2003: The single "Baby Boy" by Beyoncé featuring Sean Paul began a nine-week run at number-one on the U.S. charts.

2004: The documentary, *And You Don't Stop: 30 Years Of Hip-Hop*, premiered on the VH-1 network. The five-part series chronicled the origins and history of hip hop.

2005: An album and DVD, *Tupac Shakur: Live At The House Of Blues*, captured the rapper at his final performance which took place in Los Angeles on July 4, 1996. He was gunned down just two-months after the concert.

2013: Lauryn Hill was released from a federal prison after spending nearly three-months behind bars for tax evasion.

2015: Action Bronson cut his concert short at the UKA Festival in Norway due to health problems. He performed just two songs before leaving the stage.

OCTOBER 5

1985: LL Cool J released, "I Can't Live Without My Radio," which was the debut single from his first album, *Radio*. He later performed the pioneering hip hop song on *Soul Train* and in the film *Krush Groove*.

1990: Father MC released the single, "I'll Do 4 U" (featuring Mary J. Blige). The track sampled the1970s disco classic "Got To Be Real" by Cheryl Lynn.

1991: P.M. Dawn released the chart-topping, crossover single, "Set Adrift On Memory Bliss." The track was built upon a sample of "True" by Spandau Ballet and also sampled "Paid In Full" by Eric B. & Rakim and "Ashley's Roachclip" by the Soul Searchers. As a tribute to Spandau Ballet, the group's lead singer Tony Hadley was invited to appear in the song's music video.

1997: A remixed version of Run-D.M.C.'s 1984 classic "It's Like That" by producer Jason Nevins was released. It was an international hit that topped the charts in several countries.

2001: Sisqó portrayed a vampire named Vladimir Kortensky on an episode of the television series, *Sabrina, The Teenage Witch*.

2009: Jim Jones pleaded guilty to an assault charge. In December 2008, the Harlem-based rapper had gotten into a physical altercation with Ne-Yo's manager, Jayvon Smith, at a Louis Vuitton boutique in Manhattan.

2010: The documentary, *Wu-Tang Saga*, was released. The film was narrated by Wu-Tang Clan member Cappadonna.

2010: Waka Flocka Flame released his debut studio album, *Flockaveli*. The album spawned the singles, "O Let's Do It," "Hard In Da Paint," "No Hands" and "Grove St. Party."

2010: Rick Ross released the single, "Aston Martin Music" (featuring Drake & Chrisette Michele). The song's music video was filmed in Atlanta and featured various Aston Martin automobiles.

2015: Will Smith announced on Beats 1 Radio that he would be reuniting with his former recording partner, DJ Jazzy Jeff, for a world tour in 2016.

2015: Sean "Diddy" Comb's label, Bad Boy Records, signed a distribution and promotion deal with Epic Records.

OCTOBER 6

1992: Redman released his critically-acclaimed debut album, *Whut? Thee Album*. The album was highlighted by the hits, "Blow Your Mind," "Time 4 Sum Aksion" and "Tonight's Da Night."

1998: Pras of the Fugees released his debut solo album, *Ghetto Supastar*. The album's title track – which featured Ol' Dirty Bastard and Mýa – was nominated for a Grammy in the category of Best Rap Performance by a Duo or Group.

1998: Ol' Dirty Bastard was charged with three counts of "terrorist threats" after confronting security guards at a concert by R&B singer Des'ree at the House of Blues in Los Angeles.

2007: Soulja Boy began a five-week run at number-one on the U.S. singles chart with "Crank That (Soulja Boy)."

2008: The VH-1 network staged the 5th annual Hip Hop Honors ceremony. The fifth year inductees included Cypress Hill, De La Soul, Naughty By Nature, Slick Rick and Too $hort. The event was hosted by Tracy Morgan, and was staged at the Hammerstein Ballroom in Manhattan.

2009: Public Enemy announced an online crowdsourcing campaign to raise $250,000 for the purpose of recording a new album. The group would raise just $75,000 toward their goal. The resulting album, *Most Of My Heroes Still Don't Appear On No Stamp*, was released in 2012.

2010: Eyedea (real name Michael David Larsen) passed away at the age of 28 as the result of opiate toxicity. The freestyle rapper was a member of the alternative-style hip hop duo, Eyedea & Abilities. In 1999, Eyedea won the Scribble Jam competition.

2011: Soulja Boy's album *Promise* was banned from the 3,100 Army and Air Force base stores around the world because one of the tracks, "Let's Be Real," featured lyrics that criticized the American military.

2012: Jay-Z created a stir when he decided to take a subway to his concert at the newly opened Barclays Center in Brooklyn. The rapper and his entourage boarded a subway train on Canal Street in Manhattan.

2015: 50 Cent filed a $75 million lawsuit against his former lawyers over their legal advice and representation in a business venture. After failing to launch a line of high-end headphones with a business partner, 50 Cent decided to create his own product line. But after his former partner claimed an infringement of intellectual property rights, 50 Cent was hit with a judgement of $18 million.

2015: Hopsin released the video for the track "No Words," which mocked rappers who recorded music with incoherent lyrics.

OCTOBER 7

1993: Georgia-based rapper 12 Gauge released the single, "Dunkie Butt (Please Please Please)." It was his only hit.

1997: Chuck D published his autobiography, *Fight The Power: Rap, Race And Reality*.

2000: Lil' Bow Wow released the single, "Bow Wow (That's My Name)" (featuring Snoop Dogg). The track sampled "Dernier Domicile Connu" by François de Roubaix and "Atomic Dog" by George Clinton.

2000: Eminem was the musical guest on *Saturday Night Live*. He performed "The Real Slim Shady" and was joined by Dido on "Stan."

2001: Sean "P. Diddy" Combs was the subject of an episode of the VH-1 program, *Behind The Music*.

2003: Oakland-based rapper Paris was at the center of a controversy over the cover art of his album, *Sonic Jihad*, which pictured a large airplane flying into the White House. In the wake of the 9/11 attacks just two years earlier, the cover image was widely criticized in the media.

2010: Nelly released a fitness training video, *Celebrity Sweat*.

2013: Pitbull released the single, "Timber" (featuring Ke$ha). A huge hit, it topped numerous music charts around the world. A lawsuit was later filed by Lee Oskar of the soul-rock group War over the similarities between "Timber" and Oskar's 1978 track, "San Francisco Bay."

2015: Compton-based rapper Teriq Royal was the victim of a gunshot wound to his head. A stray bullet from an AK-47 barely missed hitting his brain. Before seeking medical treatment, he posted a video of his wounds on Facebook.

2015: Rapper Klever (real name Alex Izquierdo) was arrested in Los Angeles for brandishing a gun in a music video. He was legally barred from owning a gun because of a prior conviction in which he was found carrying a concealed firearm. Klever was a member of the 1990s hip hop group, Brownside.

OCTOBER 8

1967: Teddy Riley (full name Edward Theodore Riley) was born in Harlem, New York. The creator of New Jack Swing, he straddled the R&B and rap fields in the 1980s and '90s. In addition to his successful solo career, he was a member of the groups, Guy and BLACKstreet. Also a producer, he worked with Michael Jackson, Usher, Doug E. Fresh, Bobby Brown, Keith Sweat and Heavy D.

1968: C.L. Smooth (birth name Corey Brent Penn) was born in New Rochelle, New York. As a member of the hip hop duo Pete Rock & CL Smooth, he is best known for the hit single "They Reminisce Over You (T.R.O.Y.)." He later pursued a solo career and released his debut album in 2005, *American Me*.

1980: Nick Cannon (birth name Nicholas Scott Cannon) was born in San Diego. A successful actor, television host and musical performer, he released his first album in 2003, *Nick Cannon*. He was married to Mariah Carey from 2008 to 2015.

1985: Kurtis Blow released the single "If I Ruled The World." The track appeared on his album, *America*, as well as on the soundtrack of the film, *Krush Groove*. The song changed the face of rap music with the introduction of the sampled loop, which became a mainstay in hip hop. Blow had sampled a portion of the track "Pump Me Up" by the group Trouble Funk. (Nas scored a hit with a reworked version of "If I Ruled The World" in 1996.)

1990: Too $hort released the hit single, "The Ghetto." The song was a remake of Donny Hathaway's 1970 soul standard and featured Gerald Levert on the chorus.

1997: Yella Boy (real name Albert Thomas) of the hip hop group, U.N.L.V., was murdered in New Orleans. He was shot while sitting in his car. He was 22-years-old.

1997: Tupac Shakur co-starred in the action-thriller film, *Gang Related*. It was his final film performance. He portrayed a police detective who shot a drug dealer played by fellow rapper, Kool Moe Dee.

2002: The documentary, *The Freshest Kids: A History Of The B-Boy*, examined the history of hip hop and break dancing. The film featured Afrika Bambaataa, Fab 5 Freddy, Frosty Freeze, DJ Kool Herc and Yasiin Bey (a.k.a. Mos Def).

2007: The VH-1 network staged the 4th annual Hip Hop Honors ceremony. The fourth year inductees included A Tribe Called Quest, Missy Elliott, Snoop Dogg, Whodini, the hip hop film *Wild Style* and Teddy Riley and Andre Harrell for their contributions to New Jack Swing. The event was hosted by Tracy Morgan, and was staged at the Hammerstein Ballroom in Manhattan.

2007: Prodigy of the hip hop duo Mobb Deep received a 42-month sentence on a weapons charge. He accepted a plea deal instead of going to trial and facing a mandatory 15-year sentence.

2008: "Weird Al" Yankovic released the track "Whatever You Like," which was a parody of the song by rapper, T.I.

2009: T.I. was the subject of an episode of the VH-1 program, *Behind The Music*.

2014: Rick Ross told a New York City radio station that he had met with officials of the Miami Dolphins in an attempt to become a part-owner of the NFL team.

2015: Eminem wrote a heartfelt tribute to fallen rapper Tupac Shakur in an issue of *Paper* magazine. The article was titled: "'Whatever He Was Rapping About, It Was Urgent:' Eminem on the Genius of Tupac."

OCTOBER 9

1957: Ini Kamoze (birth name Cecil Campbell) was born in Saint Mary, Jamaica. He started recording in 1981 and is best known for the 1994 rap-reggae hit, "Here Comes The Hotstepper."

2001: Rapper T.I. released his debut solo album, *Serious*. Although the album was only a moderate seller, it helped to popularize a subgenre of rap called "trap."

2001: Bubba Sparxxx released his debut album, *Dark Days, Bright Nights*. The album spawned the singles, "Ugly" and "Lovely."

2001: Rap-metal band Linkin Park released the single, "In The End." It was the group's highest-charting single in the U.S.

2004: Queen Latifah was both the guest host and featured musical performer on *Saturday Night Live*. She performed "The Same Love That Made Me Laugh" and "Hard Times."

2007: Flo Rida released his debut solo single, "Low" (featuring T-Pain). The track appeared on his debut album, *Mail On Sunday*, as well as on the soundtrack of the film, *Step Up 2: The Streets*. A smash hit, the song sold seven-million copies in the U.S.

2012: Machine Gun Kelly released his debut album, *Lace Up*. The album featured guest vocals by Twista, Waka Flocka Flame, Young Jeezy, Bun B, Cassie, DMX, Lil Jon, Tech N9ne and others. The album spawned the singles, "Wild Boy," "Invincible," "Hold On (Shut Up)" and "Stereo."

2012: Macklemore & Ryan Lewis released their self-budgeted independent album, *The Heist*. A surprise hit, the project spawned five singles, "Wing$," "Can't Hold Us," "Same Love," "Thrift Shop" and "White Walls." The album helped the duo earn seven Grammy nominations.

2015: The BET network presented the tenth annual *BET Hip Hop Awards*. Among the winners were *2014 Forest Hills Drive* by J. Cole for Album of the Year; DJ Mustard for Producer of the Year; "Alright" by Kendrick Lamar for Best Hip Hop Video; and Scarface for the I Am Hip Hop award. The event was hosted by Snoop Dog, and was staged at the Atlanta Civic Center.

2015: Koopsta Knicca passed away several days after suffering a massive stroke. Born Robert Cooper Phillips, he was a member of the hip hop trio, Three 6 Mafia, for most of the 1990s before leaving in 2000 to pursue a solo career.

2015: Fetty Wap was ordered by his doctor to cancel an upcoming concert tour after the rapper suffered serious injuries in a motorcycle crash. He had broken his leg in three places.

OCTOBER 10

1968: DJ Skribble (birth name Scott Ialacci) was born in Queens, New York. A producer, radio personality and DJ, he had his first success as a member of the all-white hip hop group, Young Black Teenagers.

2000: The hip hop duo Philly's Most Wanted released their debut single, "Cross The Border," from their first album, *Get Down Or Lay Down*. The duo consisted of Al "Boo-Bonic" Holly and Joel "Mr. Man" Witherspoon.

2000: Ja Rule released his second studio album, *Rule 3:36*. The album spawned the singles, "Between Me And You," "Put It On Me," "6 Feet Underground" and "I Cry." The album sold three-million copies in the U.S.

2002: Jay-Z released the single, "'03 Bonnie & Clyde," which featured Beyoncé. The track sampled "Me And My Girlfriend" by Tupac Shakur. The song's music video featured Jay-Z and Beyoncé as the legendary crime duo, Bonnie and Clyde.

2003: Lil' Kim starred in the Western film, *Gang Of Roses*. She portrayed a member of an all-female gang in the Old West.

2004: LL Cool J was the subject of an episode of the VH-1 program, *Behind The Music*.

2009: The BET network presented the fourth annual *BET Hip Hop Awards*. Among the winners were Jay-Z for Lyricist of the Year; Drake for Rookie of the Year; "Every Girl" by Young Money for Track of the Year; and Ice Cube for the I Am Hip-Hop award. The event was hosted by Mike Epps, and was staged at the Atlanta Civic Center.

2012: Wyclef Jean began a recurring role on the ABC television series, *Nashville*. He portrayed Dominic "Domino" King, the president of a fictional music label.

2014: Waka Flocka Flame was arrested at Hartsfield-Jackson Atlanta International Airport after he was found with a handgun in his carry-on baggage.

OCTOBER 11

1970: MC Lyte (birth name Lana Michelle Moorer) was born in Brooklyn, New York. She released her debut album in 1988, *Lyte As A Rock*.

1970: U-God (birth name Lamont Jody Hawkins) was born in Brooklyn, New York, but raised in nearby Staten Island. A member of the groundbreaking group the Wu-Tung Clan, he also pursued a solo career beginning in 1999 with the album, *Golden Arms Redemption*.

1992: Mad Cobra released the crossover hit single, "Flex." The track employed elements of "Just My Imagination" by the Temptations.

1994: Tupac Shakur's group Thug Life released the album, *Thug Life: Volume 1*. The album was highlighted by the tracks, "Str8 Ballin'," "Pour Out A Little Liquor" and the single "Cradle To The Grave." The gangsta-style rap group had been formed in the autumn of 1994 by Tupac Shakur, his stepbrother Mopreme Shakur, Big Syke, the Rated R and Macadoshis. (A number of the album's outtakes were leaked onto the internet in 2009.)

1999: Drama released his debut single, "Left/Right" (which was also known as "Left, Right, Left").

2002: Mos Def and Queen Latifah co-starred in the romantic-comedy film, *Brown Sugar*.

2007: Belo (real name Darnell Smith) of the Chicago-based hip hop trio, Do Or Die, pleaded guilty to second-degree murder in the shooting death of a 19-year-old acquaintance. He served five-years of a ten-year prison sentence.

2010: 50 Cent establishing his own film company, Cheetah Vision. The ten-film venture was backed by $200 million in funding. The agreement included a distribution deal with Grindstone/ Lionsgate. The first film, *Setup*, starred 50 Cent, Bruce Willis and Ryan Phillippe.

2011: Bill Adler and Dan Charnas wrote the book, *Def Jam Recordings: The First 25 Years Of The Last Great Record Label*.

2011: The BET network presented the sixth annual *BET Hip Hop Awards*. Among the winners were Lil Wayne for Lyricist of the Year; "Black And Yellow" by Wiz Khalifa for Track of the Year; Lex Luger Producer of the Year; and LL Cool J for the I Am Hip-Hop award. The event was hosted by Mike Epps, and was staged at the Atlanta Civic Center.

2012: Ke$ha became the first Caucasian female to appear on the cover of *Vibe* magazine during the publication's 19-year history.

OCTOBER 12

1984: The hit "I Feel For You" by Chaka Khan was one of the first mainstream pop/R&B songs to feature rap music. Melle Mel of Grandmaster Flash and the Furious Five provided the rapping, which Khan reportedly disliked when she first heard it. The song's music video featured a number of break dancers including Adolfo Quiñones and Michael Chambers. ("I Feel For You" was written and originally recorded by Prince in 1979.)

1993: Salt-n-Pepa released their fourth album, *Very Necessary*. The group's best-selling album, it was highlighted by the hits, "Shoop," "None Of Your Business" and the Grammy-winning "Whatta Man" (featuring En Vogue).

1995: Tupac Shakur was released from prison after Suge Knight and Jimmy Iovine paid the rapper's $1.4 million bail. Shakur was awaiting his trial on a charge of sexual abuse.

1999: Solé released the hit single, "4,5,6" (featuring JT Money and Kandi). Earlier in the year, Solé was a featured artist on JT Money's hit single, "Who Dat."

2004: The VH-1 network staged the inaugural Hip Hop Honors ceremony. The first year's inductees included DJ Hollywood, DJ Kool Herc, KRS-One, Public Enemy, Run-D.M.C., Rock Steady Crew, the Sugarhill Gang, 2Pac and the Graffiti Movement. The event was hosted by Vivica A. Fox and MC Lyte, and was staged at the Hammerstein Ballroom in Manhattan.

2007: The mayor of Bridgeport, Connecticut, declared the day, "50 Cent Curtis Jackson Day." The rapper was also given an honorary "key to the city."

2009: Ice Cube released the track, "Raider Nation," which was a tribute to the NFL team, the Oakland Raiders.

2010: The BET network presented the fifth annual *BET Hip Hop Awards*. Among the winners were Eminem for Lyricist of the Year; Nicki Minaj for Rookie of the Year; Swizz Beatz for Producer of the Year; and Salt-n-Pepa for the I Am Hip-Hop award. The event was hosted by Mike Epps, and was staged at the Atlanta Civic Center.

2013: Vanilla Ice starred in the reality mini-series, *Vanilla Ice Goes Amish*. On the program, the rapper visited an Amish community in Holmes County, Ohio, where he helped to renovate homes for Amish families.

2014: Ke$ha filed a lawsuit in Los Angeles Superior Court against her producer and songwriter, Dr. Luke (a.k.a. Lukasz Gottwald). The lengthy complaint accused Dr. Luke of abuse and asked for the termination of her contract. In response, he filed a countersuit just several hours later.

2015: Trey Songs was the target of an IRS lien for the failure to pay $749,000 in taxes for the year of 2013.

OCTOBER 13

1980: Ashanti (full name Ashanti Shequoiya Douglas) was born in Glen Cove, New York. An R&B and hip hop artist, she released her Grammy-winning debut album in 2002, *Ashanti*.

1997: Shaniqua Tompkins, the girlfriend of 50 Cent, gave birth to their son, Marquise Jackson. She later sued the rapper for $50 million, claiming that he promised to take care of her financially for the rest of her life. The case was later dismissed.

1999: Puff Daddy released the hit single, "Satisfy You," featuring R. Kelly. The track sampled "I Got 5 On It" by Luniz.

2005: The reality show, *Run's House*, debuted on MTV. The program followed the home life and career of former Run-D.M.C. member Joseph Simmons, who was also known as the Reverend Run. The series ran for six seasons.

2006: Sean "Diddy" Combs was given an honorary "key to the city" by the mayor of Chicago.

2007: The BET network presented the second annual *BET Hip Hop Awards*. Among the winners were Common for Lyricist of the Year; "Party Like A Rockstar" by Shop Boyz for Track of the Year; Timbaland for Producer of the Year; and KRS-One for the I Am Hip Hop award. The event was hosted by Katt Williams, and was staged at the Atlanta Civic Center.

2007: T.I. (real name Clifford Harris) was arrested for attempting to purchase unregistered machine guns and silencers. He was caught in a federal sting as he tried to buy the weapons for $12,000. As a convicted felon, he was barred from owning guns. He later pleaded guilty and was sentenced to one-year and a day in prison.

2009: The VH-1 network staged the 6th annual Hip Hop Honors ceremony. The event honored the recordings of the Def Jam label. The ceremony was hosted by Tracy Morgan, and was staged at the Hammerstein Ballroom in Manhattan.

2010: Rapper T.I. helped to talk down a man who was threatening to leap from the roof of a 22-story building in Atlanta.

2013: *Tiny and Shekinah's Weave Trip*, a spinoff of the series *T.I. and Tiny: The Family Hustle*, debuted on the VH-1 network. The reality program followed Tameka "Tiny" Cottle-Harris and her best friend Shekinah Jo Anderson as the pair launched a hair care business.

2014: At the 28th annual Soul Train Music Awards which were staged in Las Vegas, "Loyal" by Chris Brown (featuring Lil Wayne and Tyga) won the award for Best Hip-Hop Song of the Year.

2015: Author Shea Serrano published *The New York Times* best-selling book, *The Rap Year Book: The Most Important Rap Song From Every Year Since 1979, Discussed, Debated, And Deconstructed*.

OCTOBER 14

1974: Shaggy 2 Dope (birth name Joseph William Utsler) was born in Wayne, Michigan. In the early-1990s, he teamed with Violent J (birth name Joseph Bruce) to form the horror-core hip hop group, Insane Clown Posse. The group's loyal fans are known as Juggalos.

1997: LL Cool J released his seventh album, *Phenomenon*. The album spawned the singles, "Phenomenon," "4, 3, 2, 1," "Father," "Hot Hot Hot" and "Candy." The album sold more than two-million copies in the U.S.

1997: Ma$e released his debut solo single, "Feel So Good" (featuring Kelly Price). The track sampled "Hollywood Swinging" by Kool & The Gang and included an interpolation of "Bad Boy" by Miami Sound Machine. The song's music video featured comedian Chris Tucker.

2001: Aaliyah was the subject of an episode of the VH-1 program, *Behind The Music*. The documentary focused on her career and tragic death.

2007: *The Salt-n-Pepa Show* debuted on the VH-1 network. The reality program starred two members of the 1980s female rap trio, Cheryl "Salt" James and Sandra "Pepa" Denton. The series ran for two seasons.

2007: Big Moe (real name Kenneth Doniell Moore) passed away a week after suffering a heart attack. The Houston-based rapper enjoyed his greatest success with his second album, *Purple World*. He was 33-years-old.

2008: Busta Rhymes released the single, "Arab Money." The track was banned in a number of Middle Eastern countries due to its lyrics.

2009: Busta Rhymes was ordered by a New York state court to pay $75,000 to a concertgoer who was attacked at a 2003 performance in Albany.

2010: Vanilla Ice debuted his successful reality program, *The Vanilla Ice Project*, which aired on the DIY Network.

2010: Alicia Keys and Swizz Beatz welcomed the birth of their son, Egypt Daoud Dean.

2010: A judge ruled that Bushwick Bill of the Geto Boys was permitted to stay in the U.S., despite three criminal convictions, and would not to be deported to his native country, Jamaica.

2012: Bryan "Birdman" Williams, the co-founder of Cash Money Records, paid $14.5 million to purchase a 19,000-square-foot mansion in Miami. The residence was previously owned by record producer Scott Storch.

2014: The BET network presented the ninth annual *BET Hip Hop Awards*. Among the winners were "Worst Behavior" by Drake for Best Hip-Hop Video; Iggy Azalea for Rookie of the Year; Kanye West for Best Live Performer; and Doug E. Fresh for the I Am Hip Hop award. The event was hosted by Snoop Dog, and was staged at the Atlanta Civic Center.

2015: G-Eazy and Bebe Rexha released the single, "Me, Myself & I." The track appeared on G-Eazy's album, *When It's Dark Out*.

OCTOBER 15

1970: Ginuwine (real name Elgin Baylor Lumpkin) was born in Washington, D.C. Launching his music career in the mid-1990s, he worked with Missy Elliott and Timbaland. Primarily an R&B singer, Ginuwine has recorded songs with a number of rappers.

1987: Audio Two released the track, "Top Billin'." The song was a B-side hit and appeared on the duo's album, *What More Can I Say?*

1990: Chubb Rock released the EP, *Treat 'Em Right*. The project was highlighted by the hit, "Treat 'Em Right."

1994: Snoop Dogg released the film, *Murder Was The Case*. The 18-minute clip was directed by the team of Dr. Dre and Fab 5 Freddy. The film focused on the fictional death and resurrection of Snoop Dogg, following a deal with the devil.

2002: LL Cool J released his ninth studio album, *10*. (Counting a greatest-hits package, this was his tenth album on Def Jam Recordings.) The album spawned the singles, "Luv U Better," "Paradise" and "Amazin'."

2006: Run-D.M.C. were inducted into the first class of the Long Island Music Hall of Fame, which is based in Melville, New York. The ceremony was staged at the Patchogue Theatre.

2009: Fergie announced a partnership with Avon to create her own fragrance, "Outspoken." She would later introduce three more fragrances.

2011: Hip hop entrepreneur Rick Ross opened his first Wingstop restaurant. (He had mentioned the restaurant chain in the lyrics of his 2010 track, "MC Hammer.") Ross was on hand for the grand opening of the chicken wings outlet in Memphis. By 2015, Ross owned a total of 25 Wingstop restaurants.

2011: Drake was the musical guest on *Saturday Night Live*. He performed "Headlines" and "Make Me Proud."

2013: Eminem released the track, "Rap God." According to *The Guinness Book of World Records*, the song set the record for the most words in a hit song. The track – which appeared on the album *The Marshall Mathers LP 2* – featured a total of 1,560 words over six-minutes and four-seconds. The song's music video parodied 1980s cartoon character, Max Headroom. The track was nominated for a Grammy in the category of Best Rap Performance.

2013: The BET network presented the eighth annual *BET Hip Hop Awards*. Among the winners were "Started From The Bottom" by Drake for Best Hip-Hop Video; Kendrick Lamar for Lyricist of the Year; Jay-Z for Best Live Performer; and MC Lyte for the I Am Hip Hop award. The event was hosted by Snoop Dog, and was staged at the Atlanta Civic Center.

2015: Biz Markie appeared in a television commercial for Lucky Charms cereal, and sang a reworked version of his 1990 hit, "Just A Friend."

OCTOBER 16

1997: A few months after he was ordained a Christian minister, MC Hammer debuted his new group of musicians and dancers at the World Gospel '97 festival in Barbados.

2003: Two members of the hip hop act Arrested Development sued the Fox network over the use of the group's name for the title of the television program, *Arrested Development*. The lawsuit was settled out of court.

2006: Jay-Z appeared in a commercial for Budweiser Select, after he was hired as the new co-brand director of the beer line.

2012: Pharrell Williams published his autobiography, *Pharrell: Places And Spaces I've Been.*

2014: Tyga purchased a mansion in Calabasas, California, for $6.5 million.

2015: Machine Gun Kelly released his second studio album, *General Admission*. Guest artists included Kid Rock, Lzzy Hale, Bone Thugs-N-Harmony, Yo Gotti, French Montana, Ray Cash and others. The top-10 album spawned the singles, "Till I Die," "A Little More," "World Series" and "Gone."

OCTOBER 17

1969: Wyclef Jean (birth name Wyclef Jeanelle Jean) was born in the town of Croix-des-Bouquets, Haiti, but had moved to the U.S. at age nine. In 1992, he co-founded the hip hop trio, the Fugees. Later pursuing a solo career, he released his first album in 1997, *The Carnival*.

1972: Eminem (birth name Marshall Bruce Mathers III) was born in St. Joseph, Missouri, but raised in Detroit. One of the leading figures in hip hop, he released his debut studio album in 1996, *Infinite*. He also co-founded his own label, Shady Records, and starred in the hit film, *8 Mile*. He was also a member of the group, D12, and the duo, Bad Meets Evil.

1984: Whodini released their second album, *Escape*. The album spawned the hits, "Friends," "Five Minutes Of Funk" and the rap classic, "Freaks Come Out At Night." This was one of the first hip hop albums to be certified platinum for sales of more than one-million copies.

2000: Jay-Z released the single, "I Just Wanna Love U (Give It 2 Me)." The song featured uncredited guest vocals by Pharrell Williams, Shay Haley and Omillio Sparks. The track sampled "The World Is Filled" by the Notorious B.I.G. and featured an interpolation of "Give It To Me Baby" by Rick James.

2000: The hip hop duo Reflection Eternal released the album, *Train Of Thought*. The duo consisted of Talib Kweli and DJ Hi-Tek. The album spawned the singles, "Move Somethin'" and "The Blast."

2000: Ludacris released his debut major-label album, *Back For The First Time*. The album spawned the singles "What's Your Fantasy" and "Southern Hospitality." The hit album placed Ludacris at the forefront of the Dirty South movement. (Many of the tracks originally appeared on his 1999, independently released album, *Incognegro*.)

2001: Jay-Z was sentenced to three-years of probation following the stabbing of record executive Lance "Un" Rivera at the Kit Kat Club in Manhattan. Although the rapper initially denied the charges, he later pleaded guilty to third-degree assault.

2006: The VH-1 network staged the 3rd annual Hip Hop Honors ceremony. The third year inductees included Afrika Bambaataa, the Beastie Boys, Eazy-E, Ice Cube, MC Lyte, Rakim, Russell Simmons and Wu-Tang Clan. The event was hosted by Ice-T, and was staged at the Hammerstein Ballroom in Manhattan.

2006: Sean "Diddy" Combs released the album, *Press Play*. The album spawned the singles, "Come To Me," "Tell Me," "Last Night" and "Through The Pain (She Told Me)."

2012: Flavor Flav was charged with assault and battery following a confrontation with his fiancee at their home in Las Vegas.

2012: Drake announced that he had belatedly earned his high school diploma at the age of 25. The Canadian-born rapper had dropped out of school at 15 in order to join the cast of the television series, *Degrassi: The Next Generation*.

OCTOBER 18

1970: Nonchalant (birth name Tanya Pointer) was born in Washington, D.C. She is best known for her 1995 hit, "5 O'Clock."

1986: Run-D.M.C. were the musical guests on *Saturday Night Live*. The group performed "Walk This Way" and "Hit It, Run."

1988: Tone Loc released the top-10 crossover hit, "Wild Thing." The track prominently sampled the intro of "Jamie's Cryin'" by Van Halen. The song's music video was made for less than $1,000 and borrowed the theme of Robert Palmer's popular clip for "Addicted To Love."

1991: Vanilla Ice made his acting debut in the romantic film, *Cool As Ice*. He portrayed a young rapper named Johnny Van Owen who fell in love with a straight-laced, small town girl.

1992: After changing their name from Inner City Posse, the Detroit "horror-core" rap duo Insane Clown Posse released their debut album, *Carnival Of Carnage*. The project received poor reviews and was a slow seller.

1994: Scarface released the solo album, *The Diary*. Recorded while he was a member of the Geto Boys, the album was highlighted by the singles, "Hand Of The Dead Body" and "I Seen A Man Die."

2002: The MTV musical variety show, *Scratch & Burn*, made its debut. The program combined comedy with rap music. The eight-episode series starred GQ, Jordan Allen-Dutton, J.A.Q. and Erik Weiner.

2005: Bun B released his debut solo album, *Trill*. He was forced to pursue a solo career after Chad "Pimp C" Butler, his partner in the duo UGK, was sent to prison in 2002. The album was highlighted by the hit single, "Draped Up."

2010: Several musical performers were contestants on the reality show, *Celebrity Apprentice 4*, which was hosted by Donald Trump. Country singer John Rich was selected the winner of the competition after he defeated Lil Jon, La Toya Jackson, John Rich, Dionne Warwick, David Cassidy, Mark McGrath and others.

2011: Soulja Boy (real name DeAndre Cortez Way) was arrested on felony drug and weapons charges after his vehicle was stopped in the town of Temple, Georgia. He was arrested along with the four other occupants of the vehicle.

2011: Will Smith and his wife Jada Pinkett Smith purchased a minority stake in the NBA team, the Philadelphia 76ers.

2013: Rappers Ja Rule, Toby Mac and T-Bone starred in the drama film, *I'm In Love With A Church Girl*.

2014: A concert by Kevin Gates in Sioux Falls, Iowa, was cancelled at the last minute after a "near riot" broke out in the venue's parking lot. A fight that began inside Exhibit Hall continued into the parking lot, eventually involving approximately 100 people.

2015: The security crews of Sean "Diddy" Combs and Lil Wayne got into a skirmish inside the VIP section at LIV nightclub in Miami Beach. The party, hosted by Diddy, was the final event of his annual Revolt Music Conference.

OCTOBER 19

1972: Pras Michel (birth name Prakazrel Samuel Michel) was born in Brooklyn, New York, but raised in Irvington, New Jersey. He co-founded the Fugees.

2010: AXE Body Spray terminated an endorsement deal with T.I. after the rapper was arrested and sent to prison. The following week, T.I. would also lose an endorsement deal with the cognac maker, Remy Martin.

2010: The nine-episode reality series, *K-Ci & JoJo... Come Clean*, debuted on the TV One network. The program followed former Jodeci members Cedric "K-Ci" Hailey and Joel "JoJo" Hailey as they attempted to reignite their careers.

2011: British rapper Tinie Tempah published his autobiography, *My Story So Far*.

2011: MC Hammer announced the launch of his new internet search engine, WireDoo. He made the announcement at the Web 2.0 summit in San Francisco.

2015: The Game revealed to the press that he had purchased a $250,000 Ferrari as a gift for fellow rapper, Diddy. At the time, the two men were celebrating the success of their duet hit, "Standing On Ferraris."

OCTOBER 20

1950: Graffiti artist Stay High 149 (birth name Wayne Roberts) was born in Virginia but raised in the Bronx, New York. Also using the name "Voice of the Ghetto," he tagged trains in New York City from 1970 to 1975. He died in 2012 at the age of 61.

1971: Snoop Dogg (birth name Calvin Cordozar Broadus, Jr.) was born in Long Beach, California. After he was discovered by Dr. Dre in 1992, Snoop Dogg enjoyed a quick rise to fame as a recording artist and actor. He is the cousin of R&B singers Brandy and Ray J.

1999: The hip hop film, *Thicker Than Water*, was released. The film followed two fictional street gang leaders who wanted to produce music. A number of rappers starred in the film including Krayzie Bone, Flesh-N-Bone, Fat Joe, Big Pun, Mack 10, Ice Cube, CJ Mack, MC Eiht, K-Mack and Bad Azz.

2006: The reality series, *Ice-T's Rap School,* debuted on the VH-1 network. On the program, Ice-T taught the art of rapping to eight students from the prestigious York Preparatory School in New York City. On the show's final episode, the group – named the York Prep Crew – was the opening act at a Public Enemy concert. The series ran for one season.

2008: Public Enemy were inducted into the Long Island Music Hall of Fame, which is based in Melville, New York. The ceremony was staged at the Patchogue Theatre.

2009: Jay-Z released the single, "Empire State Of Mind," featuring Alicia Keys. The song was a tribute to New York City, the hometown of both Jay-Z and Keys, and mentioned many of the city's landmarks. The track sampled "Love On A Two-Way Street" by the Moments. "Empire State Of Mind" was nominated for three Grammys and won two awards in the categories of Best Rap Song and Best Rap/Sung Collaboration.

2009: Numerous internet sites claimed that Kanye West had been killed in a car crash in Los Angeles. The rumor was not debunked until the following day.

2014: Professor Griff of Public Enemy published the book, *The Psychological Covert War On Hip Hop*.

2014: Louisiana rapper Lil Boosie changed his stage name to Boosie Badazz.

OCTOBER 21

1988: The rap duo Kid 'n Play released their debut album, *2 Hype*. The album spawned three hit singles, "Rollin' With Kid 'n Play," "2 Hype" and "Gittin' Funky."

1997: The hip hop supergroup, the Firm, released their only studio album, *The Album*. The group consisted of Nas, Foxy Brown, AZ and Cormega. (Nature replaced Cormega during the middle of the recording sessions.) The group was the brainchild of Nas, his manager Steve Stoute, Dr. Dre and the production team, the Trackmasters. The chart-topping album received limited radio airplay.

2006: Jim Jones released the single, "We Fly High." This was Jones' biggest crossover pop hit. The track sampled "Mr. Cool" by Rasputin's Stash. The song's music video featured Jones' girlfriend, Chrissy Lampkin.

2007: Kid Rock and five members of his entourage were arrested after a fight at a Waffle House restaurant in suburban Atlanta. The following year, Kid Rock was sentenced to one-year of probation and a $1,000 fine.

2012: Fergie of the Black Eyed Peas discussed her past addiction to Crystal Meth during an appearance on the program, *Oprah's Next Chapter*. Fergie attributed her drug use to the breakup of her previous band, Wild Orchid.

2013: Sean "Diddy" Combs formally launched his music-themed cable network, REVOLT.

2015: The U.S. District Court in Los Angeles dismissed a lawsuit against Jay-Z and Timbaland over the use of a sample in Jay-Z's 1999 smash hit, "Big Pimpin." The copyright infringement suit had been filed by the family of Egyptian singer Baligh Hamdi. A judge ruled that the family lacked legal standing to pursue the claim.

OCTOBER 22

1968: Shaggy (birth name Orville Richard Burrell) was born in Kingston, Jamaica, but moved to Brooklyn, New York, at age 18. After serving in the U.S. Marines, he pursued a career in music and scored his first hit in 1993 with a remake of "Oh Carolina."

1983: British rapper Plan B (birth name Benjamin Paul Ballance-Drew) was born in Forest Gate, London, England.

1985: Kurtis Blow released his sixth album, *America*. This was the rapper's first release after signing a lucrative contract with Polygram Records, which earned him the nickname "Hip Hop's First Millionaire." The album changed the face of rap music with the introduction of the sampled loop, which became a mainstay in hip hop. The album was highlighted by the hit single, "If I Ruled The World."

1987: On an episode of *The Cosby Show*, two of the characters – Theo Huxtable (real name Malcolm-Jamal Warner) and Walter "Cockroach" Bradley (real name Carl Payne) – wrote and performed a rap version of Mark Antony's speech, "Friends, Romans and Countrymen," from the William Shakespeare play, *Julius Caesar*.

1991: The hip hop duo Black Sheep released their debut album, *A Wolf In Sheep's Clothing*. The album spawned four singles, "Flavor Of The Month," "The Choice Is Yours," "Strobelite Honey" and "Similak Child."

1996: The hip hop supergroup Westside Connection – which was formed by Ice Cube, WC and Mack 10 – released the gangsta rap album, *Bow Down*. The album sold nearly two-million copies in the U.S. and was highlighted by the singles, "Bow Down" and "Gangstas Make The World Go Round." Westside Connection would later release a second studio album.

1996: Chuck D released his debut solo album, *Autobiography Of Mistachuck*. The album spawned just one single, "No."

1996: Nas released the single, "Street Dreams." The track sampled "Never Gonna Stop" by Linda Clifford and featured an interpolation of "Sweet Dreams (Are Made Of This)" by the Eurythmics. The song's music video was a tribute to the Martin Scorsese film, *Casino*, and was filmed in Las Vegas.

2012: Kendrick Lamar released his second studio album, *good kid, m.A.A.d city*. The album spawned the singles, "The Recipe," "Swimming Pools (Drank)," "Backseat Freestyle," "Poetic Justice" and "Bitch, Don't Kill My Vibe." The album received five Grammy nominations.

2013: Questlove of the Roots published the book, *Soul Train: The Music, Dance, And Style Of A Generation.*

OCTOBER 23

1989: Janet Jackson popularized the Running Man dance in her music video for "Rhythm Nation." The video was choreographed by hip hop dancer Anthony Thomas.

1991: The members of the musical duo Kid 'n Play reprised their roles as students in the hip hop film, *House Party 2*. The members of the group, Full Force, played the roles of bullies in the film.

1991: Marky Mark And The Funky Bunch released the single, "Wildside." The track heavily sampled "Walk On The Wild Side" by Lou Reed. The song was written and originally recorded by Boston rapper M.C. Spice.

1999: Eminem, Dr. Dre and Snoop Dogg were the musical guests on *Saturday Night Live*. Dr. Dre and Snoop Dogg performed "Still D.R.E." and Dr. Dre and Eminem performed "Forgot About Dre."

2002: Kanye West was seriously injured in an auto accident in West Hollywood, California. He suffered a fractured jaw which had to be wired shut. Despite his injuries, he entered a studio two weeks later to record the track, "Through The Wire."

2005: Cam'ron was shot during an attempted carjacking in Washington, D.C. While stopped at a traffic light at the wheel of his 2006 Lamborghini, Cam'ron was approached by a man who ordered the rapper to give up the vehicle. When he refused, Cam'ron was shot in both arms. He managed to drive away and reach a hospital.

2006: A scheduled concert by Jay-Z was cancelled by authorities in China. The show at Shanghai's Hongkou Stadium was called off due to what the Chinese Ministry of Culture described as the rapper's "vulgar" lyrics.

2006: Fergie released the single, "Fergalicious." The top-10 hit sampled "Give It All You Got" by Afro-Rican and interpolated "Supersonic" by J. J. Fad. The song's music video drew comparisons to the fantasy film, *Willy Wonka*.

2006: British neo-soul singer Amy Winehouse released the smash hit, "Rehab." Many top-40 radio stations in the U.S. played the official remix of the track which featured rapping by Jay-Z.

2006: Bow Wow released the single, "Shortie Like Mine" (featuring Chris Brown and Johntá Austin). The song's music video featured Reverend Run and his daughter Angela Simmons.

2007: Sean "Diddy" Combs teamed with the British beverage firm Diageo to promote Ciroc vodka. The deal gave the rapper 50-percent of the drink's profits in the U.S.

2008: The BET network presented the third annual *BET Hip Hop Awards*. Among the winners were Lil Wayne for Lyricist of the Year; Akon for Producer of the Year; DJ Khaled for DJ of the Year; and Russell Simmons for the I Am Hip-Hop award. The event was hosted by T-Pain, and was staged at the Atlanta Civic Center.

2010: The documentary, *Rubble Kings*, examined the street gangs of the Bronx in the 1970s and the social environment that produced hip hop music and culture. The film's director Shan Nicholson told *The New York Daily News*, "The backbone of this film is really the music and how hip hop culture came out of gang culture."

2011: Jay-Z provided the voice of a cartoon version of himself on the animated, Saturday morning television series, *Secret Millionaires Club*.

2014: Kurtis Blow was inducted into the Long Island Music Hall of Fame, which is based in Melville, New York. The ceremony was staged at the Patchogue Theatre.

OCTOBER 24

1983: Too $hort released his debut album, *Don't Stop Rappin'*.

1986: Drake (birth name Aubrey Drake Graham) was born in Toronto, Ontario, Canada. Before emerging as a successful rapper, he was an actor on the popular, teen television drama, *Degrassi: The Next Generation*. He later launched the annual OVO Festival in Toronto.

1987: LL Cool was the musical guest on *Saturday Night Live*. He performed "Go Cut Creator Go."

1992: Arrested Development were the musical guests on *Saturday Night Live*. They performed "Tennessee" and "People Everyday."

1993: One of the most celebrated freestyle rapping sessions in history occurred at Madison Square Garden. Big Daddy Kane invited 22-year-old Tupac Shakur and 21-year-old Biggie Smalls onstage for an unplanned freestyle performance. One of Kane's backup dancers, Scoob Lover, also contributed some raps. Mister Cee recorded the all-star performance, which was later released on vinyl.

1995: Big Pun made his recording debut when he appeared as a featured vocalist on the track, "Watch Out," from Fat Joe's second album, *Jealous One's Envy*.

2009: KRS-One published the book, *The Gospel Of Hip Hop: The First Instrument*.

2010: Eminem was selected as the winner of MTV's annual "Hottest MCs in the Game."

2014: The hip hop duo Run The Jewels released the critically acclaimed album, *Run The Jewels 2*. The duo consisted of Killer Mike and El-P.

OCTOBER 25

1968: Speech (birth name Todd Thomas) was born in Milwaukee, Wisconsin. He was the lead vocalist of the alternative hip hop group, Arrested Development. He released his debut solo album in 1996, *Speech*.

1977: The Alchemist (birth name Daniel Alan Maman) was born in Beverly Hills, California. An in-demand producer, he was hired as a DJ by Eminem in 2005.

1983: Comedian and actor Rodney Dangerfield released the novelty single, "Rappin' Rodney." This was one of the first rap songs featured on MTV. The song was co-written by James B. Moore and Robert Ford, Jr., the same team of songwriters who wrote "The Breaks" with Kurtis Blow. The song's music video featured cameo appearances by Pat Benatar and Father Guido Sarducci.

1985: Ciara (full name Ciara Princess Harris) was born in Austin, Texas. After moving to Atlanta and joining the girl group Hearsay, she later signed with LaFace Record as a solo act. Her 2004 chart-topping single "Goodies" gave Ciara the nicknames, the First Lady and the Princess of Crunk&B.

1985: The pioneering hip hop film, *Krush Groove*, was released. A semi-fictional account of the rise of Def Jam Recordings, the film starred Blair Underwood who portrayed a character based on Russell Simmons. The film featured appearances by Kurtis Blow, Run-D.M.C., LL Cool J, the Fat Boys, New Edition, Sheila E. and the Beastie Boys. Def Jam co-founders Rick Rubin and Russell Simmons both appeared in the film.

1993: NBA star Shaquille O'Neal staged a party at the Hard Rock Cafe in Orlando to launch his rap album, *Shaq Diesel*. The project was produced by Def Jeff, K-Cut (of Main Source), Erick Sermon (of EPMD) and Ali (of A Tribe Called Quest). The album sold more than one-million copies and was highlighted by the hit single, "(I Know I Got) Skillz."

2002: Rappers Cam'ron and Mekhi Phifer starred in the film, *Paid In Full*. The drama, which was produced by Roc-A-Fella Films, examined the period in the 1980s before a crack epidemic hit Harlem. The title of the film was taken from the name of an album by Eric B. & Rakim.

2010: Scott Brown released the single, "Yeah 3x." Brown was later accused of borrowing the song's melody from the 2009 hit, "I'm Not Alone," by Scottish DJ Calvin Harris. After a quick telephone conversation, Brown offered to give Harris half of the track's songwriting credits.

2014: Iggy Azalea was the musical guest on *Saturday Night Live*. She performed "Beg For It" and a medley of "Fancy" and "Black Widow."

2015: A shooting took place at Scales 925, an Atlanta restaurant owned by rapper T.I. Former NBA player Glen Rice, Jr., was shot in the leg during a confrontation that began inside the restaurant and continued into the parking lot.

OCTOBER 26

1989: Arsenio Hall introduced his alter ego, an overweight rapper named Chunky A. He released the album, *Large And In Charge*, and scored a minor hit with the funk-based single, "Owwww!"

1994: Nate Dogg was charged with robbing a Taco Bell restaurant in San Pedro, California. When the case went to trial in 1996, the jury was deadlocked by a vote of 9 to 3, which resulted in a mistrial.

1996: Dr. Dre was the musical guest on *Saturday Night Live*. He performed "Been There, Done That."

2001: Snoop Dog starred in the horror film, *Bones*. He portrayed a murdered gangster who rose from the grave to find and punish his killers.

2006: Lil' Romeo and his father Master P starred in the film, *God's Gift*. Master P also directed the film, which included appearances by Lil' Romeo's younger brother Young V and their uncle Silkk the Shocker.

2009: Violence erupted at a concert headlined by Akon and T-Pain in Melbourne, Australia. At least 18 people were injured after members of rival gangs started fighting. Additionally, dozens of fans without tickets attempted to storm the venue but were blocked by security guards.

2010: Willow Smith, the daughter of Will Smith and Jada Pinkett Smith, released her debut single, "Whip My Hair," a week before her 10th birthday. The song was a surprise hit. An official remix, which featured British rapper Tinie Tempah, was released the following January.

2012: Natina Tiawana Reed of the all-girl, hip hop trio Blaque passed away. She was struck by a vehicle in suburban Atlanta while walking across a street. She was 31-years-old.

2015: Former heavyweight champion Mike Tyson performed a rendition of Drake's "Hotline Bling" during an episode of *The Tonight Show*.

2015: The Roots were inducted into the Philadelphia Music Walk of Fame. Also inducted were Billie Holiday, Ray Benson of Asleep At The Wheel, the Trammps, Cinderella, Andrea McArdle and local deejay Harvey Holiday.

OCTOBER 27

1987: Heavy D & The Boyz released their debut album, *Living Large*. The album spawned three singles, "Mr. Big Stuff," "The Overweight Lover's In The House" and "Don't You Know."

1998: Jay-Z released the single, "Hard Knock Life (Ghetto Anthem)." It was the biggest hit of his career. The track sampled "It's The Hard Knock Life" from the Broadway musical, *Annie*. The song was nominated for a Grammy in the category of Best Rap Solo Performance.

1998: Ice Cube released the single, "Pushin' Weight" (featuring Mr. Short Khop). This was the first single from his album, *War & Peace Vol.1 (The War Disc)*.

2004: P. Diddy was parodied on an episode of the animated television program, *South Park*.

2005: Jay-Z and Nas ended their often bitter, public feud. After Jay-Z finished his performance at the annual Powerhouse concert in New York City, he invited Nas on stage and the two former rivals shook hands. The two men then performed a medley of Jay-Z's "Dead Presidents" and Nas' "The World Is Yours."

2006: A copyright infringement lawsuit filed by 2 Live Crew singer Luther Campbell against 50 Cent was dismissed by a judge in Miami. Campbell had claimed that a portion of his solo track "It's Your Birthday" had been used by 50 Cent on his hit, "In Da Club."

2009: Eminem published his autobiography, *The Way I Am*. The name of the book was taken from the title of a track from his album, *The Marshall Mathers LP*.

OCTOBER 28

1987: Frank Ocean (birth name Christopher Francis Ocean) was born in Long Beach, California, but raised in New Orleans. After breaking into music as a songwriter, he enjoyed a successful solo career beginning with his 2012 debut album, *Channel Orange*.

1993: Tupac Shakur released the single, "Keep Ya Head Up," from his second album, *Strictly 4 My N.I.G.G.A.Z.*

1997: The New Orleans hip hop group, the Hot Boys, released their debut album, *Get It How U Live!!* The all-star group consisted of Juvenile, B.G., Lil Wayne and Turk. The album was highlighted by the tracks, "We On Fire" and "Neighborhood Superstar."

1997: Ma$e released his debut album, *Harlem World*. The album featured a number of guest artists including Busta Rhymes, Jay-Z, Lil' Kim, the Lox, Total and DMX. The chart-topping album spawned four singles: "Feel So Good," "What You Want," "24 Hrs. To Live" and "Lookin' At Me." The album was nominated for a Grammy in the category of Best Rap Album.

2003: Beyoncé released the R&B/rap single, "Summertime," which featured P. Diddy. A remixed version of the track featured rapper Ghostface Killah. The song also appeared on the soundtrack album of the film, *The Fighting Temptations*, which starred Beyoncé and Cuba Gooding, Jr.

2008: Coolio starred in the Oxygen network reality series, *Coolio's Rules*. The program followed the rapper – a single father – as he raised his teenage children in suburban Los Angeles. The series featured four of his six children.

2009: After completing an eight-year stint in a New York state prison, Rapper Shyne (birth name Jamal Barrow) was deported by U.S. authorities and sent back to his native Belize. While behind bars, he converted to Judaism and legally changed his name to Moses Michael Levi.

2011: British rapper Tulisa co-starred in the slasher film, *Demons Never Die*.

2014: Young Fathers, a Scottish hip hop group, won the prestigious Mercury Prize for their debut album, *Dead*.

2014: Nicki Minaj released the single, "Only" (featuring Drake, Lil Wayne and Chris Brown). The song was nominated for a Grammy in the category of Best Rap/Sung Collaboration. The song's controversial music video was the target of protests due to its Nazi-style imagery. The track sold three-million copies in the U.S.

2014: A number of performers joined forces to launch the TIDAL music streaming service. Among the financial partners were Jay-Z, Beyoncé, Kanye West, Rihanna, Nicki Minaj, Daft Punk, Jack White, Madonna, Arcade Fire, Alicia Keys, Usher, Chris Martin, Calvin Harris, deadmau5, Jason Aldean and J. Cole.

2015: Action Bronson underwent emergency surgery in Alaska, a few days after a concert in Anchorage. While there was speculation that the surgery might have been the result of his consumption of native Alaskan foods such as bowhead whale, caribou stew and whale blubber, the rapper attributed his health scare to complications of a chronic hernia from his power-lifting days.

OCTOBER 29

1979: Lady B (real name Wendy Clark) released one of the first rap singles by a female performer, "To The Beat Y'all." The Philadelphia native also worked as an R&B and hip hop radio deejay.

1991: Ice Cube released the controversial album, *Death Certificate*. Similar to his previous album *AmeriKKKa's Most Wanted*, it explored the themes of drug addiction, ghetto life, poverty and the right to bear arms. The album was criticized for two of the tracks, "No Vaseline," a diss track aimed at the members of N.W.A. and "Black Korea," which attacked Korean-owned grocery stores in black neighborhoods. The album was banned by the Midwestern-based record chain, Camelot Music.

1991: MC Hammer released the album, *Too Legit To Quit*. For the album, he dropped the "MC" portion of his name. The album spawned four singles, "2 Legit 2 Quit," "Addams Groove," "Do Not Pass Me By" and "This Is The Way We Roll." The album sold more than three-million copies in the U.S.

1991: Black Sheep released the hit single, "The Choice Is Yours (Revisited)." The track sampled "Keep On Doin' It" by the New Birth, "Her Favorite Style" by Iron Butterfly, "Big Sur Suite" by Johnny Hammond Smith, "Impressions" by McCoy Tyner and "I'd Say It Again" by Sweet Linda Divine. "The Choice Is Yours (Revisited)" enjoyed renewed attention in 2010 after it was featured in a commercial for the Kia Soul.

1994: Lil' Boo (real name John Moore) was shot to death while protecting his nephew. A member of the Cleveland hip hop group, Gaveyard Shift, Lil' Boo was killed at his mother's home. He was 16-years-old.

1996: Faith Evans and her husband the Notorious B.I.G. welcomed the birth of their son, Christopher Wallace, Jr.

2010: Miami native Pitbull performed at a pre-game concert to celebrate LeBron James' first home game as a member of the Miami Heat.

2013: Eminem released the hit single, "The Monster" (featuring Rihanna). An international smash, it was the follow-up to the duo's first collaboration, "Love The Way You Lie." The song's music video earned three nominations at the MTV Video Music Awards.

2015: DJ Khaled was given an honorary "key to the city" by the mayor of Miami.

OCTOBER 30

1969: Snow (birth name Darrin Kenneth O'Brien) was born in Toronto, Ontario, Canada. He is best known for his 1993 crossover, reggae-style hit, "Informer."

1989: DJ and producer Baauer (birth name Harry Bauer Rodrigues) was born in Philadelphia. He is best known for his smash hit, "Harlem Shake," which was released in mid-2012 but was not a hit until the following year.

1993: Snoop Doggy Dogg released his debut solo single, "Who Am I? (What's My Name?)." The Dr. Dre-produced track sampled "Atomic Dog" by George Clinton, "Pack Of Lies" by the Counts and "P. Funk (Wants To Get Funked Up)" by Parliament, and interpolated "Give Up The Funk (Tear The Roof Off The Sucker)" by Parliament.

2001: Ja Rule released the single, "Always On Time" (featuring Ashanti). This was Ashanti's first hit single.

2002: After he was ordained as a minister, MC Hammer officiated the wedding of actors Corey Feldman and Susie Sprague. The ceremony aired on the reality series, *The Surreal Life*. (The wedding was co-officiated by a rabbi.)

2002: Jam Master Jay of Run-D.M.C. was murdered while sitting on a coach at a recording studio in the Jamaica section of Queens, New York. Another person in the studio, Urieco Rincon, was shot in the leg. No one was arrested for the crime.

2004: Eminem was the musical guest on *Saturday Night Live*. He performed "Mosh" and "Just Lose It." This was his fourth appearance on the program.

2004: R. Kelly dropped out of a double-headlining tour with Jay-Z. During a performance at Madison Square Garden in New York City, Kelly abruptly left the stage after telling the audience, "Two people were waving guns at me. I can't do no show like that." As a result of Kelly's departure, the name of the tour was changed from "The Best of Both Worlds" to "Jay-Z and special guests."

2005: Kanye West released his second album, *Late Registration*. The album employed a string section on a number of tracks and included vocal contributions by Common, Jay-Z, Lupe Fiasco, Jamie Foxx, Brandy, Adam Levine and Nas. The album spawned five singles: "Diamonds From Sierra Leone," "Gold Digger," "Heard 'Em Say," "Touch The Sky" and "Drive Slow." The album sold three-million copies in the U.S. and won a Grammy in the category of Best Rap Album.

2005: Chris Brown released his debut single, "Run It." The chart-topping track featured rap verses by Juelz Santana.

2006: Jay-Z released "Show Me What You Got," the debut single from his "comeback" album *Kingdom Come*. The track sampled "Show 'Em Whatcha Got" by Public Enemy, "Darkest Light" by Lafayette Afro Rock Band and "Shaft In Africa" by Johnny Pate. The song's music video featured professional drivers Danica Patrick and Dale Earnhardt, Jr.

2008: Marion "Suge" Knight sued Kanye West over a shooting at a Miami Beach nightclub in 2005. A gunman at a party hosted by West shot Knight in the leg, which shattered a bone. In the aftermath, Knight was forced to undergo surgery and spent months in rehabilitation. Knight also claimed that during the shooting, he lost a 15-carat diamond earring valued at $135,000. According to reports, the suit was settled out of court.

2010: Rihanna was the musical guest on *Saturday Night Live*. She performed "What's My Name?" and "Only Girl (In The World)."

2013: Drake sold his condo in Toronto for $3.75 million. His original asking price was $4.195 million.

2015: Jerry Heller, the former business partner of the late Eazy-E, filed a lawsuit against Dr. Dre, Ice Cube, Eazy-E's estate and NBC-Universal. He claimed that his portrayal in the N.W.A. biopic, *Straight Outta Compton*, was both unauthorized and inaccurate. He asked for $35 million in compensatory damages and $75 million in punitive damage, as well as 100-percent of the movie's profits. Heller was portrayed by actor Paul Giamatti.

OCTOBER 31

1967: Vanilla Ice (birth name Robert Matthew Van Winkle) was born in Dallas. He is best known for his 1990 smash hit, "Ice Ice Baby."

1972: Pharoahe Monch (birth name Troy Donald Jamerson) was born in Queens, New York. The rapper formed a duo with Prince Poetry, Organized Konfusion, before pursuing a solo career.

1993: Tupac Shakur was charged with shooting two off-duty policemen in suburban Atlanta. Allegedly, he nearly hit both men with his vehicle. Then after the officers shot at this vehicle, he shot back and struck both men. The 22-year-old rapper was arrested in his hotel room and was charged with aggravated assault. He was released after posting a $55,000 bond.

1995: LL Cool J was backed by Boyz II Men on the Grammy-winning hit single, "Hey Lover." The track sampled "The Lady In My Life" by Michael Jackson. The song's music video featured actress Gillian Iliana Waters. (Waters later starred in Dr. Dre's video for "Been There, Done That.")

1999: All nine original members of the Wu-Tang Clan were featured in the PlayStation video game, *Wu-Tang: Shaolin Style*.

2000: Jay-Z released the album, *The Dynasty: Roc La Familia*. The album spawned the singles, "I Just Wanna Love U (Give It 2 Me)," "Change The Game" and "Guilty Until Proven Innocent." The album sold more than two-million copies in the U.S.

2000: OutKast released their fourth album, *Stankonia*. The socially-conscious project spawned three singles, "Ms. Jackson," "B.O.B." and "So Fresh, So Clean." The album sold four-million copies in the U.S. and won a Grammy in the category of Best Rap Album. One of the tracks, "Ms. Jackson," won a Grammy in the category of Best Rap Performance by a Duo or Group.

2006: Flavor Flav released his first solo album, *Flavor Flav* (which was also known as *Hollywood*). He recorded the album over a seven-year period.

2006: Birdman and Lil Wayne released the collaborative album, *Like Father, Like Son*. The album spawned the singles, "Stuntin' Like My Daddy," "Leather So Soft" and "You Ain't Know."

2006: Fat Joe released the single, "Make It Rain" (featuring Lil Wayne). The track sampled "Shoulder Lean" by Young Dro (featuring T.I.). The song was nominated for a Grammy in the category of Best Rap Performance by a Duo or Group.

2006: NBA player Ron Artest released the rap album, *My World*. The project featured guest appearances by P. Diddy, Mike Jones, Juvenile, Big Kap, Nature and Capone.

2006: Authors Gabriel Tolliver and Reggie Osse published the book, *Bling: The Hip-Hop Jewelry Book*.

2007: Da Brat was involved in a confrontation during a Halloween party at the Studio 72 nightclub in Atlanta. She allegedly struck a female employee in the face with a bottle of rum. The rapper was arrested and charged with aggravated assault. She later pleaded guilty and was sentenced to three-years in prison, seven-years of probation and 200-hours of community service.

▶ NOVEMBER

NOVEMBER 1

1988: Slick Rick released his debut album, *The Great Adventures Of Slick Rick*. The album topped the R&B charts and spawned the singles, "Teenage Love," "Children's Story" and "Hey Young World."

1989: Queen Latifah released her debut single, "Ladies First" (featuring Monie Love).

1993: Flavor Flav (real name William Drayton) of Public Enemy was arrested in New York City on charges of trying to shoot his neighbor. After agreeing to drug rehabilitation, the charges against the rapper were dropped.

1996: After launching Mo Thugs Records, the members of Bone Thugs-N-Harmony released a compilation album, *Family Scriptures*, to showcase the talent on their new label. The 16-track album nearly topped the U.S. charts.

1999: Published three years after the death of Tupac Shakur, his early poetry from 1989 to 1991 was collected in the book, *The Rose That Grew From Concrete*. The book featured a preface by Shakur's mother and an introduction by his manager Leila Steinburg.

2001: Mac Dre (real name Andre Louis Hicks) was killed in Kansas City, Missouri. He was shot in a drive-by shooting after a concert. He was 34-years-old. The Oakland-born rapper owned a pair of record labels, Romp Productions and Thizz Entertainment, and recorded more than a dozen solo albums.

2003: OutKast were the musical guests on *Saturday Night Live*. They performed "Hey Ya!" and "The Way You Move."

2005: Nearly a decade after he was forced to declare bankruptcy, MC Hammer placed his musical catalogue up for sale. The catalogue was purchased in 2006 for nearly $3 million by Evergreen/BMG.

2005: Voletta Wallace, the mother of the Notorious B.I.G., published a biography of her son, *Biggie*.

2008: Debbie Nelson, the mother of rapper Eminem, published the controversial book, *My Son Marshall, My Son Eminem: Setting The Record Straight On My Life As Eminem's Mother*.

2011: Jay-Z published his autobiography, *Decoded*.

2011: Dozens of recording artists including Chuck D of Public Enemy filed a $100 million class action lawsuit in California against Universal Music Group, claiming breach of contract over the issue of unpaid digital royalties. The lawsuit was settled in April 2015.

2015: The Capitol Hill Value Village, one of the Seattle thrift shops that was featured in the music video for "Thrift Shop" by Macklemore & Ryan Lewis, closed its doors.

NOVEMBER 2

1974: Nelly (birth name Cornell Iral Haynes, Jr.) was born in Austin, Texas, but raised in St. Louis. Before launching a solo career, he was a member of the 1990s hip hop group, the St. Lunatics. Nelly scored a long string of solo hits beginning with "Country Grammar (Hot Shit)."

1974: Prodigy (birth name Albert Johnson) was born in Hempstead, New York. A member of the hip hop duo Mobb Deep, he was also a successful solo artist. His mother, Fatima Johnson, was a member of the 1960s hit girl-group, the Crystals.

1992: Rap-metal band Rage Against The Machine released the hit single, "Killing In The Name." The song's lyrics explored the topics of racism and police brutality. In 2009, the track returned to the charts and hit number-one in the U.K., following an online campaign by British deejay Jon Morter.

2002: Jay-Z was the musical guest on *Saturday Night Live*. He was joined by Lenny Kravitz on "Guns & Roses" and by Kravitz and Beyoncé on "'03 Bonnie & Clyde."

2002: Rap music promoter Kenneth Walker was shot to death while sitting in a parked van on a street in the Bronx, New York. The vehicle was struck by a total of eight gunshots.

2003: Sean "Puffy" Combs competed in the New York City Marathon. He ran the entire 26.2 mile course and raised $2 million for various children's charities.

2006: Kanye West crashed the stage at the MTV Europe Music Awards ceremony in Denmark. He interrupted the presentation of an award after losing in the Best Video category to the French duo Justice vs. Simian. Taking the microphone, West launched a profanity-filled tirade and claimed that his video for "Touch The Sky" should have won.

2010: RZA, a co-founder of the Wu-Tang Clan, published his second book, *The Tao Of Wu*.

2013: Eminem was the musical guest on *Saturday Night Live*, three days before the release of *The Marshall Mathers LP 2*. This was his sixth appearance on the program. The Detroit rapper performed the tracks, "Berzerk" and "Survival."

NOVEMBER 3

1987: Kool Moe Dee released his best-selling solo album, *How Ya Like Me Now*. The album was highlighted by the crossover hit, "Wild Wild West."

1992: The Los Angeles-based band Rage Against The Machine combined heavy metal and rap on their debut album, *Rage Against The Machine*. The politically-charged project spawned the singles, "Killing In The Name," "Bullet In The Head," "Bombtrack" and "Freedom." The album sold more than three-million copies in the U.S.

1992: Ice Cube released the single, "Wicked" (featuring Don Jagwarr). The song's music video featured Anthony Kiedis and Flea from the funk-rock group, Red Hot Chili Peppers.

1998: Mo Thugs released the single, "Ghetto Cowboy" (featuring Bone Thugs-N-Harmony). The chorus was sung by Layzie Bone's wife, Felecia. The song's music video was set in the Old West.

2001: Ja Rule was the musical guest on *Saturday Night Live*. He was joined by Ashanti on "Always On Time" and by Case on "Livin' It Up."

2001: Mary J. Blige began a six-week run at number-one on the U.S. singles chart with "Family Affair."

2006: André 3000 of OutKast provided the voice of music teacher Sunny Bridges in the animated Cartoon Network series, *Class Of 3000*. The series was set at the fictional Westley School of Performing Arts in Atlanta and ran for 28 episodes.

2008: Jax (real name Christopher Thurston) died while performing. A member of the hip hop group, Binkis Recs, he collapsed onstage at Lenny's Bar in Atlanta during the middle of the song, "Sharper Images." He was 32-years-old.

2009: B.G. (real name Christopher Dorsey) of the New Orleans hip hop group the Hot Boys was arrested in Covington, Louisiana. During a routine traffic stop, the rapper was found with three guns in his vehicle, two of which were reported stolen. Police also found a number of loaded magazines and illegal drugs. He was convicted in 2012 and sentenced to 14-years in prison.

2009: Timbaland released the single, "Say Something" (featuring Drake).

2011: Atlanta-based hip hop producer Shawty Redd (real name Demetrius Lee Stewart) was found not guilty of murder in a Georgia courtroom. He had been charged in a 2010 shooting of an acquaintance at his home.

2011: British rapper K. Koke (real name Kevin Georgiou) was acquitted of attempted murder in the shooting of a man at a London train station earlier in the year. A total of five people had been charged in the shooting. Koke had signed a contract with Jay-Z's Roc Nation just weeks before he was charged.

2015: A mansion in Miami owned by Lil Wayne was raided by Miami-Dade police in an effort to collect a court judgement of $2 million for failure to make the payments on a leased jet. The authorities confiscated much of Lil Wayne's extensive art collection.

NOVEMBER 4

1966: Kool Rock-Ski (birth name Damon Wimbley) was born in Brooklyn, New York. In 1982, he co-founded the early rap group, the Fat Boys.

1969: Sean "Diddy" Combs (full name Sean John Combs) was born in Harlem but raised in Mount Vernon, New York. A superstar in the hip hop field, he enjoyed great success as a performer, producer, business owner, actor, clothing designer and film producer. He also operated Bad Boy Entertainment.

1994: Drake made his first appearance on the long-running television drama, *Degrassi: The Next Generation*. His character James "Jimmy" Brooks was the school basketball star. The future rapper remained with the show until 2009. Drake would mention Degrassi in a number of his songs including "Ransom" and "Worst Behavior."

1997: Jay-Z released his second album, *In My Lifetime, Vol. 1*. The album spawned six singles including "Who You Wit," "(Always Be My) Sunshine" and "The City Is Mine." The album sold more than one-million copies in the U.S.

1998: The crime-drama film, *Belly*, starred a number of hip hop artists including Nas, DMX, Taral Hicks, AZ and Method Man. The film's script was co-written by Nas.

2003: Jay-Z released the single, "Change Clothes" (featuring Pharrell Williams). The song's music video featured appearances by Kelly Ripa, Naomi Campbell, Jessica White, Omahyra Mota, Mey Bun, Mos Def and others.

2003: The Black Eyed Peas released the single, "Shut Up," from the group's third album, *Elephunk*. This was the group's first hit to feature Fergie.

2015: Puff Daddy released a free album, *MMM*, in celebration of his 46th birthday. The title of the album was based on the character, Money Making Mitch, from the 2002 film, *Paid In Full*.

NOVEMBER 5

1994: A number of leading NBA players recorded tracks for the hip hop album, *B-Ball's Best Kept Secret*. Among the players-turned-rappers were Shaquille O'Neal, Malik Sealy, Cedric Ceballos, Jason Kidd and Gary Payton.

1996: The final studio album by Tupac Shakur was released, *The Don Killuminati: The 7 Day Theory*. Recorded over a 12-day period in August 1996, the album was issued two-months after he was murdered. The album sold more than five-million copies in the U.S. and was highlighted by the hits, "Toss It Up," "Hail Mary" and "To Live & Day In L.A." Intended as his final album for Death Row Records, Shakur had planned on starting his own label, Makaveli Records.

1996: Brian Green, who played the character of David Silver on *Beverly Hills 90210*, attempted a career as a rapper. Despite production help by will.i.am and members of the Pharcyde, the album *One Stop Carnival* sold poorly.

2002: The documentary, *Da Westside*, examined the rising popularity of West Coast rap.

2004: The documentary, *Fade To Black*, was released. The film captured what was billed as Jay-Z's final concert. Staged at Madison Square Garden in New York City, the concert also featured Missy Elliott, Twista, P. Diddy, Mary J. Blige, Pharrell Williams and many others.

2006: Sir Mix-A-Lot portrayed a cartoon version of himself on *The Simpsons*. In the episode titled "Treehouse of Horror XVII," he sang a parody of his hit "Baby Got Back," which he reworked as "Baby Likes Fat."

2008: Kanye West released the single, "Heartless." The song was later a hit for three other artists: the Fray, Kris Allen and Dia Frampton.

2009: 50 Cent introduced the men's fragrance, "Power by 50." The product was initially sold at Macy's stores. The rapper introduced the cologne at an in-store appearance at Macy's in Herald Square.

2010: The Black Eyed Peas released "The Time (Dirty Bit)," the first single from their album, *The Beginning*. The song sampled "(I've Had) The Time Of My Life" by Bill Medley and Jennifer Warnes.

2013: Eminem released his eighth studio album, *The Marshall Mathers LP 2*. The album spawned five singles, "Berzerk," "Survival," "Rap God," "The Monster" and "Headlights." The album won a Grammy in the category of Best Rap Album and sold nearly three-million copies in the U.S.

2014: Dr. Dre and Jimmy Iovine were honored at *The Wall Street Journal's* annual Innovator Awards. Earlier in the year, the two music moguls had sold their Beats Music and Beats Electronics businesses to Apple. Eminem made a surprise appearance at the ceremony as he took the podium and presented the award to Dre and Iovine.

2014: Jay-Z announced the purchase of the premium champagne maker, Armand de Brignac. The sale price was not disclosed. Bottles of the champagne – nicknamed Ace of Spades – were previously featured in the music video of his track, "Show Me What You Got."

NOVEMBER 6

1996: For the first time, Vanilla Ice publically discussed the infamous conversation he had with Marion "Suge" Knight on a 15th floor hotel balcony. Appearing on ABC's *20/20*, Vanilla Ice explained how he was pressured to sign over a substantial portion of the copyright of his mega-hit, "Ice Ice Baby."

1996: The crime-action film, *Set It Off*, was released. The low-budget film featured Jada Pinkett Smith, Queen Latifah and Dr. Dre, and grossed more than $40 million in the U.S.

2001: Christian rapper TobyMac released his first solo album, *Momentum*, which he recorded after his group DC Talk went on a hiatus. The Grammy-nominated album was certified Gold by the RIAA for sales of 500,000 copies.

2001: The Oakland-based hip hop group, the Coup, delayed the release of their album, *Party Music*, due to its controversial front cover which featured the destruction of the World Trade Center. The album was subsequently issued with a different cover.

2002: 50 Cent released his first hit single, "Wanksta." The track was the second single from the hit soundtrack of the Eminem film, *8 Mile*. The song had originally appeared on 50 Cent's underground mixtape, *No Mercy, No Fear*.

2007: Chris Brown released his second album, *Exclusive*. The album spawned the hit singles, "Wall To Wall," "Kiss Kiss" (featuring T-Pain) and "With You." The album sold nearly two-million copies in the U.S. The following year, he released an expanded version of the album, *Exclusive: The Forever Edition*. It contained four extra tracks including the top-10 hit, "Forever."

2008: 50 Cent hosted the MTV reality series, *The Money And The Power*. The program featured 14 contestants who competed to win a $100,000 investment from 50 Cent to start a business. The contestants were judged by a panel that included Tony Yayo, Lloyd Banks, Chris Lighty, Ryan Schinman, DJ Whoo Kid, LL Cool J, Miss Info and Aubrey O'Day. The series ran for one season.

2011: The television series, *Hell On Wheels*, debuted on the AMC network. Set in the American West after the Civil War, the program co-starred Common as a former slave named Elam Ferguson who worked as a security agent for a railroad construction company.

2013: More than fifty R&B and hip hop artists performed at a variety of music venues across New York City as part of a week-long celebration to commemorate the 40th anniversary of the Universal Zulu Nation and the 39th anniversary of hip hop.

2013: Jay Z was sued for sampling a very brief portion of the 1969 track "Hook And Sling" by Eddie Bo, which appeared on the rapper's 2009 Grammy-winning hit single, "Run This Town." A judge dismissed the lawsuit in December 2014.

2013: Eminem appeared on the cover of the Marvel comic book, *Mighty Avengers #3*. The cover featured Eminem sitting on the front stoop of his childhood home in Detroit. Seated next to him was the Armored Avenger.

2015: Republican presidential candidate Ben Carson debuted a 60-second radio ad that featured rapping. The advertisement aired on urban radio stations in eight cities.

NOVEMBER 7

1988: British rapper Tinie Tempah (birth name Patrick Chukwuemeka Okogwu) was born in South London, England. Of Nigerian descent, he scored a pair of number-one British hits from his debut album, *Disc-Overy*.

1989: Queen Latifah released her debut album, *All Hail The Queen*. The album spawned the hits, "Wrath Of My Madness" and "Ladies First" (featuring Monie Love).

1995: Goodie Mob released their debut album, *Soul Food*. The Atlanta-based quartet consisted of Cee Lo Green, Big Gipp, Khujo and T-Mo. The album helped to popularize Southern Rap and featured the very first use of the term "Dirty South." The album spawned the singles, "Cell Therapy," "Soul Food" and "Dirty South."

1998: Sticky Fingaz of the group Onyx climbed into a boxing ring to fight skateboarder Simon Woodstock at the MTV Sports & Music Festival in Memphis.

2001: The documentary film, *Scratch*, chronicled the history of the hip hop DJ. Directed by Doug Pray, the film explored the world of deejay culture as well as various deejay techniques from extending breaks to scratching. A number of pioneering DJs were featured in the film including Afrika Bambaataa, the Beat Junkies and Grandmixer D. ST. of "Rockit" fame.

2002: Nelly was criticized for promoting a commercial product – a style of Nike shoes – in the lyrics and music video of his hit single, "Air Force Ones" (featuring Kyjuan, Ali and Murphy Lee).

2003: Slick Rick was released from prison. He had been jailed for trying to enter the U.S. through Florida. Denied bail, he had spent the previous 17-months behind bars and faced deportation back to his native country of England due to a past felony conviction.

2008: Black Eyed Peas member will.i.am provided the voice of the hippopotamus, Moto Moto, in the hit animated film, *Madagascar: Escape 2 Africa*. (His bandmate Fergie provided the voice of an unnamed female hippo.)

2010: Wiz Khalifa was arrested and charged with a felony count of trafficking in marijuana. Police had searched his tour bus following a concert at East Carolina University. Nine others were also arrested. Khalifa was released after posting a $300,000 bond.

2012: Waka Flocka Flame announced that he would be running for the U.S. presidency in 2016.

2013: The childhood home of Eminem – which was featured on the cover of his album *The Marshall Mathers LP* – was destroyed by fire. No one was living in the boarded-up dwelling at the time.

NOVEMBER 8

1971: Tech N9ne (birth name Aaron Dontez Yates) was born in Kansas City, Missouri. Launching his rap career in the early-1990s, he also co-founded a record label, Strange Music.

1977: Khia (full name Khia Shamone Finch) was born in Philadelphia. A producer and rapper, she released her breakthrough album in 2002, *Thug Misses*.

1978: Shyne (birth name Jamal Barrow) was born in the country of Belize but raised in Brooklyn, New York. The rapper was a protege of Sean "Puff Daddy" Combs. Shyne is best known as a co-defendant along with Combs in a 2001 shooting trial. While Combs was found not guilty, Shyne was convicted on five of eight charges and sentenced to nine-years in prison. After his release, he was deported to Belize.

1997: Erykah Badu performed an all-acoustic concert on the program, *MTV Unplugged*.

2002: Eminem's semi-autobiographical film, *8 Mile*, was released. He played the role of Jimmy "B-Rabbit" Smith, Jr., a working-class factory worker in Detroit who yearned to make it as a rapper. The film was a box office hit that earned more than $115 million in the U.S. The film's soundtrack album, *Music From And Inspired By The Motion Picture 8 Mile*, included five tracks by Eminem including the chart-topping hit, "Lose Yourself." The album sold more than three-million copies in the U.S.

2011: Heavy D (real name Dwight Arrington Myers) passed away at the age of 44. The Jamaican-born rapper suffered a fatal blood clot in his lung while battling pneumonia. He collapsed outside of his home in Beverly Hills and later died at a hospital.

2011: The musical video game, *The Black Eyed Peas Experience*, was released.

2011: Pusha T released the single, "What Dreams Are Made Of." The track sampled a speech by professional wrestler Ric Flair.

2013: Xzibit began his recurring role on the CBS television series *Hawaii Five-0*. He portrayed the leader of a weapons-running gang.

2015: Mary J. Blige debuted her radio show, *Real Talk*, on Apple Music's Beats1 Radio.

NOVEMBER 9

1969: Roxanne Shanté (birth name Lolita Shanté Gooden) was born in Queens, New York. She is best known for her 1985 hit, "The Real Roxanne."

1969: Sandra "Pepa" Denton of the 1980s female rap trio Salt-n-Pepa was born in Kingston, Jamaica, but raised in New York City. She co-founded the group in 1984.

1970: Scarface (birth name Brad Terrence Jordan) was born in Houston, Texas. Originally known as DJ Akshen, he enjoyed his first success as a member of the gangsta rap group, the Geto Boys. As a solo artist, he released a series of hit albums in the 1990s including *The Diary* and *The Last Of A Dying Breed*. In 2000, he was named the president of Def Jam South.

1976: Sheek Louch (birth name Sean Divine Jacobs) was born in Brooklyn, New York. As a member of the Lox, he was known as Donnie Def Jam and Donnie G. He also co-founded the label, D-Block Records.

1978: Singer and actor Sisqó (birth name Mark Althavean Andrews) was born in Baltimore. He is best known for the 1999 hit, "Thong Song."

1992: Digable Planets released the single, "Rebirth Of Slick (Cool Like Dat)." The track sampled "Blow Your Head" by Fred Wesley and the J.B.'s, "Stretching" by Art Blakey and the Jazz Messengers, "Foodstamps" by the 24-Carat Black, "Impeach The President" by the Honey Drippers and "On The Subway" by the Last Poets. The song won a Grammy in the category of Best Rap Performance by a Duo or Group.

1993: The Wu-Tang Clan released their highly-acclaimed debut album, *Enter The Wu-Tang (36 Chambers)*. The album spawned the singles, "Protect Ya Neck," "Method Man," "C.R.E.A.M." and "Can It Be All So Simple." All nine members of the group provided raps on the album.

1996: The single "Hot Diggity" by BLACKstreet featuring Dr. Dre began a four-week run at number-one on the U.S. charts.

1998: The Black Eyed Peas released their debut single, "Joints & Jam," which featured the lead vocals of Ingrid Dupree. (Fergie would not join the group until 2002.)

1999: The RIAA named *CrazySexyCool* by TLC the best-selling hip hop album of the 20th century, with sales of more than 11-million copies.

1999: Missy "Misdemeanor" Elliott released the hit single, "Hot Boyz" (featuring Lil' Mo). The remixed version of the track featured Nas, Eve and Q-Tip. The song's music video featured Nas, Eve but not Q-Tip, and included cameo appearances by Mary J. Blige, Ginuwine and Timbaland.

2002: Eve was the musical guest on *Saturday Night Live*. She performed "Gangsta Lovin'" and "Satisfaction."

2002: Eminem began a remarkable twelve week run at number-one on the U.S. singles chart with "Lose Yourself."

2004: Lil Jon & The East Side Boyz released the single, "Lovers And Friends" (featuring Usher and Ludacris). The track sampled "Lovers And Friends" by Michael Sterling.

2005: Rapper 50 Cent starred in the semi-autobiographical film, *Get Rich Or Die Tryin'*. Samuel L. Jackson turned down an offer to co-star in the film.

2007: Ludacris played the role of DJ Donnie in the Christmas comedy film, *Fred Claus*.

2013: Rihanna set a chart record in the U.K. when she reached number-one on the singles chart for seven consecutive years. She was the first female artist to achieve the feat.

2015: Waka Flocka Flame gave the weather report on Channel 19 in Columbia, South Carolina. He sang part of the report.

2015: Pusha T of the hip hop duo Clipse was appointed the president of the New York-based label started by Kanye West, G.O.O.D. Music.

NOVEMBER 10

1970: Warren G (birth name Warren Griffin III) was born in Signal Hill, California. The West Coast rapper is best known for his 1993 duet hit, "Regulate." Also a producer, he worked with MC Breed and 2Pac.

1971: Big Punisher (birth name Christopher Lee Rios) was born in the Bronx, New York. Usually referred to as Big Pun, the Latino rapper enjoyed success in the 1990s as a solo artist. In 1998, he joined the rap collective, Terror Squad. Morbidly obese at the time of his death, he suffered a fatal heart attack in 2000 at the age of 28.

1978: Eve (birth name Eve Jihan Jeffers-Cooper) was born in Philadelphia. An actress and singer, she released her debut album in 1999, *Let There Be Eve...Ruff Ryders' First Lady*.

1984: Melle Mel of Grandmaster Flash and the Furious Five provided the rapping in the first number-one U.K. single to feature rap music, "I Feel For You" by Chaka Khan.

1994: Tupac Shakur punched director Allen Hughes during the filming of *Menace II Society*. The rapper was arrested, spent 15-days in jail and was fired from the film. Shakur, who was playing the role of an aspiring college student named Sharif Butler, was replaced in the film by actor Vonte Sweet.

1996: Yaki Kadafi (real name Yafeu Akiyele Fula) was murdered inside an apartment building in Orange, New Jersey, at the age of 19. The rapper was a co-founder of the hip hop group, Outlawz. A close associate of Tupac Shakur, Kadafi claimed he could identify Shakur's killers. Kadafi's murder went unsolved.

1998: Method Man released his second solo album, *Tical 2000: Judgement Day*. The project, which explored apocalyptic theories, was highlighted by the tracks, "Judgment Day," "Torture" and "Perfect World." Donald Trump made a cameo appearance on the album.

2009: The documentary film, *Dirty: The Official ODB Biography*, was released.

2012: Rihanna was the musical guest on *Saturday Night Live*. She performed "Diamonds" and "Stay." This was her fourth appearance on the program.

2014: Nicki Minaj was criticized for using Nazi-inspired images in the music video for her hit, "Only." She later apologized.

2015: Will Smith starred in the sports-thriller film, *Concussion*. He portrayed a real-life pathologist who spent years publicizing the risk of head injuries among NFL players.

NOVEMBER 11

1981: The music video for "Young Turks" by Rod Stewart featured hip hop dancer Cool Pockets of Chain Reaction.

1999: A major exhibit was unveiled at the Rock and Roll Hall of Fame in Cleveland, "Roots, Rhymes & Rage: The Hip-Hop Story." The exhibit showcased the evolution of hip hop music from its origins in the 1970s to the gangsta rap era of the 1990s. The night before the opening, a VIP party featured performances by Nas, Public Enemy, OutKast, Grandmaster Flash, Slick Rick, Doug E. Fresh and Cleveland's own Bone Thugs-N-Harmony.

2001: Renowned New York-based graffiti artist A-One (real name Anthony Clark) died in Paris after suffering a brain hemorrhage. He was 37-years-old.

2003: Anthony "Wolf" Jones, a longtime affiliate of Sean "Puff Daddy" Combs, was murdered in Atlanta. Jones and another man were both shot and killed outside the Chaos nightclub following a dispute over a woman.

2004: Eminem released his fifth album, *Encore*. The album spawned six singles, "Just Lose It," "Mosh," "Encore," "Like Toy Soldiers," "Mockingbird" and "Ass Like That." The album sold more than five-million copies in the U.S.

2005: Rappers RZA and Xzibit co-starred in the thriller film, *Derailed*. While RZA portrayed an ex-convict, Xzibit played a scam artist. The film grossed more than $55 million.

2005: Hip hop group De La Soul teamed with Nike to introduce the Dunk High Pro SB – De La Soul athletic shoes. The heels of the shoes featured a hologram of the artwork from the cover of the group's album, *3 Feet High And Rising*.

2009: British rapper Plan B (real name Ben Drew) co-starred in the thriller film, *Harry Brown*. He scored a top-10 U.K. hit with a track that was featured in the film, "End Credits" (which was a collaboration with the duo Chase & Status).

2014: Big Bank Hank (real name Henry Lee Jackson) of the pioneering rap group, the Sugarhill Gang, died of cancer at the age of 57.

NOVEMBER 12

1973: The Universal Zulu Nation was founded. Often called "the Organization," the group emerged from a reformed New York City gang, the Black Spades, and promoted an Afrocentric view of culture and music. The movement's leader was DJ and rapper Afrika Bambaataa.

1974: Afrika Bambaataa introduced the term "hip hop." He declared that the "Four Elements" of hip hop were DJing, Breaking, Graffiti Artists and MCing.

1991: Tupac Shakur released his debut album, *2Pacalypse Now*. The album explored social and political issues on tracks such as "Trapped," "Brenda's Got A Baby" and "If My Homie Calls." Considered controversial at the time, the album was criticized by Vice President Dan Quayle.

1996: Eminem released his debut album, *Infinite*, on a tiny Detroit record label, Web Entertainment. He was 24-years-old at the time. The album sold approximately 1,000 copies.

1996: Snoop Doggy Dogg released his second album, *Tha Doggfather*. The album spawned the singles, "Snoop's Upside Ya Head," "Vapors" and "Doggfather." The album sold two-million copies in the U.S. This was the final album he released under the name, Snoop Doggy Dogg.

1996: Lil' Kim released her debut solo album, *Hard Core*. She was previously a member of Junior M.A.F.I.A., a group organized and mentored by the Notorious B.I.G. The album spawned the singles, "No Time," "Crush On You" (Remix) and "Not Tonight" (Ladies Night Remix). The album sold two-million copies in the U.S.

2002: The city of Atlanta declared the day, "TLC day," as a tribute to Lisa "Left Eye" Lopes who was killed in a car crash earlier in the year.

2002: Jay-Z released the album, *The Blueprint²: The Gift & The Curse*. The album spawned three singles, "'03 Bonnie & Clyde," "Hovi Baby" and "Excuse Me Miss." The album sold two-million copies in the U.S.

2003: Cam'ron and Dame Dash appeared on *The O'Reilly Factor* to debate the merits of rap music with the principal of a Philadelphia elementary school.

2004: Redman starred in the horror flick, *Seed Of Chucky*. Redman portrayed a film director who was murdered by an actress he refused to cast.

2006: The BET network presented the first annual *BET Hip Hop Awards*. Among the winners were "What You Know" by T.I.; Chamillionaire for Rookie of the Year; Common for Lyricist of the Year; and Grandmaster Flash for I Am Hip-Hop Icon Award. The event was hosted by Katt Williams, and was staged at the Fox Theatre in Atlanta.

2015: Soulja Boy discovered that he had been scammed out of more than $175,000. The thieves used fraudulent credit cards to purchase dozens of the rapper's Souljaboard brand of hoverboards, which he sold online for $1,500.

2015: *Billboard* magazine published the list, "The 10 Best Rappers of All Time." Topping the ranking was the Notorious B.I.G.

NOVEMBER 13

1989: Salt-n-Pepa released the single, "Expression," which appeared on their third album, *Blacks' Magic*. This was the first single to reach number-one on both the U.S. pop and rap charts.

2001: Graffiti artist Andrew "Zephyr" Witten and the brother of the late graffiti artist Dondi White published the book, *Dondi White Style Master General: The Life Of Graffiti Artist Dondi White*.

2001: The action film, *Ticker*, co-starred Ice-T and Nas. While Ice-T portrayed a terrorist leader, Nas played a police officer named Art "Fuzzy" Rice.

2004: Ol' Dirty Bastard (also known as ODB) died in New York City at the age of 35. He collapsed at RZA's recording studio, 36 Chambers Records. An autopsy attributed his death to a lethal mixture of cocaine and the prescription drug Tramadol, an opioid pain medication. The night before his death, he failed to show up at a Wu-Tang Clan performance.

NOVEMBER 14

1977: Obie Trice was born in Detroit. The rapper is best known for his work at Shady Records, including the solo album, *Cheers*. He later founded his own record label, Black Market Entertainment.

1982: Boosie Badazz (birth name Torrence Hatch) was born in Baton Rouge, Louisiana. He was formerly known as Lil Boosie. He had his first success with the album *Ghetto Stories*, a collaborative effort with rapper Webbie.

2001: The hip hop comedy film, *The Wash*, followed the exploits of a group of car wash employees. The film starred DJ Pooh, Snoop Dogg and Dr. Dre. Also appearing in the film were Ludacris, Xzibit and Eminem.

2003: The film documentary, *Tupac: Resurrection*, chronicled the life of fallen rapper Tupac Shakur.

2003: Jay-Z released *The Black Album*. He announced at the time that it would be his final album. The project featured a different producer on every track and was highlighted by the hits, "Change Clothes," "Dirt Off Your Shoulder" and "99 Problems." The album sold nearly four-million copies in the U.S. and was nominated for a Grammy in the category of Best Rap Album.

2004: At the 32nd annual American Music Awards, the winners were: Jay-Z for Favorite Rap/Hip-Hop Male Artist; OutKast for Favorite Rap/Hip-Hop Band, Duo or Group; and *Speakerboxxx/The Love Below* by OutKast for Favorite Rap/Hip-Hop Album. Kanye West stormed out of the ceremony after he lost the Best New Artist award to country singer Gretchen Wilson.

2009: Young Money, an all-star studio group, released the single, "BedRock." The hip hop group was formed by members of the record label Young Money Entertainment and consisted of Nicki Minaj, Drake, Lil Wayne, Gudda Gudda, Tyga and Jae Millz as well as guest singer Lloyd.

2009: The Black Eyed Peas were the musical guests on *Saturday Night Live*. The group performed "I Gotta Feeling," "Meet Me Halfway" and "Boom Boom Pow."

2011: Dr. Dre announced he would take a break from music after he finished producing albums for Kendrick Lamar and Slim The Mobster. During this period, he worked on a new business venture: Beats By Dre headphones.

2014: Machine Gun Kelly co-starred in the romantic-drama film, *Beyond The Lights*. Billed as Colson "MGK" Baker, he portrayed a fictional rapper named Kid Culprit.

2014: Buddha Monk, a close friend of Wu-Tang Clan founding member Ol' Dirty Bastard, published a biography of the late rapper, *The Dirty Version: On Stage, In The Studio, And In The Streets With Ol' Dirty Bastard*. The book was released on the 10th anniversary of the rapper's death.

NOVEMBER 15

1967: E-40 (birth name Earl Stevens) was born in Vallejo, California. The rapper co-founded the hip hop group the Click and released his debut solo album in 1995, *Major Way*. He also started his own label, Sick Wid It Records.

1968: Ol' Dirty Bastard (real name Russell Tyrone Jones) was born in Brooklyn, New York. A co-founder of Wu-Tang Clan, he pursued a solo career beginning with the 1995 album, *Return To The 36 Chambers: The Dirty Version*. He passed away in 2004.

1988: B.o.B (birth name Bobby Ray Simmons, Jr.) was born in Winston-Salem, North Carolina. He scored his breakthrough hits in 2010 with "Nothin' On You" and "Airplanes."

1988: West Coast rapper King Tee released his debut album, *Act A Fool*. The album spawned the singles, "Act A Fool" and "Bass."

1990: EPMD released the hit single, "Gold Digger." The track sampled several songs including "It's A New Day" by James Brown and "Think (About It)" by Lyn Collins.

1990: German producer Frank Farian publically admitted that Rob Pilatus and Fab Morvan did not sing on any of the tracks on the Milli Vanilli album, *Girl You Know It's True*. The following week, the lip-synching duo would be stripped of their Grammy for Best New Artist.

1994: Method Man released his solo album, *Tical*. The album spawned three singles, "Bring The Pain," "Release Yo' Delf" and the Grammy-winning remix "I'll Be There For You"/"You're All I Need To Get By." Method Man was the first member of the Wu-Tang Clan to issue a solo album in the wake of the group's debut hit album, *Enter The Wu-Tang (36 Chambers)*.

1996: A court in Los Angeles granted Ice Cube a restraining order against a female fan that had been contacting him for the previous two-years. The fan was ordered to stay a minimum of 100-feet from the rapper and his family.

2002: Ja Rule and Kurupt co-starred with Steven Seagal in the action film, *Half Past Dead*. The rappers portrayed a pair of prison inmates named Nick Frazier and Twitch.

2003: Missy Elliott was the musical guest on *Saturday Night Live*. She performed "Pass That Dutch" and "Work It."

2008: The single "Live Your Life" by T.I. Featuring Rihanna began a four-week run at number-one on the U.S. charts.

2008: Beyoncé was the musical guest on *Saturday Night Live*. She performed "If I Were A Boy" and "Single Ladies."

2009: Pioneering U.K. rapper Derek B. (real name Derek Boland) passed away at the age of 44, after suffering a heart attack. He was one of the first British hip hop acts to appear on the U.K. music program, *Tops Of The Tops*, and on the cover of *Smash Hits* magazine.

2011: Drake released his second studio album, *Take Care*. The album spawned eight singles beginning with "Marvins Room." The album sold more than two-million copies in the U.S. and won a Grammy in the category of Best Rap Album.

2014: Kendrick Lamar was the musical guest on *Saturday Night Live*. He performed "i" and was joined by Chantal Kreviazuk and Jay Rock on "Pay For It."

NOVEMBER 16

1983: The soundtrack of the pioneering hip hop film, *Wild Style*, was released. While the film was mostly overlooked at the time, the accompanying album was instrumental in the rise of rap music. Although the album produced no hit singles, it was highlighted by tracks such as "Cold Crush Brothers At The Dixie" by the Cold Crush Brothers and "MC Battle" by Busy Bee Starski vs. Rodney Cee.

1993: Domino released his debut single, "Getto Jam." The track sampled "Sing A Simple Song" by Sly & The Family Stone.

1996: During a concert by the Roots at Irving Plaza in New York City, Ol' Dirty Bastard performed a few songs as a guest artist but then refused to leave the stage. After getting into a scuffle with the group's MC, Black Thought, ODB finally exited the stage by jumping into the audience.

1997: Violent J of the rap duo Insane Clown Posse was arrested after a concert in Albuquerque, New Mexico, after he used a microphone to repeatedly strike a member of the audience who had jumped onto the stage. The rapper was released after posting a $5,000 bond.

1998: Singer and actress Queen Latifah published her autobiography, *Ladies First: Revelations Of A Strong Woman*.

1999: Dr. Dre released his second solo album, *2001*. The album – which was issued seven years after his debut disc *The Chronic* – spawned three singles, "Still D.R.E.," "Forgot About Dre" and "The Next Episode." The best-selling album of Dr. Dre's career, it sold eight-million copies in the U.S.

2000: Joe C. (real name Joseph Calleja) passed away in his sleep at the age of 26. The diminutive rapper toured regularly with Kid Rock.

2002: Nelly was the musical guest on *Saturday Night Live*. He performed "Hot In Herre" and was joined by Kelly Rowland on "Dilemma."

2003: At the 31st annual American Music Awards, the winners were: 50 Cent for Favorite Rap/Hip-Hop Male Artist; Missy Elliott for Favorite Rap/Hip-Hop Female Artist; Lil Jon & The East Side Boyz for Favorite Rap/Hip-Hop Band, Duo or Group; and *Get Rich Or Die Tryin'* by 50 Cent for Favorite Rap/Hip-Hop Album.

2004: Snoop Dogg released the album, *R&G (Rhythm & Gangsta): The Masterpiece*. The album spawned the hits, "Drop It Like It's Hot" (featuring Pharrell Williams), "Let's Get Blown" (featuring Pharrell Williams), "Signs" (featuring Charlie Wilson and Justin Timberlake) and "Ups & Downs."

2004: The Sugarhill Gang sued the Beastie Boys for allegedly using an unauthorized sample of "Rapper's Delight" on the track, "Triple Trouble."

2010: Florida rapper Trick Daddy published his autobiography, *Magic City: Trials Of A Native Son*.

2010: Late night talk show host Jimmy Fallon performed a folk-rock parody of "Whip My Hair" by Willow Smith on *The Tonight Show*. Fallon was accompanied on the track by rock legend Bruce Springsteen.

2010: Eric B. and Rakim were inducted into the Long Island Music Hall of Fame, which is based in Melville, New York. The ceremony was staged at the Patchogue Theatre.

2010: Rapper/producer Swizz Beatz announced his new sneaker line in collaboration with Reebok.

NOVEMBER 17

1955: Graffiti artist Futura 2000 (birth name Leonard Hilton McGurr) was born in New York City. A pioneering tagger, he began spray-painting subway cars in the early-1970s. His work was later exhibited in numerous art galleries.

1967: Ronnie DeVoe (full name Ronald Boyd DeVoe, Jr.) was born in Boston, Massachusetts. He was a member of the new jack swing / hip hop trio, Bell Biv DeVoe. The group had been formed by members of the R&B boy band New Edition.

1973: Lord Infamous (birth name Richard Dunigan) was born in Memphis, Tennessee. He was a founding member of the hip hop group, Three 6 Mafia. Lord Infamous is the half-brother of rapper DJ Paul.

1998: Chuck D settled a legal dispute with the estate of the late rapper, the Notorious B.I.G., over the unauthorized use of Chuck D's voice on the Notorious B.I.G. track, "Ten Crack Commandments." The song had sampled a portion of Public Enemy's 1991 track, "Shut 'Em Down." Although Chuck D had originally asked for at least $2 million in damages, details of the settlement were not released.

1998: Tommy Boy Records, the legendary hip hop and dance music label, released the 5-CD box set retrospective, *Tommy Boy's Greatest Beats 1981-96*. In 1981, the label had scored its first with "Planet Rock" by Afrika Bambaataa & Soul Sonic Force.

1999: Snoop Dogg and Davin Seay published the book, *Tha Doggfather: The Times, Trials, And Hardcore Truths Of Snoop Dogg*.

2009: Coolio published a cookbook, *Cookin' With Coolio: 5 Star Meals At A 1 Star Price*.

2013: During the London stop of the Vans Warped Tour, rapper George Watsky climbed onto the stage rigging and then jumped nearly 40-feet into the audience. He injured himself and two audience members. Remarkably, Watsky was able to finish the rest of the tour.

2014: Pitbull released the single, "Time Of Our Lives" (featuring Ne-Yo). The track sold more than one-million copies in the U.S.

2015: Timbaland published his autobiography, *The Emperor Of Sound: A Memoir*.

NOVEMBER 18

1977: Fabolous (birth name John David Jackson) was born in Brooklyn, New York. The prolific rapper released his debut album in 2001, *Ghetto Fabolous*. In 2006, he founded his own label, Street Family Records.

1985: The debut album by 17-year-old LL Cool J, *Radio*, was released by Def Jam Recordings. Previously, the label had only issued 12-inch singles. The million-selling album spawned the hits, "I Can't Live Without My Radio," "I Need A Beat," "I Want You," "Rock The Bells" and "You'll Rock." LL Cool J had dropped out of high school to record the album.

1997: Soul/hip hop singer Erykah Badu released a live album, *Live*. The project was highlighted by the Grammy-nominated track, "Tyrone." The album sold more than two-million copies in the U.S. and earned a Grammy nomination in the category of Best R&B Album.

1997: Erykah Badu and André 3000 of OutKast welcomed the birth of their son, Seven Sirius Benjamin.

2001: Jay-Z performed an acoustic concert at the MTV studios in New York City for an episode of the program, *MTV Unplugged 2.0*. The rapper was backed by the group, the Roots. The performance was later released on the album, *Jay-Z: Unplugged*.

2001: Mary J. Blige was the subject of an episode of the VH-1 program, *Behind The Music*.

2003: Eminem was involved in a controversy when an amateur recording he made at age 16 surfaced and came into the possession of *The Source* magazine. After a judge ruled that the magazine was permitted to release only a 20-second snippet of the allegedly racist track, reporters attended a press conference to hear the recording. Earlier in the day, Eminem issued a statement which in part read that the track – which was recorded following the breakup with his African-American girlfriend – was "made out of anger, stupidity and frustration when I was a teenager."

2005: Rapper DMX was sentenced to 70 days in jail for a parole violation after he was arrested the previous year for trying to steal a car from an airport parking lot. He was released on December 30 after serving 42-days of his sentence.

2006: At the 35th annual American Music Awards, the winners were: T.I. for Favorite Rap/Hip-Hop Artist; Bone Thugs-N-Harmony for Favorite Rap/Hip-Hop Band, Duo or Group; and *Strength & Loyalty* by Bone Thugs-N-Harmony for Favorite Rap/Hip-Hop Album.

2006: Ludacris was both the guest host and the featured musical performer on *Saturday Night Live*. He performed "Money Maker" and was joined by Mary J. Blige on "Runaway Love."

2012: At the 40th annual American Music Awards, the winners were: Nicki Minaj for Favorite Rap/Hip-Hop Artist; and *Pink Friday: Roman Reloaded* by Nicki Minaj for Favorite Rap/Hip-Hop Album.

2015: A fake concert promoter scammed officials at Alabama State University by promising to bring Lil Wayne to the campus for a homecoming concert. Lil Wayne learned of the scheduled concert only a few days before it was to take place. The university was forced to issue refunds to ticket buyers.

NOVEMBER 19

1974: Buckshot (birth name Kenyatta Blake) was born in Brooklyn, New York. He was the leader of the hip hop collective Boot Camp Clik and the group Black Moon.

1984: At age 16, rapper LL Cool J released his first record, the 12-inch single "I Need A Beat." The single was released by Rick Rubin's new label, Def Jam Recordings. Selling more than 100,000 copies – mostly around New York City – the record gave the label its first success.

1989: Tyga (birth name Michael Ray Stevenson) was born in Compton, California. The rapper released his breakthrough album in 2012, *Careless World: Rise Of The Last King*.

1990: The members of the duo Milli Vanilli were stripped of their "Best New Artist" Grammy after admitting to lip-synching the tracks on the album, *Girl You Know It's True*.

1992: Dr. Dre released the single, "Nuthin' But A 'G' Thang," featuring Snoop Doggy Dogg. (The "G" in the title stood for "Gangsta.") It was the first single from Dre's debut solo album, *The Chronic*. The track sampled "I Want'a Do Something Freaky To You" by Leon Haywood, "B-Side Wins Again" by Public Enemy and "Uphill (Peace Of Mind)" by Kid Dynamite. "Nuthin' But A 'G' Thang" was nominated for a Grammy in the category of Best Rap Performance by a Duo or Group.

1992: OutKast released their debut single, "Player's Ball." The remixed version of the track sampled "Over You" by the Main Ingredient.

1993: Tupac Shakur and his road manager Charles Fuller were charged with weapons violations and sodomy following an incident with a female fan at the Parker Meridien Hotel in New York City. Both men were later convicted of first-degree sexual abuse but were acquitted of the more serious charges.

1996: DJ Shadow released his debut album *Endtroducing*, an all-instrumental project that consisted mostly of samples.

1996: Flesh-n-Bone became the first member of Bone Thugs-N-Harmony to release a solo album. The album *T.H.U.G.S.* spawned three singles, "World So Cruel," "Nothin But Da Bone In Me" and "Playa Hater." Another track, "Reverend Run Sermon" featured a sermon by the rapper-turned-preacher from Run-D.M.C.

2000: Snoop Dogg was the subject of an episode of the VH-1 program, *Behind The Music*.

2007: Rapper and actor Percy Romeo Miller (a.k.a. Lil' Romeo) signed a letter of intent to play basketball for the University of Southern California. Miller was a starter on the 2008 team alongside future NBA player DeMar DeRozan.

2012: The reality series, *Marrying The Game*, debuted on the VH-1 network. The program examined the turbulent relationship between the Game (real name Jayceon Taylor) and his fiancee, school teacher Tiffney Cambridge. The series ran for three seasons.

2015: Snoop Dogg handed out 1,500 free turkeys at the Forum arena in Los Angeles ahead of the Thanksgiving holiday.

NOVEMBER 20

1983: Future (birth name Nayvadius DeMun Wilburn) was born in Atlanta. He released his debut album in 2012, *Pluto*.

1990: LL Cool J released the crossover hit single, "Around The Way Girl." The track sampled "All Night Long" by the Mary Jane Girls, "Risin' To The Top" by Keni Burke and "Impeach The President" by the Honey Drippers.

1992: Sega released the home video game, *Marky Mark And The Funky Bunch: Make My Video*.

1998: A remixed version of the rock hit, "Another One Bites The Dust" by Queen, was a hit on the R&B charts. The new rendition – which was remixed by Wyclef Jean – featured rap verses by Free and Pras. The track was featured in the film, *Small Soldiers*, and was also included on Pras' debut album, *Ghetto Supastar*.

2001: The second album by the duo Timbaland & Magoo, *Indecent Proposal*, featured one of the final recordings by Aaliyah before her death, "I Am Music."

2003: Kool Moe Dee published the book, *There's A God On The Mic: The True 50 Greatest MCs*.

2007: Webbie released the single, "Independent" (featuring Lil Phat and Lil Boosie). The track sampled Webbie's 2003 release, "Bad Bitch."

2011: At the 39th annual American Music Awards, the winners were: Nicki Minaj for Favorite Rap/Hip-Hop Artist; and *Pink Friday* by Nicki Minaj for Favorite Rap/Hip-Hop Album.

2013: Jay-Z was the anonymous buyer of a $4.5 million painting by Afro-Latin artist Jean-Michel Basquiat, according to *The New York Post*.

2015: Aspiring rapper Jimmy Winfrey (also known as Peewee Roscoe) pleaded guilty to 6 of 27 counts related to the shootings of two tour buses owned by Lil Wayne. Winfrey was allegedly driving his Camaro on Interstate 285 in Atlanta when he fired at the buses, causing $20,000 in damages. He was sentenced to ten-years in prison and ten-years of probation.

NOVEMBER 21

1992: Paperboy released his debut single, "Ditty." The track sampled "Doo Wa Ditty (Blow That Thing)" by Zapp and "Funky President (People It's Bad)" by James Brown. The single was nominated for a Grammy in the category of Best Rap Solo Performance.

1995: LL Cool J released his sixth album, *Mr. Smith*. The album was highlighted by the hits, "Doin' It," "Loungin" and the Grammy-winning track featuring Boys II Men, "Hey Lover." The album sold more than two-million copies in the U.S.

1995: Tupac Shakur and Tha Dogg Pound handed out 2,000 Thanksgiving turkeys at the Brotherhood Crusade building in Los Angeles.

1995: Kris Kross released the million-selling single, "Tonite's Tha Night," featuring background vocals by Trey Lorenz. (The 12-inch remix featured Redman.) The track appeared on the duo's third and final album, *Young, Rich & Dangerous*.

1998: The Beastie Boys were the musical guests on *Saturday Night Live*. They performed "Three MC's And One DJ" and "Sabotage." Beastie Boys member Adam Horovitz also appeared in a comedy skit with Jennifer Love Hewitt.

1999: Dr. Dre was the subject of an episode of the VH-1 program, *Behind The Music*.

2006: At the 34th annual American Music Awards, the winners were: Eminem for Favorite Rap/Hip-Hop Male Artist; The Black Eyed Peas for Favorite Rap/Hip-Hop Band, Duo or Group; and *Monkey Business* by the Black Eyed Peas for Favorite Rap/Hip-Hop Album.

2006: Jay-Z released the album, *Kingdom Come*. He had originally planned to issue the album under his real name, Shawn Carter. The album spawned four singles: "Show Me What You Got," "Lost One," "30 Something" and "Hollywood." The album sold two-million copies in the U.S. and was nominated for a Grammy in the category of Best Rap Album.

2007: Chris Brown co-starred in the romantic-comedy movie, *This Christmas*. The title was taken from a Donny Hathaway song which Brown performed in the film.

2008: A mansion in Malibu, California, belonging to Marion "Suge" Knight was sold "as is" by a bankruptcy court for $4.56 million. Knight had listed the home the previous year for $6.2 million.

2010: At the 38th annual American Music Awards, the winners were: Eminem for Favorite Rap/Hip-Hop Artist; and *Recovery* by Eminem for Favorite Rap/Hip-Hop Album.

2011: The Grammy Hall of Fame announced its class of 2012 inductees, which included the first rap song to receive the honor, "The Message" by Grandmaster Flash & The Furious Five featuring Melle Mel & Duke Bootee.

NOVEMBER 22

1988: Eazy-E released his debut solo album, *Eazy-Duz-It*. The album spawned three singles, "Eazy-Duz-It," "Eazy-Er Said Than Dunn" and "We Want Eazy." The album sold more than two-million copies in the U.S.

1994: Redman released his second album, *Dare Iz A Darkside*. The album spawned two singles, "Rockafella" and "Can't Wait." Later in his career, he would rarely perform any of the tracks from the album.

2002: The Michigan State Spartans basketball team began their season with a win over North Carolina-Asheville. Kyle Myricks, one of Michigan's players, suffered a severe foot injury before the start of the season and left the team. He soon adopted the stage name Stalley and launched a career in rap music.

2005: At the 33rd annual American Music Awards, the winners were: Eminem for Favorite Rap/Hip-Hop Male Artist; Missy Elliott for Favorite Rap/Hip-Hop Female Artist; The Black Eyed Peas for Favorite Rap/Hip-Hop Band, Duo or Group; and *The Massacre* by 50 Cent for Favorite Rap/Hip-Hop Album. The ceremony was hosted by Cedric the Entertainer.

2005: Lil' Romeo teamed with his brother Valentino Miller (known at the time as Young V) and his cousins, C-Los, Lil' D and Willie J, to form the rap group, Rich Boyz. The group would release just one album, *Young Ballers: The Hood Been Good To Us*. The album was issued by Guttar Music, a label started by Lil' Romeo and his father Master P.

2008: MC Breed (real name Eric Breed) passed away at the age of 37. He had battled kidney disease for a number of years. The Michigan-based rapper released 13 albums during his career beginning with *MC Breed & DFC* and scored his biggest hit with the single, "Ain't No Future In Yo' Frontin'."

2008: Ludacris and T-Pain were the musical guests on *Saturday Night Live*. They performed "One More Drink" and "Chopped & Skrewed."

2009: At the 37th annual American Music Awards, the winners were: Jay-Z for Favorite Rap/Hip-Hop Artist; and *The Blueprint 3* by Jay-Z for Favorite Rap/Hip-Hop Album.

2010: Kanye West released his fifth album, *My Beautiful Dark Twisted Fantasy*. A critical success, the album spawned four singles: "Power," "Monster," "Runaway" and "All Of The Lights." The album won a Grammy in the category of Best Rap Album.

2011: Various internet websites reported that Too $hort had died. The rapper went on Twitter to debunk the hoax.

2011: Loon (born Chauncey Lamont Hawkins) was arrested in Brussels and later extradited to the United States where he was prosecuted for a number of drug offenses. The rapper was convicted in 2013 and sentenced to 14-years in prison.

2015: At the 43nd annual American Music Awards, the winners were: Nicki Minaj for Favorite Rap/Hip-Hop Artist; and *The Pinkprint* by Nicki Minaj for Favorite Rap/Hip-Hop Album. The ceremony was hosted by Jennifer Lopez.

NOVEMBER 23

1972: Kurupt (birth name Ricardo Emmanuel Brown) was born in Philadelphia. A rapper and actor, he was also a member of the hip hop supergroup, the HRSMN. In 2002, he was named the Executive Vice President of Death Row Records.

1983: The influential film, *Wild Style*, was released. Featuring hip hop and graffiti artists, the movie starred Fab 5 Freddy, Lady Pink, the Rock Steady Crew, the Cold Crush Brothers, Queen Lisa Lee of Zulu Nation, Grandmaster Flash and Zephyr. The film followed a fictional South Bronx graffiti artist named Shy Zoro (portrayed by real life artist George "Lee" Quiñones) as he painted the stage backdrop for a rap and break dancing concert.

1993: Snoop Doggy Dogg released his debut album, *Doggystyle*. A defining West Coast rap album, it spawned the singles, "Who Am I? (What's My Name?)," "Gin And Juice" and "Doggy Dogg World." Selling more than four-million copies in the U.S., it was the best-selling album of his career.

1996: Future rap star 2 Chainz (real name Tauheed Epps) played his first game as a member of the Alabama State Hornets basketball team. A six-foot-five forward, he played 24 of 29 games during the 1996/97 season and scored 71 points. The team's opening game was against George Marshall University.

1998: Will Smith released the single, "Miami," from his debut solo album, *Big Willie Style*. The track sampled "And The Beat Goes On" by the Whispers. The song's music video cost an astounding $2 million and earned an MTV award in the category of Best Male Video. The clip featured actress Eva Mendes, who co-starred with Smith in the film, *Hitch*.

2008: At the 36th annual American Music Awards, the winners were: Kanye West for Favorite Rap/Hip-Hop Artist; Three 6 Mafia for Favorite Rap/Hip-Hop Band, Duo or Group; and *Graduation* by Kanye West for Favorite Rap/Hip-Hop Album.

2009: 50 Cent wrote, produced, directed and starred in the crime-drama film, *Before I Self Destruct*.

2009: Taco Bell settled a lawsuit with 50 Cent over the unauthorized use of his image in an advertising campaign. The restaurant chain reached a confidential settlement with the rapper.

2014: At the 42nd annual American Music Awards, the winners were: Iggy Azalea (who was nominated for six awards) for Favorite Rap/Hip-Hop Artist; and *The New Classic* by Iggy Azalea for Favorite Rap/Hip-Hop Album. The ceremony was hosted by Pitbull.

NOVEMBER 24

1992: Young Black Teenagers, an all-white hip hop group, released their best known single, "Tap The Bottle."

1992: The Pharcyde released their debut album, *Bizarre Ride II The Pharcyde*. The album spawned four singles, "Ya Mama," "Passin' Me By," "4 Better Or 4 Worse" and "Otha Fish." The album was far more lighthearted than most of the West Coast gangsta rap of the era.

1998: Redman released his fourth album, *Doc's Da Name 2000*. The album spawned three singles, "I'll Bee Dat!," "Da Goodness" and "Let Da Monkey Out." The album sold more than one-million copies in the U.S.

1998: Released two years after the death of Tupac Shakur, the compilation album *2Pac Greatest Hits* sold more than five-million copies in the U.S. The project earned a Grammy nomination and spawned two singles, "Changes" and "Unconditional Love."

2008: John Forté was pardoned by President George W. Bush. The rapper and producer had been arrested in 2000 at the Newark International Airport while carrying $1.4 million of cocaine, and was subsequently sentenced to 14-years in prison. Forté is best known as a producer and MC who worked on the Grammy-winning album by the Fugees, *The Score*.

2008: Kanye West released his fourth album, *808s & Heartbreak*. The album spawned the singles, "Love Lockdown," "Heartless," "Amazing" and "Paranoid." The album sold nearly two-million copies in the U.S.

2009: Comedian Bill Cosby released a rap album, *Bill Cosby Presents The Cosnarati: State Of Emergency*.

2013: At the 41st annual American Music Awards, the winners were: Macklemore & Ryan Lewis for Favorite Rap/Hip-Hop Artist; and *The Heist* by Macklemore & Ryan Lewis for Favorite Rap/Hip-Hop Album.

2014: Cheryl "Salt" James and Sandra "Pepa" Denton of the rap group Salt-n-Pepa performed their 1988 hit "Push It" in a television commercial for Geico Insurance.

2015: Paddle8 auction company announced that Wu-Tang Clan had sold the one and only copy of their new album, *Once Upon A Time In Shaolin*. It was purchased for a reported $2 million by 32-year-old pharmaceutical executive Martin Shkreli, who was free to either keep the album for himself or post the tracks on the internet.

NOVEMBER 25

1968: Erick Sermon was born in Brentwood, New York. He was a member of the hip hop trio EPMD, which released their first album in 1988, *Strictly Business*. Also a solo artist, he released his debut album in 1993, *No Pressure*.

1997: Will Smith released his first solo album, *Big Willie Style*. The album spawned the hit singles, "Men In Black," "Just Cruisin'," "Gettin' Jiggy Wit It," "Just The Two Of Us" and "Miami." The album sold six-million copies in the U.S. Smith had previously recorded five albums as part of the hip hop duo, DJ Jazzy Jeff & The Fresh Prince.

1997: The hit compilation album, *In Tha Beginning... There Was Rap*, was released. The album featured remakes of early rap classics including, "Rapper's Delight" by Def Squad, "6 In The Mornin'" by Master P, "Big Ole Butt" by P. Diddy and "Sucker M.C.'s" by Wu-Tang Clan.

2001: Salt-n-Pepa was the subject of an episode of the VH-1 program, *Behind The Music*.

2002: Snoop Dogg starred in the MTV comedy series, *Doggy Fizzle Televizzle*. The debut episode featured appearances by Colin Farrell, Samuel L. Jackson, Killer Mike, Big Boi, George Clinton and Bootsy Collins. The series ran for eight episodes.

2012: At the 25th annual Soul Train Music Awards which were staged in Las Vegas, "Mercy" by Kanye West (featuring Big Sean, Pusha T and 2 Chainz) won the award for Best Hip-Hop Song of the Year. The ceremony included a tribute to *Soul Train* founder Don Cornelius.

2014: Nelly began hosting a reality series on the BET network, *Nellyville*. The series followed the daily life of the rapper. The program took its name from Nelly's 2002 hit album.

NOVEMBER 26

1996: LL Cool J released a hip hop remake of the 1983 hit by Rufus and Chaka Khan, "Ain't Nobody." The track was included on the soundtrack of the comedy film, *Beavis And Butt-Head Do America*.

1996: After leaving Death Row Records in March 1996 and launching Aftermath Entertainment, Dr. Dre released the first album on his new label, *Dr. Dre Presents: The Aftermath*. The album spawned two singles, "East Coast, West Coast, Killas" and "Been There, Done That."

2003: Soulja Slim (real name James Adarryl Tapp, Jr.) was murdered at the age of 23. While standing in the front yard of his mother's home in New Orleans, he was shot once in the chest and three times in the face. A suspect was arrested but released after authorities were unable to find any witnesses to the crime.

2005: Chris Brown began a five-week run at number-one on the U.S. singles chart with "Run It!"

2010: The Black Eyed Peas released their sixth studio album, *Beginning*. The album spawned the singles, "The Time (Dirty Bit)," "Just Can't Get Enough" and "Don't Stop The Party."

2010: Romeo Miller, also known as Master P, founded the label, No Limit Forever Records. The label would release albums by Master P, Louie V. Mob, Money Mafia, She Money, Maserati Rome and others.

NOVEMBER 27

1970: Skoob (birth name William Hines) of the hip hop duo Das EFX was born in Queens, New York. He was also known as Books.

1973: Twista (birth name Carl Terrell Mitchell) was born in Chicago. In addition to his successful solo career, he co-founded the hip hop group, Speedknot Mobstaz.

1977: British rapper and actor Mike Skinner (full name Michael Geoffrey Skinner) was born in Birmingham, England. He is best known as the lead singer of the U.K. hip hop group, the Street.

1981: The newly formed Tommy Boy Records released its first 12-inch single, "Jazzy Sensation" by Afrika Bambaataa & The Jazzy 5. The label had been launched by Tom Silverman with a $5,000 loan from his parents.

1983: British rapper Professor Green (birth name Stephen Paul Manderson) was born in Upper Clapton, London, England.

1992: Onyx released their debut single, "Throw Ya Gunz." The song sampled "Escape-Ism" by James Brown, "It's A New Day" by Skull Snaps and "Nautilus" by Bob James.

2008: Soulja Boy released the hit single, "Kiss Me Thru The Phone," which appeared on his second album, *iSouljaBoyTellem*. He was backed on the single by Sammie. The track sold two-million copies.

2011: At the 24rd annual Soul Train Music Awards which were staged in Atlanta, "Moment For Life" by Nicki Minaj (featuring Drake) won the award for Best Hip-Hop Song of the Year. The ceremony included a tribute to Heavy D, which featured performances by Doug E. Fresh, Kurtis Blow, Whodini, Naughty By Nature and Common.

2013: The musical-drama film, *Black Nativity*, was released. It featured an all-black cast, which included hip hop artists Tyrese Gibson, Mary J. Blige, Jacob Latimore and Nas.

NOVEMBER 28

1974: Singer apl.de.ap (birth name Allan Pineda Lindo) of the Black Eyed Peas was born in Angeles City, Pampanga, Philippines. He moved to the United States at the age of 14.

1974: Styles P (birth name David Styles) was born in Yonkers, New York. He released his debut solo album in 2002, *A Gangster And A Gentleman*. He was also a member of the hip hop group, the LOX, which included Jadakiss and Sheek Louch.

1979: Chamillionaire (birth name Hakeem Seriki) was born in Washington, D.C., but raised in Houston. A successful solo artist, he also recorded several albums with fellow Houston rapper Paul Wall and was a member of the hip hop group, the Color Changin' Click. Chamillionaire enjoyed his biggest hit with the 2006 Grammy-winning single, "Ridin'."

1984: Trey Songz (birth name Tremaine Aldon Neverson) was born in Petersburg, Virginia. The hip hop/R&B performer released his debut solo album in 2005, *I Gotta Make It*.

1988: Neneh Cherry released the chart-topping, crossover single, "Buffalo Stance," from her debut album, *Raw Like Sushi*.

1995: The album *Str8 Off Tha Streetz Of Muthaphukkin Compton* by Eazy-E was released eight-months after his death. He had recorded nearly 60 tracks during the sessions, 14 of which made it to the album. The project spawned the singles, "Tha Muthaphukkin' Real" and "Just Tah Let U Know."

2004: 50 Cent released "Disco Inferno," the debut single from his second album, *The Massacre*. The track was nominated for a Grammy in the category of Best Rap Solo Performance.

2008: All five original members of Bone Thugs-N-Harmony performed at Club Nokia in Los Angeles. This was the first time all of the original members had been onstage together since the incarceration of Flesh-n-Bone in 2000. The reunited group later released the album, *Uni5: The World's Enemy*.

2009: Jay-Z and Alicia Keys began a five-week run at number-one on the U.S. singles chart with "Empire State Of Mind."

2010: At the 23rd annual Soul Train Music Awards which were staged in Atlanta, "Love The Way You Lie" by Eminem (featuring Rihanna) won the award for Best Hip-Hop Song of the Year.

2015: Music mogul Percy Miller, better known as rapper Master P, starred in the reality series, *Master P's Family Empire*. The program aired on the Reelz network.

NOVEMBER 29

1979: The Game (birth name Jayceon Terrell Taylor) was born in Los Angeles. Aided in his career by Dr. Dre, the Game released his breakthrough solo album in 2005, *The Documentary*. He later launched his own record label, Blood Money Entertainment.

1993: Legendary radio station WQHT Hot 97 in New York City went on the air. With its slogan, "where hip-hop lives," the station helped to popularize and define modern rap music.

1994: Mary J. Blige released her second album, *My Life*. Most of the tracks were co-produced by Puff Daddy. The album was highlighted by the tracks, "You Bring Me Joy," "My Life," "Be Happy" and a remake of Rose Royce's "I'm Goin' Down."

1995: Busta Rhymes released his debut solo single, "Woo Hah!! Got You All In Check." He was later sued by the Sugarhill Gang for copyright infringement over the song's lyrics which were allegedly similar to the group's 1980 track, "8th Wonder."

2005: Chris Brown released his debut album, *Chris Brown*. He was 16-years-old at the time. The album spawned the hits, "Run It!," "Yo (Excuse Me Miss)," "Gimme That" and "Say Goodbye." The album sold two-million copies in the U.S.

2010: PBS aired the documentary, *Copyright Criminals*, which examined the conflict between traditional copyright laws and the art of sampling by rap artists.

2011: Drake released the hit single, "The Motto." The song's music video was a tribute to slain Kansas City rapper, Mac Dre. The track sold more than three-million copies in the U.S.

2013: The hip hop group We Are Toonz launched the "NaeNae" dance craze with the release of their single, "Drop That #NaeNae." The dance was inspired by comedian Martin Lawrence's character on the television sitcom, *Martin*.

2013: Jay-Z introduced the men's fragrance, "Gold Jay Z."

2015: At the 29th annual Soul Train Music Awards which were staged in Las Vegas, "Alright" by Kendrick Lamar won the award for Best Hip Hop Song of the Year; and Jidenna won the award for Best New Artist. The ceremony opened with the program's host, Erykah Badu, pretending to take a telephone call from Iggy Azalea and saying, "what you're doing is definitely not rap."

NOVEMBER 30

1981: New Wave rock band Adam And The Ants flirted with rap music on their British top-10 single, "Ant Rap." This was one of the very first rap singles to land on the U.K. charts. The drum-heavy track was not a hit in the U.S.

1984: Egyptian Lover (real name Greg Broussard) released one of the first West Coast rap albums, *On The Nile*. The album was highlighted by the single, "Egypt, Egypt."

1986: The documentary, *Big Fun In The Big Town*, examined the rising hip hop scene in New York City. The project featured interviews with pioneering rappers Run-D.M.C., Grandmaster Flash, LL Cool J, Doug E. Fresh, Roxanne Shanté, Biz Markie, MC Shan, Mr. Magic and Schoolly D as well as spoken-word pioneers the Last Poets. The film first aired on Dutch television and was issued on DVD in 2012.

1988: LL Cool J staged a concert in the African nation of Ivory Coast. Halfway through his performance, the stage was stormed by fans and fights broke out in the audience.

1989: Professor Griff of Public Enemy released his debut solo album, *Pawns In The Game*. He recorded the album with his group, the Last Asiatic Disciples. The project was highlighted by the hit single, "Pawns In The Game."

1994: Tupac Shakur was robbed of money and jewelry and then shot five times by three men as he arrived at Quad Recording Studios in Manhattan. Shakur initially suspected that rival rappers were responsible for the attack. The incident occurred just one day before the announcement of the verdict in his sexual abuse trial. Despite undergoing surgery, Shakur appeared in court the following day. (In 2012, Jimmy "The Henchman" Rosemond admitted his involvement in the shooting.)

1995: Rapper and producer Stretch (real name Randy Walker) was killed in a drive-by shooting in Queens, New York. He was 27-years-old. With his death coming exactly one year after the Quad Recording Studio shooting of Tupac Shakur, there was speculation that two attacks were somehow related.

1998: Fergie began a four-year run as the co-host of the teen musical program, *Great Pretenders*, which aired on the Fox Family network. She joined the Black Eyes Peas shortly after the program was cancelled.

1999: Sisqó, who began his professional career as a member of the R&B group Dru Hill, released his debut solo album, *Unleash The Dragon*. The album was highlighted by the smash hit, "Thong Song," and sold more than five-million copies in the U.S.

2003: British rapper Asher D published his autobiography, *So Solid: My Dangerous Life With So Solid Crew*.

2004: Jay-Z teamed up with rap-metal band Linkin Park on the collaborative CD/DVD, *Collision Course*. The project featured six mash-up tracks by the two artists. The album was a surprise hit and was highlighted by the Grammy-winning track, "Numb"/"Encore."

2005: After reuniting and releasing their first new single in a decade, the Fugees launched an 11-date European tour that began in Vienna, Austria, and ended in Zurich, Switzerland.

2013: Rick Ross (real name William Leonard Roberts II) won a lawsuit filed against him by Los Angeles-based rapper and drug kingpin, "Freeway" Ricky Ross. Rick Ross was accused of committing copyright infringement by borrowing Ricky Ross' name and public reputation. Ricky Ross had demanded $10 million in damages.

▶ DECEMBER

DECEMBER 1

1991: Hitman (real name Ricky Heard) of the San Francisco-based hip hop group RBL Posse was killed. He was shot in the head while sitting in his car. He was 24-years-old.

1992: Positive K released the single, "I Got A Man." He performed both the male and female vocals on the track. The track sampled "Rescue Me" by A Taste Of Honey, "Spread Love" by Take 6, "High Power Rap" by Crash Crew, "Mama Used To Say" by Junior and "Get Up And Dance" by Freedom.

1995: Tupac Shakur was convicted of sexual abuse in an incident involving a female fan, but was acquitted of the more serious sodomy and weapons charges. He was sentenced to 18 to 54 months in prison. His road manager Charles Fuller was also convicted and was sentenced to four months in prison and five years of probation.

1999: Jay-Z was accused of participating in the stabbing of record executive Lance "Un" Rivera during a record release party at the Kit Kat Klub in New York City. He later pleaded guilty to a misdemeanor and was sentenced to three years of probation.

2000: Three 6 Mafia released their highest-charting album, the platinum-selling *When The Smoke Clears: Sixty 6, Sixty 1*. The album spawned the singles, "Sippin' On Some Syrup," "Tongue Ring" and "Who Run It?"

2001: Shakira and Bubba Sparxxx were the musical guests on *Saturday Night Live*. Sparxxx performed "Ugly" and "Lovely."

2007: Alicia Keys began a five-week run at number-one on the U.S. singles chart with "No One."

2010: Property belonging to Marion "Suge" Knight was sold at an auction, which aired on an episode of the A&E program, *Storage Wars*. The auction took place following a bankruptcy filing by Knight.

2013: At the 26th annual Soul Train Music Awards which were staged in Paradise, Nevada, "Bad" by Wale (featuring Tiara Thomas) won the award for Best Hip-Hop Song of the Year.

2015: The number-one album on *Spin* magazine's "The 50 Best Hip-Hop Albums of 2015" was *To Pimp A Butterfly* by Kendrick Lamar.

DECEMBER 2

1983: Action Bronson (birth name Arian Asllani) was born in Flushing, New York. The rapper released his major label, debut album in 2015, *Mr. Wonderful*.

1993: Salt-n-Pepa released the hit single, "Whatta Man" (with En Vogue). A top-10 hit, it sold more than two-million copies in the U.S. (The song was a remake of a 1968 soul hit by Linda Lyndell.) The music video featured cameo appearances by Tupac Shakur and Treach.

2003: Twista released the chart-topping track, "Slow Jamz," featuring Kanye West and Jamie Foxx. The song was included on Twista's album, *Kamikaze*, as well as on West's debut album, *The College Dropout*. The song's music video featured cameo appearances by John Legend, Consequence, Aisha Tyler, Mike Epps and Common. The track was nominated for a Grammy in the category of Best Rap/Sung Collaboration.

2015: Kanye West won "The Shoe of the Year" award at the 29th Annual Achievement Awards sponsored by *Footwear News*. He appeared at the ceremony in New York City to accept the prize for his Adidas brand Yeezy Boost 350s.

DECEMBER 3

1978: Trina (birth name Katrina Laverne Taylor) was born in Miami. She released her debut album in 2000, *Da Baddest Bitch*.

1991: M.C. Brains released his debut single, "Oochie Coochie." The track sampled "UFO" by ESG, "South Bronx" by Boogie Down Productions, "Let The Words Flow" by Chill Rob G and two songs by James Brown, "Get Up Offa That Thing" and "Get Up, Get Into It, Get Involved."

2007: Spice 1 (real name Robert L. Green, Jr.) was shot in the chest by carjackers while sitting in a vehicle outside of his parents' home in Hayward, California. He survived the shooting.

2012: British rapper Tulisa released her debut solo album, *The Female Boss*. The album was highlighted by the chart-topping U.K. hit, "Young."

2013: Adidas announced a collaborative deal with Kanye West. Soon after, West announced the release of the Adidas Yeezy Boosts.

2013: The Grammy Hall of Fame announced its class of 2014 inductees, which included two hip hop songs, "Rapper's Delight" by the Sugarhill Gang and "Walk This Way" by Run-D.M.C.

2014: Gerardo "Rico Suave" Mejia starred in the VH-1 reality series, *Suave Says*. The program followed the Latin rapper as he attempted to educate his children about the entertainment industry.

DECEMBER 4

1966: Masta Ace (birth name Duval Clear) was born in Brooklyn, New York. As a member of the hip hop collective Juice Crew, he recorded the influential single "The Symphony." Pursing a solo career, he released his debut album in 1990, *Take A Look Around*. He was also a member of the Crookston Dodgers.

1969: Jay-Z (birth name Shawn Corey Carter) was born in Brooklyn, New York. A successful rapper, producer and entrepreneur, he co-founded the Rocawear clothing line, co-founded Roc-A-Fella Records, founded Roc Nation and was the former president of Def Jam Recordings. In 2008, he married singer Beyoncé.

1973: Pimp C (birth name Chad Lamont Butler) was born in Port Arthur, Texas. He co-founded Underground Kingz (UGK) along with fellow rapper Bernard "Bun B" Freeman. Pimp C passed away on his birthday in 2007.

1979: Polygram Records released the first-ever, major label, rap single, "Christmas Rappin'" by Kurtis Blow.

1986: Run-D.M.C. were the first rap act featured on the cover of *Rolling Stone* magazine.

1990: Monie Love released the single, "It's A Shame (My Sister)" (featuring True Image). The track sampled "It's A Shame" by the Spinners and "He's The Greatest Dancer" by Sister Sledge.

1990: Brand Nubian released their debut album, *One For All*. The politically-charged project spawned five singles beginning with "Brand Nubian." The hip hop group had been formed in New Rochelle, New York, by Grand Puba, Sadat X, Lord Jamar and DJ Alamo.

2001: Fat Joe released his fourth album, *Jealous Ones Still Envy*. The album spawned the singles, "We Thuggin'," "What's Luv?" and "Opposites Attract (What They Like)." This was the biggest-selling album of Fat Joe's career.

2007: Pimp C (real name Chad Butler) was found dead in a Los Angeles hotel room. A coroner attributed the death to "respiratory depression" from a combination of sleep apnea and an accidental overdose of Promethazine and Codeine. Pimp C was 33-years-old.

2010: Diddy-Dirty Money – a group consisting of Sean "P. Diddy" Combs, Dawn Richard of Danity Kane and singer-songwriter Kalenna Harper – were the musical guests on *Saturday Night Live*. They performed "Coming Home" and "Ass On The Floor."

2011: Philadelphia-based rapper Tommy Hill (real name John Wilson) died two-days after he was struck by gunshots during a robbery outside of a bar. Also known as Tommy Butta, he recorded several albums with the group, R.A.M. Squad.

2013: Fazer (real name Richard Rawson) of the British hip hop group, N-Dubz, declared bankruptcy.

2014: Pharrell Williams was awarded a star on the Hollywood Walk of Fame.

2015: The Pimp C album, *Long Live The Pimp*, was released exactly eight-years after his death. The album featured guest appearances by Bun B, Lil Wayne, Nas, Juicy J, Slim Thug, A$AP Rocky and others.

2015: When Big Sean returned home from an overseas trip, he discovered that burglars had broken into a safe and stolen $150,000 worth of jewelry and an unspecified number of unpublished songs. The rapper had spent the previous week in the United Arab Emirates to watch his friend Lewis Hamilton compete in the annual Abu Dhabi Grand Prix. (Hamilton came in second place, losing by 8 seconds.) Big Sean told the press that he suspected the robbery was an inside job.

2015: Offset, a member of the hip hop group Migos, was released from jail after spending nearly eight-months behind bars. He was arrested on multiple charges the previous April following a concert at Georgia Southern University, but had been repeatedly denied bail. Offset was sentenced to five-years of probation, a $1,000 fine and banishment from four counties in Georgia. Another member of Migos, Takeoff, pleaded guilty to possessing less than an ounce of marijuana and was sentenced to 12-months of probation.

DECEMBER 5

1990: Interscope Records issued its first single, "Rico Suave" by Latin rapper Gerardo. The song was a top-10 crossover hit. The label quickly became a rap and rock music powerhouse.

1998: Lauryn Hill was the musical guest on *Saturday Night Live*. She performed "Doo Wop (That Thing)" and "Ex-Factor."

2003: Lil' Romeo co-starred in the Jessica Alba film, *Honey*. Romeo played the role of a young dancer named Benny. The film featured performances by hip hop artists Jadakiss and Ginuwine and soul singer Tweet.

2008: The film *Cadillac Records* chronicled the rise of Chess Records in the 1950s. The film starred Mos Def as Chuck Berry and Beyoncé as Etta James. Beyoncé's rendition of "At Last" earned a Grammy in the category of Best Traditional R&B Vocal Performance.

2009: Rihanna was the musical guest on *Saturday Night Live*. She performed "Russian Roulette" and "Hard."

2011: The reality series, *T.I. & Tiny: The Family Hustle*, debuted on the VH-1 network. The program followed the daily life of rapper T.I., his wife Tameka "Tiny" Cottle-Harris and their children.

2012: "The Message" by Grandmaster Flash and the Furious Five topped *Rolling Stone* magazine's list of "The 50 Greatest Hip-Hop Songs Of All Time." At number two was "Rapper's Delight" by the Sugarhill Gang.

2013: The number-one album on *Spin* magazine's "The 40 Best Hip-Hop Albums of 2013" was *Yeezus* by Kanye West.

2014: Beanie Sigel was shot in the abdomen while standing outside of his home in Pleasantville, New Jersey. He was seriously injured. Sigel was previously shot in 2006.

2015: Kanye West and Kim Kardashian welcomed the birth of their second child, a son named Saint West.

DECEMBER 6

2002: Fat Joe and Anthony "Treach" Criss starred in the crime film, *Empire*.

2005: T-Pain released the controversial single, "I'm 'n Luv (Wit A Stripper)" (featuring Mike Jones). The clean version of the song was reworked as "I'm 'n Luv (Wit A Dancer)."

2008: T.I. was the musical guest on *Saturday Night Live*. He performed "Whatever You Like" and "Swing Ya Rag."

2011: Azealia Banks released her debut single, "212" (featuring Lazy Jay).

2013: Beyoncé became the most nominated female artist in the history of the Grammy Awards, after passing the former leader, country singer Dolly Parton.

2014: Nicki Minaj was the musical guest on *Saturday Night Live*. She performed a medley of "Only" and "All Things Go" and was joined by Skylar Grey on "Bed Of Lies."

DECEMBER 7

1978: Mr. Porter (birth name Denaun Porter) was born in Detroit. Also known as Kon Artis, he was an original member of the rap group, D12. He also appeared as a featured artist on a number of hip hop hits by Eminem, Young Buck, Method Man and others.

1991: MC Hammer was both the guest host and featured musical performer on *Saturday Night Live*. He was the first hip hop artist to host the program. He performed "Too Legit To Quit," "Addams Groove," and "This Is The Way We Roll."

1993: Ice Cube released the album, *Lethal Injection*. The album spawned the singles, "Really Doe," "You Know How We Do It" and "Bop Gun (One Nation)."

2002: The film, *Bomb The System*, was released. The fictional movie followed a group of young graffiti artists in New York City. A number of real-life graffiti artists worked on the film including Lee Quiñones, Cope2 and Chino BYI.

2003: Mary J. Blige married producer Kendu Isaacs in a private ceremony at her home in New Jersey.

2010: Nicki Minaj released the single, "Moment 4 Life" (featuring Drake). The track sampled "Confessin' A Feeling" by Sly, Slick and Wicked. The song was nominated for a Grammy in the category of Best Rap Performance.

2012: The Los Angeles Police Department apologized to the relatives of the Notorious B.I.G. for releasing the late rapper's autopsy information without first informing his family. The 23-page document included previously undisclosed details.

2013: At least four people were shot following a concert by Meek Mill at the MoodSwing Nightclub Lounge in Wilmington, Delaware.

2015: Snoop Dog partnered with King Ice, a men's jewelry maker, to introduce the Jungl Julz line of products which included rings, pendants, bracelets and cigar tips.

2015: Kendrick Lamar was nominated for 11 Grammys, the second-most ever for a single artist in one year. Michael Jackson received 12 nominations in 1984.

DECEMBER 8

1966: Bushwick Bill (birth name Richard Stephen Shaw) was born in Jamaica. A member of the Geto Boys, he also enjoyed a successful solo career beginning with the album, *Little Big Man*. A dwarf who stood just 3-feet 8-inches tall, he lost an eye during a 1991 shooting.

1986: Salt-n-Pepa released their debut album, *Hot, Cool & Vicious*. The project was highlighted by the hits, "The Showstopper," "I'll Take Your Man," "Tramp" and a bonus track that was added to the album in 1987, "Push It." This was the first album by a female rap act to reach platinum status for sales of one-million copies.

1992: Arrested Development released the single, "Mr. Wendal." The song examined the plight of the homeless. The track sampled "Sing A Simple Song" by Sly & The Family Stone.

1993: Will Smith portrayed a con man in the comedy-drama film, *The Six Degrees Of Separation*. This was Smith's first of many blockbuster feature films. At the time of the film's release, he was in the middle of the third season as the star of the popular sitcom, *The Fresh Prince Of Bel-Air*.

2011: The number-one album on *Spin* magazine's "40 Best Rap Albums of 2011" was *XXX* by Danny Brown.

2012: Ne-Yo was the musical guest on *Saturday Night Live*. He performed "Let Me Love You (Until You Learn To Love Yourself)" and "She Is."

2014: Detroit-born rapper Earl Hayes murdered his estranged wife, VH-1 television star Stephanie Moseley, and then committed suicide inside the couple's Los Angeles apartment. He was 34 and she was 30.

2014: P. Diddy allegedly punched rapper Drake three times while the two men were outside of the popular LIV nightclub in Miami Beach, according to *The (New York) Daily News*. During the scuffle, Drake aggravated an old shoulder injury and was hospitalized.

DECEMBER 9

1974: Canibus (birth name Germaine Williams) was born in Kingston, Jamaica. He was a member of the hip hop acts, Sharpshooterz, the Hrsmn, Cloak-n-Dagga, the Undergods and T.H.E.M.

1991: Hip hop dancer Kuriaki (Lorenzo) was shot and killed in front of his home in the town of Mount Vernon, New York. He was a member of the award-winning break dancing group, Rock Steady Crew.

2000: Eminem released the smash hit single, "Stan." The song prominently sampled "Thank You" by Dido. The song's lyrics followed the exploits of an obsessive fan named Stan. Dido co-starred in the song's music video as Stan's wife. Eminem performed the track at the 2001 Grammy ceremony in a duet with Elton John.

2003: Nick Cannon released his debut album, *Nick Cannon*. The album was highlighted by the tracks, "Your Pops Don't Like Me (I Really Don't Like This Dude)" and "Gigolo" (featuring R. Kelly).

2006: Akon and Gwen Stefani were the musical guests on *Saturday Night Live*. Akon performed "I Wanna Love You."

2007: Soulja Boy (real name DeAndre Cortez Way) was sued by William Lyons of Mo Thugs Family who had created the Souljah Boy stage name in 1996. The lawsuit was settled out of court.

2007: Snoop Dogg's reality series *Father Hood* debuted on the E! network. The program followed the daily life of the rapper, his wife and three children. The series ran for two seasons.

2014: J. Cole released the album, *2014 Forest Hills Drive*. The album spawned five singles: "Apparently," "G.O.M.D.," "Wet Dreamz," "No Role Modelz" and "Love Yourz." The album was nominated for a Grammy in the category of Best Rap Album and sold more than one-million copies in the U.S.

DECEMBER 10

1954: Pioneering hip hop performer DJ Hollywood (birth name Anthony Holloway) was born in Harlem, New York. He was one of the first DJs to rap over the instrumental breaks of records and is often credited with coining the term, "hip hop." (Some sources attribute the origin of the term "hip hop" to DJ Hollywood's musical partner, Lovebug Starski.) A local star during the 1970s, DJ Hollywood often performed at multiple clubs on the same night. In 1980, he released his debut single, "Shock, Shock, The House."

1993: While still a high school student, a young Lauryn Hill portrayed a Catholic schoolgirl named Rita Louise Watson in the hit film, *Sister Act 2: Back In The Habit*. In the movie, Hill performed two songs, "His Eye Is On The Sparrow" and "Joyful, Joyful." (In 1991, she had appeared on the daytime soap opera, *As The World Turns*, and portrayed a troubled youth named Kira Johnson.)

1994: The Beastie Boys were the musical guests on *Saturday Night Live*. They performed "Sure Shot" and a medley of "Ricky's Theme" and "Heart Attack Man."

1995: The Human Beat Box (real name Darren Robinson) of the Fat Boys died at the age of 28. Weighing approximately 450 pounds at the time of his death, he suffered a massive heart attack following a session at a recording studio.

2007: Will Smith was honored at Grauman's Chinese Theatre in Hollywood. He left imprints of his hands and feet in the sidewalk outside the legendary venue. He was first and only hip hop artist to receive the coveted honor.

2011: Karryl "Special One" Smith of the Oakland-based hip hop duo, the Conscious Daughters, passed away at age 44 after suffering a fatal blood clot in her lungs. She had formed the duo in 1993 with Carla "CMG" Green.

2015: Rihanna staged her 2nd annual Diamond Ball. The black-tie fundraising concert was held at Barker Hangar in Santa Monica, California, and featured a performance by Lionel Richie. The annual event raised money for Rihanna's Clara Lionel Foundation, which she founded in 2012.

2015: MTV selected *To Pimp A Butterfly* by Kendrick Lamar as "the Best Hip-Hop Album of the Year." Drake came in second place with *If You're Reading This It's Too Late*.

DECEMBER 11

1979: The Sequence, a pioneering all-female rap group, released the hit single, "Funk You Up." The group had been discovered by Sugarhill Records co-founder Sylvia Robinson in Columbia, South Carolina, after a concert by the Sugarhill Gang. The track was later sampled in Dr. Dre's 1995 hit "Keep Their Heads Ringin'."

1983: The Art Of Noise, one of the pioneers of modern electronic music, released the influential single, "Beat Box." The syncopated, percussion-heavy track became the unofficial theme of early break dancers.

1985: Members of the Chicago Bears NLF championship team recorded the rap song, "The Super Bowl Shuffle." The single sold more than half a million copies, mostly in Chicago, and nearly reached the national top-40 charts.

2006: Legendary daredevil Evel Knievel sued Kanye West for featuring a character named Evel Kanyevel in the music video for his track, "Touch The Sky." Knievel claimed that the video infringed on his trademarked name and likeness. The lawsuit was settled out of court.

2007: Bow Wow and Omarion released the collaborative album, *Face Off*. The album spawned the singles, "Girlfriend" and "Hey Baby (Jump Off)."

2007: Rappers Ja Rule and Paul Wall co-starred in the horror film, *Furnace*.

2009: Chamillionaire joined singers Nick Jonas, Aaron Lewis and Zac Brown at a free concert in Texas in the wake of the terrorist attack at Ft. Hood that left 13 dead and 31 wounded. The event was billed as Fort Hood Community Strong.

2011: Director Jason Swain premiered his documentary about a 1991 hip hop concert at the City College of New York, which ended in tragedy. The film, *9 Lives*, examined the events which led up to a stampede that resulted in nine deaths and more than 30 injuries. Jason Swain was the brother of one of the dead concertgoers, Dirk Swain.

2014: Rihanna staged her 1st annual Diamond Ball. The black-tie fundraising concert was held at the Vineyard in Beverly Hills, California, and featured performances by Rihanna and Big Sean. The annual event raised money for Rihanna's Clara Lionel Foundation, which she founded in 2012. The proceeds were used to purchase $2 million of medical equipment for a hospital in Barbados.

2014: The Oscar-winning track "Glory" by Common and John Legend was released. The song served as the theme of the Civil Rights film, *Selma*. Common also appeared in the film as James Bevel, a Civil Rights leader in Selma, Alabama.

2015: Willow Smith, the daughter of Will Smith and Jada Pinkett Smith, released her debut album at the age of 15, *Ardipithecus*.

DECEMBER 12

1999: The VH-1 network issued its list of "The 40 Greatest Hip Hop Songs of the '90s." At number-one was "Juicy" by the Notorious B.I.G. featuring Total. Coming in at number-two was "California Love" by Tupac Shakur featuring Dr. Dre.

2000: Shade Sheist released the single, "Where I Wanna Be" (featuring Nate Dogg and Kurupt). The track sampled "Waiting For Your Love" by Toto.

2003: Nick Cannon starred opposite Christina Milian in the teen comedy film, *Love Don't Co$t A Thing*, which was an updated version of the 1987 film, *Can't Buy Me Love*. Cannon portrayed an intelligent but socially awkward nerd named Alvin Johnson.

2006: R&B singer Tyrese released his first rap album, *Alter Ego*. For the project, he referred to himself as Black-Ty. A number of R&B and rap acts made guest appearances on the album including Snoop Dogg, the Game, Method Man, Lil Scrappy, Lil Jon, R. Kelly and Mannie Fresh. The album spawned a pair of singles, "One" and "Turn Ya Out."

2012: The city of Pittsburgh declared the day, "Wiz Khalifa Day."

2012: A fundraising concert for the victims of Hurricane Sandy was staged at Madison Square Garden. The superstar lineup included hip hop acts Kanye West and Alicia Keys as well as rock acts Paul McCartney, Bruce Springsteen, the Who, Billy Joel and Jon Bon Jovi.

2014: Nick Cannon filed for divorce from his wife of six-years, Mariah Carey. The split was finalized the following April.

2014: The number-one album on *Spin* magazine's "The 40 Best Hip-Hop Albums of 2014" was *Run The Jewels 2* by Run The Jewels.

2015: *Billboard* magazine named the Notorious B.I.G. the greatest rapper of all time.

2015: Chance The Rapper was the musical guest on *Saturday Night Live*. He teamed with Jeremih Chance on "Somewhere In Paradise" and with Jamila Woods on "Sunday Candy."

DECEMBER 13

1975: Spoken-word artist Gil Scott-Heron was the featured musical performer on an episode of the first season of *Saturday Night Live*. He performed "Johannesburg" and "A Lovely Day."

2002: Nick Cannon starred in the film, *Drumline*. Cannon portrayed Devon Miles, a drummer in the marching band at the fictional Atlanta A&T University.

2003: OutKast began a nine-week run at number-one on the U.S. singles chart with "Hey Ya!"

2005: Beyoncé released the single, "Check On It," which featured Bun B and Slim Thug. The track had been recorded for the soundtrack of a film starring Beyoncé, *The Pink Panther*, but was ultimately not included in the project.

2006: Snoop Dogg co-starred in the adventure-fantasy film, *Arthur And The Invisibles*. He portrayed the role of Max, the leader of the Koolamassai.

2008: Kanye West was the musical guest on *Saturday Night Live*. He performed "Love Lockdown" and a medley of "Heartless" and "Pinocchio Story."

2008: Soulja Boy released the hit single, "Turn My Swag On," which appeared on his second album, *iSouljaBoyTellem*. In 2009, hip hop producer Greg Street scored a U.K. hit with a remixed version of the song.

2011: Kanye West and Jay-Z performed their hit song, "Niggas In Paris," a total of ten times at the Staples Center in Los Angeles. The night before, they performed the song nines times.

2015: Swagg Huncho (real name James Johnson, Jr.) of the hip hop group, 3 Problems, died of a gunshot wound to his head. His body was found in the backyard of a home in St. Louis. He was 18-years-old.

DECEMBER 14

1968: King Tee (birth name Roger McBride) was born in Compton, California. The pioneering rapper is best known for the 1988 single, "Payback's A Mutha."

1981: Ed Koch, the mayor of New York City, announced the allocation of $22.4 million to construct razor wire fences around the city's subway yards in an effort to battle graffiti artists.

1990: Heavy D & The Boyz scored a crossover hit with the single, "Now That We Found Love." The song was originally recorded in 1973 by the O'Jays. In 1978, a reggae version of the song by Third World reached the top-10 in the U.K.

1996: Rappin' Ron (real name Rohnie Louis Royster) of the hip hop group, the Dangerous Crew, died in a car crash in Oakland. He was 22-years-old.

2005: Kanye West was an opening act for the Irish rock band U2 during their very successful Vertigo world tour. West appeared at a total of 16 shows.

2007: Will Smith starred in the science-fiction film, *I Am Legend*. Smith played the role of Robert Neville, a U.S. Army virologist. The film was a remake of the 1971 Charlton Heston classic, *The Omega Man*. A smash hit, *I Am Legend* grossed nearly $600 million worldwide.

2010: Diddy-Dirty Money – a group consisting of Sean "P. Diddy" Combs, Dawn Richard of Danity Kane and singer-songwriter Kalenna Harper – released the studio album, *Last Train To Paris*. The album spawned the singles, "Angels," "Hello Good Morning," "Loving You No More" and "Coming Home."

DECEMBER 15

1990: EPMD released their third album, *Business As Usual*. The album was highlighted by the hit singles, "Gold Digger," "Rampage (Slow Down, Baby)" and "Give The People." The album also marked the recording debut by Redman who was featured on two tracks, "Hardcore" and "Brothers On My Jock."

1992: Dr. Dre released his first solo album, *The Chronic*. It was Dre's first project after his departure from N.W.A. The album featured Snoop Doggy Dogg on a number of tracks and was highlighted by the singles, "Nuthin' But A 'G' Thang," "Fuck Wit Dre Day" and "Let Me Ride." The album earned two Grammy nominations and sold nearly six-million copies in the U.S.

1995: The New Zealand-based duo OMC, which consisted of Alan Jansson and singer Pauly Fuemana, released the international hit, "How Bizarre." In the U.S., the song received much airplay but did not chart because it was not available as a commercial single. The song's music video featured a break dancer.

2001: Jonell released the single, "Round And Round" (featuring Method Man).

2005: Foxy Brown held a news conference to discuss her hearing loss. She had not been able to hear a human voice over the previous six-months. After undergoing surgery, she regained her hearing the following year.

2006: Will Smith starred in the drama film, *The Pursuit Of Happyness*. The film was based on the real-life story of Chris Gardner, an out-of-work salesman who was homeless for one year. Will Smith's son, Jaden, appeared in the film as Gardner's son.

2006: 50 Cent co-starred in the Samuel L. Jackson film, *Home Of The Brave*. The rapper portrayed a soldier named SPC Jamal Aiken.

2009: The Black Eyed Peas released the hit single, "Imma Be." The track was featured in the film, *The Hangover Part II*.

2010: Harlem-based rapper G. Dep (real name Trevell Coleman) walked into a police station and admitted to murdering a man during a robbery in 1993. Following a trial in 2012, G. Dep received a sentence of 15-years to life in prison.

2014: 50 Cent announced that he had signed a $78 million deal with Frigo Revolution Wear to promote a line of upscale men's underwear.

DECEMBER 16

1973: Hit producer Scott Spencer Storch was born in Philadelphia. He began his music career as a member of the Roots. As a producer, he worked with scores of artists including 50 Cent, Beyoncé, Tupac Shakur, Snoop Dogg, the Game, T.I., Chris Brown, Christina Aguilera, Dr. Dre, Nas, Lil Wayne, Pink and Jessica Simpson.

1978: Kaine (birth name Eric Jackson) of the Ying Yang Twins was born in Atlanta. The duo first hit the charts in 2000 with "Whistle While You Twurk."

1995: Gunshots were fired at Tha Dogg Pound's trailer during the filming of a music video for their single, "New York, New York." The video featured monster-sized figures of Daz Dillinger, Snoop Dogg and Kurupt knocking over skyscrapers in Manhattan, which inflamed the East Coast / West Coast hip hop rivalry. The song was met with an answer record, "L.A., L.A.," by New York City hip hop duo Capone-N-Noreaga featuring Mobb Deep and Tragedy Khadafi. (Several years later, Kurupt claimed that "New York, New York" was not intended as a diss song.)

1997: *The Source* magazine released the first of its 13 compilation albums, *The Source Presents: Hip Hop Hits*.

2000: Pimp C (real name Chad Butler) was arrested at Sharpstown Mall in Houston, Texas. He was charged with aggravated assault with a deadly weapon following a confrontation inside a shoe store. He was later convicted of the charge. After committing multiple parole violations, he was found in contempt of court and would serve nearly four-years of an eight-year prison sentence.

2000: K-Ci (real name Cedric Hailey) of the group Jodeci allegedly exposed himself while onstage at the Jingle Ball concert at the Shrine Auditorium in Los Angeles, and was charged with multiple counts of lewd conduct and indecent exposure. He later pleaded no contest to four charges of lewd conduct.

2000: Jay-Z was the musical guest on *Saturday Night Live*. He performed "I Just Wanna Love U (Give It 2 Me)" and "Is That Your Chick."

2002: Ja Rule released the single, "Mesmerize" (featuring Ashanti). The track sampled "Stop, Look, Listen (To Your Heart)" by the Stylistics. The song's music video was inspired by a scene from the hit film, *Grease*.

2010: Cam'ron and Vado were both barred from entering Canada. The rappers were scheduled to perform in Montreal.

2011: Slim Dunkin (real name Mario Hamilton), an up-and-coming Atlanta rapper, was killed in a fight over a piece of candy. He was shot in the chest at a recording studio. The shooter was later found guilty of aggravated assault with a deadly weapon and was sentenced to 25-years in prison. Dunkin was a member of Brick Squad Monopoly and was also affiliated with Waka Flocka Flame.

DECEMBER 17

1991: In a landmark legal ruling, Biz Markie was forced to recall all copies of his album, *I Need A Haircut*, after failing to get prior permission to use a sample on one of the tracks, "Alone Again." A New York federal court ruled against the rapper, who sampled a portion of a 1971 hit by Gilbert O'Sullivan, "Alone Again (Naturally)." Suddenly, record companies started making sure they had secured sampling permissions *before* an album was released. Reissues of *I Need A Haircut* did not include the track, "Alone Again." Biz Markie's follow-up album was humorously titled, *All Samples Cleared*.

1991: MC Hammer released the single, "Addams Groove," which was the theme song of the hit film, *The Addams Family*. Most of the film's cast appeared in the song's music video.

1992: Arrested Development staged an acoustic concert at the Ed Sullivan Theater in New York City for an episode of the program, *MTV Unplugged*. The 18-track set was released the following year on the album, *Unplugged*.

2000: Eminem was the target of an internet hoax which claimed he had died in an auto accident, enroute to a party.

2002: The state of New York officially declared November as "Hip Hop History Month." The resolution was introduced by Senator Pedro Espada, Jr., of the 32nd state district.

2005: When a pair of *Saturday Night Live* cast members – Andy Samberg and Chris Parnell – performed a novelty-styled hip hop song, "Lazy Sunday," the duo became an internet sensation. The two *SNL* writers who wrote the song, Akiva Schaffer and Jorma Taccone, later teamed with Samberg to form a musical trio, the Lonely Island. The men later scored a hit with the Grammy-winning rap song, "I'm On A Boat," which featured T-Pain.

2013: Beyoncé released the single, "Drunk In Love," which featured her husband Jay-Z. The song won two Grammys in the categories of Best R&B Performance and Best R&B Song. The song's music video won the award for Best Collaboration at the MTV Video Music Awards.

2014: Brooklyn rapper Bobby Shmurda (real name Ackquilla Pollard) was arrested and charged with conspiracy to commit murder and reckless endangerment. He pleaded not guilty to the charges.

2015: Remy Ma and Papoose were married at a ceremony in Connecticut. Among the wedding guests were Keyshia Cole, Ice-T and Fat Joe. The ceremony was filmed for an episode of the program, *Love & Hip Hop: New York*.

DECEMBER 18

1961: R&B singer Angie Stone (birth name Angela Laverne Brown) was born in Columbia, South Carolina. As a member of the Sequence, she scored the first hip hop hit by an all-female group with the single, "Funk You Up." Then following a stint in the R&B trio Vertical Hold in the early-1990s, she launched a successful solo career.

1970: DMX (birth name Earl Simmons) was born in Mount Vernon, New York, but raised in nearby Yonkers. Also known as Dark Man X, he enjoyed a successful solo career which was highlighted by the 1999 album, *...And Then There Was X*. Also an actor, he appeared in a number of films including *Romeo Must Die*, *Exit Wounds*, *Belly* and *Cradle 2 The Grave*.

1972: DJ Lethal (birth name Leor Dimant) was born in Riga, Latvia. After a stint in the hip hop group House Of Pain, he spent 15 years as the DJ in the popular rap-metal band, Limp Bizkit.

1984: The Fat Boys released their debut album, *Fat Boys*. The hit album was highlighted by the tracks, "Fat Boys," "Jail House Rap," "Human Beat Box" and "Can You Feel It?"

1992: LL Cool J co-starred in the Robin Williams comedy film, *Toys*. The rapper portrayed a former soldier.

2001: Nas released one of the most infamous diss tracks in rap history, "Ether." On the track, Nas compared Jay-Z to the character J.J. Evans from the sitcom *Good Times* as well as the cartoon cigarette mascot, Joe Camel. Jay-Z responded with his own diss track, "Supa Ugly," which included verses about having an affair with Nas' girlfriend.

2003: Nas (real name Nasir Jones) was charged with assault after he allegedly hit a man in the head with a bottle. The incident occurred a week earlier in the VIP section of the Cielo Club in New York City. Nas was arrested and released after posting the $7,500 bail.

2009: Fergie of the Black Eyed Peas co-starred in the musical-drama film, *Nine*.

2010: Eminem and Lil Wayne were the musical guests on *Saturday Night Live*. This was Eminem's fifth appearance on the program. Eminem performed "Won't Back Down," Lil Wayne performed "6 Foot 7 Foot" and the two rappers teamed up for a performance of "No Love."

2010: A high school football team coached by 2 Live Crew leader Luther Campbell won a state championship in Florida. Miami Central Senior High School defeated Orlando Dr. Phillips in the finals by a score of 42 to 27.

2011: Yung Joc was the victim of a robbery at the offices of his record label, Swagg Team. The thieves took $70,000 worth of studio equipment as well as a computer drive that contained a number of completed tracks that were intended for Yung Joc's next album.

2013: Ludacris (real name Christopher Bridges) purchased a mansion in the Hollywood Hills section of Los Angeles for $4.8 million.

2015: Walmart reportedly removed a Rick Ross album from its shelves following a complaint by a journalist. The album, *Black Market*, included the track "Free Enterprise," which contained lyrics that allegedly threatened Donald Trump.

DECEMBER 19

1987: Following a rap concert at Municipal Auditorium in Nashville, two teenagers were trampled to death and 27 people were injured while trying to exit the building. Some of the attendees reported hearing gunshots. The charity fundraising concert had featured Public Enemy, Eric B. & Rakim and N.W.A.

1998: Nick Cannon made his first appearance on the Nickelodeon comedy program, *All That*. In all, he would appear on 31 episodes from 1998 to 2000. He later starred in the spinoff series, *The Nick Cannon Show*.

1999: Michigan-based rap duo Insane Clown Posse staged their first Juggalo Championship Wrestling event at St. Andrews Hall in Detroit. On the bill were classic wrestlers such as King Kong Bundy, the Iron Sheik and Abdullah the Butcher.

2001: The film, *Too Legit: The MC Hammer Story*, made its debut on the VH-1 network. While Hammer was portrayed by Romany Malco, Tupac Shakur was played by Lamont Bentley and Suge Knight was played by Anthony Norris.

2006: After signing with Def Jam Recordings, Nas released his eighth album, *Hip Hop Is Dead*. The album spawned the singles, "Hip Hop Is Dead" and "Can't Forget About You." The album was nominated for a Grammy in the category of Best Rap Album.

2007: West Coast rapper Nate Dogg suffered a debilitating stroke, which left him paralyzed on the left side of his body.

2008: Will Smith starred in the drama film, *Seven Pounds*. Smith played the role of Tim Thomas, an aeronautical engineer who attempted to save seven lives after taking seven other lives in a car crash. The film grossed almost $170 million.

2014: The BET series *106 & Park* aired its final episode. Nicki Minaj was the last guest on the show. A number of current and past cast members appeared on the episode including Terrence J, Rocsi, DJ Enuff, Big Tigger, Julissa Bermudez, Miss Mykie, Paigon, Shorty Da Prince, Keshia Chante, Bow Wow, AJ Calloway and Free. The series ran for 14-years.

2014: The reality television series, *Caught On Camera With Nick Cannon*, premiered on NBC.

2015: Nicki Minaj was criticized by the Human Rights Foundation after she performed at the annual Show Unitel Boas Festas in the city of Luanda, Angola. The foundation had accused the country's leadership of repeatedly violating the rights of journalists and activists. Minaj was reportedly paid $2 million for her appearance.

DECEMBER 20

2005: Mary J. Blige released her seventh studio album, *The Breakthrough*. The album was highlighted by the singles, "MJB da MVP," "Be Without You," "Enough Cryin'," "One" and "Take Me As I Am." The album topped the pop charts and sold more than three-million copies in the U.S. Blige would earn seven Grammy nominations and win the awards in the categories of Best Female R&B Vocal Performance, Best R&B Song and Best R&B Album.

2010: Magnolia $horty (real name Renetta Yemika Lowe-Bridgewater) was murdered at the age of 28. She was a passenger in a vehicle that was struck by a hail of gunfire in front of an apartment complex in New Orleans. Both $horty and the driver of the vehicle, Jerome Hampton, died at the scene. As the first female rapper signed to Cash Money Records, she released her debut album in 1997, *Monkey On Tha D$ck*.

2013: Lord Infamous (real name Richard Dunigan) of the hip hop group, Three 6 Mafia, passed away after suffering a heart attack in his sleep while staying at his mother's home in Memphis. He was 40-years-old.

DECEMBER 21

1999: DMX released his third studio album, *...And Then There Was X*. The album spawned the singles, "What's My Name," "Party Up (Up In Here)" and "What These Bitches Want." The best-selling album of DMX's career, it was nominated for a Grammy in the category of Best Rap Album.

2001: Method Man and Redman starred in the comedy film, *How High*. The rappers portrayed a pair of pot-growing stoners at Harvard University.

2011: Flavor Flav teamed with two business partners to open a restaurant in Sterling Heights, Michigan. But after seven months in operation, Flavor Flav's Chicken & Ribs closed its doors the following June. This was Flav's third attempt at operating a restaurant.

2012: South Korean rapper Psy made history when his music video for "Gangnam Style" became the first clip in YouTube history to reach one-billion views. Released just five months earlier, the video surpassed Justin Bieber's "Baby" as the most-watched clip on the website.

2013: The single "The Monster" by Eminem featuring Rihanna began a four-week run at number-one on the U.S. charts.

2014: Birdman appeared on the cover of the Marvel comic book, *The Amazing Spider-Man*.

2015: A trio of rappers – Killer Mike, Big Boi and T.I. – filed a formal brief with the U.S. Supreme Court arguing that rap lyrics should be protected as free speech under the First Amendment. The brief was filed in defense of a high school student from Mississippi who was punished after he wrote a rap song about his teachers.

DECEMBER 22

1960: Luther Campbell (full name Luther Roderick Campbell) was born in Miami, Florida. He was also known as Luke Skyywalker and Uncle Luke. As the leader of the controversial rap group 2 Live Crew, he was often targeted by state and federal authorities after the release of the album, *As Nasty As They Wanna Be*. He later pursued a solo career.

1992: The owner of Metropol nightclub in Pittsburgh was forced to cancel a concert by Ice-T after the local police refused to work as security guards at the show. The police officers were protesting the rapper's song, "Cop Killer."

1999: LL Cool J co-starred in the sports-drama film, *Any Given Sunday*. Directed by Oliver Stone, the film featured an all-star cast that included Al Pacino, Cameron Diaz, Dennis Quaid, Charlton Heston and Ann-Margret.

2011: On MTV's list of "The 12 Best Hip-Hop Christmas Songs Of All Time," the number-one song was "Christmas In Hollis" by Run-D.M.C.

2013: A 24-year-old man was shot and killed at a Rich Homie Quan concert at the Red Zone bar in Columbus, Ohio. There was another shooting at a previous Rich Homie Quan concert just six-weeks earlier at the same nightclub.

2015: Travi$ Scott (real name Jacques Webster) pleaded guilty to a charge of reckless conduct after he started a stampede during his performance at the Lollapalooza festival in Chicago. He was placed under court supervision for a period of one year.

2015: Drake was named Artist of the Year by *Spin* magazine.

DECEMBER 23

1985: A large fight erupted during a concert by LL Cool J at a roller rink in Baltimore. During the melee, three people were shot and one person was trampled.

2005: Foxy Brown (real name Inga Marchand) was handcuffed and threatened with a 30-day jail term after she stuck her tongue out at a judge following a warning about chewing gum. Brown was in court to make a plea on charges of assaulting two employees of a nail salon.

2009: DJ Omega Supreme (real name Andre Kyles) of the hip hop duo Organized Konfusion died of cancer.

2013: Ricky Spicer of the Cleveland-based soul group, the Ponderosa Twins Plus One, sued Kanye West over a sample on the rapper's hit single, "Bound 2." The lawsuit was settled in 2015.

2015: Chicago rapper King Louie (real name Louis Johnson, Jr.) was shot in the head while sitting in a vehicle. The 27-year-old recovered from his injuries.

DECEMBER 24

2007: Jay-Z announced that he would not be renewing his contract to remain the president of Def Jam Recordings. The two sides could not agree on financial terms.

2012: Capital STEEZ (real name Courtney Everald "Jamal" Dewar, Jr.) of the hip hop group, Pro Era, died at the age of 19. He committed suicide by jumping from the rooftop of the Cinematic Music Group building in Manhattan.

2014: Kanye West was named *GQ* magazine's "Most Stylish Man of 2014."

DECEMBER 25

1992: Ice-T and Ice Cube starred in the crime-thriller film, *Trespass*. While Ice-T portrayed a gang leader named King James, Ice Cube played a hitman named Savon.

2006: James Brown, the most sampled musical artist of all time, died of pneumonia. The Godfather of Soul's music can be heard in countless rap songs by artists ranging from Big Daddy Kane to Public Enemy.

2015: Bronx-based rapper French Montana announced he was donating $1 million to a local charity that aided children and schools.

2015: Ludacris married his longtime girlfriend Eudoxie Agnan. The private ceremony took place in Georgia.

DECEMBER 26

1981: Drama (birth name Terence Cook) was born in Sylacauga, Alabama. He is best known for his 1999 hit single, "Left/Right" (which is also known as "Left, Right, Left").

1989: Wrecks-n-Effect released their debut full-length album, *Wrecks-n-Effect*. The project was highlighted by the tracks, "New Jack Swing" (featuring Teddy Riley) and "Juicy." One of the trio's members, Brandon Mitchell, passed away the following year.

1993: During a P.M. Dawn performance at the Sound Factory nightclub in Manhattan, KRS-One and his posse jumped onto the stage, stopped the concert and pushed the members of the group off the stage. Allegedly, KRS-One was responding to comments made by one of the members of P.M. Dawn in *Details Magazine*.

1995: The Notorious B.I.G. provided the backing vocals on a single by Michael Jackson, "This Time Around."

DECEMBER 27

1998: Busta Rhymes was arrested in Manhattan after police found an unregistered gun in his car.

1999: After bumping into another patron at a New York City nightclub, Sean "Puff Daddy" Combs and his entourage got into an altercation. Combs was visiting the club with his then-girlfriend, Jennifer Lopez. At a trial in 2001, Combs and his bodyguard Anthony "Wolf" Jones were both acquitted of all charges. Another member of Combs' entourage was not as fortunate: Jamal "Shyne" Barrow was convicted of first degree assault and sentenced to ten-years in prison.

2002: Queen Latifah starred in the hit musical film, *Chicago*. She won an Oscar in the category of Best Supporting Actress for her portrayal of a corrupt matron at the Cook County Jail named "Mama" Morton. In the film, she performed the jazz song, "When You're Good To Mama."

2005: DJ Kool Herc wrote the foreword of Jeff Chang's award-winning book, *Can't Stop Won't Stop: A History Of The Hip-Hop Generation*.

2007: Tragedy Khadafi was convicted of selling narcotics. Sentenced to a four-year prison term, he was released in June 2010.

DECEMBER 28

1989: Bell Biv DeVoe released their debut single, "Poison." The hip hop / new jack swing group had been formed by three members of the R&B boy band New Edition, Ricky Bell, Michael Bivins and Ronnie DeVoe.

1991: A total of nine people were crushed to death and more than 30 others were injured during a stampede at a hip hop concert. Organized by Heavy D and Sean "Diddy" Combs, the concert – which followed a celebrity basketball game – drew nearly 5,000 people to a gymnasium at the City College of New York that seated only 2,700. In 1999, a court ruled that Heavy D and Combs were 50-percent responsible for the incident while the college was responsible for the other 50-percent.

1995: 2Pac released the single, "California Love" (featuring Dr. Dre and Roger Troutman). Considered 2Pac's comeback hit, it was issued after his release from prison. The chart-topping single was nominated for two Grammys in the categories of Best Rap Solo Performance and Best Rap Performance by a Duo or Group. A remixed version of "California Love" was included on his 1996 double-album, *All Eyez On Me*.

1999: One day after Sean "Puff Daddy" Combs was arrested in New York City on weapons charges, he declared: "I do not own a gun nor did I have possession of a gun that night. I had nothing to do with a shooting in this club. I want to make this 100 percent clear."

1999: Jay-Z released the album, *Vol. 3... Life and Times of S. Carter*. The project spawned the singles, "Do It Again (Put Ya Hands Up)," "Things That U Do" and "Big Pimpin." The album sold more than three-million copies in the U.S.

2013: Doe B (real name Glen Thomas) was shot and killed at Centennial Hill Bar & Grill in Montgomery, Alabama. During the melee, seven other patrons were shot – two fatally. Signed to T.I.'s record label Hustle Gang, Doe B was working on his debut studio album at the time of his death. He was 22-years-old. Authorities arrested two suspects in connection with the shootings.

DECEMBER 29

1994: Lisa "Left Eye" Lopes pleaded guilty to charges of arson. Earlier in the year, she had set fire to a million-dollar mansion in Atlanta owned by her boyfriend, NFL player Andre Rison. She was sentenced to five-years of probation and ordered to undergo mental health therapy.

2011: Members of the Sugarhill Gang, the estate of Sugarhill Records founder Sylvia Robinson and others filed a lawsuit against Universal Music Group, charging that the label had failed to pay royalties since 1995.

2015: Kanye West was named *GQ* magazine's "Most Stylish Man of 2015." He also won the award in 2014.

DECEMBER 30

2004: Rapper Lil' Zane teamed with MAM Group to form the record company, 3 Mill Entertainment (3ME). The label was later renamed U.S. Entertainment and then Money Making Muzik (MMM). Acts on the label included Lil' Zane, Shawty, Soulja P, Indyspensablz, D Phlo, the Triple M Boyz and Young Crunk.

2005: Pimp C (real name Chad Butler) of the hip hop duo UGK was released from a Texas prison. He was granted parole after serving half of an eight-year term for an aggravated assault conviction.

2008: Soulja Boy was robbed at his home by a group of heavily-armed masked men. The rapper claimed that he shot at least one of the robbers.

2015: Justin Combs, the 22-year-old son of Sean "Diddy" Combs, announced the launch of Tonite, an entertainment event and music management company. He formed the venture with a classmate from UCLA, Kene Orijoke.

DECEMBER 31

1977: Asian rapper Psy (birth name Park Jae-sang) was born in Seoul, South Korea. He is best known for his 2012 international smash hit, "Gangnam Style."

1993: A New Year's Eve concert by artists from the golden age of rap was staged at the Apollo Theater in Harlem. The lineup included Kurtis Blow, Grandmaster Flash, Melle Mel, Biz Markie, Kool Moe Dee, Whodini and show's host Doug E. Fresh.

1997: Will Smith married actress and singer-songwriter Jada Pinkett. The couple had first met in 1994 on the set of Smith's hit television show, *The Fresh Prince Of Bel-Air*, when she auditioned for the role of Smith's girlfriend. Although she failed the audition, she became Smith's real-life girlfriend the following year. The couple were married in a ceremony at Cloisters Mansion near Baltimore.

1999: Sisqó released the single, "Thong Song." A huge hit, the track was nominated for four Grammys. The song's music video was filmed on a beach in Miami during Spring Break.

2001: The documentary, *Tupac Shakur: Thug Angel*, was released. Directed by Peter Spirer, the film examined the life and art of the late rapper.

2002: 50 Cent and his entourage were arrested outside of the Copacabana nightclub in Manhattan. The rapper had just arrived at the venue for a performance when police swarmed his limousine. The rapper and his entourage were charged with two counts of criminal possession of a weapon.

2005: Obie Trice was shot two times while driving on Interstate-95 in his hometown of Detroit. One of the bullets struck the rapper in the head. He managed to exit the interstate and then wave down a police car.

2006: The Black Eyed Peas performed for more than one-million people at Ipanema Beach in Rio de Janeiro, Brazil.

2007: During the middle of a New Year's Eve performance at the House of Blues, the Game announced that his next album would be his final release.

2010: Russian multi-billionaire Roman Abramovich hired the Black Eyed Peas to perform at an extravagant New Year's Eve party at his estate on the Caribbean island of St. Barts. The group was paid an undisclosed sum.

2013: Rick Ross filed a copyright infringement lawsuit against the duo LMFAO, the group's publishing company Kobalt Music Publishing America, Kia Motors and others. Ross claimed that the lyrics of LMFAO's smash 2010 hit "Party Rock Anthem" were based on his 2006 single, "Hustlin'," which was written by the team of Ross, Jermaine Jackson and Andrew Harr.

2014: Kanye West teamed with Paul McCartney on the track, "Only One." The song was a tribute to West's young daughter, North, who appeared in the song's music video.

▶ NOTES

A wide variety of source material was used to compile this reference book. Both traditional and internet sources were employed in an effort to verify information and dates.

MAGAZINES
Billboard
Blaze
Cash Box
Details
Ebony
Entertainment Weekly
Esquire
Forbes
Goldmine
GQ
Melody Maker
Mojo
Newsweek
Paper
People
Q
Rap Pages
Rolling Stone
The Source
Spin
Time
Vibe
Wax Poetics
XXL

BROADCAST NETWORKS
BBC
BET
MTV
VH-1

NEWSPAPERS
The Atlanta Journal-Constitution
The Boston Globe
The Chicago Sun-Times
The Chicago Tribune
The Cincinnati Enquirer
The Cleveland Plain Dealer
The Columbus Dispatch
The Daily Mail
The Detroit News
The Guardian
The Los Angeles Times
The Miami Herald
The Nashville Tennessean
The New York Daily News
The New York Post
The New York Times
The Philadelphia Inquirer
The St. Louis Post-Dispatch
The Seattle Post-Intelligencer
The Times of London
The Toronto Star
The Toronto Sun
USA Today
The Village Voice
The Wall Street Journal
The Washington Post
The Washington Times